REVEAL

REVEAL

ROBBIE WILLIAMS
BY CHRIS HEATH

BLINK
bringing you closer

Published by Blink Publishing
3.08, The Plaza,
535 Kings Road,
Chelsea Harbour,
London, SW10 0SZ

www.blinkpublishing.co.uk

facebook.com/blinkpublishing
twitter.com/blinkpublishing

Hardback – 978-1-911274-91-9
Trade Paperback – 978-1-911600-25-1
eBook – 978-1-911600-26-8

A CIP catalogue of this book is available from the British Library.

Designed and set by seagulls.net
Printed and bound by Clays Ltd, St. Ives Plc

1 3 5 7 9 10 8 6 4 2

Picture credits: Chapter 1 © Leo Baron; Chapter 2 © Gwen Field; Chapter 3
© Ayda Williams; Chapter 4 © Hamish Brown; Chapter 5 © Ayda Williams;
Chapter 6 © Ayda Williams; Chapter 7 © Ayda Williams; Chapter 8 © Gwen Field.

Blink Publishing is an imprint of the Bonnier Publishing Group
www.bonnierpublishing.co.uk

This is a book about Robbie Williams. It's an intimate and close-up account of his life as he has lived it, and of the things that he has done, and of what he has thought along the way. Because of who he is, and how he is, and how frank and open he instinctively prefers to be, it describes moments and shares information that you might not normally expect in a book with a photograph of a modern-day celebrity on its cover. Some of these will be silly, some heartrending, some funny, some unpleasant, some uncomfortably honest or disconcertingly blunt, some tender and uplifting, some ludicrously self-obsessed, some touchingly generous and open-hearted, some dispiriting, some life-affirming, some infuriating, and some transcendentally joyous.

Before anything else, here's a story about a song that he recently tried to write. It may seem, to begin with, quite a dark story, because it is one in which he is unsparing about his frustrations and his shortcomings and his failures, as he himself briefly recaps his own life story in a most brutal and bleak way. It serves as a good introduction to one side of who he is, and to the churning cauldron of doubts and obstacles that can fill his head.

But it's also a story in which, by following and facing these fears, somehow he will discover something magical. It spoils nothing to come in this book if I point out, at the very start, that this will be happening, in small ways and large, over and over again. There are no happy endings in lives that are still being lived, because we all remain vulnerable to capricious fortune and our own frailties. But if on one level this book is the ongoing chronicle of a troubled man's quest for the rich life the world already assumes he has, then even if this account dwells at least as much on the struggles as the triumphs, that shouldn't cloud the news that for the most part these days his quest is going extraordinarily well.

* * *

June 2016

He explains his life into the microphone. One version of it, anyway:

So I wasn't going to get married, I wasn't going to have kids, it was my life to fuck up. And I was doing an excellent job of it. And I was never going to sell out because I never bought in, and I never feel comfortable in my own skin. And I was never going to get rid of the anxiety. Fuck, I've got so much anxiety.

Today Rob is at RAK Studios in London with the songwriter Johnny McDaid. It can be an intimate process, songwriting, often with far more time spent exchanging experiences and thoughts than actually crafting lyrics or melodies. Johnny has suggested that they see what happens if Rob just speaks, over some music, some of the pitilessly truthful stuff he's been sharing. No one need ever hear it. Rob has agreed to try.

I know when you're younger you think things must get better, because when you're young, you're immortal, this shit just looks forever, right? But I've done a bit of time on the planet, and it doesn't disappear. I walked through the horizon and I'm still right here.

Part of Rob's current anxiety, an anxiety that has been building and building, is about his forthcoming album. He has written so many new songs – even he's not quite sure how many; maybe 60, maybe 70, maybe 80 – but he's still looking for something he can't quite find. Not just something that's good, not just something that feels special and that feels true, but something that feels *undeniable*. Something that feels like a hit.

I'm jealous and petty and insecure, and oversensitive, undereducated. I think my success is a glitch in the matrix. And, oh yeah, it hurts way more than it should do when you call me fat … talentless … embarrassing.

It doesn't seem very likely at all that this song will turn out to be what he's looking for. But he's doing it anyway.

As he'll put it later, 'I was trying to be honest.'

Because maybe you're saying what I think about myself. And I wouldn't treat anybody the way I treat me. I can name all my faults so easily. And trying to stay positive is so hard. There is no escape.

Over the years, he has written a fair few songs that have been pitiless and unflinching about the man singing them. 'He throws himself under the bus,' notes Johnny, 'before anybody else gets a chance to.' But although self-laceration has been one of Rob's richest subjects, it has usually been a little more heavily disguised than this, or dressed up in metaphor, or camouflaged by humour, or presented in a weird type of sardonic bombast all of his own where Rob has a way of making self-criticism sound like boasting.

But this is more like an unadorned transcription of his bleakest thoughts.

I have self-medicated with drugs, drink, women, TV, the internet, cigarettes. Is it unshakeable DNA that has me rooted to the spot, or am I my forefathers' forefather?

Only at the very end of this dark soliloquy is there a tiny moment of uplift, a very slight triumph-through-adversity my-power-comes-from-my-weakness twist:

Well, actually, my vulnerability has been my strength. I've achieved what I've achieved because of it. And I did it all because I thought I couldn't.

After all that unremitting flagellation, it's not much.

Still, what's been created today is quite an achievement: a distilled three-minute autobiography eloquently told through his doubts and fears and insecurities. They call the song 'I Am Me', after another section that repeats: *Wherever I am, that's where I'll be … I am me.* It obviously isn't anything like the kind of special, universal hit single Rob was after, but sometimes creativity resists being harnessed and commanded to head off in a particular direction.

That other search will have to continue.

* * *

Rob is always writing songs.

He knows some people probably assume that he's the kind of pop star who is eternally sauntering around doing pop star things, and that every now and again some new songs are gathered together for him – maybe with a little bit of input from the star, maybe not – and a record is made. There are plenty of pop stars like that in the modern era, and for some of them this kind of arrangement works wonderfully well.

But actually Rob is the other kind, and he has been ever since he first started writing songs in the mid-1990s. The kind who is always writing, simply because that's what he does. The kind who busies himself laying out pretty much every triumph, every failing, every up, every down, every fantasy, every fear, every love, every hate, every dumb and smart thought, every ambition, every dream, every resonant memory, every boast, every joke, every clever quip and bad rhyme, every hope and every disappointment … all of this, all of whatever part of the mess and majesty of his life comes to mind, in song after song after song. In far more songs, in fact, than anyone will ever hear.

For instance, even though he didn't tell many people at the time, towards the end of 2006 he retired. He gave up being a pop star. And even though he'll now concede that one reason he didn't tell too many people was because somewhere buried deep inside he must have known that he would return, eventually, for nearly three years he told himself that his pop star days were behind him. And *even then* he never stopped writing songs. It just never seemed to cross his mind that he should. At the time, if you visited him in his new life as an ex-pop-star hermit, and if you maybe hinted that there was something strange about the fact that he nonetheless always had new songs to play for you, and that as often as not there'd be some songwriting friends staying in the house, he'd just look at you as though you were being a bit annoying. Couldn't you understand that what he had retired from was something else entirely? From being, if he was forced to put it into words, 'Robbie Williams, pop star', and all that came with it. What he had retired from was everything out *there*. Why on earth should that mean he would stop writing songs? This was something he could do here, safe at home, with his friends. Without anyone else even having to know. This was just what he *did*.

So he writes because he writes. But even so, as he discovered when he did return, if you are a successful pop star for long enough, then there are certain kinds of pressures that change over time, and that grow and grow. There is a magical time in successful pop careers where you're just freewheeling, where everything you do seems to work effortlessly, where it seems as though each time you whisper even the simplest word, the whole world's ears listen. Song after song seems to hit some universal spot, and for a while you almost don't know how to miss.

And then one day, almost as though some random cog in some distant celestial mechanism has clicked into another setting, it stops. This happens to *everybody*, however talented, however famous. There are no exceptions. From then on, great success and acclaim and riches may continue to flow, but it will never again be as easy as it once was.

* * *

So it is now June 2016, and in under five months' time he is scheduled to release the first Robbie Williams album of new pop songs in four years; his first such album as a pop star in his forties. That pressure has been growing. Writing songs for self-fulfilment and self-expression may be a great joy, but writing songs that will be judged by whether they satisfy some standard that is hard even to explain or define, that's more stressful.

He carries around with him all the songs he has been writing, on and off, for the last four years, on the laptop that accompanies him wherever he goes. (Well, to be more precise, the latest version of that laptop. More often than would seem likely, some damage has just been done to the current laptop – it usually involves being dropped, or a mishap involving bathwater – and a tech guy is up at the house, transferring his data onto a brand new one.) Rob's always trying out on people whichever songs are currently on his mind – often the most recent, but sometimes older ones which may have bubbled back up into his thinking. Some are written with his old songwriter partner Guy Chambers, some with members of his live band, some with old friends from Stoke, some with the producer Stuart Price, and some with various other people who he has run into or had recommended by other friends. (Here's a telltale fact: Rob is far more comfortable trying to write a song with someone he doesn't know than, say, going out to dinner with them.) Even if less than half of these songs have ever been serious contenders for a place on a new Robbie Williams album, it's a lot of writing.

The question that he keeps asking himself, and those around him, even when it's not explicitly stated, is: are any of these hits? There's plenty that he's proud of, plenty he likes, plenty he's sure are objectively good. But there are no big prizes in pop music for quantity, or for hard work, or even consistency – the search is for a song that will cut through and that will endure. Maybe he's already got them. It's so hard to know.

Time is nearly up, but he's still searching. Even so, just when you'd think he'd be making the obvious mistake of trying to force out something too crass or commercial or one-dimensional, songs still go where they go. Some days you start out looking for a hit, and you end up with a load of talking and swearing, and an excoriating compendium of the negative thoughts running around inside your head. There's always tomorrow.

* * *

The very next day, he and Johnny McDaid return to RAK Studios to work some more on 'I Am Me'. Weirdly, Rob has emailed a quote to Johnny by the writer Marianne Williamson that Johnny had, quite separately, come across and already read this same week. It's a quote about fear:

Our deepest fear is not that we are inadequate. Our deepest fear is that we are powerful beyond measure. It is our light, not our darkness that most frightens us.

So that is the kind of thing they are discussing and these are the kinds of thoughts in the air. At one point, Rob goes to the bathroom, and as he returns he hears Johnny playing some chords on the piano. Rob just starts singing.

I love my life
I am powerful
I am beautiful
I am free.

'An empowerment song to myself, because that's not how I felt,' he explains. 'I'm a depressive that's struggled with happiness, and I've overcome that now to be in the position where I can sing: *I love my life*. And I know, intuitively, that there's many people out there that feel the same way.'

That is his rationale, here in the moment, anyway. They're certainly not the usual kind of words he would sing. Pop music may be full of self-empowering positivity, often to a fault, but the Robbie Williams catalogue is not. And perhaps he only feels able to do so right now, in this room, because he knows that they'll be balanced by the spoken catalogue of his shortcomings he recited yesterday.

I love my life
I am wonderful
I am magical
I am me.

This is obviously the chorus. It has taken them about five minutes. So now they have a song.

But it's just another song, one more on the computer. There's something special about it, but it's not what he needs. All that dark dialogue – that's not exactly going to be part of a hit single. And there's another problem. That chorus. Rob knows that there's something powerful about it. And when he sung it, he meant it. But he also can't imagine singing those words about himself – not in public, not as Robbie Williams, telling the world that he loves his life.

'What kept coming back,' he says, 'was: "You can't do that, because it seems egoic."'

There's other kinds of boasting that are an essential part of what he does, but not something like this. It's just not the kind of thing he'd do.

* * *

The one part of all this that doesn't bother him is the part that would bother almost anyone else: the thought that he'd been too honest in those verses. That he'd said too much. That he had exposed things it would be safer to keep hidden.

That's one thing that rarely seems to worry him, and it never has. Maybe there's more truth there than a sensible person would share, but throughout his career he's been sharing more truth than a sensible person would share. You could even say it's one of the distinctive counter-logical foundations upon which he's built his whole career.

Most people try to protect themselves by clutching their secrets close, but there is another way. If you reveal your secrets, share your stories, before anyone else can discover them, then they're so much harder to use against you.

And also, this way, even as you share them, they remain yours.

1

September 2016

It is 7:30am. Some mornings are quiet, some less so. Today seems to be a father-and-daughter rap flashback Monday. At the breakfast table in the Williams family's Los Angeles home, Teddy – Theodora Rose Williams, who will be four next week – is eating waffles and raspberries, and in front of her the video to LL Cool J's 'I'm Bad' is playing. It's followed by Public Enemy's 'Don't Believe The Hype', then Kris Kross's 'Jump'.

'Daddy used to love this one,' her personal VJ, who is 42½ years old, tells her. 'Do you like it, Ted? They used to wear everything back to front.'

'Why?' asks Teddy.

'Good question.'

After Will Smith's 'Gettin' Jiggy Wit It', Rob cues up a final selection. 'This one's a good one,' he promises, and OutKast's 'Hey Ya!' begins.

'Daddy wishes he'd written this one,' he says.

* * *

Today is also her father's first public day of work to promote his forthcoming album, *The Heavy Entertainment Show*. He is to be one of the guest celebrity judges on British *X Factor*, for which he needs to spend most of the day being filmed at Sharon Osbourne's house. After breakfast, in preparation for this, he goes back to bed.

During this second sleep, he has a dream. His wife, Ayda, had bought a house in Las Vegas, and he remembers remarking, even inside the dream, how surprised he was to discover that this new house had its own stage. That was far from the only odd thing about it. 'There was a table full of footballers at the housewarming,' he recounts. 'Loads of other tables, too, but no one I knew apart from the footballers.' It was all very uncomfortable. 'I tried to get into it,' he says, 'but I don't like surprises. Though Wayne Rooney was very nice.' And while the front part of the house didn't look so unlike his Los Angeles mansion, something even stranger happened when you walked through to the other side.

'At the back,' he explains, 'it joined to Tunstall market.' Tunstall being the area of Stoke-on-Trent where he grew up.

Rob explains all this in a car heading down from the Hollywood Hills towards Sharon Osbourne's, all quite matter-of-factly. If he doesn't seem to find it all that odd to have dreamed himself in a surreal mansion with a performance space and a portal back into his childhood, it may be because he's got used to weirder things happening all the time, asleep and awake.

Michael Loney, the one of his managers who tends to be with Rob day-to-day when he's working, mentions that he has also had a disquieting dream last night. His also involved Rob. Michael dreamed that Rob and his band had to take a helicopter to a private gig in France today, but that he had completely forgotten to tell Rob about any of it. When he woke up, he actually had to look at his calendar, just to make sure that it wasn't true.

A broader discussion of disturbing dreams follows.

'Yeah,' says Rob. 'I have dreams every now and again that Ayda breaks up with me. She's so cold and divorced from emotion …'

'You don't have relapse dreams still, do you?' Michael asks.

'Well, I don't consider them to be relapse dreams,' Rob says. 'They're just me using drugs.'

He's had a cold for a couple of days and has been complaining of feeling ill. Michael asks him whether he's feeling better or worse than yesterday.

'Maybe better?' Rob allows, tentatively. 'But you know when you don't want people to expect too much of you, so you say "worse"?'

* * *

Sharon Osbourne's house is the one with the Never Mind The Dog Beware Of The Owner sign outside it. She comes to say hello while Rob is having make-up done in one of the upstairs rooms.

'I've got a cold and don't want to give it to you,' he says, 'so let's rub elbows.'

Elbows duly rubbed, they chat about real estate and decorating. (Sharon and Ozzy – though he's away on tour – have just moved into this house.)

'I'm not in control of these decisions,' Rob says. 'I have a wife, and I gave her my testicles ten years ago. She keeps them in a jar by the bed.'

He tells Sharon, who has her own all-female-panel TV show here in America, about Ayda's recent appearances as one of the hosts on *Loose Women*.

'Does she love it?' Sharon asks.

'She does, yeah,' Rob says. 'She does. And I like her being on it. I mean, she talks a lot, but, you know, nothing that I can't handle. Nothing that we don't talk about publicly, anyway.'

They chat about friends and enemies, and Rob tells her that he recently ran into Piers Morgan, someone he has had a long contentious relationship with. 'I used to think that you should shout and rave and call them things,' he says. 'I used to think that you speak your version of truth to power … but I'm a dad now. And also they're not going to hear it, it's not going to change anything, it's just going to cause a problem for yourself. So might as well be nice.'

'It doesn't cost anything to be nice,' says one of the *X Factor* executives who has also come into the room.

'Apart from your dignity,' says Rob. 'But I lost that in 1991 anyway. So that's all right.'

A while after Sharon and the *X Factor* people leave, Rob suddenly says, 'Yeah, it was the "Do What U Like" video.' 'Do What U Like' was Take That's first single; at the end of the video the five of them lie face down on the floor, naked, while a young woman rubs jelly across their arses with a mop.

There's a pause.

'When I lost my dignity,' he adds, just in case that wasn't absolutely clear.

* * *

The chain of events that led to Rob making nice with Piers Morgan began at somewhere called the Dan The Man Gym, a children's play gym where Rob and Ayda had taken their son Charlie. (Charlton Valentine Williams, who will be two next month.) There they ran into Simon Cowell's partner, Lauren Silverman, and she invited them to her birthday party the following night at the Chateau Marmont hotel. That's a place Rob would go when he was single, and not a place he ever particularly wants to revisit, but he thought he should at least show his face. He hadn't thought too hard about who else might be there.

'And then there's Piers Morgan through the crowd,' he says. He had a quick decision to make. Piers Morgan has said many poisonous and patronising things about Rob over the years, and Rob has not always failed to find a hateful response. Occasionally he may have even got in his retaliation first. And now here they were. 'Of course I'm in a difficult position then because I'm at a party where he's been invited, and I can't do rude or violent,' Rob explains. So he decided to go completely the other way. 'I went and gave him a hug. And he was, "Robbie, are we feuding at the moment or are we not? I don't know where we are with that." I said, "Look, you know, when all the bad media stuff was happening for me and at me, you became the poster child for all of it – so you represented all of that bad bit." And he said, "I understand that." And I said, "I'm a bit older now." And he went, "… and wiser." And I went, "Yeah, and wiser." I made nice.'

When dinner was served, they were seated next to each other at a table, with Simon Cowell and Lauren, and Ayda, and Nicole Scherzinger. They chatted, and Rob complimented Morgan on things he had read him saying about terrorism that Rob considered brave. Nothing bad happened.

'Interestingly, it was like a weight off my shoulders not having to hate someone,' Rob reflects. 'One person less. It was weirdly gratifying, being nice to him.'

Afterwards, as Rob expected might well happen, Morgan wrote about the encounter in his column in the *Mail on Sunday*.

This was how he saw it:

Robbie and I have had a rather chequered past together. I was Take That's official biographer but we fell out when fame and fortune went to his head and he disappeared up his backside. Or maybe that was me … !

So things could have been a little tense, but fortunately our wives chatted first and it turned out they share the same Pilates instructor in London … always an effective ice-breaker.

Robbie offered me his hand.

'How are you, mate?'

'I'm good, mate. It's been a while …'

'It certainly has! I've calmed down a bit now.'

'Me too.'

We both chuckled, then had a lengthy chat about life, the universe and my opinion columns. 'I admire the way you stick your neck out about stuff like Isis and guns,' he said, 'but are you not worried someone's going to have a pop at you one day?'

'People have been wanting to kill me for 30 years,' I replied.
'True,' he nodded. 'Well, if anyone succeeds, I'll sing Angels at your funeral.'
'Cheers mate, very good of you.'
'Least I can do.'

According to Rob, most of this was true, though he says that Piers Morgan asked him if he would sing 'Angels' at his funeral, rather than Rob offering out of the blue. And he notes how Piers Morgan didn't mention the poster child bit, though doubtless Morgan took that as an apology for how he was made to unfairly represent the collective sins of others. Never mind that sometimes they put you on the poster because you're the star of the show.

* * *

As he has his make-up done, Rob shares some surprising news. About ten days ago, he had Botox for the first time.

'Botox and fillers,' he explains. 'It was a traumatic experience. It really hurt.' He says that it took about eight days to settle down; before then, there were bits of his face where the Botox hadn't kicked in. 'Ayda thought that I was always angry with her but I wasn't.'

I ask him why he did it.

'Because if you stay in a barbershop long enough you're going to get a haircut,' he says. 'And I live in Los Angeles. And I'm forty-two. And why not? I like it. I've got a flat forehead.'

* * *

For some TV shots which will at first mask, and then reveal, who the mystery celebrity judge is, Rob is filmed in dungarees, pruning the foliage with shears, pretending to be Sharon Osbourne's gardener. The film crew have an extra idea that they like – that he should be sprayed with a hose. They ask Rob whether that sounds weird to him.

'Does a bit,' he replies, 'because then I'll get my tits wet. And I'm trying my best to be a pop star.'

He and Sharon sit and watch as the contestants perform in front of them, twice each, in the garden. By their second performances, it's dark. In a break, there's some chat about the different singers, and Michael mentions that one of them didn't get all of the notes right.

'She got most of them right!' Rob protests. 'That's what I work on. If I get seventy-five per cent right, I've had a good performance.'

A while later, while they're still filming in the garden, Ayda arrives with Teddy and Charlie to say hello, and the whole shoot halts for a moment. That's when Teddy, surrounded by maybe fifty people making a TV show in a Los Angeles garden, somehow completely takes over, starting to sing 'Let It Go', with so much possession that pretty much everyone gathered here joins in.

'Well done, baby,' says Rob.

* * *

Rob spends the next day back at his own house doing filmed interviews, first in the studio, then at the edge of his expansive lawn, with the city behind him, talking about each song on his album. Work complete, he sits with the kids as they have their supper. They watch some of *Mary Poppins* on YouTube and then, this rap video phase enduring, he puts on the Beastie Boys' 'Intergalactic' video.

'Do you like this, Ted?' he asks.

'Yes,' she answers, then reconsiders. 'I don't like it when he's singing.'

'Shall I play a song with me on it?' he suggests.

'Yes,' she says.

'Which one?' he asks.

'Did you sing "Let It Go"?' she replies hopefully.

'No, I haven't got that,' he says, and puts on the 'Candy' video. Charlie looks enraptured, but Teddy has a question about the on-screen action.

'Did you fall in love with her?' she asks, pointing to one of Rob's co-stars.

'No!' says Rob. 'The only woman apart from you I love is Mummy.'

He has another idea.

'Do you want to see lots of people watching Daddy?' he asks.

'Yes.'

He puts on the beginning of the Knebworth show.

'And all of those people,' he explains, 'have come to see Daddy. A sea of people …'

She peers close as he sings 'Let Me Entertain You'.

'Is that you?' she asks.

'Yeah.'

After a few minutes, he pauses it.

'What do you think, Ted?'

She appears to consider her response to this question with some care. There is something she very much wants to say to her father, and she feels that this is the moment to say it.

'Now,' she says, 'can I show you the rainbow sweeties?'

* * *

Rob will tell this last story many times over the next few months – between songs onstage, and during TV and radio and print interviews. Of course there are almost endless layers here: the entwined spirals of conceit and modesty, self-deprecation and rampant egotism involved in telling a story notionally against yourself that's nonetheless designed to entertain and so, I suppose, to make people like you more.

Over time, he changes the story, too. He rarely says 'rainbow sweeties'. It's a bit confusing. You could say that Teddy slightly messed up there – didn't think hard enough about what would play best as a chat-show anecdote. For a while he has her say 'can I have some cake?', though sometimes he prefers 'can I watch *Peppa Pig*?' (Both things that Teddy has said many times, though not this time.)

Anyone who picks up on these contradictions probably imagines that the whole thing is made-up. It's not. It happened. But like many other things in the world, in entertainment what actually happened is just a good first draft of the truth.

* * *

REVEAL

April 2006

In his Cape Town hotel, Rob tries to enjoy some fresh air from the balcony of his room. He's 32, and in South Africa on the first leg of a tour that will last the rest of the year. But already he seems somewhat frayed.

Right now, down in the courtyard below, some of the other hotel guests are simply standing there, staring up at him, as you might regard an interesting piece of architecture or a full moon. As though they have no conception that the object of their gaze also has eyes, and that he can see them, too.

'Go and look at someone else,' he beseeches.

But he says it under his breath, too quietly for them to hear. No good would come of saying it any louder.

* * *

Looking back, what should have been one of his great moments of triumph is also the exact moment when Rob believes it all really began to crumble inside. On 19th November 2005, tickets went on sale for Robbie Williams' Close Encounters tour: his biggest tour yet, and also his longest. Even though he'd approached, or occasionally reached, meltdown on previous tours, and with worrying frequency, he had agreed to this tour because the opportunity was too big not to. Success has its own logic, and this is simply how success works if you leave it to its own devices. When you're given the chance to go beyond what you have done before, that's what you do.

'It seemed,' he remembers, 'the part of the jigsaw that's obvious. It was the next step, the natural conclusion. At that moment I was for all intents and purposes the biggest pop star on the planet, and the next step was to go bigger and be bigger and do bigger. And there didn't seem like any other option. This was what I'd always done. Just follow the momentum.'

On that first day, when tickets went on sale, 1.6 million were sold, a feat that remains in *The Guinness Book of Records* as the most tickets sold by one person in a single day. But Rob wasn't elated. He was terrified. And confused.

'It didn't add up in my head,' he says. 'That so many people should turn up and it generate that much money. I didn't feel worthy of performing to that many people, and I didn't feel worthy of receiving that much money.' He laughs. 'Not that I was going to give it away. But what was happening in my career didn't sit well with my chronic lack of self-esteem. It felt like: I'm not capable of mentally doing this or physically doing this.'

He had asked his friend Jonny Wilkes to come on tour with him, ostensibly so that they could perform two songs in the middle of the set together and do a little onstage tomfoolery, though for Rob it was more for the overall support and company Jonny could offer: 'I'd sort of kidnapped Jonny to be my walker and hold my hand, shoulder some of the glare.' But after the tickets went on sale, Rob called a meeting with his management. He told them that he wanted to cancel the whole tour. 'I'm really sorry but I've got to pull out of this,' he announced. 'I know it's going to be too much for me.'

Rob then headed to Jonny's house, to let him know. But as soon as Jonny opened the door, he told Rob his latest news – how he'd just been offered a 12-month stint in a touring production of *Guys and Dolls* but that of course he'd turned it down because the two of them would soon be off on their own touring adventures.

Most likely Rob would have found another way to talk himself round – there had been other moments like this where he had declared that everything must be cancelled and had then backtracked, and there will be more to come – but for now he used this.

'We weren't going on tour,' he explained to Jonny, 'but we are now.'

* * *

He knows that people struggle to understand what it is that he finds so hard about doing something that seems so fundamental to who he is and what he does: performing in huge concerts, night after night. We are raised on the stories of the Michael Jacksons, the entertainers who say that they feel more at home onstage than off it. And Rob is well aware that if there is a kind of entertainer who appears, from the outside, not just comfortable up there, but thriving on it – bathing in, and orchestrating, the attention and appreciation of the transfixed hordes around and below – he most certainly looks like a textbook specimen.

He also knows that when people are told that, for Rob himself, being up onstage often doesn't feel the way that they're convinced it must – especially as they often feel they've seen evidence with their own eyes to the contrary – this information is, at best, an annoying and confusing distraction. At worst, people simply don't believe it. Don't believe *him*. They think it's some weird cry for (even more) attention, some kind of perverse outsize humblebrag.

So he'd ask that if you care to consider it at all, forget all that. Forget what your instincts tell you about showbiz and entertainment, and what you imagine someone who you believe seems to belong onstage is feeling.

'It happens to be,' he points out, 'a completely unnatural environment.'

Just try to think about it, if you can, from first principles. Think of it just as a group of people – everyone, including the audience and the performer – and how they find themselves to have been arranged in relationship to each other on this particular evening in one particular space on this planet.

Imagine that someone has picked sides for an after-school game and it has somehow gone horribly, horribly wrong.

'There's eighty thousand of them,' he explains. 'There's one of you.'

* * *

The real endurance test, the run of shows that continues week after week, doesn't begin until early June, but now, in April 2006, there are these few early dates in South Africa. I fly out to meet him there two days before the first show in Durban. He's been in the country for a while, rehearsing the new tour production, and filming a video for his next single, 'Sin Sin Sin'. When I arrive, it's immediately clear that he's in an odd frame of mind. In his hotel room, he simultaneously watches Leicester beat Crystal Palace, plays me new songs he's written, has a massage for a bad groin, and tells me about how, when he heard that his summer Wembley concerts were cancelled because of construction delays with the new stadium, he couldn't hide his glee, even though he knew it wasn't how he was supposed to be reacting. (The dates will be moved to the Milton Keynes Bowl, so, whatever weird sense of victory he was feeling, it will be a hollow one.)

Then, once the masseuse has gone, he rather obsessively reads to me some pieces of writing he has done. They're mostly horror stories about his dating life – bleak, despairing and intermittently vengeful. He tells me he thinks that they're the beginning of a book. After I leave him, he stays up late into the night compiling an eclectic playlist of party tunes that includes 808 State's 'Pacific State' and Billy Idol's 'Dancing With Myself', for no more reason, it seems, than that he thought it had to be done.

* * *

The next day he is scheduled to visit some orphaned children, in order to draw attention to the work UNICEF is doing here for families affected by AIDS. He's doing this because he has an ongoing relationship with UNICEF – officially, he is known as a UNICEF UK ambassador, though 'ambassador' is a term that embarrasses him. But he has done trips with UNICEF before. He was introduced to UNICEF by Ian Dury, whom he met through their shared make-up artist Gina Kane, and who told Rob he was looking for somebody 'to pass it on to'. In 1998 they went to Sri Lanka together, in 2000 Rob went to Mozambique, and in 2003 he visited child protection programmes in Russia. But this current visit has a dual purpose. He and Jonny Wilkes recently dreamed up, as a kind of fantasy wish-fulfilment, a football match involving celebrities and legendary football players; it is taking place next month under the name Soccer Aid, and its proceeds are going to UNICEF. So today he needs to make one of those films that will be broadcast during the Soccer Aid coverage, both to educate TV viewers about the kinds of things UNICEF does and as an appeal to send in money.

Even though this is probably a good diversion from the start of the tour, he doesn't find these things easy. First there is a briefing from UNICEF in one of the hotel function rooms, He wears sunglasses throughout, not just because he's had a late night – 'I don't normally get up for another four hours,' he'll apologise as he enters the room – but for another reason he'll explain to me later on: 'I didn't want anybody to read my eyes because my eyes were saying, "Oooh, please – help me out here." It's another one of those things where you wish you were in a band. That it was you and The Edge doing it ...' He's often fantasised about being in a band, and has occasionally tried to form one, and he's always given the same reason: because in a band at least people are looking somewhere else for some of the time. (The downside of being someone who people pay attention to is exactly the same as the upside: people pay attention to you.)

The children we will visit today, the Zondi family, live some distance outside Durban in a place called Umbumbulu. They lost their father a few years back and their mother much more recently; they'd stopped going to school and were seen foraging for food until a childcare worker associated with UNICEF started visiting and helping the household to function once more. In the car, one of the UNICEF workers teaches Rob the Zulu word for hello – *sawubona* – and he repeats it. But he sits mostly in silence, and he'll later tell me that, as we were driving, he was carving up pie charts in his head of whether his reasons for being here are more selfish or selfless, going over and over it: 'Is the "look at me ..." percentage of the pie chart bigger than the humanitarian reasons?' He couldn't be sure. 'Who fucking knows?' he concludes afterwards. 'All I know is this – that I do it regardless of what I think and feel, and I do it regardless of what other people think and feel. And when I got there, that all went out the window.'

We leave the paved roads, losing an unwanted police escort that after some complicated negotiations with UNICEF has agreed to shadow us no further, and start meandering down dry, red earth tracks that wind up and down and around the hills, dwellings spread here and there. When we arrive at our destination, Rob bonds with the brothers by quizzing them about football, the shared international language of men. He asks them how old they are. Mboniseni is 18, Mlungisi 14. (Their sisters, Balungile and Khethiwe, are nine and six.)

'I'm thirty-two, which is very, very old,' he tells them. 'I'm a singer from England.'

After he's chatted with the kids for a while, the UNICEF people cut in – they have an agenda here, of course, and theirs is ultimately the reason Rob's here. They ask the children to talk about the death of their parents, and what has happened since. It's doubtless necessary, but also uncomfortable. Maybe it's that Rob and people in his world are used to the intrinsic moral imperfections and incongruities of the entertainment universe, but nonetheless unrealistically expect that the world of charity and aid wouldn't have its own equivalents. Even so, sometimes the contradictions of what is required here show themselves a little too blatantly. A few minutes later, Rob is filmed at the parents' simple graves, a short walk from the house, narrating to camera the story of the Zondi family and how UNICEF has helped them. But by now we have gathered quite a crowd, mostly local kids who Rob has been playing football with and who understandably seem excited by the strange roadshow that has come into their lives. But their high spirits are not what is needed right now.

'Sorry, guys,' says the cameraman. 'I can hear all the laughing in the background.'

'Just misery, please,' mutters Rob quietly, embarrassed.

Back in the house, Rob sits with the four children. Mlungisi starts touching Robbie's tattoos, seemingly enchanted and mystified by them.

'It's my grandfather,' Robbie explains, as he fingers one of them.

'You like him?' asks Mlungisi.

'Yes. A lot.'

He points to the design on his left shoulder: 'This is from New Zealand and it's a traditional Maori prayer, and it protects me and my family.' Then he guides Mlungisi around some others – the Staffordshire knot on the back of his right hand ('this is the town where I was born'), the cursive 'B' just behind and below his left ear ('that's my grandma, Betty'). He moves on to the large letters down his forearms: 'My mother hates tattoos, so this says I LOVE YOU ... MOTHER – she doesn't hate those.' Then he lifts a sleeve of his t-shirt to show one more. 'The lion!' exclaims Mlungisi, grabbing at his right arm.

They ask him whether his tattoos cost money.

'Yes,' he says. 'They're expensive, but they're with me for life. It's difficult to explain, but it's like my armour. It protects me.' He points again around his body: 'My religion, my family, my town, my mother … everything that protects me.'

They say their goodbyes (for now – they are invited to the show tomorrow night), and Rob tells Mboniseni he likes the way he wears his cap at a jaunty angle. He then worries that this message isn't getting through.

'What's the Zulu word for "jaunty"?' he asks.

* * *

Before the first show of the tour, he meets with the Zondi children again, and shows them round backstage.

He tries to tell them about the concert. 'I'm really scared,' he explains to them. 'Honestly, truth to God. I'm a tiny person. And that out there is huge.'

He makes it sound sweet and funny, and I'm sure they don't for a moment imagine that he might mean it. But after they go to get some food – they are entranced by the chocolate fountain that has been set up – Rob goes into the band room, and tries to start a conversation about which songs can be dropped from the set. 'The long and the short of it is, we have a five-month tour,' he says. 'The setlist for me is too long.' Part of his argument is that he assumes they must have put extra songs in, knowing he would do this. As he makes his case, someone in the throng, chatting on their phone, gives whomever they are talking to a commentary on what is happening: 'I'm just listening to Rob whittling his set down to an opening song and a closing song.'

The show itself goes without a hitch, and everyone gathers back at the hotel. If anyone imagines that when a touring party gets together to relax the conversations tend to be about momentous issues of the day or even important matters relating to the tour, they quite probably have never been on a tour. Tonight, there is an improbably intense discussion about what kind of crisps James Bond would eat (Rob's ultimate verdict is smoky bacon) which leads him to talk about his eternal hunger for chocolate. (When someone here doesn't quite seem to get it, Rob spells it out. 'I'd eat these curtains if they were made of chocolate. I'd eat my own knee if it were made of chocolate.') Then, not long after the crisps and chocolate debate, there is a long conversation about TV shows from yesteryear, which leads to an ensemble singalong of the theme tunes to *Top Cat*, *Hong Kong Phooey* and *The Flintstones*, and then a solo rendition from Rob of the theme to *Sons and Daughters*. ('Where the fuck did that come from?' he quite reasonably asks.) Someone mentions *The A-Team* and Rob reflexively says, 'First thing I ever recorded with a video recorder.' Then he reminisces about a particularly disturbing episode of *Tales of the Unexpected* where someone was shadowed all the time by a man they couldn't see.

'That's fucked me up until this day,' he says. 'Looking in cupboards …'

The tour has begun.

* * *

Perhaps it could have all been fine. At times in South Africa, the discomfort he was clearly showing could have been nothing but teething problems. After the first show he told me, 'At least I didn't come offstage and think: 'I don't want to do that for five months'.'

But that may also have been part of the bluff that Rob was trying to work even on himself, because after it all spins horribly out of control he will explain that, deep down, right before the start, he already knew.

'This huge operation was in place and there was no way of backing out,' he says. 'And I kind of just didn't have the heart for it anymore. It was kind of like being on the *Titanic*. Like: I don't know where this ship is going to sink … but it's definitely letting in water.'

* * *

January 2016

The Williams family and their ten dogs move into their new Los Angeles home on New Year's Eve. It's a house big enough that even Rob is somewhat taken aback. 'The "slack-jawed" has just about stopped,' he says when I arrive a few days later, as Teddy dashes past in a princess dress that she got for Christmas.

Whether because his default setting is worry, or because it's useful to have something to motivate you, he claims that being here is also a little unnerving.

'I come downstairs in this big house,' he says, 'and there's two security on, four cleaners, a nanny, a chef ... and that's just in this house. I've got two other houses. It's all right when I'm on tour, but when I've not been on tour for a while, it makes me restless and worried. Which also keeps me sober-ish, and in the gym, and focused, and bothered.'

The plan for the next ten days is to write songs with Guy Chambers, the songwriting partner with whom he wrote most of his first five albums, and with whom he reunited in recent years after a long estrangement. Guy is arriving tomorrow. This is supposed to be their final push to come up with even better songs than they already have for the album he'll release in the autumn.

'I just hope he comes up with the goods,' says Rob, sort of playfully, and sort of not.

Still, priorities. He goes down into the basement where the engineer Richard Flack is setting up the studio. They talk, and Richard suggests they might think about buying a particular expensive set of speakers.

'I've just bought a tennis-ball machine for a grand,' Rob objects. 'It fires three hundred and fifty balls,' he adds, by way of explanation.

Richard, who is not given to grand emotional gestures, slightly raises an eyebrow.

'Not at the same time,' Rob clarifies.

* * *

Come a new year, come a new series of *Celebrity Big Brother*. When, in interviews, Rob patiently explains that for the most part the only television he enjoys watching is reality TV, I think people often think he's just trying to be funny or silly. He's not. He'll watch the occasional film, and the occasional documentary, and he'll very occasionally get interested in a TV drama, but quite genuinely the majority of his viewing is reality TV.

Celebrity Big Brother is one of his and Ayda's favourites, and every night when it is on they watch the latest episode in their bedroom before going to sleep. Generally, anyone staying in the house is invited; the two of them sit in bed and anyone else can pull up a chair around the bed to face the drop-down screen.

Already, Ayda explains, this season has provided talking points in the Williams family.

'It's my running joke with Rob,' she says, 'that every time we turn on the television, I kid you not, he has slept with someone on TV – whether it's a commercial for anti-HIV medication, or it's a crime-scene show, or something from the nineties, Rob has slept with someone on TV. So we turn on *Celebrity Big Brother* ...'

At first it seemed like there was going to be a slight twist on this theme, in that Rob was only going to be implicated indirectly. Darren Day, one of the house guests, was talking about his reputation as a love rat, and mentioned Anna Friel.

'So I said,' Ayda continues, '"Oh my God, you've kind of slept with Darren Day because you've slept with Anna Friel ..."'

As she tells it, for a moment Rob didn't say anything, as though considering whether, or perhaps how exactly, to explain. Because while the every-time-we-turn-on-the-television rule had indeed worked its wonders again, Ayda was looking at the wrong part of the screen. Better just say.

'Babe,' he says. 'Danniella Westbrook.'

* * *

The next morning is Teddy's first day at school, and Rob is awake to accompany her at 7:45. Over breakfast, he explains to her the five-second dropped-food rule, and then muses blearily whether the Kardashians might be one sign of the apocalypse. He seems to be serious about this. 'But,' he adds, by way of acknowledging that there may very well be good and bad in almost everything, 'I can't knock the hustle.'

With that, he beckons Ayda – 'okay, Mummy, let's go' – and he leads Teddy towards the car, a half-eaten, peanut-butter-covered bagel in her hand.

Around lunchtime, Guy arrives. Rob takes the long walk with him down to the bottom of the garden, Los Angeles spread below, and, beyond, in the hazy distance, the ocean. At the furthest end of the garden is a tangerine tree, and this journey to get a tangerine becomes a kind of ritual. Whenever Rob wants to talk to someone, he suggests this tangerine-walk.

Guy talks about the New Year festivities he was part of at Babington House, the country house affiliated to the Soho House private members' club empire which hosted a particularly exclusive gathering of the well-known and well-connected. At one point, there was a group singsong and Guy played the piano. 'Adele wanted to sing "Angels",' he says. 'And she did.' But then, he says, there was a slightly embarrassing moment when it became clear that Guy didn't know any of her songs well enough. He tried to cover up: 'I said let's do 'Mamma Mia'!'

Down in the studio, Rob explains to Guy about his current no-flour, no-sugar diet, which he was set on to after Hugh Jackman came to his last show in Melbourne and recommended someone. (This explanation actually includes the phrase 'my friend Wolverine's nutritionist'.)

Recently, though, he explains, it hasn't been going so well.

'I had a cake relapse,' he tells Guy.

'At Christmas?' says Guy, as though to say: well, that's no big deal – a seasonal setback like that is nothing to worry about.

'Well, yeah,' says Rob, 'but the door isn't shut yet, and I was hoping it would be. And it was for a year and a half. And now I'm a bit scared.'

'What kind of cake was it?' Guy asks.

'*All* of the cakes,' Rob clarifies.

'How many cakes did you do?'

'Well, there's a lot of cakes about at Christmas,' says Rob, and starts listing: 'Christmas cakes … red velvet cakes … my daughter's *Frozen* cake which she hadn't eaten yet – I had about a quarter of that the other day.'

This morning, in fact, I had listened as Teddy quizzed him about this, more puzzled than upset.

'I had a little bit,' he explained to her. 'But I had a little bit quite often.'

* * *

Guy says that he has 12 ideas, by which he means pieces of music that he has already recorded, if only in a rudimentary form, in his London studio. He suggests trying four a day.

'And if you don't like any of them,' he says, 'we'll start something from scratch.'

They begin writing, though sometimes it's quite hard to tell how committed Rob is, as even when he's excited he still often multitasks. Right now, at the same time as he thinks up lyrics, he is watching footage of Elton John singing 'Pinball Wizard', with the volume muted, on YouTube. A few minutes later he shows Guy a photo of Elton John wearing gigantic boots which presumably conceal some kind of stilts.

'Can you imagine the show starting like that?' he says. 'It'd look fucking great.'

* * *

'Are you hiking anymore?' Guy asks. During previous writing sessions in Los Angeles, he and Rob would often break to go for a hike, but this week Rob hasn't suggested it. It turns out there's a reason.

'I went apeshit with a paparazzi,' Rob explains. 'I tried my best to provoke him to get out of the car. We were hiking every day in the same place, TreePeople. And I was coming back and we'd put baby girl in the car and this day I could see a Volkswagen with the window open this much.' He knew it was a paparazzo, filming him, Ayda and, most importantly, Teddy. And he was correct in his assumption. 'I went over with my phone to film them filming us, and as I got there I just lost it. I wanted to provoke something in him so that he would hit me first, so I went over and cunted him off left, right and centre. He was a Scouser – I called him a Scouse cunt.'

What did he say?

'"Less of the 'Scouse'."'

It escalated from there. After some more back and forth, the man told Rob, 'You're a worldwide tit.' (Which, now, he clearly thinks is hilarious, though back then nothing was.)

'I went, "Seventy million albums, you cunt!" It was the only thing I could think of. But I was so enraged. I was that angry – I would never have ever said "Scouse cunt". Never ever *ever*. But I was that angry it came out before I'd recognised I'd done it. I could see how that happens. I was filming him, but I couldn't get the phone to work, and as soon as the conversation had ended, he wanted me to get rid of the film, because I was calling him a paedophile because he was taking pictures of kids.'

Ayda, who has come down to the studio, offers her own observations. 'It didn't go well, the fight. You let yourself down,' she says to Rob, and then to us: 'Rob did not show his best side.'

What he learned from this experience is that he's not quite sure how to control his rage in these circumstances: 'When a lens comes out and it's your daughter or it's your son, and you can't protect them from it, it's primal. You want to kill them. And you tell them that you want to kill them. And then you realise that you can never say or do that again in front of the children. Getting back into the car after that event took place, I realised that I could never ever behave that way ever again.'

That is the long answer to Guy's question.

This is the shorter one: 'I haven't been hiking since.'

* * *

Because of the time difference between London and Los Angeles, whenever something newsworthy occurs on *Celebrity Big Brother* – which is to say newsworthy according to the British tabloids – Rob is often likely to read about it online before he and Ayda have watched the relevant episode. Today, Rob discovers, browsing the internet down in the studio, that the papers have just such a story. And this one involves him. On the latest episode, Darren Day is apparently filmed telling Danniella Westbrook that Rob once phoned the home in Chelsea where he and Anna Friel lived together, and asked Anna Friel out.

'I did know I'd done that,' he concedes. 'My recollection now is somewhat murky, but I didn't know she was still going out with Darren Day.'

That night, five of us watch in the bedroom. Darren Day says on the screen that when he answered the phone Rob pretended to be someone called 'Derek from Go! Discs'. (Go! Discs was an independent record label enjoying some success back in the 1990s.) Rob immediately realises that what Day is saying is true. It all comes back to him.

'A man answered and I panicked, and said it was Derek from Go! Discs,' he says. 'I was probably on the phone in front of a bunch of CDs.'

When Darren Day tells her this story inside the Big Brother house, Danniella Westbrook's reaction is to say 'he's got some balls'.

'And she would know,' Rob mutters.

* * *

One afternoon, Guy starts talking about a mid-range 1970s music star, largely forgotten now, who has fallen on difficult times.

'He's really sad, that guy,' says Guy.

'Sad?' asks Rob.

'Yeah,' Guy continues. 'He had a major breakdown. He had terrible anxiety about being a pop star. It was like Beatlemania – he couldn't leave his hotel room for years. And he went nuts and had a breakdown. And you see him now and you can see on his face that something terrible happened to him.'

'*I* don't leave my hotel room!' Rob points out, indignantly.

'Well, you're not sad,' says Guy, then, in the tone of a man who isn't quite sure how he has found himself in a slightly awkward spot, readjusts this a little. 'You don't have a sad-looking ...' he says, then halts again. He has a third try. 'You don't look *destroyed* by who you are ...' he tells Rob.

'No,' Rob agrees. 'But it is angles and lighting.'

* * *

Rob tells Guy he has to take a break in a moment for a business meeting. 'I'm going to rob a bank,' he declares. 'And the bank's called show business.'

The meeting takes place outside by the pool with David Enthoven – who, with Tim Clark at their company IE, has managed Rob since 1996 – and with Michael. Rob explains to them the idea he has for a biographical one-man live show, something that he woke up thinking about this morning. 'Talking about my life, being really honest ... the frailties, my hatreds – who I hate, why I hate – what my actions have led me to,' he says. 'It could be *Never Explain, Don't Complain*.' After making a case for it as a piece of storytelling and entertainment, he allows that there is another reason why he's thinking about this. 'I just think that with my bad back, and how much physical exertion it takes to do these shows ...' he says, trailing off. 'Because I do a show and go to bed, that's what happens: do a show, go to bed, go to the gig, stretch, do a gig, come back, watch YouTube, fall asleep, until it's time to do the next gig. So I wonder if there's a clever way of having another branch of entertainment – another idea of a show?'

They listen carefully, and discuss the idea back and forth. Rob fills out more of the details, and then says, 'There will be pathos and there will be moments of shit that fucking happened: you were that scared that you slept with a starting pistol and CS gas ... but I can make it funny and humorous too.' As for the audience, he says: 'They come to a theatre and sit down. There's no bouncing. They listen.' He offers one final flourish: 'And if it's good enough, and it stands up by itself, maybe other people can play me eventually.'

He looks around the table, hoping for some enthusiastic reinforcement of this idea.

'Or not,' he adds.

* * *

Over the next few days, more songs are written, and some of them seem good, but as ever Rob is getting stressed about whether they've got the song they need. Chris Briggs, his long-term A&R man, who sits on the sofa during most of these sessions, only intervening occasionally with a deceptively casual comment, says that Adele wrote a hundred songs before she found 'Hello'. Rob counters that he doesn't think that's true.

A while later, he looks up from his computer screen, on which he has just read some useful and relevant information, and announces, 'Adele wrote thirty-four songs.'

'Where did you find that bit of information?' asks Guy, assuming that Rob must have been searching through Adele interviews online. But there are easier ways.

'I just asked her,' Rob says.

* * *

June–August 2006

On the surface, the Close Encounters tour was going well enough. The stadiums were full, the reviews suggested that he wasn't annoying anyone who wasn't annoyed by him already, and he kept turning up. 'There was a job to be done, there was a lot of people in front of me,' he says. 'And it kind of got to the point where everybody was going to be bankrupt if I pulled out. But it was ultimately my choice to try and get myself up there and do it.' Sometimes you find yourself so far from home that the only option is to keep right on going in the direction that you're going in.

Behind the scenes, it was more obvious that he was struggling. The first steroid-injection-in-his-arse of the tour came in Berlin. As the tour continued, it happened progressively more and more, as he kept searching for enough borrowed energy to get himself onstage. Once he was up there in front of the audience, he switched to a different crutch. 'The amount of times I went to the drum riser and had a triple espresso was unbelievable every night,' he says.

* * *

As the tour went on, how were you feeling?

'Britain was looming, and for whatever reason on that particular tour, the thought of the UK being on the horizon absolutely terrified me. To a certain degree I'd say the rest of the tour was a success. Not internally, because I was just in a place where my job was making me unhappy. It was having the opposite reaction to what I would hope that my life as that person would have. And it was isolating and lonely, and I found the responsibility of having that many people to perform in front of overwhelming. Stadiums full of people would come to see me. And like I've said before, my self-worth wasn't big enough to accept the challenge. Or I didn't have enough self-worth to believe in myself.'

But it's not as though, as you went round the world, people were going, 'God, he's lost it, he's shit.' It was, externally, still a huge success. Did that make it better or worse?

'It was confusing. I suppose that I was in the middle of a breakdown, and no matter what I would have been doing at that point, I would have found it equally hard to rise to the challenge of being anything.'

What happened when you got to Britain?

'I froze internally. Throughout my career it has always been kind of easier to be a pop star in a country where you don't know what they're saying about you. I can't read German. In England I froze and felt physically incapable to do the job that I was being paid handsomely to do.'

What did that mean?

'It meant that I was terrified. It was beyond stage fright, into this new stratosphere of complete terror. It's so isolating to be the person that's got to go and do this thing that's the last thing you want to do. It's like being asked to jump out of a plane without ever having had to jump out of a plane before without a parachute and then in mid-air try to find somebody that's got a parachute and hold on to them. But in reality you'd be jumping out of the plane, and there'd be no one there with a parachute.'

But you'd still do it every night?

'I had to. There were "I'm not going on" moments, but I was being begged and pleaded that if you didn't go on, "it's going to cost this much". There was a moment at Leeds on the first night where I looked right to the back of the bowl and then looked on the ground close to me. There was this rivet in the corrugated iron that had been put down on the turf for the vehicles travelling over it, to stop everything get muddy. And I thought: *Everything here, including this little rivet to that last person that I can't see on the horizon is here for me*. And I was already freaked out, and that compounded my freak-out. Afterwards, I got into the chopper to fly back to Manchester and was shaking uncontrollably. The next night was being filmed live. In the hotel I was, "I don't care how much it's going to cost, I can't do it." I remember Max Beesley telling me about having a panic attack when he was drumming for George Michael at the first MTV awards: "Brother, I was onstage and I thought: what if I just stop. This whole thing is relying on me being able to do this." At the time I thought, "What a weird schism to have." But then I got exactly that. What if I just stopped? What if I just told them what was going on, and walked offstage?'

But you didn't?

'No. But the night that it was on TV, I actually struggled to walk to the stage. My legs were bandy. They just wouldn't work. It felt as though I was walking towards death. And then I shot up through the stage – *bmmmmfffff!* – and a performance happened.'

You know how it is: a lot of people will read something like this and they'll think: *I was at that show* or *I watched it on TV, you were fine. Why are you being so melodramatic about it?* How can you explain it to them?

'I can't.'

But you get what it is that they can't understand?

'Yeah. Completely. All I can say is that the breakdown that I was having was incredibly real, and the extreme force of the stage fright and the panic and terror was real. So much so that the last thing I wanted to do was to get up onstage. And then whatever happens as soon as that trapdoor opens and I go through the middle, it's on. I think I just channelled the terror. I mean, what nobody realises is that the more cocky and arrogant that I look onstage, the more terrified I am. I saw some old footage of me walking towards stage and I've got a black suit on and I'm skinny and I've got black glasses on and I'm walking like I'm ten men, and I look like I'm rock hard. And I remember at the time knowing that I was being filmed and in my head thinking, "If they only knew what was going on right now ..." And I knew that I would look back on this footage and know exactly how I felt – walking towards the stage pretending to be really confident, and how terrified I felt. And that was a few tours before this one.'

Once you realised you were having a bad time of it, did you have a plan of what you thought you would do ultimately?

'No, because I was just spiralling. There wasn't any "figure this out". There wasn't any "what's going to happen?" or "what will you do ultimately?" or "what does this mean?" I think I was just spiralling towards death, which became more evident as the months passed by. I say that in hindsight, because I don't know in June that that's happening, I'm just stuck in the middle of something that feels overwhelming.'

Were you thinking to yourself, 'Oh shit, I've really fucked up here, this is terrible'? Or were you just thinking: 'I don't give a fuck right now'?

'I wanted to be numb because I was scared of what was happening to me, I think. And maybe the one thing that it did do was made me numb.'

Were you thinking: I just can't wait for this tour to end?

'Well, it just felt like it never would.'

* * *

After the final British date, he finally had a break.

He flew back to Los Angeles. The next day I received an email update:

Oh my god ... we came close (or I came close) to fucking up everything ... but by the skin of my teeth etc ... I'm fucked ... but home ... bouncing off the walls with boredom and worrying about trying to reconstruct my already fragile peace of mind ... in the words of Des'ree:

* 'Life? Oh life! Do, do, do, do.'*

* * *

January 2016

At breakfast, I tell Rob the overnight news: David Bowie has died.

'That sucks,' he says. 'That's really sad.'

Right now, he doesn't say anything else about it. Because it's early, and because it's hard to know what to say, and because Teddy has decided to have a meltdown about the fact that Charlie's cereal bowl is better than hers.

* * *

Rufus Wainwright is in town and is coming up today to write. In preparation for Rufus' arrival, Guy is working on a track based around a fairly obscure Serge Gainsbourg sample he has found, an instrumental called 'Je n'avais qu'un seul mot à lui dire' from a 1967 film called *Anna*.

'This happiest of days,' says Rufus when he walks in. 'Depressing.'

'Yes,' says Rob. 'Super sad.'

After everyone has caught up a little, Guy says, 'So we've got this idea ...' and turns to Rob. 'Shall we tell him the concept?'

'Yeah,' says Rob.

There's a silence for a few seconds.

'Do you want me to tell him?' says Guy.

'Yes,' says Rob.

Guy explains. 'Rob traditionally always starts his shows with "Let Me Entertain You",' he begins, 'and ideally would like to start with something else. We wrote "Let Me Entertain You" specifically as an opening song when we wrote it and now, after many, many years, it would be really cool when we do the stadium tour next year ...'

'It's so difficult to put it somewhere else other than at the beginning,' Rob says, both interrupting and digressing, 'because if you put it fifth or sixth in, or at the end, you've already done it – you've already entertained them.'

'But we think we can put it in second,' Guy explains, '*if* there's a song before it that announces the show. We want a show announcer: *This is the Heavy Entertainment Show.* That's what the album's going to be called. And it would be cool if there was a song on the album that's called that.'

'Well, that's the idea that we just had ten minutes ago,' Rob explains. 'But that would be fucking great.'

* * *

Guy plays Rufus what they have.

'You can't help but think about David Bowie,' says Rufus, and he sings, a cappella.

Goodbye Ziggy Stardust
The sun's setting down on us.

'I don't know,' he reconsiders. 'You don't want to get too weird about it.'

Rufus and Rob starts extemporising for a while around this first melody, coming up with rough lyrics, and then Guy mentions that he also has a melodic and lyrical idea. He sings it, using nonsense words wherever he has no real ones:

Welcome to the heavy entertainment show
Where the nehnehneh and the nehnehno.

It's more rhythmic and direct, and immediately trumps what has come before. With that, they're off; ideas fly back and forth and soon the song, 'The Heavy Entertainment Show' – which will indeed, within a few months, become the title track of Rob's next album – is taking shape. When a collaboration like this doesn't work, there's nothing more awkward, but when it does it can be kind of magical to experience. And I think a substantial part of the value of these collaborations for Rob – when they do work – is not just in what he gets out of his collaborators but in the way it makes him focus and dig deep for the best he can find inside himself.

* * *

In the middle of all this, Teddy and Charlie are brought down to the studio to say hello. Teddy immediately declares that she has some firm views about what should, and should not, be happening in here.

'Don't sing!' she instructs her father.

'It's what I do!' he protests, and introduces her to Rufus.

'Daddy …' Teddy persists.

'Yes, darling,' he says.

'I don't *want* you to sing,' she says. 'No singing.'

'I'm going to sing,' he explains. 'I'm in the studio – it's what I *do*. I'm going to sing what we've got. I'm practising.'

'No, thank you,' Teddy says, decisively. 'Don't practise.'

'Well, how will I ever get good?' Rob asks her.

Then the track restarts and he sings anyway – the latest verse, one that won't even exist by tomorrow:

Welcome to the heavy entertainment show
Come and brave the wave of my overflow
Welcome to the heavy entertainment show
It's fun above but more below.

After he sings, Teddy comes over and gives her father a hug.

'I'm so proud of you,' she tells him.

* * *

Late in the day, Rufus comes up with a strange and idiosyncratic lyric that will become the song's opening line:

Good evening children of cultural abandon.

It inspires three further lines that not only set up the vainglorious braggadocio at the song's heart, but which are also clearly influenced by the shock of today's news:

30

You've searched for a saviour, well here I am
And all the best ones are dying off so quickly
Well, I'm still here, enjoy me while you can.
'I think that's great,' says Guy. 'It's quite touching.'

'And egoic,' adds Rob, as though ticking off a list of the most important virtues. 'And narcissistic.'

Rufus is only here for this one day, so his input will end here. The song isn't finished, and will have all kinds of additions and changes made to it over the next few days, but its core has been established, and it's clearly something that's working. There's a sense of satisfaction in the air as the session breaks up. And the day itself isn't over.

* * *

Tomorrow is Guy's birthday, but he is throwing a dinner party tonight at the house he is renting nearby in the Hollywood Hills with his brother Dylan. There's about a dozen people gathered around a large dining table, and after the food has been eaten, a glass is chinked for silence, and Guy asks whether his guests might do a musical turn. He clearly means Rufus and Rob. Rob immediately looks quietly horrified at the thought. When Rufus sits at the piano, and Guy says, 'My good friend Rufus would like to sing a song he's written,' Rob reframes this scenario to the rest of the table: 'Guy's making him sing a song.'

Rufus explains that the song he will play was written with his five-year-old daughter: 'The first ever Wainwright/Cohen collaboration.'

'Better be good!' shouts Guy.

'It's a nice sentiment for this evening,' says Rufus. 'It's called "Unfollow The Rules". She came up with that.'

It's a fairly amazing song, and he doesn't hold back in performing it. As Rufus does this, Rob realises two things. First, he's going to have to sing. Second, that he wants to do it well. So once Rufus has finished, Rob suggests to Guy that they perform 'Blasphemy'.

The idea clearly takes Guy aback. This song has a particular place in their mutual history. It was written and recorded as a demo in a Hollywood studio in late 2002 and was the final song of their collaboration before they split up. They haven't performed it together since that day in the studio; not even in private. And while Guy clearly wants to do it, he isn't confident that he even knows the song well enough. And so there is a short interlude in the night's entertainment while he quickly refreshes his memory by listening to the record. Then they're ready.

'This is a bit of a weird song for me,' Guy tells the room from behind the piano. 'This was the last song me and Rob wrote together.'

'We had a massive falling out,' Rob reminds everyone, perhaps unnecessarily.

'It's a bit weird that we're playing this song now,' says Guy. 'But, hey, it's fine.'

And they begin. Later tonight, back home, in the lift going up to the second-floor bedrooms – Rob's new house, just like his old one, has an elevator, and while he inherited each from the previous owners, rather than demanded that they be installed as part of some mad pop-stars-don't-do-stairs caprice, he does tend to use them – the very last thing Rob will say to me before going to bed will be: 'I'm genuinely so in awe of Rufus and his talent that I thought, "I'd better do this right."' And he does. 'Blasphemy', a complicated and despairing tale of dysfunctional relationships, is clearly a song that means a lot to him. He's always saying, and sometimes proving, that he can't remember the lyrics of some of his most famous songs (and always has a teleprompter onstage for this very reason), but 'Blasphemy' has reams of lyrics and he remembers every single one. And, perhaps spurred by his combination of respect for, and competition with, Rufus, he sings it with an intense beauty.

What happens next simply seems to happen, without much forethought, just because it somehow needs to. 'I feel like we should do a David Bowie song,' says Rufus, and there's a chorus of approval round the table. 'I don't know them very well,' he adds.

Guy, still at the piano, begins to play 'Changes', but Rob halts him, and says that he'd rather do 'Kooks'.

'Do you know "Kooks"?' he asks Guy.

Guy does, and begins to play it – and, quite naturally, without any discussion of what each of them will do, Rob and Rufus start harmonising. There's something incredibly moving about this scene, the two of them just sitting at the dinner table, singing this with so little fuss, yet with so much weight – an accidental, unpremeditated heartfelt celebration and wake. And it sounds incredible. It feels a privilege to be part of.

'David Bowie … David Bowie,' says Rob quietly when they finish.

This time, when Guy starts playing 'Changes', Rob starts singing, reading the lyrics from the screen of Guy's computer. In the chorus Rufus joins in, Rob singing the 'ch-ch-changes', Rufus the lines in between. As they sing, Rob raises his arms and pumps them skywards. Then, over Guy's piano outro, Rob gently claps his hands and mutters 'David Bowie' one last time.

* * *

A couple of days later, Rob comes across a David Bowie reminiscence written by the British journalist Dylan Jones; part of it recalls time that Jones and Bowie spent together at the Halkin hotel in London around 2002:

We spent a good hour discussing exactly why Robbie Williams was famous … He seemed to be somewhat bewildered by Robbie's success, as to him he appeared to be little more than an old-school musical song-and-dance man. Bowie had spent most of his career following his instinct and hoping it would collide with public taste, and so when he was presented with a phenomenon that he didn't understand (like Robbie Williams), he wanted to get to the bottom of it. Bowie was incensed that Robbie had co-opted so much of the John Barry Bond theme You Only Live Twice for Millennium … he wondered how on earth he had got away with it.

'I woke up at about five,' Rob says the next morning at breakfast, 'feeling sad that David Bowie doesn't like me.'

Rob wonders whether it was what happened at NetAid that made David Bowie feel that way. NetAid was a big charity show that took place at Wembley Stadium in 1999 to fight poverty, and they were both on the bill. It was one of the key landmarks in Rob's ascendance: 'One of those steps like Tom Jones at the Brits, Michael Parkinson – I went onstage and was greeted with just like this wave of "this is the person that everybody loves the most". A wave of euphoric love. And I conducted it.' Rob played just five songs – five top-five singles: 'Let Me Entertain You', 'Millennium', 'Strong', 'Old Before I Die' and 'Angels'.

'And then David Bowie came on and did a very not very well-picked set if he was looking to please the crowd,' Rob remembers – Bowie included songs from his latest album *Hours* – '… and it didn't go down very well.'

So maybe it was something to with that.

But it's a weird feeling. 'I'm, like, oh, I'm mourning your loss – this has made it difficult,' he says.

Later, down in the studio he returns to the subject.

'Did you read the Bowie thing that Dylan Jones from *GQ* was talking about today?' he asks Guy. 'Where they had long conversations about how unbelievable my success was?'

Rob mentions now that he was already aware of other vaguely disparaging comments that Bowie had made about him in the past. Specifically, Bowie once told the BBC: 'I know about Kylie and Robbie and *Pop Idol* and stuff like that. You can't get away from that when you hit the shore, so I know all about the cruise ship entertainment aspect of British pop.'

'I can remember going, "Owww … !",' he says to Guy. But then Rob's also well aware of how often he's spoken freely like that, more concerned with being interesting and honest than careful and diplomatic.

'I also have those thoughts about people,' Rob says.

'You have it about *yourself*,' Guy points out.

'Yeah,' he concedes.

* * *

September 2006

In the midst of the Close Encounters tour, Rob also released a new single and a new album. He'd recorded the album over the previous year, much of it in the studio set up at one end of the master bedroom at his Los Angeles house, with a cast of collaborators, mostly friends of his: 'The best fun I'd ever had recording. I saw it as a gap-year record where I had loads of fun with me mates, and we went "Look!".' There were a handful of unlikely cover versions, and all kinds of eclectic styles visited, including plenty of rap. 'And I thought the fun would translate. It was like, "Woah, this sounds like *me* – this is what I really, really do! Brilliant! I've found it." I was making a record that would impress a fifteen-year-old me.'

He decided to call the album *Rudebox*, after the most aggressive rap song on it, the song that had also been chosen as the first single. The very first night they played this song in concert, near the end of the show in Hampden Park, he realised that this particular adventure might not play out in the way he'd expected it to. It felt as though a whole stadium-full of dubious Scots collectively took a step back, bemused at what they were hearing. He remembers finding it funny, but a little worrying, too.

More damaging was what happened in the press, or at least in one specific and influential part of it. Ironically, especially given the reputation it has since gathered as some kind of mythic disaster, the album would get quite a few very good reviews. But *The Sun*'s chief pop writer at the time, Victoria Newton – someone who, coincidentally or otherwise, Rob had verbally abused at a recent party in Los Angeles – pre-empted all of that with a very firm view of 'Rudebox', the single, given over two pages, with the headline:

Robbie's single is the worst song EVER.

The story's subtle subhead pushed the knife in a little further:

SINGER'S NEW RAP – WITH A SILENT C

And then came the article itself:

Robbie Williams' new track Rudebox is not only the worst song by him I've heard, it's the worst record I've EVER heard (and believe me, I've had to listen to some sh*te in the past) … try to imagine you and your mates messing around in your bedroom with a drum machine while comedy 'rapping' over the top. The *only difference is that Robbie is actually allowed to release this rubbish because he has a record deal ... Rudebox? Rudeb****x more like.*

It set in place a narrative that could never really be turned around.

* * *

'I think perception was a motherfucker on that album,' he says. 'They'd been waiting for ages to give me a good kicking, you know, and kind of putting the boot in here and there, but then it was like a collective "Quick! He's down! Jump on him! Kick him in the head! Make sure he's gone! Do it again! And do it again! ... And do it again! ... And do it again!"'

Why do you think that was?

'It was a moment of perceived weakness in a glittering career.'

So, whether it really was or it wasn't, why do you think they were looking for that?

'Well, that's what they do, isn't it? That seems to be their MO. It's been said a million trillion times: build them up and knock 'em down.'

He laughs.

'They're hardly decent enough to build 'em up these days, you know.'

No matter that the album sold over two million copies – disappointing by his own elevated standards, but huge by most others. Later the story spread that EMI Records had to dispose of a mountain of unsellable *Rudebox* stock by shipping it to China where the CDs were broken up and used in road surfacing. That was what *Rudebox* became: an album so catastrophic that it ended up with its every dumb conceit and clunky, white b-boy folly crushed under the wheels of unknowing Chinese commuters. (No matter whether or not the story was true, and it almost certainly wasn't. 'I'm pretty sure it's a complete fabrication,' says Tony Wadsworth, who was chairman and CEO of EMI at the time, pointing out that by 2006 CDs could be manufactured to order so quickly that there was simply no reason to gamble by producing huge amounts of stock in advance.)

That was how *Rudebox* was to be remembered: as Robbie Williams' legendary folly and failure. It's a narrative that Rob would frequently play along with in the years to come. He's never one to shy away from self-laceration, particularly when it offers an opportunity to entertain. And there was plenty of humour to be mined here. What difference does it make that in truth there are few, if any, of his albums that he likes better, and certainly none that he feels is a closer representation of his character and his taste? As a rule it's been easier, and funnier – and maybe a little less painful, too – just to play along.

* * *

January 2016

Even here in his private life, just as it is in interviews and onstage, *Rudebox* is used as an all-purpose comedy prop and punchline.

One day Rob complains to Ayda, quite seriously, 'Teddy's pushing me away.' He's initiating the kind of discussion that all parents have when a growing child's behaviour evolves, sometimes day by day, as they explore and test out and try to understand the world around them.

'Maybe,' Ayda suggests, 'she's finally heard *Rudebox*.'

* * *

This morning, Rob reads *Everyone Poops* to Teddy at breakfast, then goes to talk with a therapist, something he does periodically, whenever he feels the need. Today's visit is to someone he hasn't spoken with before.

'I did a lot of talking,' he says afterwards, 'but I really liked him.'

He details some of the things they talked about: 'How I don't want to be social and how I panic when I'm out. Not so much here as in the UK. And when I'm getting on a plane and I get out of the car at the airport, I'm shitting myself.' Then he adds: 'I was kind of talking about spending. I'm terrified of all the money going, because I don't know how to be a grown-up.'

He laughs, but then he continues.

'And I'm serious. I've not ironed anything, not washed anything, not sorted out a bill, not been to the supermarket – my progress with all of that kind of stuff was stunted. And with the kids here, if the money goes, I don't know how to do it. I'd figure out how to pretty quickly, but ...'

He realises how it sounds. That *these* are the things he is worried about. 'I *know*,' he acknowledges, 'it's, in real terms, a "my heart bleeds ..." kind of problem. But in real terms, for me, this has been my life.'

And if you are Robbie Williams, what's the point in going to a therapist and talking about someone else's problems?

* * *

Later that afternoon, sitting with Michael and David, Rob has a request. It's happened again.

'I need a new computer, Michael,' he says, and shows him the crack right down the side of his current one.

'Have you been throwing your computer around again?' David asks him, more amused than anything.

'Mate, I've dropped it five times in the last two weeks,' says Rob.

But he shares with some excitement his new discovery – that this, and the many similar mishaps that have preceded it, might not be *completely* his fault.

'The therapist said, "When you were a kid, did you lose things, drop things, couldn't concentrate on stuff ..." I was like, "Yeah!"'

He's excited by what this might imply.

'So,' Rob declares, as though this means that, in one sense at least, he may have been almost completely absolved of responsibility for any of this, 'it's a *thing*.'

* * *

The following day, the producer Stuart Price comes round to play tennis. Rob mentions that he started therapy yesterday. 'He was, "Were you diagnosed with depression when you were fifteen, sixteen?"' says Rob, and laughs at the absurdity of someone imagining that was the kind of thing that commonly happened back then in Britain.

'Yeah, we didn't have that in England,' Stuart agrees. (Stuart's also English.)

'It wasn't until I got to rehab,' Rob says. '"What? I can *call* it something?"'

Stuart wins the tennis, then Rob gets his revenge at the pool table. Afterwards they take the tangerine-walk with Chris Briggs and David. On the walk Rob gives David a different, more succinct account of his therapy session:

'I went in talking about Ayda and the kids, and came out having to fix my self-esteem.'

Everyone laughs.

'No,' he says, 'that's genuinely what's happened.'

* * *

December 2006–February 2007

In early December, Rob emails me from Australia:

Fuckin orrible year … nearly over … then I can get on with business of putting my head back together … it's time for a big change … and eventually this whole tour and what it's done to my head will be a massive (spiritual) gift.

But for now … etc.

* * *

The Close Encounters tour's final leg had begun at the end of November.

'Australia was really rough,' he remembers. 'I didn't go to sleep. I'd been given tablets for my ADHD, and of course these tablets contain speed, and of course I'm an addict, so one wasn't going to do it, two wasn't going to do it, three wasn't going to do it, until I'm having handfuls at a time. And it's just like taking a bag of Pro Plus: jittery and dirty and uncomfortable and spacey and paranoid and crazy.'

The final show was in Melbourne on 18th December 2006.

'Zero sleep,' he says, 'and I had to go and perform in front of eighty thousand people or whatever it was. And it was just so embarrassing. Letting me down, letting them down, letting the people I work for down. And also, having had some pretty successful gigs that year, knowing what I was capable of, whether I thought I was worthy or not. And I just wasn't that night. I just didn't have any energy. I was fucked. But there was no massive backlash about the shows being shit. I turned up and gave everything that I'd got, albeit in an altered state.'

After that, it was back to Los Angeles once more. Now, at last, he had all the time and space he needed to relax and recover and recuperate.

But that's not what happened.

'There was no kind of relief,' he says, 'because I knew that there was going to be some sort of payment – spiritually, physically and mentally – for what I'd just been through.'

When your world has started to unravel, sometimes it can be hard to make it stop.

* * *

After any tour finishes, it can be difficult for a while.

'Even if you come off tour and you're sober, it's a horrendous comedown anyway. At eight o'clock your body switches on and goes, "Hey! HEY EVERYBODY! Let ME ENTERTAIN YOUUUUUU!!!!!" And you don't know *what* to do. You're bouncing off walls for, I'd say, at least a month after a tour like that. Because everything's structured: "At such-and-such o'clock you go here, you do this …"'

This time, he was in a much bigger mess.

'I suppose there was…' – he considers what the right word is, then settles on it – '… a breakdown.' Then chides himself for even dancing around it. 'Of course,' he says. 'Of course there was.'

Once the tour was done, what were you thinking?

'I'm not thinking by then. I've taken that many chemicals that I'm altered … maybe beyond maybe repair. I'd ingested that much stuff that I was crazy.'

You came back to Los Angeles. What happened?

'It's not difficult to get whatever you want, it's always there somewhere – you just scratch the surface and something appears. It's funny – when you're not looking for anything, nothing comes to you. I've noticed that in all my years of sobriety: I'm not in a loo where somebody's doing coke, I'm not being offered ecstasy – when you're out of the loop you're out of the loop. Totally unaware. Blissfully unaware. But the moment you engage, you find it instantly. So I'd come back to Los Angeles and was buying some very expensive drugs. I was addicted to Adderall. I was doing coke by myself in my room. All use of coke for me is useless because it instantly gives me this weird head-click thing where I cluck like a chicken. And I don't go up, I just go sideways. It's not like the enjoyable bit of supercharged blessing-to-the-ego thousand-miles-an-hour chatter, it's just sadness and me by myself in a room feeling paranoid and jittery.'

That doesn't make it sound a very attractive thing to do.

'No.'

So when you start doing it in that circumstance, why are you doing it?

'Because it was an addiction. They say in AA and therapy and rehab that if you relapse you pick up from where you left off and more, and I did – that's exactly what happened. There was something beautifully hedonistic about 1995, 1996 that will never again be recaptured – there was a sexiness and an out-of-control. There were a lot of hellish nights, but there was also a lot of reckless abandon, *sex and drugs and rock'n'roll is all my brain and body needs* and a place that I was hoping to probably get back to. I think I tried to go and recreate that again. And I didn't quite manage it. Didn't manage it at all. It was just not in my make-up anymore to be able to go and do those things. Sadly enough, it is kind of writing a suicide note to yourself, going on that path. I didn't instantly know, but it was a fraction later than instant, as these things often are. You know, there's a corruption of reality, there's a corruption of sense where you stop and addiction in earnest kicks in. Yeah, it was a place where I was … I'd say slowly dying, but I was rapidly dying. When your left arm goes numb, that's normally what's happening.

A fan of mine gave me some Seroquel – I think it's maybe something to do with schizophrenics or something. Anyway, the heavy mixture of cocaine and that was incredibly trippy in the worst way. I couldn't use my legs. I fell into the bathroom and took the casing off the light switch and bust up my eyebrow and then sort of lay on the floor as this pool of blood trickled out. And I just lay there. I'd turned the light on, though, which was a plus. So at least I could see what was going on.'

Did it make you consider what you were doing?

'I'd got to the point where I didn't care if I was alive or dead. Not the healthiest place to be. Understatement. But because of my addiction and what I was taking, it led me to a place where I didn't care.'

So did you think you were in danger?

'Yeah. I knew that I was fucked.'

And what were you thinking in your head?

'I was thinking, "I'm dying and I'm not bothered."'

That's a pretty sad thing to be thinking.

'Oh, it's horrendous. You know, I went to some very, very dark places. The darkest I think you can go. And if there are levels past there, I never want to visit them.'

Why do you think you didn't care?

'I think the ability to care is taken away in the addiction. That's why so many people die from addiction. It was the biggest load of apathy that I will ever have.'

How would you spend your days?

'Getting over the night before.'

And how would you spend the night?

'Go again. Doing whatever.'

And the rest of the time?

'There was no rest of the time. That was it.'

* * *

Strangely, pretty much the only thing Rob didn't do, even as bad as it got, was drink.

One reason, he reflects, is – if he is honest with himself – pure vanity.

'Drink,' he says, 'makes me *huge*.'

But there was also maybe some kind of vestigial pride, too – that this was one achievement that he could still stubbornly cling on to: 'I've come this long without having a drink – I'm not having a drink now.'

And maybe also, he says, it was a way of deluding himself that things hadn't got that bad. If he'd been drinking, well, then he might have had to face up to the fact that he *really* had a problem …

* * *

In early February I was passing through Los Angeles and I went to see him.

'I remember, yeah.'

You weren't good.

'Yeah, I was crazy.'

There were phone calls and then suddenly you went to meet someone in the street outside the house.

'Yeah, there were Escalade windows dropping down and packets being delivered and me giving money, and it just felt like I was a crackhead because there was no sort of conversation with this person. It was very much business: done, move on. Normally I'd have conversations with dealers.'

I remember you had a weird way of being secretive – you'd kind of say, 'I'm going to go and take a load of coke on my own now'.

'Yeah.'

It was as though, even then, you were offering the director's commentary on this terrible time you were having.

'Yeah, I've got a compulsion to tell the truth. Mainly.'

And I remember you spent a lot of time in bed while I was there, constantly talking to me about pages in Gary Barlow's autobiography that you were particularly annoyed about.

'Yeah. When you're taking a shitload of Adderall you can obsess about things. And one of the things that I was particularly obsessed about before I went into rehab was Gary Barlow's autobiography.'

I think you felt outraged at some of it, as though it was unfair.

'Was I? Well, unless he'd written, "I was an absolute cunt to Robbie Williams and I'm going to take this opportunity to apologise and I can't wait to make it right …" then that's what I would have thought then.'

It was a very troubling visit. In fiction, when someone is on a downward slide like this, the story is always looking for that moment when the lead character suddenly realises what they are doing. For the moment when the scales drop from their eyes, and they become *aware*, and the healing can begin. But one of the great conundrums with Rob is that in all kinds of difficult situations, including this one, he can show great awareness of his predicament, and show that he understands how you see it, and talk to you about it perfectly frankly, and pre-empt the smart thoughts and wise advice you might have about it, just as he did to me at times that evening up at his house. And in fact his self-awareness actually seems to make the situation worse, because it undercuts the hope that he'll suddenly come to his senses, that he'll suddenly *realise*.

What might he be expected to realise when he quite clearly already knows?

* * *

Could you tell that people around you were worried?

'Oh yeah. People around me were worried. And it was going to take an intervention to get me to rehab and save my life.'

A few days after my visit, his managers Tim Clark and David Enthoven were due in Los Angeles. They had told Rob they were coming to have a meeting with him. But he was pretty sure what that meant. He might have been half out of his mind, but he wasn't stupid. 'I'd been to rehab before, and they're such brain-numbingly boring places. That was the last place I wanted to go to. Also it would mean that I would have to stop my dependency on what I was taking, and I was deep in the addiction.'

But he also *knew*.

Tim and David were scheduled to be there on a Wednesday, so Rob really went for it on Monday. He'd worked it out: he could have Tuesday to get himself together, ready to face their music on Wednesday.

But on Tuesday he was lying on a sofa, recovering, when he heard the door downstairs, and he heard their booming voices coming his way.

'As soon as I heard their voices I thought, "The game's up, I'm going to rehab,"' he says.

'Robert, you look like shit …' David began, but Rob stopped him there. He didn't need to hear the arguments, the rationale, the persuasions. He'd rather skip that bit.

'You don't have to say that … Dave, fucking hell! I'll go to rehab – you don't have to be a knob,' Rob interrupted. 'I'll go, I'll go … I'll go.'

They told him that there was a private plane waiting. The car was outside. 'I think they were expecting an argument,' he says.

Did you know that there would be an intervention?

'An intervention or death, yeah.'

Were you kind of relieved when it came?

'I was just really annoyed. Mega mega annoyed that I'd gotten myself into such a state that I had to go and do what I had to go and do. Yet again my feet were doing something that I didn't want to do, which was taking me to a car that was going to take me to a plane to take me to rehab. And there I was on this aeroplane being flown to Arizona, kicking the fucking seat in front of me so many times because I couldn't believe I'd allowed myself to get in that position again. I fucking hated it. Absolutely hated it.'

What would have happened if you hadn't gone?

'I'd be dead now. Absolutely. I'd be fucking dead.'

How?

'Overdose. And it could have been the Wednesday or the Tuesday. The Tuesday that they came and took me in, it could have been that night.'

* * *

January 2016

In the studio, he's working on another song, this one called 'My Intentions Are Good'. He suggests a lyric – *You must be able to read my mind* – and then explains precisely what it means.

'Sometimes,' he says, 'I think the voices in my head are so loud that you can hear them. It's like I can't believe when I'm on television and being interviewed that people outside can't hear my voice going, "You're on telly! You're on TV! You're gonna fuck it up! You're gonna fuck it up! You're on the television!" That's what my head's doing.'

Everyone laughs.

A while later, he mentions that he's been having dreams about not being able to sleep.

* * *

One day, over a late breakfast, Rob explains that he won't be down to the studio for a little while.

'I've got to go and have a blood test,' he says.

'Just to make sure he's human,' Ayda clarifies.

* * *

At the end of Guy's visit, there's a listening session. Four new songs have been finished. One of them, 'The Heavy Entertainment Show', will become the title track of the new album. Two of them, 'Best Intentions' (the final version of 'My Intentions Are Good') and 'Time On Earth', will end up on the album's deluxe edition. The fourth, a manic disco-funk song called 'Wicked Wonderchick' that moves back and forth between KC and the Sunshine Band and Gorillaz, never quite finding its place, is cast aside.

* * *

Meanwhile, *Celebrity Big Brother* continues.

'I was watching and thinking how much I liked Darren Day,' Rob says. 'He's got a really bad rap. He's just a bloke like me. That probably would have a better life if he didn't drink or do drugs. Well, would definitely be more husband material if he didn't drink or do drugs. I'd fuck this whole thing up if I did coke or drank, so I know how that goes.'

He decides that there's something that he needs to do. Once Day is evicted (he comes third), Rob films a video that he'll send to him.

It opens with a close-up of Rob sitting on his bed, smiling.

Rob: *Darren, it's Robbie Williams here, sending a video message of apology for the whole phoning your house whilst you were going out with Anna Friel and asking her out. A terrible thing to do. Um, by a man a thousand moons ago who had his head up his arse. I'm apologising and really hope that you receive my apology and it's accepted. It made me feel shit that I made you feel shit. And I bet you I made you angry, and I bet you I'm on the cunt-list ... and I don't want to be on that list. I'd like to be taken off it. I'm really, really sorry. And ...* [the camera zooms out to show Ayda sitting next to him] *... here's my wife.*

Ayda: [waving] *Hi, Darren. Well done. Can I just say, this is like Robbie's fifteenth video message to you, keeps trying to redo it, because he really, really wants to apologise. So on his behalf, I'm really sorry he was such a wanker. I totally get it. He's not a wanker anymore ...*

* * *

February–March 2007

'The first time you go to rehab, it's terrifying, because it's the unknown. And the second time it's *terrifying* ... because you know.'

* * *

The private plane took him to Arizona.

'I've only been to "hardcore" rehabs,' he says. 'I don't go to luxury rehabs. And it isn't swimming pools and TVs and luxury meals and five-star accommodation. It's basically a youth hostel where you have to go to meetings about sobriety every hour of every day, and you are cut off from civilisation – no phone, no TV, no music, no books other than spiritual and getting better, no radio, nothing to entertain you. It was just so fucking boring. You are left to deal with yourself, and you've been trying to run away from yourself for so long that you uncomfortably have to confront it. And I would say that it was not something that I wanted to confront head-on – I wanted to confront it sideways or the easiest way possible. I remember the first rehab that I went to I wanted to be a good boy and do everything that I had to. This time, not so much. I didn't throw myself in. I was resistant to the process.'

Did part of you not want to get better or did you just not want to be bothered with … ?

'I wanted not to do drugs. And the compulsion to use goes away pretty quickly when you are in a hospital or when you are taken away from all means of getting anything. While I was in it, the compulsion to use was paramount, and the only thing that I thought about. But come four days into being in a treatment facility, that compulsion had gone. It was about putting days together between me and it, and it was successful for that.'

As soon as you pulled away from what you'd been doing, how did you feel? Were you relieved? Happy? Worried what to do next?

'I was immensely depressed, because the drug use had been self-medication.'

Did you feel as though there was anything particular deep down that you felt you were depressed about?

'There's no depressed *about*. That's not what depression is. It's just ill. I was ill and I was trying to make myself not ill. Or not feel ill. I think people understand depression a bit more than they used to. Look, from sixteen I'd started taking drugs and drinking. Seventeen, eighteen, it became a problem. Nineteen I *knew* it was a problem. And since nineteen I've tried to be sober, and I'd been mainly successful at being sober. There have been blips and periods in between me trying to be sober, but for all intents and purposes I've been sober since I was twenty-one, twenty-two. Obviously with some smoking and the whatever. But the stuff that makes it impossible to be me, that would give me a divorce, lose my home, lose my life, lose my career, I've been very successful at staying away from those things.'

Basically staying away from alcohol and what people think of as hard drugs?

'Yeah. And once I'd got a week under my belt … once you get the compulsion to use out of the way, you can get in a slipstream, and you're just in it, and that's your life, and it becomes normal. And quite quickly, not being off my head became normal again.'

* * *

That's what was happening on the inside. On the outside, Rob's trip to rehab was viewed rather differently. He went away the day before the Brit Awards – a Brit Awards at which the resurgent four-piece Take That would cement and celebrate their comeback with the Best British Single award for 'Patience'. All of this was the last thing on Rob's mind – 'I hadn't a fucking clue the Brits was on,' he points out. But in the UK, the news from America was widely seen as an attention-seeking bit of melodrama, and even as a moment of jealous petulance intentionally planned to steal his former bandmates' thunder.

This dovetailed with a fairly condescending and thoughtless perception of what had sent Rob to rehab. The official statement that was issued was this: *Robbie Williams has today been admitted into a treatment centre in America for his dependency on prescription drugs. There will be no further comment on this matter.* That was all – or maybe even more than – anybody needed to know.

But how this information was filtered to the public through Britain's media was remarkable. Though there were also lurid melodramatic headlines (front page of the *Mirror*: GET ME INTO REHAB BEFORE I TOP MYSELF), mostly the story was treated as some kind of semi-comic publicity stunt. The Brit Awards' host, Russell Brand, who might have been expected to show a little more sensitivity, made repeated jokes about it all from the stage.

A lack of real knowledge of what is going on in any given situation is only a small impediment to a media that has stories that need writing, and one instinctual fallback is to scour the record for what is known, and extrapolate fancifully from there. And so some stories pointed to an addiction to his antidepressants. But the most popular theme was about caffeine. During his tour, in an astonishing attempt either to redirect the narrative or seize the bull by the horns, Rob had actually done an interview with *The Sun*'s Victoria Newton, his *Rudebox* tormentor. Three days of big stories followed (the first was headlined: 'If you're married you have to keep it in your pants … I can't do that!'), and she made the following observation:

It was clear his new addiction is CAFFEINE. During the two hours I spent with him he downed six strong espressos. If that's his normal rate of coffee drinking, he would average out at an incredible 36 a day.

Once Rob was in rehab, this back-of-the-envelope calculation became the new truth. The tabloid assertion was that he had been habitually consuming 20 Red Bulls and 36 double espressos in a single day, and this was regularly spouted as the principal reason for his treatment. He had been drinking plenty of both, though not to these absurd levels, and of course these were very far from his main problems. But that became the story. The dominant narrative really did seem to be that poor, delicate, self-obsessed Robbie Williams, miffed that his boyband ex-colleagues were doing so well, had gone away for some self-indulgent pampering because he'd been overdoing the caffeine. This insulting absurdity led, for instance, to the helpful article the following week in the Glasgow *Herald*, headlined: *Why There's No Need To Fear Our New Favourite Drug; Robbie Williams Is Seeking Treatment For His Espresso Habit, But Is Coffee Really So Bad? Not If We're Careful.*

The overall spirit of the coverage was summarised by a quote in the tabloids from his long-term bête noire, Take That's ex-manager, Nigel Martin-Smith: 'He's very theatrical. His whole life is one huge soap opera … He might be after a bit of sympathy. If I was a Robbie fan I wouldn't be worried. He'll go to his rehab, have a lie-down and a couple of Anadins and he'll be fine.'

Perhaps one blessing of how Rob really was is that he was in no state to be reading any of this lazy, presumptuous, callous bile. Not yet, anyway.

'It's horrendous in there,' he says. 'It's absolutely horrendous. It's not something that you would choose to do to upstage somebody. You've got to be pretty fucked to go there.'

* * *

You had to share a room? How many people?

'Five. It was fine. I quite liked the company, to be honest.'

What does a day consist of?

'You get up at seven, have breakfast, and then the first thing you do is group for an hour and forty-five minutes, and then you break for not too long and then you go and do lots of different lessons: eating, anger, compassion, self-worth etc., etc. All day. And then you have homework. Life story. Keep a diary of how you'd gotten there. There was something to do every night.'

And you'd do it seriously and diligently?

'Yeah.'

And it was useful?

'Yeah. The very act of doing something that was disciplined was useful. Then you'd be asked: the most significant people in your life, write a paragraph or a few paragraphs about what they mean to you – it was all stuff like that. Then lectures on eating properly. Then you get taken out to an AA group.'

When you write stuff, would people comment on it?

'You'd all sit in a room, in a circle and read it out.'

That's quite heavy.

'Oh yeah. Especially when your story's the least of the heaviness that surrounds you. You're also dealing with a lot of people that have been sexually abused and they go into detail about that – oh, Jesus. All sorts.'

And would other people there give you feedback on what they thought about your situation?

'I suppose you get more sympathy, empathy, more than feedback. It wasn't like I was deluded about what my problem was. I was quite erudite when it comes to therapy talk.'

* * *

Another snapshot of life in rehab for a 33-year-old pop star who has now been famous for nearly half his life:

'In rehab, one of the big things I was kind of worried about on the way there was, I've never washed my clothes. How do I get my clothes washed? And I managed to meet an addict who was obsessed with washing clothes. So I didn't even have to do it in rehab, I just gave it to this person that had a problem with washing clothes and they washed my clothes for me. I don't know if that's a good or a bad thing. For me personally, when I was in rehab, it was a good thing. I got lucky.'

* * *

When you are in rehab, and it is known that you are in rehab, people try to contact you. They seem to imagine this would be a good time to reach out to you, and that you might want to hear what they have to say. In Arizona, says Rob, he got a lot of abusive letters, and he'd think, 'Jesus Christ, I nearly died three nights ago!'

One letter he received was from someone explaining that she didn't like him that much because she liked Neil Diamond much better. But she felt he'd appreciate being told that 'your problem is that you've got too much time on your hands, that's why you're in rehab'. She also mentioned that she needed a white van to help her pack some stuff, so maybe he could use some of his spare time by coming round to help her?

Rob's father handled that one for him.

'My dad sent her a letter back, pretending to be from my management, saying, "Thank you very much. We have passed your letter and concerns on to Neil Diamond."'

* * *

Recovery and celebrity can make uncomfortable bedfellows. He realised that quite early on, though only after he'd got over the initial shock of what it would feel like to address his problems.

'I can remember going to my first AA meeting – it was at Chelsea and Westminster Hospital – and thinking, "What the *fuck*? What??? I give up *this* for *this* – no fucking way." I wasn't at death's door then.'

And what were you seeing?

'Well, it was the opposite of fun. I think you've got more of a crack at it at the meetings out in Los Angeles when you're first going. There are more people of a young age, and there's hope. In London the meetings were very, very dour. Very, very dour.'

What had made you go to the first one?

'Knowing I was a bit fucked and knowing Dave Enthoven. He took me. But I just wasn't at that point ... God, it was boring. And it was too long. An hour and forty minutes, those meetings.'

Did you talk in the first one?

'I think I did, yeah. I wanted to join in. I never found that difficult, telling them how I felt. But there was quite a few meetings I went to where the paparazzi attention was actually driving me crazy, and I'd sort of share about that and I'd be in tears, and that particular bit probably wasn't the right bit to share there. One time there was a guy doing his chair who said, "I've seen these *famous* people in these rooms, I've seen one of them cry into his hands about the problems that they've got ..." I was like, "That was *me*! At *that* meeting!" And people would just come up and say the wackiest things to me afterwards: "You're probably going to need to be a bit more mature about this whole paparazzi thing ..." There was quite a few judgements. They had no comprehension. There is a general level of "it's their fault for being famous ..." and "that's the price you pay ..."'

* * *

This last visit to rehab in Arizona didn't proceed smoothly. Three weeks in, Rob was unsettled by an incident involving another vulnerable patient; his subsequent unanswered questions about, and challenges of, what transpired left him feeling rattled and unsafe. He also couldn't see why it was being recommended that he should stay for nine weeks when it became apparent to him that a number of other patients were only staying for four. So he announced that he would also only stay four weeks.

'The first time I said this, they went, "I suggest you write an essay about a future relapse." The next day they tried again to convince me to stay and I said I wasn't going to, and they said, "Well, write an essay on your death." When my counsellor asked me to write a letter about my death, I lost all respect for him. I was, "I'm going early because you're saying 'write an essay about your death' which I think is a tool to keep me here, and the worst one you could use."'

In the end, after three weeks, triggered by what he saw as an insufficient response to these and other concerns, he packed his bags. Just as he was storming out, his mother, Jan, arrived in a taxi on a visit for family week.

'I was, "Look, love you loads, we're going, some shit's gone down, I'll tell you about it in a minute, get in the car."' Mother and son checked into a hotel, then flew back to Los Angeles; they did family week with a therapist there instead.

He wants to be clear – he is glad that he went to rehab, and grateful that it gave him space he needed to separate himself from the drug addiction he had at that time. And he is aware that without rehab that very well might not have happened. But he now thinks that if he ever had to go back again, he would choose somewhere where he had a bedroom and a television and he could use his computer: 'I would still spend all day in class, I'd still spend an awful lot of my time with the people that are there. But there would be more of a chance of me staying if I could have something of the outside world inside. I'd go to wherever they allow you to watch the television and have a nice bedroom to yourself.'

Ayda, who has been listening to the end of this conversation, offers an alternative suggestion.

'You're going nowhere,' she says, 'because you're not going to have a problem.'

* * *

Once you were out, how quickly or slowly did you work out what your plan was, going forward? Did you immediately know that you wanted to get off the relentless rollercoaster you'd been on?

'What I knew was, what I did for a living was making me ill. So that's easy maths. I've just made a shitload of money, I don't have to do this, I'm not going to.'

So you'd just stay home, writing songs, and living?

'Yeah. And trying to make friends, trying to be a friend. Filling my time. Falling in love.'

2

May 2016

In room 117 of the Soho Hotel, Rob is still sleeping. Ayda, who is to make her fourth appearance as a host on *Loose Women* today, left hours ago for production meetings, make-up and so on. In a connecting room, Michael and Craig Doyle – Craig is one of Rob's regular revolving security roster – wait. Eventually Rob blearily sticks his shirtless torso round the door to ask for breakfast, and to check that Michael saw his recent Shakespeare tweet. ('Bard Motherfucker', it said). And he asks Craig for a lighter.

He's smoking again. This is a surprise. He smoked until he was 38. Up to then, as various landmarks in his life approached he often talked of quitting, but never did. He only tried once, and when he did he succeeded.

Or as he puts it, 'The only time that I gave up was the time that I gave up.' And he says that he stopped simply by stopping.

He details the circumstances behind this recent slip. 'Five days into my diet,' he says. This latest diet was masterminded by Amelia Freer, who he'd gone to, impressed by the difference she'd made to Sam Smith. Also, he was concerned that all the chewing gum and Berocca he'd been having were exacerbating his eczema. So he'd decided to do it properly.

'The first day,' he says, 'went: a shot of Epsom salts, which keeps everything regular, a couple of eggs, nothing for five hours, vegetable broth, nothing for five hours, steamed vegetables, nothing until the next morning.'

He didn't like it.

'It was really fucking difficult. But my level of self-loathing was such that I seemed to be able to muddle through.'

Three days in, he was craving a cigarette, something he hadn't done at all for years. 'Never. Never. Went past people outside of buildings where people were smoking, thinking, "They still make them?"' After five days, he cracked. He's been smoking for eight weeks now. The first five of those, in secret.

He describes the ritual he adopted in their new Los Angeles house. 'I would go downstairs and outside the back door.' Go to the bathroom where he had Listerine and hand sanitiser stashed. 'And I would go out and take my clothes off. Take my top off anyway.' For a few weeks he got away with it. Maybe six cigarettes a day. Six visits. Even with the kind of occasional blunder that maybe you make when you know you're doing something wrong: 'One morning I gargled hand sanitiser by mistake. Just got it the wrong way round.'

He knew he needed to come clean with Ayda. Just not yet. 'I was trying to get brave enough to tell her, but couldn't find that moment. Plus I was enjoying being naughty for a little bit. I felt really guilty … but I also felt like a sixteen-year-old off to a rave.'

A few weeks ago they moved to England, and he adapted accordingly. He'd get up in the morning with jet lag, an hour and half before Ayda, and sneak out. 'The shoes I was wearing seemed to be really loud, so I had to walk really slowly to the living room at Compton Bassett, get out of the door window, and go and smoke outside. But then it would hit me so hard that I would instantly have a panic attack – I was literally high and low at the same time. Sometimes I couldn't get back into the house for the first minute.'

Finally, he was ready to tell her. They were watching *Mob Wives* at the time, the reality show based around a group of American housewives with purported Mafia connections – a show whose key storyline recently has been about the health problems of one wife, Angela Raiola. 'And just as I was about to, Big Ang died of lung cancer,' says Rob. 'And Ayda was so gutted about Big Ang dying of lung cancer – and so was I, because I like Big Ang. So I couldn't do it then. So then I was going to wait until she went away to go to work, in Manchester on a drama, and then I was going to tell her on the phone, so she could process it before she got home. And then I didn't do that.'

Eventually the guilt got too much. He just told her.

'She was absolutely gutted. Because it was something that was in my past, that she'd worried about for a long time.' Nonetheless, it might have been worse: 'She was so upset, but she's very understanding. She gives me adequate grief – she doesn't go a thousand per cent with the grief, she just gives me enough to let me know that I'm not out of the doghouse but the doghouse is a safe padded place.'

He's now agreed that he has until after Soccer Aid, four weeks away, to stop.

'It's going to be difficult. I think it's patches and a vape for a little while. But, look, I'm forty-two. I've got two kids. It's a really good idea to not smoke.'

* * *

Loose Women is filmed just over the river at the South Bank Studios. Coldplay's recent hit, 'Adventure Of A Lifetime', is on the radio, a song he says that he's only just begun to appreciate at all. 'It's not a song I'd want in my armoury. And there's quite a few Coldplay songs I'd want in my armoury, like "The Scientist" and "Clocks".'

He mentions that, along with the smoking, he's also recently developed a new habit.

'I'm sleep-eating,' he says. 'And quite a lot. The first couple of nights I was …' – he acts out being woozily confused – '… "Did I get up and eat last night … ?" And then I'd have a Polaroid snapshot in my head of a grape going into peanut butter. I think it's happened, like, six nights. We locked ourselves in and I still got out. On the door in the bedroom at Compton Bassett there's four locks, so I thought I'll put four locks on because Ayda will definitely hear me unlocking four locks. She didn't. Anyway, some nights is just a snapshot of what I've done, and then a couple of nights I get up and Ayda says "where are you going?" and I say "sleep-eating" and off I go.'

What do you eat mostly?

'Flapjacks made of seeds. And dates. And nuts.'

We near the studio.

'One night I ate brownies,' he adds.

* * *

After greeting Ayda and chatting in the canteen with today's guest, Rylan, he watches the show on the TV monitor in the dressing room. On-screen, today's panellists talk about their first celebrity crush. 'It wasn't Robbie?' Ayda is asked.

'No, no. Mine was Tom Cruise. This is before the couch, I'd like to say … that's when all of me wept inside …' And soon she is talking about her grandmother's superstition that one should never have a hat on the bed. 'Rob really laughs at me … My grandmother: "No hat on the bed, never" … Now Rob does not share the same irrational suspicions I have of luck and these things. He just likes to throw the cap on the bed.' She acts out how, when this happens, she'll immediately remove the offending headwear then brush the bed manically as though she can somehow undo the memory, and the bad luck, of it being there. 'It looks insane,' she says. 'He just laughs at me.'

'She seems incredibly relaxed to me today,' says Rob, watching. 'I don't know if she is.'

It cuts to adverts.

'Have you listened to the new Radiohead album?' he asks. *A Moon Shaped Pool* came out the previous week. 'Is it so sublime you'd have to buy it twice?' he asks drily, and says he just doesn't get them. Though he does find Thom Yorke's voice incredible. 'He could sing "Baa Baa Black Sheep" and you would be like, "Wow. *Is* there any wool?" You would be contemplating if there was any wool, and what that means.'

He goes outside for a cigarette, and says that Teddy thinks that when Ayda goes to work she is going out singing: 'I think she thinks everybody's mum and dad goes singing.' He mentions a recent meal with Adele, and their conversation about the craft of live performance. 'So I said, "How long are you onstage for?" She says, "An hour forty-five." I said, "Babe, that's perfect – you don't need to do longer than that. I'm always being convinced to do two hours, but an hour forty-five is perfect," She went, "Yeah, your show could have been twenty minutes shorter."' He laughs merrily. 'I think that Adele sort of thinks that anything other than the absolute truth is a lie. And why would you bother saying it unless it's the absolute truth?' To be quite clear, he doesn't say this like it's anything other than admirable.

Back on the show, the loose women, having discovered that Ayda never had a hen party, throw her one, here and now. Rylan is interviewed, and mentions that he and his husband didn't sell their wedding to anyone.

Rob turns to me. 'We did,' he laughs.

'I think when we got engaged on Christmas,' says Ayda on-screen, ' I think Rob thought "engagement" was the final frontier. I don't think that he thought that there was "wedding" after that. He was, like, "You got the ring – we're done!"'

In the dressing room, Rob listens, nodding. He turns to Gina, his regular make-up artist who is here today doing Ayda's make-up. 'I genuinely did think "I'd got the ring",' he tells Gina. 'Her mate gave her a wedding magazine two weeks after getting the ring, and I was, "What are you doing with that?"'

'It came as a surprise to him that there was a wedding to follow,' Ayda continues onscreen. 'After the engagement he was, "I don't know why we're talking about weddings – we got engaged."' She explains that he was eventually prevailed upon to come around. On her birthday he agreed to set a date, but it had to happen before he went away for work. 'We did the whole thing in six weeks,' says Ayda. 'My dogs were my bridesmaids.'

* * *

Afterwards, there is a *Loose Women* debrief in the green room. Rob slips in but hangs at the back. Eventually the conversation turns back to marriage, and their stumbles on the way.

'Can I just say?' says Rob, 'I was never, ever getting married. Ever. When I got to twenty-seven, I made a proclamation. All the way through my twenties I'd wanted somebody to fix me. And then at twenty-seven, I went, "Actually, I'm never getting married – this is perfect." Then we got engaged, and I was, "I've done the difficult thing."'

'Yeah, you were not prepared for …' says Ayda.

'I was not prepared for *actual* marriage,' he agrees.

'I was going to tell the thing about the magazine,' she says, 'but I didn't want you to look like a dick.'

* * *

August 2010

Rob and Ayda were married on 7th August 2010 in the garden of his Los Angeles home.

'Great day,' he says. 'Best day of my life.'

It was supposed to be a secret – his friends and family were told that he was throwing a big party to celebrate 20 years in the business, but he knew people had figured it out. Inevitably, rumours began to spread more widely. A couple of days before, Rob spoke to someone he knew in the media, and they did him the favour – a favour they would try to call in soon enough – of spreading the false story that the wedding was indeed about to happen this weekend, but that it was to take place on Catalina Island, a few miles offshore. That story – *Secret ceremony on romantic US island tomorrow* – was on the cover of the next day's *Sun*, and reporters set out to sea in preparation.

Even so, by the time the real ceremony was taking place, there were five helicopters hovering over his property.

'A split second after we'd got married and gone into our bedroom,' he notes, 'there was a long lens into our bedroom – the two of us just sat on the chaise longue, taken through the window from a helicopter.'

One more tender moment, this one on the most special day of his life liberated to be shared in grainy colour with the world.

* * *

But there were much better photos than this: in focus, and showing almost everything that happened that day, even behind closed doors, over 37 pages, for anyone who had £2 to spare. Given Rob's historic struggles with the media, and the endless battles he has fought to salvage some privacy, one decision made at this time might seem surprising: they sold coverage of the wedding to *Hello!* magazine.

There was a kind of clear rationale behind the decision. Rob knew what would inevitably happen on this day, whether they allowed someone access or not. As far as Rob was concerned, *Hello!* may have been writing the cheque, but they were doing so on behalf of all of the media. 'The reasoning behind that was: we can have several helicopters over wherever we are and have it be greatly saddening and impinge on our wonderful day. Or that can happen and they can pay for it. That helped in the knowledge that they're all going to be hugely desecrating something that's supposed to be sacred. It paid for the ring, and paid for the day.'

Aside from all the photos, *Hello!*'s coverage took the traditional form: copious lists of people, places and products, and the key romantic notes spelled out, albeit in a reasonably Rob-and-Ayda way. Wedding cake? A three-layer cake (red velvet, carrot cake, and vanilla and coconut). First dance? Harry Connick Jr's version of 'It Had To Be You'. There is also a substantially sanitised account of their early dating life, in which Rob describes how he proposed the previous Christmas, a proposal inspired by the way, early in their relationship, it seemed as though each time he split a deck of cards, the queen of hearts would come up.

'Because I'm into mysticism and signs and all that kind of stuff,' he explained, 'it filled my heart and made me stop worrying about whether I was with the right person.'

So he persuaded Ayda to go for a drive early on Christmas Day, saying he wanted to go down to Coffee Bean, their preferred coffee shop in the Valley. On their way, they pulled up at the main house, which was being renovated at the time, and Rob asked her to get out of the car. This was the exact spot where they had first met four years before, when she had arrived at the house in a friend's car on a blind date. He gave her four playing cards, the four queens, and on each he had written one word in black marker pen: *Will. You. Marry. Me?* He dropped to one knee; she said yes.

* * *

'I didn't want to get married at all,' says Rob. 'At all. *Ever*. It changed on the day, a complete transformation – just everybody turning up with your best interests at heart and loving you was incredibly special. I can't even put into words how lovely the day was. Best day ever.'

* * *

May 2016

Rob waits in another *Loose Women* dressing room while Ayda changes. He's been thinking about Ayda's birthday next week, and he says that he has decided what he's going to put on her birthday cake:

Congratulations – you're the oldest person I've ever slept with.

Is it true?

'No!' he scoffs.

* * *

In the car, they have a personal debrief.

'It felt like you were incredibly relaxed,' he says.

'It's such a whirlwind while it's happening, I never know if I'm being funny or if it's good,' she says. She points out that she's never done live TV before. 'It's a weird mixture of euphoria and fear. But more euphoria. I love it. It's comfortably outside my comfort zone. You get to be yourself wild, but protected at the same time.'

He's going to drop Ayda off to have lunch and shop with his manager David Enthoven's wife, Maren, while he spends a couple of hours in the studio with Guy Chambers. First, sitting together in the back seat, they record a wedding message on an iPhone for one of Olly Murs' friends – 'You don't know what you're doing!' they chant in unison at the end. Then Rob starts looking ahead, but not looking forward, to Soccer Aid. When he and Jonny came up with the idea, it was as a one-off, to fulfil a childhood dream, and he was pleased that they could make some money that would help some people in the process. But now it keeps coming around, and he dreads it. 'It starts in January, worrying about it. I only meant to do it once, and it's ten years in.' He says he'll do what he needs to do – 'it's such a big thing that keeps UNICEF UK going ...' – but he talks as though it's a troublesome blot on his year.

'I'd love to watch it at home,' he says, 'but the whole process makes me feel so awkward, and I think about it months before it comes up, and it constantly plagues me. It's actually a nightmare of mine to have to be that social with people for that length of time. I feel that socially awkward that a lot of people look at me that I'm a bit weird. And it's evident to a lot of people that I'm not very comfortable in my skin around a lot of people. Which compounds the sort of anxiety. It's not in my locker to do it. It keeps coming back, and now it's a *thing*. It's definitely a thing.'

He says that he gets psychosomatically ill beforehand. Last year he convinced himself he had a tropical disease, and even insisted on going to the Hospital for Tropical Diseases to get checked out. 'Just panicking about being a figurehead, and being around a lot of people,' he says. 'It's not my comfort zone, to say the least.' This time he's trying to work out a way of making it more manageable – keeping to himself more, sidestepping a lot of the social requirements that panic him. But he doesn't sound too optimistic. He says that in recent times his social skills have got worse.

I counter that it looks, from the outside, as though they've got better.

'I've got it worse than anybody else!' he proclaims defiantly, but also self-mockingly, and laughing. He said he had to do a Soccer Aid interview recently and that being inauthentic for 40 minutes gave him 'a brain quake'. For instance, he was asked his favourite Soccer Aid memory, and he immediately realised what the true answer would have been.

'At Keele services afterwards,' he says. 'Having a ploughman's sandwich at the garage. Because I hadn't had carbohydrates for a week. A ploughman's sandwich, some Ribena and a pack of Skips, heading back to London.'

* * *

At Guy Chambers' London studio, Rob listens to a new spoken-word intro recorded by the comedian Steve Furst for the new album's intended title track, 'The Heavy Entertainment Show'. He's not sure whether this version is better than the one he did in LA, a ludicrously over-the-top preamble in the style of a boxing announcer:

Ladies and gentleman! … The world's greatest entertainer! … Weighing in! … At 200 million pounds! … Reigning light and heavy entertainment champion of the world! … Here, tonight, in peak musical condition! … Mr Robbie Williams!

In the end they will decide the song works better without either. Meanwhile, he decides he wants to fix a lyric. At the moment there's a characteristically daft verse that goes:

I am notorious
For making all the crowd sing the chorious

You know how it goes.

He thinks the last line could be better; an idea is batted around until it becomes *I just made up that word!* Obviously better. He goes into the vocal booth to sing it.

Walking around the studio, Rob passes a dictionary lying on a table, and does what he often likes to do when a dictionary is around – as he thinks about something or someone in the world, he thrusts his hand in, so that it settles on a random place on a random page, just to see what word his finger alights upon.

His object of thought today: Noel Gallagher.

The word his finger finds: 'knocker'.

Guy and Richard work on the track and don't need him for the moment, so Rob gets on the internet where he reads the breaking news about Ayda's latest *Loose Women* appearance from earlier today.

The headline is I Felt Like A Fake Fiancée.

* * *

Today's travel is taking place in the Bentley he bought at the end of last year. He's particularly proud of the number plate, which he tracked down after reading an article about it.

E IS BAD.

'People look at the reg and they look at Craig and they don't look in the back, which is handy,' he says. 'I'm going round in the car thinking I'm doing an ironic statement about ecstasy, but I don't think people are getting that bit.'

We wait for Ayda, idling in front of Chelsea's ground. Rob points to a pub across the road, and says he got very drunk there during the recording of his first album, *Life Thru A Lens*. 'That was the Elton John day,' he says. Later on that day, he was so drunk when he turned up at Elton John's house with a cassette of his new songs to play him, that Elton John had him taken to rehab.

'How was the studio?' asks Ayda.

'I didn't do a lot,' he says. 'But I did do enough to justify going.'

The car heads west to their country home. On the way, he tells Ayda that he's done something that they have clearly agreed many times before is unwise. He read about himself online. 'I checked some comments yesterday,' he says. 'There's a lot of people still unimpressed with me.' He explains what he believes led him there: 'I think I went, consciously or unconsciously, to see if anybody's noticed I've lost weight.'

'I'm skipping that whole party,' says Ayda. 'I'm not playing the game. I don't want to. It hurts too much. I'm not one of those people who don't give a fuck what people think – I do give a fuck what people think. I'm not cool. I'm not impervious. I'm not going to be that person who can get past it.'

Rob says that he read an article in the *NME* – 'I skimmed it' – which he considered a kind of sarcastic defence of his new record contract; he has recently signed to Sony. 'It was along the lines of "he's shit, but he's our shit".'

It's a reasonable summary. The article, titled *In Defence of Robbie Williams*, begins: *No, look, come back, please – come back. Hear me out. The thing people always forget about Robbie Williams is that he's really not that bad.* It then offers a catalogue of criticisms, before pivoting to: *But what Robbie Williams is, what he will always be, is a proper pop star. Egotistical. Insecure. Contradictory. Absurd. Kind of embarrassing, but always compelling.*

Soon Rob is on to other memories, other blunders. 'Did I tell you about when I introduced Ayda as "my wife Adele"?' he asks. 'We were at an Olly Murs FIFA party. And I was, "Hi guys, this is my wife Adele." Just the wiring in my brain.'

'We get confused a lot,' says Ayda.

* * *

January 2007

If you wanted the film of the Robbie Williams story to have a pleasing, logical redemptive arc, then it would go like this: he would burn himself out horribly on his 2006 tour, hit bottom, go to rehab, and then once he has recovered, clear-headed and straight and carefully re-establishing his place in the world, that is when he would meet the woman with whom everything would at last make sense: love would blossom, light conquer darkness, joy vanquish fear, and they would gambol merrily, hand in hand, into the happy life that awaited them.

It didn't quite happen like that.

Rob and Ayda actually met for the first time several weeks before he went to rehab, on a Friday night in the third week of January, right when he was at his messiest. A mutual friend had set the two of them up. What the friend had told Rob – words that would hover in, and mess with, his head for a long time – was this: 'I've got a friend for you, she's fucking crazy but she might be fun for an evening.' Not the most promising of introductions. Nor was he in the best state to be meeting anyone. 'I Googled her – she was obviously very attractive,' he recalls. 'But I was also doing a lot of pills that were making me antisocial. On top of me being antisocial anyway. So we had plans but I flaked. So she'd given up on me. And then I left her a message days, weeks, later, and it made her laugh. And we made plans to meet. But I wasn't leaving my house, so she had to meet me at my house, which I think freaked her out a bit.'

This – and be warned, it's not quite as romantic as it might be – is how Rob prepared for the date which would eventually change his life: 'Earlier, a dealer had come round that I was sleeping with, and she'd given me all these pills – morphine, Adderall, Vicodin, a few more things. So I'd slept with the dealer, taken a bunch of pills.'

A while later, Ayda, who'd been at a party, was dropped off just outside Rob's house by a friend, right at the spot where, three years later, Rob would propose. But if they were destined to be together, there were few early signs. 'Porsche door opens,' Rob remembers, 'and out of the back seat clambers this girl. She's wearing a dress with pockets and it makes her look frumpy, and my first thought was, "Oh, she's put on a lot of weight." In she came, and she's had a few red wines. Ayda's different on red wine than she is on white wine – and she's different on rum and different on tequila. On red wine she's kind of bolshy New York Jew. I'm normally quite good with that situation of putting people at ease and being charming in a one-on-one situation, but I don't think the situation suited her, being at a stranger's house, and coming from a party where she was a few sheets to the wind, and I think I freaked her out. I think she was, "I'm not sure about this guy." Normally I can cut through that, put people to ease, but I just couldn't at that moment, and it wasn't working out for me, so I thought I'd take her back to her party.'

To get *rid* of her – that's the reason he went with her in the car: 'She doesn't know that I'm just planning to drop her off and go.'

And then something shifts, if only at first very slightly.

'She says a few funny things in the back of the car,' Rob explains, 'so I think I'll go in with her. It's this tech party with tech people – I've never experienced anything like it before. Now, looking back, it was like *Revenge of the Nerds*. It was very *cold*. The boys didn't want me to be there. And normally my pop star currency holds weight, whether that be in America where nobody knows me, or where people do know me – because even the currency of being someone somewhere normally makes it all right for you to be there. This particular time, it didn't. It just wasn't working. I wasn't very welcome. And the music was weird – quite binary and industrial, and not something that I was into. No melody, no vocal. Strange. The women were very nice, but the men, I felt as though I was on their turf and I wasn't welcome.'

His default way of dealing with such uncomfortableness at the beginning of 2007 was not necessarily the wisest.

'So,' he continues, 'I got tucked into a lot of drugs. Anyway, I took a turn for the worse, because I started to cluck like a chicken. And there was a moment in the jacuzzi where Ayda had gone and got changed and she came into the jacuzzi and she's wearing this Ursula Andress bikini and she had a killer body. I was, in my mind, "Oh wow, that dress was doing nothing for me." I was in my underpants. So I was in the jacuzzi with a very, very hot girl in Hollywood doing a Hollywood thing. But then I got ill, started to cluck, had to leave, embarrassingly. I had a great pair of Bathing Ape trainers on and I left one of them there, never to be returned. Favourite pair of trainers – shell-toe, orange stripe, white. I had to leave quickly – I was embarrassing myself.'

Ayda escorted her one-shoed, clucking date back to his house.

'And dutifully Ayda nursed me,' he says. 'And I played my records to her. Well, she says I did, but I know it was lots of things that I loved. But she nursed me and took care of me and was exactly what I needed at that moment, a bit of loving. She saw me at my worst the first night. And, quite interestingly, liked it.'

After that, they were together for the next three weeks: 'Ayda didn't leave my house, apart from to go to work. I've got these pills, the Adderall, and we eat cake every day, nothing else – I want to lose weight but I want to eat fun so I decide that all the calories would go to cake. We had these eclairs from the Glen, so the fridge would just be full of these eclairs. At breakfast we'd have an eclair, lunch we'd have an eclair. I was taking so much speed that I didn't need to eat anything really, so we just ate cake. For weeks.'

And then he split up with her.

* * *

In retrospect, Rob thinks that whatever link joins him and Ayda, the bond that has carried them through, was formed on that first evening, just after they'd arrived at the tech party. What united them, and made them realise for the first time that the way they thought and the way they saw the world and the way they *were* might just mesh in an unusual way, first showed itself as they shared their similar discomfort and perspective on what was in front of them.

'There was a moment,' he says, 'when we'd just arrived, when we were stood by the wall and we were looking at the party and I said something funny and took the piss out of the party, because there was a particular guy that was just being too much, and it made Ayda laugh. I made her laugh and she made me laugh. And in that moment I realise in hindsight we both fell in love – it was a universal connection, deeper than anything I've experienced before. We just got on like a house on fire.' Not that he was prepared to acknowledge or embrace the significance of what happened that night until much, much later. 'I'd set in stone the fact that I wasn't going to get married and I wasn't going to be in a relationship,' he says. 'So it wasn't until I was in a committed relationship with this person that I'd had that moment with that I realised that that *was* that moment.'

Looking back, he knows how easily he might never have realised.

'It's *Sliding Doors* moments, isn't it?' he says. 'I often think that's true about getting sober: the elevator door to sobriety opens and if you don't step into it that day, you're going to miss it for another three or four months. Or you might miss it for another four years. Or you might miss it for your life. It's the same sort of thing happened with Ayda – a door opened, and I refused to be open to the possibility of a different way of life. And it was a hair's breadth away from all of this not happening.'

* * *

The way he explains it, one of the reasons he split up with Ayda is that he'd been told she was crazy, and so he assumed that sooner or later the craziness would show itself, and he was finding it hard to see past this: 'There's a hole being filled by the presence of this person ... *but she's a crazy person*. She's hot ... *but she's a crazy person*.' In fact, it was almost as though the longer her craziness failed to show up, the more annoyed he was, as though this was a deliberate, mischievous trick on her part. How *dare* she keep hiding her craziness? 'I remember being with her thinking, "This is all good and proper, but I'm waiting for the crazy ... I'm meeting with a representative of yours because the crazy's coming."' (For the record, he says, 'Sure there was a crazy there – but it wasn't any more than yours or mine or anybody else's.' Certainly not the extreme, disqualifying character flaw he'd been primed to expect.)

Also, he knew that Ayda seemed to like him, and this meant that, in the fatalistic dating mindset he'd developed, he might as well pre-empt the inevitable ritual that he knew would come sooner or later. 'I've made a plan to never get married,' he explains, 'so she's doomed. And for years and years and years, alls I seemed to be doing was upsetting people that'd get close to me, that'd want to be in a relationship with me. So I seemed to be having these non-relationships with people that I'd have to *end* and upset them, whether it had just been three dates, five dates, six dates. So I'm, "Fuck me, I know how this goes, it's so fucking painful." People would quite quickly put all their eggs into my basket, and it would seem I would have to have that conversation fifteen times a year. I was frustrated that I had to do the same thing all the time. It's not a pleasant thing, breaking somebody's heart. But I'm always breaking somebody's heart that I've been knocking about with for two weeks.'

Best, if that's the way it is, to get it over with. The final straw as far as Rob was concerned – another insight into the troubled and troubling logic at work in his mind – came one evening when some regulars were up playing a game on his football pitch.

'So we're three weeks into this relationship,' he remembers, 'and one of the guys at football says, "Oh, my wife was with your girlfriend …" And I'm, like, "*Girlfriend* … ?" "Yeah, Ayda, she's your girlfriend, right?" "She's not my *girlfriend*."' That sent every bell ringing in his head – this beautiful woman he'd just spent every free moment of the past three weeks with, entwined together at his house, eating eclairs and whatever else, had somehow developed the deluded notion, or had at least been giving people the impression, that she was his *girlfriend*?

Quite obviously, he had to do something. So he phoned her up, said he couldn't see her anymore, and offered an excuse.

'There's been an intervention,' he explained. 'I've been taken to rehab.'

This was a complete lie. A few days later, he would be taken to rehab for real, and maybe the idea came so easily to mind because somewhere in the fog of his mind he knew it might be coming. But right now 'rehab' was just an excuse, a handy way of getting out of something.

And that, as far as he was concerned, was that.

* * *

May 2016

In the morning, Rob appears in the kitchen of his Wiltshire house and announces that he's not yet awake.

'I did sleep-eating again last night,' he says. 'Millionaire's shortbread.' Pause. 'I ate a lot.'

In the background, the Super Furry Animals are on *Soccer AM*. They look pretty rugged and weathered. The screen flashes to a picture of them when they were young and somewhat fresher-faced, posing on a tank. Two screenwriters, Ant and Casper, are at the breakfast table. They're here to discuss a prospective TV project with Rob and Ayda. For raw material, Rob is trying to point out anything interesting or unusual about his life, past or present. Even still half asleep, the picture of the tank on TV reminds him of something he feels he needs to share with them.

'Tanks are quite cheap,' he says. 'I looked into having a tank for here.' He explains that, in the end, he found other reasons not to. 'I just knew that it would rip up the ground,' he says. But he seems somewhat disappointed by his failure to follow through, by the way overblown whim bowed to practicality. 'So that's not truly eccentric, is it?' he says.

He tells the cook about his night binge and she explains that it was a kind of faux millionaire's shortbread, a little healthier than the real thing.

'But there was chocolate and caramel,' he points out.

Not so, she says. The 'caramel' is actually made from dates, and the 'chocolate' is raw cocoa.

'Oh,' he says. 'Okay.' He seems confused by the idea that he might not have fucked up as badly as he thought he fucked up, as though it's difficult to recalibrate in that direction.

Teddy rushes in, wanting to play. Momentarily Rob negotiates a delay. 'This is Daddy's favourite programme,' he says, gesturing towards *Soccer AM*. But then he gives in, and children's programming takes over.

* * *

Men who spend too much time in the English countryside tend to adopt hobbies. Rob's latest is metal-detecting. He started a few weeks ago – he bought a Garrett Ace detector for about £300 and a handheld pointing stick. 'Let me show you my pennies,' he says, with improbable enthusiasm. '1922. 1910. 1959.' All from the grounds here. He's looked them up, and believes one of them is worth four dollars. He's been thinking about carrying it around as his lucky penny. 'But then I'll lose it,' he worries.

He deflects my observations about whether there might seem something slight discordant about a multimillionaire with a metal detector, given the sense that it's a pastime often driven by the dream of finding a fortune. He has his reasons, and they're actually quite solid and authentic.

'When I was a kid, in the house I grew up in, there was a little section that was overgrown,' he says. 'And I got a shovel and started to dig, and found an old path that was there from the owner before the owner before the owner before. And I found it really exciting – a glimpse into another past, a glimpse into another dimension, a glimpse into another reality.'

And that's what he'd like more of. Recently, he had a try in the farmer's field next door, though not with great success: 'I thought, "I'll go over to that mud bit, because it'll be easier to dig up." And it wasn't mud, it was all cow shit. I'd been there quite a bit before I realised I was deep in cow shit.'

Still, for the time being, this new hobby has changed his perspective on the world around him. 'I used to look out of windows on car journeys thinking "that'd be good to BMX down", or to jump off. Then it was "that'd be good for rollerblading". And now I look at fields and think, "I bet you there's loads of things I could find in there."'

Nonetheless, he says that there is a downside to his new favourite distraction. For some reason, as he searches the ground below, the mind above wanders into unwelcome places.

'I'm locked into a syndrome where I go metal-detecting, and when I'm digging the holes, I can't stop thinking about everybody that I've upset during my life.' He says that he really tries not to. He'll keep saying to himself: 'I'm not thinking about it, I'm not thinking about', over and over.

'And then the shovel goes in, and it starts. And as I'm digging these holes, I'm literally worried about the holes that I've dug for myself. My brain idles at self-hatred, self-loathing. So I branch off into "oh, here's a reason ..." My brain now, when the shovel hits the earth, goes to worrying about people that I've upset. It is funny, where my mind goes. I think of people that I was at school with. Right now when I metal-detect, it's Taylor Swift.'

'Stop metal-detecting for a while?' suggests Casper.

'Yeah, I suppose so,' says Rob, as though this is the least likely solution for him to adopt. 'I had a whole afternoon, digging holes, worrying about upsetting Taylor Swift.'

At the 2013 Brit Awards, Rob was interviewed live on air at a table in the audience by James Corden. (He hadn't been sitting at the table at any other time, by the way – he'd just been led out there and sat down to have this conversation. Even the real stuff's often fake.) At the time Taylor Swift had a reputation, fairly or otherwise, for having a steadily flowing stream of ex-boyfriends, many of whom she was reputed to have written post-break-up songs about. Another factor may or may not have been that Rob had been annoyed earlier in the evening by the way her security detail would, quite unnecessarily, bully people out of the way in the backstage corridors to create a clear pathway for their star. But mostly he was trying to be less boring than most of what he was experiencing that night, and that's not the frame of mind in which he speaks most carefully. The conversation between Rob and James Corden took place immediately after Taylor Swift's huge pyrotechnic-filled production number for 'I Knew You Were Trouble'.

This is how the interview progressed:

James Corden: 'What about that? Did you enjoy that, Rob?'

Rob: 'She's really fit.'

James Corden: 'I'll say. Robbie Williams is here, everybody. How are you, sir?'

Rob: 'I'm really good. That was really good – what a great tune.'

James Corden: 'It was terrific, wasn't it?'

Rob: 'It'll be my go soon, won't it, really?'

Rob says that he's never actually been told that she is annoyed at him, but he assumes she is. Firstly, because, if he is honest, he would be. 'I reckon Taylor Swift's deeply offended about stuff because I got deeply offended about stuff,' he reasons. 'When people said nasty mean things about me, it really upset me. There's lots of things that I'm deeply offended about.' He also feels like he's been given a clue to that effect second-hand: 'Since Calvin Harris started going out with Taylor Swift, he doesn't email me back anymore.'

I ask whether, if he ran into her, he'd apologise.

'It depends what I'd get,' he considers. 'Because I couldn't have somebody telling me off.' But he expects other people to hold a grudge precisely because he does. He offers an example. 'There's whatshisname from Primal Scream. The lead singer. Bobby Gillespie. He said that he'd like to set me on fire "but shit doesn't burn". This is in '99. When I see him, I'm going to hurt him. I will hurt him.'

'I fancy your chances against Bobby Gillespie,' says Ant.

'Yeah, me too,' says Rob.

But seriously, I say, if Bobby Gillespie had walked in yesterday at the *Loose Women* studio, you wouldn't really, would you?

He concedes that I may be right.

'Probably not, now. But there was a long time when I would have.'

* * *

'You know my nickname is Jeanine,' says Ayda to Ant and Casper.

Jeanine is the archetypal pushy and controlling rock star wife in *This Is Spinal Tap*.

'I haven't called you Jeanine for a while,' says Rob. 'Ayda is actually the gatekeeper to all of my choices. I can't do anything without going through Ayda first.'

'I haven't Jeanine'd it much recently,' she says. 'I gave up.'

'No, *I* gave up!' says Rob.

'But you don't listen,' says Ayda. 'Because there was that time when you tweeted that photo of yourself, like, naked.'

'Oh,' he concedes. 'Yeah. Yeah.'

'I was, "You're going to look like a dick – do not tweet a picture of yourself naked."' She acts out his incoherently annoyed and defiant response. 'I was, "Don't get mad at me – I'm just telling you. People are going to hate on that picture. You're going to look stupid. I hate it when I see people do that." And then you got really cranky, and you posted it anyway.'

'I posted it out of spite,' Rob concedes. 'And then instantly regretted it.'

'And spent the next three days really depressed,' says Ayda. 'People were slagging him off.'

It happened a couple of years back. 'It was all out of oversensitivity towards my weight and being called a fatty, and wearing those words day-in, day-out. And then I lost two pounds – "look at me!".'

'He was completely naked,' says Ayda. 'Just cupped his penis. That was it.'

'And my tweet was "can my bell-end break the internet"?'

'It was after Kim Kardashian did "Kim Kardashian breaks the internet",' says Ayda.

Rob's tweet, however, did not break it.

'It offended a lot of people,' says Ayda.

'And I looked like a twat,' he says.

Casper wonders why they even read any of these reactions.

'Twitter's fine,' Rob argues, weakly. 'Facebook's not.'

'I may be addicted to finding things out about myself where I go, 'Yeah … I hate myself …' Rob concedes.

'"This confirms that I'm shit",' says Ayda. 'The good ones he doesn't even take on board. He goes looking for the bad ones to validate how bad he feels about himself. This is where we'll go head-to-head on it, and I'll go Jeanine – "Stop!" Because he will be depressed for, like, three days, hating himself …'

'Yeah,' he acknowledges.

'He's addicted to it,' says Ayda. 'There must be some sort of modern phenomenon.'

'I'm not saying it doesn't hurt,' says Casper. 'It's terrible.'

'That's why I don't read it,' says Ayda. 'Because I'm too sensitive. Because I know that I'm not impervious to those things.'

'It's narcissistic, but in a different way,' Rob argues. 'It's not narcissism where I'm going, "Oh, here's somebody that loves me." Because they have no effect whatsoever. I'm genuinely looking for the ones where they hate me.'

'You're looking for the hate,' says Ayda. 'You're looking for the pain.'

'It is a narcissism,' he reconsiders. 'But not in the way people think.'

'It's a self-obsession,' says Ayda, 'but not in the way of "I'm so awesome". It's the self-obsession of "I'm so shit".'

'I believe my own press,' he summarises. 'But only the press where they hate me.'

* * *

The morning continues.

'Jeanine versus Robbie,' asks Ant, 'how often does Jeanine win?'

'Jeanine's usually right,' says Ayda. 'Does Jeanine win all the time? No.'

'Jeanine wins most of the time,' Rob interjects.

'I don't think Jeanine does,' Ayda disagrees.

'I don't have my password for my Twitter,' Rob points out, 'because I can't trust myself to not cause an international incident. I send it all to Michael.'

'Yeah, Jeanine is several people, by the way,' says Ayda. 'Jeanine is not just me.'

'But today I'm getting my password,' he says. 'It's like being twenty-one and getting the keys.'

'Are you really?' says Ayda, sounding slightly alarmed. 'Why now?'

'Because I'm doing that much tweeting that I don't want to have Michael have to do ten things a day to take him away from doing important stuff.'

I ask whether he's truly ready.

'Yeah,' he says confidently. Then he adds: 'Probably not. I don't think the world's ready for it.' He explains the problem as he sees it. 'I would have the habit of breaking an acorn with an axe.'

'I don't want to fight people,' says Casper, by way of contrast.

'That's good,' Ayda agrees. 'I'm more "forget about it". He's...' – she gestures towards Rob – '... more "fight people".'

'It takes a lot to piss me off,' says Casper.

'It actually does with me, though,' says Rob.

'Yeah?' says Casper.

Ayda looks as though something preposterous has been said. 'No, babe ...'

'Yeah, it does!' he insists. 'But by the time I'm pissed off, it's way too late. It's: beware the temper of a caged man.'

'Yeah,' she agrees, coming round to his description. 'Your patience runs out, then you get really mad. Like a mad man. Then I try to pull you back. I think that's when I'm Jeanine. Where else am I Jeanine?'

'What I wear,' says Rob.

'Yeah,' she agrees.

'The money. How we spend it.'

'Yeah,' she says. 'Yeah.' She explains about the clothes. 'He would wear ... Rob has this thing, every few months, about an everyday suit. Even though he has a clothing line, so he's trying to promote himself as a fashion brand, Rob will walk around in the same stained grey sweatsuit everywhere, and then he'll go, "You know I saw this picture of this Japanese fighter ... I'm just going to wear Japanese suits ..." He'll get these custom-made Japanese suits that cost thousands and thousands – "This is all I'm ever wearing for the rest of my life." That lasts about two seconds. He was also quite partial to the nineties jean for a very long time. He's progressed, though.'

'I didn't know that the game was up, with the nineties jean,' he says, with mock ruefulness.

'You know,' Ayda continues, 'with the very flared bottom.'

'I totally understand Michael Jackson and the pyjamas,' Rob digresses. 'He just used to wear pyjamas all the time.'

This conversation is interrupted by Teddy, who has created a hybrid plastic ice cream which she hands to Rob.

'I love your dress, baby girl,' says Ayda, and then chases Charlie around the sofa.

Rob puts on first-leg play-off match between Derby and Hull, and talks about his forthcoming plan 'to start not smoking'. As though this is somehow something different from actually stopping smoking. Charlie tips a glass of water over Ayda's computer, but no damage is done.

* * *

March 2006

'I spent a lot of my twenties wanting a maid, really,' he tells me. 'I thought I wanted a relationship but I just wanted somebody to fix and nurse me, and I'd take her hostage for six months. Your brain's all scrambled at that period in your life, when you're twenty-three, twenty-four, you've just left home, there's new stuff to contend with, and you want to be in a relationship because they look brilliant – that's what you want to do and that's what you need to do because you've heard all the songs about it and seen all the movies and it looks great. Little did I know that I was nowhere near being in a relationship with anybody. I only had a couple, and after that couple I pretty much realised that until I was ready it was going to be a pain in the arse for the other person.'

But you did a lot of auditioning.

'Yeah. I did a lot of auditioning.'

What was that for?

'Well, it was for a lot of reasons. Company. Instant gratification. With a view to long-term gratification.'

Is it fair to say that while obviously you had your fair share of company and instant gratification, you'd often very intensely think that maybe someone could be something more than that … and then, very quickly afterwards, very intensely decide that they were not?

'Yeah. You want something to happen, though. You're willing it to be the match. But also I hadn't had the luxury of having that amount of time off before. There's always been something in the way – a tour or a record or promotion or a hotel or a fan or a person in a bar, ad nauseam. And I needed that break to give someone … give someone a good go.'

It seemed to me like you needed some kind of way of both giving someone else a chance, and giving yourself a chance. I'm not sure you really used to give either them or yourself too much of a chance before. Is that fair?

'Yeah, I was always expecting to be completely and utterly bowled over, like the movies. And because I didn't think that I was getting that feeling, I'd move on very quickly. And I was kind of like, "Yeah, I've done relationships – I don't like them."'

* * *

Rob sometimes now talks as though, as thankful as he is to have found his new life, the carefree single life he led before worked perfectly well. Perhaps at times it did, but certainly not always. One of the essays he shows me in South Africa begins with an account of a visit to New York the previous month with, as he explains, a bad back: *I'm despondent. Women have been trying to play me like a fool and because I've been going out more often it's happening more regularly. I'm not kidding – I'm fucked off. Bad back, heavy heart.* He veers back and forth between sounded jaded about anyone he might meet – he despondently characterises them as spies playing the long game in a cold war – and whooping himself up into a fever of hope and belief: *Then, in she walks … I love her. We will have babies. Beautiful football playing book reading babies … She has one of those faces people go and have plastic surgery to look like. Please carry my seed?* But soon enough, in this story and in pretty much everything he writes at the time, he finds his way back to bitter disenchantment, as though dating is just a pointless repetitive machine designed to tease you with a dream that's never real before it crushes you with another reminder of just how disappointing the world usually is.

All of which might be true, except that he sounds stuck in a loop, no longer ready to give anyone – including himself – much of chance. He might be spot on about each and every fault he sees in the people he encounters, even if he seems less aware of any equivalent shortcomings he might himself have or how he sometimes doesn't notice in himself the failings he's so quick to judge others for, but there's something so jaded and despondent about it all, and that's the tone I remember when I first read these essays.

It made me think that this is the person who wrote the line *before I fall in love I'm preparing to leave her,* but five or six years of disappointments later.

* * *

Eventually you seemed to be declaring: I'm not going to have a long-term relationship with anyone.

'Yeah, I remember thinking, "I'm never going to have a long-term relationship and I'm not going to have children."'

You'd present it as if it was a positive, like you'd seen through the nonsense, wouldn't you?

'Well, you're supposed to be monogamous in a relationship. Traditionally that's the accepted view of what happens, and what you must be. And I didn't feel capable of that. There were also not many good adverts around me for great relationships that you'd want to be in. It all looked like a series of arguments and discomfort, and complaining about the other half while the other half wasn't there. And I think I'd wanted to be in a relationship for so long and be loved and love that I'd got to the point where I was: actually, no. I don't think I can do monogamy. I'm just going to have sex.'

Was that fine and good, or soul-destroyingly empty, or … ?

'It wasn't soul-destroying, but I can't really remember. I remember feeling put out by the fact that I became the golden goose that nobody wanted to sleep with because they wanted to marry me. I'd been living in this big house, and in the other bedrooms were my mates, shagging, and in my bedroom was me chatting with no end result. Everyone else seemed to be shagging, and I wasn't. I seemed to be plagued with this. It was infuriating that everybody didn't want to be "like everybody else". What that meant to me was: Oh, you want a relationship with me because of what I've got, what I've accrued.'

They might also have liked you.

'Yeah. They did too, but it didn't seem honest to me. And it was frustrating, because it seemed to happen every single time. I could have given them a script and gone "this is what you're going to say ... this is what I'm going to say".'

So it made you fairly cynical about all that?

'Well, I was cynical about everything. I was really cynical about my profession. There was no magic in it. I'd demystified absolutely everything, including Hollywood, big films, big actors, show-people, getting onstage. Nothing was any good. Everything was a lie. I'd taken a bitter pill where I was bitter about showbiz.'

From the outside, the contradiction was heartbreaking – that you had all this incredible success in so many ways, but it clearly wasn't doing anything for you that made you happy or satisfied or fulfilled.

'No.'

Were you as aware of that contradiction as the people around you were?

'Yeah. But that seemed to be a running theme throughout my whole career. Buying my first million-pound house, with massive patio doors that opened to a lake of mine, and just melodramatically, figuratively dropping to my knees and going "this isn't making me happy". That just ran alongside getting in the car and turning up and doing what I was doing.'

And did you despair as to whether there would ever be a way through that?

'It's really isolating. Because the only person I kind of knew that was doing it on that sort of scale was Elton John, and he enjoys it. I was, "Why is he doing two hundred and fifty gigs a year?" Why is he doing that? *How* can he do that? And I asked him, and he said he enjoyed it. And I didn't understand that.'

The most baffling answer of all!

'Yeah. And there wasn't anybody to go to who could say to me, "Oh, you're going through this – this is what this is."'

But what could they have said to you at this point that you would have listened to and believed?

'Not much. Not much.'

I mean, if the Rob that existed then came to you now and said *this is how I'm feeling*, what would you say to him?

'You've got this completely wrong. Your brain's muddled. There is a way out of this. You can get to the place that you would like to be. Don't pull the trigger. Don't jump off the bridge. Figuratively speaking. If you can get to the person who's trying to jump off the bridge to kill themselves and really have them understand: you're going to be killing the wrong person. I'm not saying you've got to kill anybody else, just that in two months you'll be killing the wrong person.'

And if someone had said that to you back then, would you have been able to listen?

'Probably not, because I would have thought: "They don't know. Because I'm unique and special and different." Special in a dysfunctional kind of way. Maybe if there had been somebody on my level that I could have consoled with, maybe I would have. If they'd gone, "I know exactly what you mean. I know it's making you mad. I know that when a) and b) happens, c) and d) happens to you, and it's because of this. And you're not alone – you're not crazy, there is a reaction that's happening, and it's okay, and it's gonna get better. It's going to take time."'

* * *

One of the other essays from 2006 was actually called 'I Don't Want To Be Like All The Other Girls'. Its overall mood is similar: *I'm disillusioned ... let me tell you a story involving cokeheads, adulterous and crap humans ...*

This time some of the barbed asides are pretty funny – 'I'm introduced to a young actress, who will remain nameless,' he writes. 'Not that I'm protecting her anonymity, she's just rubbish at acting' – and there are weird tangents, as when he gets the Friday-night convoy of cars coming back to his house to pull into a lay-by because he's sure he's seen some UFOs. It's also probably the first time in the English language that a potential romantic partner has been described using the phrase "mutant sexy carp".

Yeah that's right ... mutant sexy carp. It took me twenty minutes to come up with that ...

But soon he is explaining the essay's title:

I always get the same line: 'I don't want to be like all the other girls!' Right. For your information ALL THE OTHER GIRLS say 'I don't want to be like all the other girls', leaving ... that's right ... NO other girls ...

That's what's happening and has happened for the last five or so years. Girls think that by being 'different' I'm going to want them more ... I am not. SLEEP WITH ME! You'll have more of chance, at least you'll be original ...

I see very little honesty in the 'other girls' statement ... To me it means this: (imagine game show host commentary) 'OK, so you've got a date with Robbie Williams. That's safe, are you going to gamble and see if you can go for Robbie's Millions? ... we'll be back after the break'.

Later, he returns to this theme:

... if I hear the 'I don't want to be like the other girls' statement again I'm going to boil and eat my own cock.

There are other essays, with other stories, but generally in a similar vein. And for every moment of inspired humour, levity or digression, there's two of frustration, anger and bitterness. Maybe these are just the days he's chosen to write about, and there are other much better days, but it really doesn't sound like he's having much fun. And in this state of mind, it's quite hard to imagine, given the resigned and distrustful mindset he seems so ready to impose upon any potential romantic encounter, what someone could possibly do to make him believe that she's not the way he already expects and assumes that anybody who comes close to him will be.

* * *

August 2016

Rob was lying awake in bed in London's Mandarin Oriental hotel early one morning a couple of weeks ago, Ayda asleep next to him, thinking about his album. Worrying about his album. They'd been living in a hotel because their new London house is still being renovated, and this wasn't the easiest way to live with two young children. Also, Ayda had had a sudden rich run of work, acting as an aide to Donald Trump in the written-and-filmed-the-same-day Brexit TV comedy *Power Monkeys*, and as a strung-out girlfriend in the drama *Paranoid*, and had become a semi-regular member of the *Loose Women* panel. He was happy for her, and had been trying to pay back the kind of support she has always shown him, but he'd also been feeling a little aimless. He'd been trying to do some more songwriting, still chasing one more special song, but he hadn't liked many of the results. 'I was sort of out of ideas and all writ out. Mostly, I was just sort of in hotel rooms and waiting about.' It'd left him a little low. 'Had to go up on my sleeping pills to get to sleep,' he explains, 'and that was making me confused and depressed.'

But on this particular morning, an idea came to him, and so he wrote the following email:

Hi mate. I've written at least 70 songs for my new album.

I'm being picky as fuck.

And if I stand with my hand on my heart there's 7, maybe 8, I can stand by.

I'm still writing and me and Johnny have a good connection that I'm looking forward to exploring.

That being said, if you have any spare bangers I'm up for having a listen.

Those nuggets are soooooo hard to come by so I totally understand if you're saving them for yourself!

Death to your enemies x

Later this year, when he starts doing interviews in which he'll tell people about this email, he'll paraphrase and boil down what he emailed to a single-sentence distress call: 'Hey mate, do you have any spare hits?' He will also describe, in what will become an increasingly baroque and elaborate set-piece monologue, the panicked break-of-dawn mindset of self-loathing and insecurity in which the email was sent: 'I was sort of neurotically obsessing about the album, and I was, "You're running out of time, fatty! Come on!

Find a hit! Get a hit! You're 42, fatty! Sort it out! Pull your finger out! Morning, fatty! Why are you sitting down to pee again?…'"

The email's recipient was Ed Sheeran. Rob doesn't know Ed Sheeran well, but a couple of years ago he accepted an invitation to sing 'Angels' with Sheeran at one of Sheeran's solo Wembley Stadium shows. (It fell through when the only date Rob was free was also the only date when Elton John could appear.) But they have met briefly. 'And he told me the first album that somebody ever bought him, his auntie, was *Life Thru A Lens* – and it meant a lot to him,' Rob says. 'And that means a lot to me.'

By way of reply, Ed Sheeran sent Rob a demo of himself singing a song he'd co-written called 'Pretty Woman'. Rob loved it, but also felt like it could go somewhere else, so with Sheeran's blessing he has since added a chorus to it. He's sure this one is a keeper: one more song for the album.

* * *

He's now back in Los Angeles. Back off the sleeping pills, back on his diet.

'No oil on anything,' he explains. 'It's oil that adds fuckery to your poundage.'

* * *

Still, there were some highlights to the last few months in Britain. One unexpected one was Soccer Aid, which he had been dreading. 'I cut an awful lot of things out of the itinerary that I would normally do – and in doing so it became very doable,' he says. 'I did what was necessary and it was enjoyable.'

He even caved on his insistence that he didn't appear on the pitch. Turns out that Sam Allardyce, who was managing the English team, is a difficult man to say no to. 'I played the last ten minutes – and I shouldn't have done,' says Rob. 'Nobody wants to hear me when I say, I'm going to put my back out. Especially Sam Allardyce. The time before I played I fucked up my back so badly for the rest of the tour – I was in so much pain … just the motion of putting my foot through a ball fucks my back.' But

Rob went on, and nothing bad happened. 'I didn't fuck up. I controlled the ball and I passed it and it got to the feet of the person I was passing it to. But I was so anxious, because I wasn't fit.'

Even so, he's no longer looking for a way to sidestep his involvement.

'The day after,' he says, 'I was: I could do that again. So Soccer Aid can continue with my participation, which is good.'

* * *

One day in London, Michael explained to Rob that he had a surprising question to ask him.

The obvious but rarely acknowledged truth about many, if not most, music industry award ceremonies, is that long before any award is publicly announced a kind of shadowy negotiation takes place, which generally involves the floating of a carefully worded conditional question along the lines of: *If we were to give so-and-so the so-and-so award, would he or she turn up to receive it?* In this kind of deniable way, Michael needed to discuss with Rob how he felt about the prospect of being given the Godlike Genius Award at this year's *NME* Awards.

Rob's relationship with the *NME*, which in its heyday was the weekly music paper which dominated a certain kind of music taste- and opinion-making in Britain, is a complicated one. There is probably no way of being treated that Rob is more sensitive to, and that raises his hackles more swiftly, than being patronised and condescended to. One harsh but understandable summary of his relationship with the *NME* over the last quarter of a century, not only in times when they thought that they hated him but also in those (occasional) times when they thought that they liked him, would be that it has been an endless drip-drip barrage of condescension. For a long time, certainly, the *NME*'s coverage epitomised a certain mindset. 'There was a sort of indie fundamentalist mentality that was with us all the way through the nineties that was very apparent to me,' says Rob, 'where I was literally looked down upon during conversations with a lot of people – you know, people scared it was going to rub off on them. Whatever "it" was. You know, the bluecoat thing. It's like, I was the underclass. Because of who I was. And it was so apparent, so hurtful.' Sometimes the condescension tipped over into pure nastiness. 'I was voted "the worst human being on the planet" when Osama Bin Laden had just done 9/11,' he points out. '"Feel" was voted the worst song of the year.'

This history would account for the strength of Rob's initial reaction when he heard what was potentially now being proposed.

'It was very northern,' he says. 'It was very sweary, very absolute: "Those fucking cunts can go and fuck themselves, no way am I fucking having a fucking award from those fucking cunts. I hate those fucking cunts." And then I went to the toilet.'

When he returned, Rob had changed his mind. He'd decided that he wanted it to happen.

'But really I'd only changed my mind because I'd plan on doing something controversial,' he says. And he remains unsure which option he prefers. 'I'm conflicted. Do I go and take the award and tell them all to fuck off? Or do I just not take the award? If it is offered?'

There must, I suggest, be an elegant way of having your cake and eating it.

'Yeah,' he agrees, laughing. 'I won't find that.'

* * *

There are few more unlikely places Rob might be found than at the *NME* Awards. But there is one.

In 2010, a few days after Take That had announced their reunion, the original five of them back together, Rob appeared on Liverpool's Radio City breakfast show with Jason Orange and Mark Owen. During the interview, he was asked whether Take That would be playing Glastonbury. This is how the conversation continued from there:

'Absolutely not, no,' Rob replied. 'Definitely not … No, there's gonna be no Glastonbury. Not for me, no. They pay you about five pence, to be honest.'

'I would love for us all to go to Glastonbury,' Mark countered. 'I'm going to try and convince the lads, I'm going to get the caravans, and I'm going to try and convince us all to go and have a day out at Glastonbury. Just for a day off.'

'Yeah, Rob,' echoed Jason. 'They pay us five pence, but what about the other reason for doing it? Apparently it's a spiritual place and …'

'It's a shithole,' Rob interrupted. 'Yeah, it is. Full of dickheads.'

Someone in the studio protested, saying that he goes every year.

'Yeah, well, you must be a dickhead,' Rob declared. 'That enjoys shitholes.'

Rob had been to Glastonbury three times. The first time, in 1994 as an off-duty member of Take That quietly stretching his wings, he kept his head down. The second time, the following year, he made a bigger splash, playing the off-his-head bleached-haired tooth-blacked-out boyband renegade, dancing onstage with Oasis during that brief honeymoon period when Oasis had taken him under their wing. He has never forgotten the scorn he faced on those first two visits. 'There was an utter pervasive contempt. The rest of Glastonbury was: "What the fuck are you doing here, you cunt?" It sort of shapes you.' Back then, he wanted to be embraced: 'You want to be okay with the big boys and you want to be accepted by the bullies.' It's a feeling that, once you get past it, you hate yourself for ever having felt, and you want the bullies to know that you'll never care what they think about anything ever again.

The only time he was actually booked to appear onstage was for an early-evening performance in 1998. 'There was a militant indie energy where everything else was scum and beneath them,' he says. 'And I was the poster boy for the scum. So then to go and perform at Glastonbury, I was overwhelmed with all those thoughts and feelings of not being good enough, not being worthy, not being cool enough. All of those things that are important when you're a teenager or in your early twenties. Yet there I was, about to go onstage in front of what I thought were the enemy. Because they're all here to see guitar bands, and I'm the pop twat from Take That.' In truth, his performance was a triumph – unexpectedly, he was embraced by the crowd. 'I found it to be a euphoric, but confusing, feeling,' he says. And not one that completely overcame the way he considered that he was made to feel just for being there.

That's how Glastonbury remained cemented in his mind over the years, representing and encapsulating the kind of ethos and spirit, not a million miles away from the *NME*'s, that doesn't respect or acknowledge the worth of what someone like him does. Despite what he said on the radio, I don't think his antipathy is really about the money at all. (Glastonbury does pay less than many other festivals, but principally because it is permanently set up to raise money for a range of causes.) I think it's more that he doesn't want to be paid less money while simultaneously being condescended to.

Anyway, given all that, it seems somewhat improbable that one of the places Rob found himself this summer, in his wellies and orange raincoat, was backstage at Glastonbury.

The simple explanation, he says, was 'I was made to go by Ayda'. But the rather more complicated and surprising upshot was that he found himself enjoying it. 'Look,' he concedes, 'I'm really glad I went – I had a great time.' He and Ayda were there to see Adele, and they watched her performance on a raised platform on the side of the stage with 'the great and the good': Stella McCartney, Mary McCartney, James Corden. Though he had no desire to announce his presence or draw attention to himself, it turned out that the audience could see him up there, and so events took an unexpected turn. 'Adele went off for her encore,' he says, 'and that's when the audience decided to start singing "Angels". So I was caught in a really awkward moment.' It was Adele's gig, and he would have hated to have done anything to undermine that. But he also realised that if he didn't acknowledge the crowd and what they were doing at all – and he did think it was sweet that they were doing it – then they would think awful things about him. He further realised that if he acknowledged the crowd too enthusiastically, the other people around him on the friends-of-Adele platform wouldn't be too impressed. He did his best to cover all options:

'I quickly went and conducted a little of the singing and then hid in the middle of the other people on the platform.'

Nonetheless, he was surprised to discover that the whole experience of being there changed how he felt about the festival. 'Interesting to go not off my head on cocaine and ecstasy, or having to perform there,' he says. 'There's an energy there that's really special.' And he realised something else, too. Perhaps his previous disparaging words will preclude an invitation coming his way, but he's now decided that he would really like to play there.

'I think I'd smash it,' he says. 'I'd like to play on the "Robbie Williams, he shouldn't be doing the main stage … !" I'd like to embrace that and go and give the audience an amazing time.'

* * *

Right now, Rob does have one new song of his own that he is excited about, one he thinks will be on the album. It's another song written with Johnny McDaid. (McDaid is a member of Snow Patrol, and has also co-written some of Ed Sheeran's biggest hits.) It's called 'Speaking Tongues' and is about a weekend he spent in Ibiza back when he was still in Take That: a travelogue of violence, drugs, sex and madness.

'Happy times,' says Ayda, drily.

Rob had gone to the island with some ravers he knew from Warrington. He talks through some of the true incidents referred to in the song. 'I did meet some lads called the Diamond Dogs that were sort of travellers from festival to festival – they were making their way to Rio to go to the carnivals, and I think they did that by dealing. Then there was this girl that followed me through the streets and she wanted sex. I think she was from Preston. And we went back to her hotel but the hotel owner wouldn't let me upstairs. It was sort of panto – I was "please" and then I got on my knee and went "*please*" and he punched me in the face. Then I was out on some rocks, jumping into the sea, and somebody came up and said, "Look, there's a gang of lads collecting together in San Antonio that are coming up to kick your face in."'

Because you were in Take That?

'Yeah. So I whistled down a taxi, to save us all the grief. I was thinking how much people have wanted to beat me up throughout the years. When I recount stories, it's *always* "people wanted to beat me up ..." I was saying to Stuart Price, I think it must be like conkers – if mine is a six and you beat it, yours is instantly a seven. And I was a high-numbered conker. But I don't think Gary Barlow went to a lot of places where he was in danger. And I don't think any other members of Take That's faces begged to be punched. Howard doesn't have the same sort of stories, and neither does Jay. But wherever I went, people wanted to beat me up.'

Do you think maybe you exuded the sense that you needed taking down a peg or two?

'Yeah.'

Weirdly, before he was famous, before he was even in Take That, he once saw an example of this kind of behaviour as an observer, and remembers how much it puzzled him.

'We were in an under-sixteens nightclub in Stoke where somebody from Grange Hill was doing a PA. And I can remember somebody from my school that I was with came over to me and said, "I've just spat on him!" And I remember in that moment thinking, "Why did you do that?"'

And then, two years later, you're the man to be spat on?

'Yeah,' he says. 'There was a lot of being spat on.'

* * *

This new Ibiza song also describes a confusing, drug-fuelled religious encounter:

And a reformed gangster got me and he said that he'd found God
He looked me in the eyes and he started speaking tongues.

'I was in a swimming pool,' Rob explains, 'and I'd been up for a couple of days and a guy came over and put his hand on my shoulder and said, "Jesus has sent me to speak to you." And I had a breakdown in the pool.'

Why?

'I don't know.'

Did you sort of believe him?

'Yeah. I thought God had sent him to speak to me. He took me back to his apartment and then started reading some Bible stuff and started speaking in tongues. He was a reformed gangster that had done bad and found God. He said, "You've been on the devil's dandruff, haven't you?" I went, "Yeah." I spent a bit of time with him and then I left. And that night I said I wouldn't do any coke, but I drank a Poco Loco, which were twenty-five quid a glass in '93, full of mescalin and ecstasy and acid. Then I left Ibiza and I had to catch a connecting flight to Barcelona, and then Barcelona to Manchester, and Manchester to Gary Barlow's house to start singing some backing vocals for a Take That album. I knocked on the door and he answered and I said that I'd found God, and I collapsed. I went to bed in Gary's bed and slept for two days.'

* * *

That lunchtime, we watch Barcelona versus Liverpool on the TV in the big cinema room at one end of the house.

After a while I mention that I'm not really buying Messi's blond look.

'No,' Rob agrees, 'but I wasn't really buying my blond-hair look.' He's referring to the style he adopted on this last tour: a kind of silver-blond upwards-heading quiff, dark and short at the sides.

'But it was a change,' he reflects. 'Something different.' By which he means that he is a pop star, and in the world of pop, change for change's sake is often a virtue.

'It's a *look*,' he points out, 'even though it might be wrong.'

* * *

One of the few current artists whose music Rob has recently found diverting are the Sleaford Mods, the Nottingham duo whose sparse, roughshod, caustic and satirical songs are, late in their career, getting the attention they deserve. 'Isn't it amazing,' Rob reflects, 'that the voice of disenfranchised youth is forty-seven years old? That that energy doesn't exist in modern music? Where's the seventeen-, eighteen-year-old version of that? Why's it got to be a forty-seven-year-old man doing that? Where's the disenfranchised youth?' He answers his own question. 'They all want to sing Beyoncé covers on *The X Factor.*'

Perhaps inevitably, and in a way Rob perhaps not only expects but almost respects, anyone persuasively inhabiting that role is not likely to warm to someone like Rob, or certainly not to how they perceive him to be. And so it has proved. The Sleaford Mods – in this case presumably, singer and lyricist Jason Williamson – recently tweeted this:

If I look at Robbie Williams in a photo for too long it sends me into a rage.

Rob simply retweeted the sentiment, along with a reply:

Rage? I can never get past shame. #goals x.

* * *

One of the many debates that seem to be constantly fomenting inside Rob's head is between two different kinds of pop star he could be. In the most simplistic terms, it could be seen as a battle between the part of him that wants to write and sing big instant songs that some people might find cheesy and uncool, and that part of him that wants to write and sing the kind of songs that might be more easily praised for their sophistication and smartness and credibility and artistic experimentation. He goes back and forth.

This debate is constantly resurfacing, and was recently stirred up by a conversation he had with the producer Stuart Price. Rob has been intermittently writing with Stuart, but he also respects his counsel. When he played Stuart some of his other new songs, for Stuart some of them clearly strayed over some invisible but, to him, clear line of what he considers acceptable, or at least wise, for an artist like Rob. There's three songs in particular: 'Disco Symphony', 'Funk With Us' and 'Marry Me'. The first two are big, instant, catchy pop songs written with Guy, both of which Guy imagines as big singles; the third, written with Rob's drummer Karl Brazil and others, is as sentimental as you'd imagine from the title. They're songs that Rob himself has been going back and forth in his head about. With songs like these, he is often less concerned that they won't connect with an audience than worried that they will, and worried whether, if they are as successful as he thinks they have the potential to be, he will come to dislike singing them night after night, year after year.

But as negative as Rob can be himself about these kinds of songs, Stuart's misgivings have inspired him to come to their defence – and, by extension, to a defence of one whole part of who he is and what he does.

'I think they're cheesy,' he says, pointing out that in this simple, objective judgement he and Stuart agree. 'But I don't *mind* cheesy.' By the same measure, he knows that 'Rock DJ' and 'Candy' are certainly cheesy. 'And they came out of my heart and my soul and my mind. It's *my* cheesy. I own it! It's what I did.' Something Stuart said while they were listening to 'Disco Symphony' has made him think hard. 'If that's the artist you want to be …' Stuart said. 'What do you *want*?'

It's made him, at least for this moment, realise something, even though it's probably not what Stuart was encouraging him to realise:

'I want to be Mr Saturday Night!' Rob declares. '*That's* what I want. I want Saturday night and I want Christmas. I said this ages ago: Freddie Starr on *Des O'Connor*, Morecambe and Wise, *The Two Ronnies*, Oliver Reed on *Wogan*, Dean Martin. Stuart was talking about: "What did you want when you started your solo career?" I wanted to do coke and sleep with women and be Oasis. But I don't want that now. I haven't got the energy, or the inclination.'

Stuart also made another argument, using Sam Smith as an example. Stuart said that on his way to success Sam Smith tried every possible style, but finally he settled on doing what he enjoyed – and that is what has translated. Stuart's suggestion is that Rob should do the same: do what he enjoys, and it will translate.

Rob could have answered by pointing out that he enjoys all these kinds of music that he makes – the cheesy, the club, the cerebral, the mournful, the mature, the inventive, the crooned, the rapped – and that is why he makes them all. But instead he answered with a single word: one man's conversation-ending personal rejoinder to *do what you enjoy and it will translate*.

'*Rudebox*,' he replied.

Still, in the end, with so many songs, the final culling is brutal. 'Speaking Tongues', for instance, is set aside. And of these three Rob was debating with Stuart, only 'Marry Me' will end up on the album, and only on the deluxe version. The most controversial omission will be 'Disco Symphony', especially after Kylie Minogue records a vocal that turns it into a duet.

'I love that track,' he says. 'It's so daft and whimsical and silly and poppy – I love all those things. And then I've got a side of me that's "I don't want to sing that for the rest of my life: *dance dance dance, dance dance dance*".' He offers a comparison: 'I don't want to sing "Candy" for the rest of my life – and I'm going to have to.'

He tells people he's keeping 'Disco Symphony' in his back pocket, saving it for something special, for its right moment, but that's also another way of saying that he just doesn't want to deal with it right now.

* * *

The best day Rob and Ayda have had since they got back to Los Angeles was round at David Hockney's studio. Through a chance web of connections, they were invited over, and they arrived mid-morning, presuming that they wouldn't stay long. They only left at six in the evening because they had to put the kids to sleep. All afternoon, they just talked and talked; at one point Hockney painted something on his iPad there and then, and sent it to them.

Rob found himself peppering Hockney with questions.

'I wasn't socially uncomfortable or anything,' he says. 'It was great to sit down and ask him things. Like, is there jealousy amongst artists? Who thinks "fucking hell, fuck David Hockney"? Tons of questions about his mind, and the whys and the wherefores.'

Hockney also, as he is famously known to do, gave his pro-smoking diatribe, listing all the smoker artist geniuses who lived to ripe old ages.

Hockney was, says Rob, 'such a fantastic smoker' that even Ayda had one in his company. 'And not only is he an unapologetic smoker, one after another after another, but when he's finished, he just drops it on the floor. Not drops it, it just falls out of his hand. And he just gets another one out.' Rob and Ayda have since agreed that if Hockney ever takes up their invitation to visit them at home, Hockney will be the first and only person allowed to smoke in their house.

It was a special day: 'It felt like we were with somebody important on the planet,' Rob explains. 'There was like a beautiful heavy weight of a light being – I don't know how to describe it but when I came away I was in a very content daze of having had a moment – not expecting to feel that way, but then leaving thinking I've just done something really special with somebody really, really special.'

One of the questions Rob asked David Hockney was this: 'Do you ever struggle with confidence? With self-worth?'

'And he didn't,' says Rob. 'And I said, "Well, I do." And he said, "Well, how do you do all the things that you've done onstage?"'

The answer that Rob gave, that came from somewhere inside his head and that he just blurted out – the answer that made him laugh and which made David Hockney laugh, too – was this:

'Well,' he said, 'I'm very brave.'

It was a funny answer to that particular question, but it stuck in Rob's head. Because he recognised that it just might also be the truth. It will become something that he repeats over and over during the next few months in interviews, when asked to explain the complications and contradictions of what he does and how he feels about them. He'll explain that he has come to realise that the confidence he has always hoped will come, the confidence that people mistakenly imagine he already has when they watch him from the audience, may never show up. But he also realises that long ago he found something to cover that up, to get him through, to pull off doing what it is that he does. And it has belatedly struck him, not without some surprise, that a good word to describe what that is, to describe the resource he falls back on when the confidence won't come, just might be bravery.

* * *

April 2007–June 2008

A couple of weeks after he returned from rehab, Rob texted Ayda and said he'd like to see her. He told her he was coming round. Then he kept sending texts delaying his arrival time, and eventually cancelled. A friend – who is a friend no more – told him it would be a mistake to 'go back there'. Looking back, Rob wonders whether the friend just didn't want any interruption to good times of all the guys hanging out together.

That night, when he eventually blew her off, he said he was too tired and going to bed, but the next day at work Ayda saw a photo on Perez Hilton of Rob, much later that night, leaving a club with a blonde.

Even so, when three weeks later Ayda and her mother happened by chance to be visiting someone just across the road on Rob's estate, she figured she should let him know in case he saw her and it seemed weird. He suggested she drop by. They talked, and he showed her his new LOVE tattoo on his right fist. Things slowly clicked back into place, and they were together for the next three months.

Then, one day in early June, she was heading out for a meeting. He asked her for a cuddle before she went. And after that she didn't hear from him for three weeks. All her clothes were at his house, and when eventually she asked to come round to pick them up, he had them brought round by his security in garbage bags.

'I think we split up three times,' says Rob.

Always you?

'Always me, yeah.'

Why?

'Well, I was incapable of being in a relationship. This person was deeply in love with me, and I thought *that* was crazy. She was really kissy and cuddly and smoochy – it's a lovely thing now – and if she could have got inside me she would have done, she was that in love with me. And it was … "oh, get off".'

* * *

In August 2007, ten or so weeks after their second break-up, they ran into each at a friend's birthday party. After that, Rob started texting and calling again, and somehow the forces that were pulling them together prevailed once more over the reasons Rob kept finding to keep them apart. This time it would last nine months. There are holiday photos from this period which, when you look at them, you would assume are the beginning of Rob and Ayda's true and enduring romance. They went travelling together to Egypt, and to France, and to Holland and to Mexico. In Mexico, they rented a boat. On the boat with Ayda and all their friends, Rob says that he had one thought that he now knew with certainty.

It is not the thought that you are imagining it would be. That you are imagining it should be.

'I knew at the end of the holiday,' he says, 'that I was going to have to finish with her.'

Why? Just because you weren't going to be with anyone?

'Yeah. I wasn't going to be with someone. Not destined to be in a relationship. So much so that I was thinking about having a vasectomy.'

You really seriously thought about that?

'Yeah. I was, "I might as well have a vasectomy because I'm not having any kids and I don't want any shooting off by accident." That was definitely in the pipeline. So to speak.'

I'd argue that there were two particular ways back then in which people could disqualify themselves in your eyes – either by being in love with you, or not being in love with you.

'Yeah. And I could have completely missed that the basis of our friendship was incredible … well, I did a few times, before I didn't.'

* * *

He knows how close it came to not happening, how he might not have done what he did. He knows how perilously and bafflingly close he came to living a completely different life from the one he has been living for the last ten years.

The flash in which it became clear to him what he must do hit him at the Chateau Marmont hotel in Los Angeles. It was towards the end of June 2008. Rob, a single man once more – he and Ayda had finally split two weeks earlier – was out for the evening. On the patio he saw Cameron Diaz and Drew Barrymore talking together at a table. He wasn't there to meet them, but he knew them well enough to sit down and have a chat.

'I just said, "Oh, I just had to break up with someone, it's terrible …"' he remembers. 'And then I went through Ayda's good points. I started to talk with such enthusiasm and love about this person that I'd just broken up with. And Cameron Diaz said, "It doesn't sound like it's over to me."'

And that was it. That was the moment. After everything that had gone before, that was all it took.

'I had a moment of clarity,' he says. 'It was also terrifying, but it was a moment of clarity that I must go back to this girl and do right by her. So my feet took me straightaway off from the Chateau to Ayda's house, and there she was curled up in bed. She'd lost so much weight and looked so ill.'

When they had split up, Ayda had nowhere to live because her mother Gwen had rented out the guesthouse where Ayda had been living. She'd refused Rob's offer of a hotel, and had moved in with her mother, sharing a bed.

'I came through the door and just saw how thin she was, and I was just like "fucking hell". She was sort of in bed, distraught, cowering, in pain, thinking, how could she have got this so wrong?'

Was she immediately pleased to see you?

'Yeah. And then I was into something I didn't think I was capable of doing. But there I was.'

Did you apologise?

'I can't remember. But it was definitely: "I can't fuck this person about again."'

If Ayda hadn't stuck with it, do you think you'd have ever found yourself to this place?

'To a place of a relationship? Maybe not.'

And what do you think the other life would have been like?

'Rudderless. Directionless. There would have been "what's the point?" to an awful lot of stuff. There is a point now, and it makes everything make sense. And it's sad to think that – that I could be forty-three and I could be childless and relationshipless. Who knows what would have happened along the way, but another path I could have taken was that I'd be here alone.'

* * *

August 2016

The bad news comes in waves. Rob's manager David Enthoven had been ill, but it was assumed to be his hepatitis C returning, as it periodically does. Now Rob has heard that David has cancer and it cannot be treated. David has been far more than just a manager to Rob. Someone who overcame his own very serious addiction issues, he helped Rob through his problems, and has kept a constant eye on him. He has long been the person who Rob is most likely to call whenever faced with a dilemma or a difficult decision, the man whose advice and counsel he has relied upon.

Rob sits on the outside terrace of his Los Angeles house, trying to process it all. He has just spoken with David in London; David is, typically, still in good spirits, still giving advice. Rob is scheduled to fly to London in about a week's time; he will see him then.

'It's an all-consuming, pervasive thing,' says Rob. 'I've just not known it before.'

He sits with Ayda, talking through everything. To distract himself, he runs through songs for his album on the computer. One of them is a slow, powerful song he wrote with Guy the previous year. He's not been sure about it. It's called 'Last Song Ever', and the strange lyric that came out of him when he wrote it is suffused with mortality and fear, and of moments lost. He's been worried that it's just too morose, and has even tried to rewrite it. But today, anyway, it feels different.

Won't you hold me now, just before I stop breathing?
I know I promised I wouldn't leave here without you.

'You should call it "David's Song",' Ayda suggests.

And that is what, from then on, it becomes.

* * *

The next morning is Rob and Ayda's wedding anniversary.

'Mummy and Daddy got married six years ago today,' Rob tells Teddy when he comes downstairs in a Tommy Cooper t-shirt. 'Hi, mini-me,' he greets Charlie. When Ayda appears, she shows the kids a video they've put online, a montage of wedding-day images set to 'It Had To Be You'. 'The best day of my life ever,' she tells them.

Rob and Ayda exchange presents: a Keith Haring drawing that served as his business card for Rob, a David Hockney print for Ayda, *The Red Chair*, showing the balcony they were on when they visited him.

'That's amazing,' says Ayda, though there is dissent.

'No, it's not,' counters Teddy. 'I wanted a princess on it! You didn't put a princess on it!' Then she changes tack, says that she wishes she was bigger and could sit in one of the grown-up chairs.

'There's plenty of time to get bigger,' her father counsels. 'You should enjoy being small.'

Rob and Ayda then do something they only do very occasionally: go away for the night, just the two of them – no children, no security. They stay at a ranch north of the city. On their way back home, they receive an unwelcome update. David has taken an unexpectedly quick turn for the worse. It might just be days.

Rob is torn between wanting to stay here, where he's safe and where his children are, and wanting to be there, but he takes an overnight flight and the following day is at David's bedside. David dies three days later.

* * *

The following week, Rob goes into the studio one more time with Johnny McDaid. They've been wondering what to do with that song they wrote a couple of months ago, the one with the brutal spoken verses and the 'I love my life …' chorus that he can't imagine himself singing. Rob knows that for the song to have a real life, it will need a different verse, but that's as far as his thoughts have gone. 'There was just something about this chorus that was making me scared that I wasn't going to be able to match it,' he says. 'We were a bit too scared and apprehensive to tackle it, in case it didn't fulfil its potential.' The last time he had a song like that, a song that he knew could be big but which he just couldn't finish, was 'Rock DJ', and that took forever.

But with Rob's blessing, Johnny has sketched out some new music for the verse with another songwriter friend, Gary Go, and the three of them meet in the studio. Suddenly there's a big melodic verse. And suddenly Rob can see a way for the song to make sense – a way in which he can sing those lyrics of empowerment but also, in a way, not sing them, too. It would be a song addressed to his children, expressing his hopes for them, and the chorus – those words that feel too uncomfortable if he were singing them to himself – will be the words that, if he raised his children in the ways he was counting on himself to do, one day his children would sing to him. The verses will explain this, and set it up:

Tether your soul to me
I will never let go completely
One day your hands will be
Strong enough to hold me
I might not be there for all your battles
But you'll win them eventually
I'll pray that I'm giving you all that matters
So one day you'll say to me:
'I love my life …'

Finally it made sense. This, he could sing. Ironically, says Johnny, at this point he and Gary Go began to wonder whether still singing *I love my life* was just too much. They were worried that it would still be misinterpreted.

But now Rob was sure. 'He said, "This is what I want my kids to say, this is the gift I want them to have – I want them to say it fearlessly, and I'm going to say it fearlessly".'

When I see Rob a few days after this writing session, back in Los Angeles, he takes me outside the back door where he likes to sit and smoke, and opens his computer. Most often when he plays a new song to anyone for the first time, by doing so he is asking a question, even if the question is unspoken. Not this time.

He simply announces it as a fact. 'A hit's turned up,' he says.

Then he plays it.

'It's odd,' he reflects, 'that it's turned up as the last song.'

* * *

In the months to come, many interviewers will ask Rob, often prompted by 'David's Song', about David Enthoven. And Rob will simply explain.

'He saved me many times. He was very sage. He had the best advice. He was my spiritual father. And also a dear, dear friend – I just loved his company, being around him, and being with him. He made me feel safe. He was an addict – he had a problem with heroin and other substance abuse – and then he got clean and he got sober, and he did it by the book, and he kind of grasped it and he got hold of it and understood it, and lived his life accordingly. And he, because of that, saved my life a couple of times. Because addiction has taken me to a place where my life could easily have ended. And he was the guiding hand that put me back on the tracks. And with love guided my career and guided my health. There will always be a huge hole. But David was very courageous. And if there's anything that he'd want me and the people that I work with to be, it's courageous. And go forward with kindness and laughter – as much laughter as you can. What I picked up from him leaving this planet is that we must be courageous and we must be kind and we must be full of laughter and we must carry on.'

Part of how loss works is that you can never fully imagine its contours ahead of time. It can be simultaneously so big that you don't notice it has completely enveloped you and surrounded you, and yet can sneak up on you in multiple other ways, in places and incidental moments you'd never thought to steel yourself against. Two months later, when Rob plays his first public concert since David's death, there will be a short-lived panic when Rob's laptop goes missing. And then someone will realise. When Rob went onstage, it had been left behind in the dressing room. And they will also realise why. It was usually David who would get that.

And those kinds of reminders, from the tiny to the immense, they'll keep coming.

'The whole process of it and the dealing with it, it's just a strange silence every time you think about it or every time you talk about it,' he says. 'There's no answer, and there's no big enough a word for it.'

* * *

Thirteen days after he dies, David Enthoven's funeral is held at St Luke's in Chelsea. The church is overflowing with mourners, just one morning's echo of the generosity and goodwill with which he lived. After Tim Clark's heartfelt and eloquently direct eulogy, which closes with the words 'I know his legacy of kindness, laughter and an unwavering sense of duty will live on – now give each other a big hug', Rob steps in front of the congregation to sing his farewell. He is wearing his pink suit – 'befitting', he will explain after, 'of the man and his energy'. What he begins to sing, his voice gently aching over Guy's desolate guitar, is 'Moon River'.

'I think if I'd sung first before Tim's thing I might have been fine,' he'll say later, 'and then seeing the rock that is Tim be emotional sort of set me off. I found it difficult to get through the song. Just kept my eyes down, didn't look at the congregation. I felt like I was going to run out of the words running out of my mouth – I didn't feel strong enough for them to form.'

But they do, and what comes out is all the more graceful and poignant for its fragility. Someone had recently sent Rob something he'd never heard before – Henry Mancini's original demo of 'Moon River'. 'It's so beautiful, and there's so much shit going on in the world, and it reminded me of how much beauty we're capable of. I sent it to David and he sent me an email back saying, "I've got tears running down my face – you got me, old boy".'

After the service, everyone mingles on the lawns and pathways outside. Even here, it seems there's a few people who want to take some of Rob's time in a way that is certainly not appropriate on an occasion like this. So he looks wary when a small old man approaches him to say hello, until he explains that he was at school with David – Rob softens a little – and that his name is Mike d'Abo and that he wrote the songs 'Handbags And Gladrags' and 'Build Me Up Buttercup'. He talks about what David was like when he was young – the bolder friend who would encourage him to do the things he didn't yet know how to dare to do, even if in the beginning that just meant throwing stones at the ducks. Always the instigator.

D'Abo moves off; someone else comes up to Rob and says, 'He really loved you.'

'Yeah …' Rob replies, voice breaking. 'And I really loved him.'

'You enriched his life.'

'And he saved mine.'

3

September 2016

He's back in London, ready for it all to start again. The interview that will begin this new campaign, and this new phase of his public life, is to be with *The Sun*. Yesterday, whether by chance or to in some way prime himself, he lay on the bed in his London hotel suite, and rewatched some of the Hugh Grant and Steve Coogan testimonies from the Leveson inquiry.

Before their journalist arrives, Rob reminisces about the very first time he spoke with *The Sun*, back when he was in Take That, and how he and his bandmates were advised they should 'be cagey'. 'We went into that interview shitting ourselves that we're going to get it wrong,' he says. 'And I'm forty-two, and I'm still shitting myself that I'm going to get it wrong. But you can't get it right.'

The Sun's interviewer, Jacqui Swift, is eager, nervous and friendly, and once they get started she seems most comfortable exchanging mutual stories of anxiety. It's hard to work out whether this is a tactic, or just how she is, or whether there need necessarily be a difference. Rob obligingly explains a wide range of his general worries, and then says: 'Right now am I anxious? Not right now in this moment. But it's only quarter to one. There's a lot left of the day.' And then, for the first of many times over the next few months, he uses the line he came up with in front of David Hockney: 'My level of self-esteem or my level of real confidence has always been chronically low, but I've still managed to take myself to the places that I've been in my career. And if I look back at it, I haven't been confident but I've been fucking brave. I give myself a pat on the back for that.'

Swift asks him whether Ayda is like the strong women he grew up with, and Rob laughs. 'She's not a strong woman,' he says. 'I think that's why I'm attracted to her. She's insecure and neurotic, and her neurosis fits my neurosis. That being said, she's unbelievably strong, she just doesn't know. She's super-strong, super-smart, super-funny. Actually my attraction to her is not only her amazing personality but her neuroses and how broken she is as a person and her weaknesses. And our weaknesses combine to make us strong. When I feel weak, she's there to support me, and when she feels weak, I'm there to support her. And that makes me feel good that I'm able to do that for her. But she mainly does it for me.'

Then Swift asks whether Rob is friends with Take That – this is clearly a way of asking about Take That but the answer she gets, maybe a more interesting one, is about Rob and friendship. 'I'm kind of like a lone wolf,' he says. 'Which kind of makes me sound appealing, but it's not – I'm sort of like an agoraphobic wolf. In fact I'm not – I'm like an agoraphobic rabbit. So am I friends with anybody? Not really. I'm an insular person – I'm not kind of friends with anybody, except for the wife.'

The journalist is perfectly friendly, and doesn't seem to have any particularly malicious agenda. Once she has gone, Rob tries to work out what her big focus will be. Maybe some stuff he said about Liam Gallagher, he suspects.

It'll turns out to be this:

'I DON'T TAKE COKE BUT I DO THINK ABOUT ECSTASY'
Robbie Williams speaks about his battle with depression and drugs ahead of new album release

This comes from a part of the conversation where Rob was asked whether he needs to think about being and staying sober every single day, and he explained that he doesn't really, then ran through, perhaps unnecessarily, how this applies to each kind of temptation he might theoretically face. The quote in the article which has been compressed by the headline is this: *'I don't want to drink and I don't want to take coke, I'm really pleased I don't take coke but I DO think about ecstasy,'* he admits.

Like the rest of the article, by the standards and values of the medium it is in, it shows a genuine attempt to convey fairly Rob's world and his opinions. But there is very often a certain kind of use of language, and of nuance, and of pure meaning, that gets lost in this process, and that is the case here. There is a way that people are expected to think and talk in the popular press, with a certain melodramatic directness and lack of complexity, their words hewing to narratives and archetypes established long before they open their mouths, their thoughts reshaped and resized as headline-friendly pronouncements. This is so routine, and so well established, that I wonder if those who shepherd these stories even notice the distortions and adjustments, however insignificant, that this requires. And perhaps any harm done is modest. But, for purposes of comparison, here is what, back in the real world, sitting on a sofa in the Soho Hotel and probably being too honest as he tries to make sure that his first interview goes well, Rob actually said:

'I don't want a drink, because I don't want to drink. I don't want to take coke because I'm really pleased that I don't take coke. I think about ecstasy but I also think about the two days later when you want to off yourself. There's not really anything that I want to take or do. That's today, talking to you. That was also yesterday. I don't know what happens in the future. I don't know if there's a place where … you remember as a kid you stood on a Coke can and you'd touch it and it just crumples? Who knows when I'll crumble? Today, quarter to one or whatever time it is, I'm happy on my water.'

* * *

The phone-hacking scandal which triggered the Leveson inquiry appears to have spread its tendrils wide, and given that Rob was one of the most famous British celebrities in the years when such practices were most rampant, it would have been surprising if he hadn't been affected. And it seems he was. At one point the police contacted him to say that they'd found numbers relating to him, and came to see him at the flat he used to have in Chelsea Harbour. (Ironically, Rebekah Brooks lived in the same complex, and it was in the bin in the underground garage there that her husband disposed of a computer.) The police went through some phone transcripts with Rob, but he found that the way they were talking to him didn't give him confidence, and he couldn't quite work out what their fundamental agenda was. He also felt sure that the hacking had got much closer to him than what he was shown – though one blessing, at least, was that for so many of those years he didn't have his own mobile phone. People he knew subsequently encouraged him to join the lawsuits, but he didn't have enough faith that anything worthwhile would come of it.

Nonetheless, he can see the difference in the tabloids these days: 'They don't have that particular tool in their black arts anymore. There isn't as many kiss'n'tells. There isn't a daily thing where somebody gets fucked over because something private was said on a private call. The landscape of the tabloids is different.'

It's particularly different for him, but he realises that's also as much just down to the passing of time, and the caravan having moved on.

'Their energy,' he says, 'isn't concentrated on me as much as it used to be.'

* * *

In two days' time Rob is to play a full concert with his band at the Camden Roundhouse, as part of the iTunes festival. Even though he hasn't done a show like this for a long time, he's not really one for rehearsal when he sees no need to rehearse. There's no complicated production or choreography in this show, and he has performed all of the songs before. (Due to whatever negotiated exclusives are to come, the only two previews of his new album allowed are the two he has sung on recent tours: 'Motherfucker' and 'Sensational'.) And he will have a teleprompter with the lyrics on it. What's to rehearse? Even so – more, I think, to show willing and solidarity at the beginning of this campaign than because he feels any real need – this afternoon he does go down to the Wimbledon studio where the band are rehearsing. But he stays less than an hour, and is in the car, going there and back, for far longer than he actually rehearses.

On the journey back into the centre of town, he talks about how he misses the kids – Teddy, Charlie and Ayda won't be joining him for another month, when their new London house should be ready – and he describes the fourth birthday party they just threw for Teddy at home in Los Angeles. Someone was hired to appear as Ariel from *The Little Mermaid*. 'Teddy absolutely loved her and was besotted and just held her hand and followed her around – it was great,' he says. 'It was literally like if the Fonz had turned up when I was four – that would have been amazing.'

Though come to think of it, he says, he did have something happen once that was a *little* like that. When they lived in a pub when he was tiny, his sister phoned from the downstairs to the upstairs, pretending to be Daisy Duke from *The Dukes of Hazzard* and then Sandy from *Grease*. 'And I was super-thrilled. I can remember: "I'm speaking to Sandy from *Grease*!"'

Now that it's late enough in California, he FaceTimes the house, and talks through Teddy's breakfast with her – 'You did dippy poo poo but not princess porridge?' – before hanging up and playing to me on YouTube the speech where Eisenhower warns about the threat posed by the military industrial complex. He tells me that his new favourite TV show, a rare drama that he likes, is *Narcos*: 'Ayda's started calling me "Pablo" and I've started calling her "Tata".' Then he tries to think of an American rock star who is funny, but he can't come up with one.

* * *

Even for a one-off show, it seems, Rob's body clock adapts to touring mode, a regime where his whole twenty-four hours is centred around feeling as he needs to feel in the middle of the evening when he has to take the stage. Consequently, today he sleeps past lunchtime and into the afternoon. At half past three, Gary Marshall, his head security person, goes into his bedroom to wake him. Gary offers Rob two options: they can leave the hotel at four o'clock in time to have a half-hour rehearsal, or leave at half past four to go straight into hair and make-up, without rehearsal.

Gary reports back that Rob neither took off his eye mask nor said anything at all in response. This is presumed to be his way of choosing option 2.

Rob appears, bleary-eyed, from the bedroom at 4:15. 'Yeah,' he drawls. 'I had a big sleep.' He explains that he slept so late because he was awake between five and ten this morning, watching episodes of *Politically Incorrect* and *The Howard Stern Show*, and old Marilyn Manson interviews. His father, Pete, who took the train down from Stoke this morning after only being asked to perform in the show three days before, has been waiting in the security room that connects with Rob's suite for a few hours. When his son eventually appears, Pete asks how he's feeling.

'Um …' he considers. 'Trying to be confident.' He pauses, thinks some more. 'Trying to persuade myself that I'm a confident person that does my job well.'

Playing live has become easier for him in recent years, after the low points of 2006. But that doesn't mean that the insecurities and fears that used to torment him have been vanquished. It's more that he has found strategies to deal with them – and this is an ongoing process. In the car, Rob fills out further the unsettling narrative running round his head this afternoon.

'I woke,' he says, 'and I'm shitting myself, and then I had a talk to myself, started to walk with a swagger. And hopefully my brain and mind will catch up with the swagger. Then you go downstairs and you get in the lift, and you're aware that you're going to go and do the first thing of the first thing that's hopefully huge. And if it isn't, you might be destroyed internally.'

And he laughs, both because he knows it sounds so melodramatic and because it's true.

* * *

There is a way he likes to explain the problem of – and also, on a good night, the solution to – what can happen when he stands in front of an audience.

'I just hope I step onstage,' he says, 'and Robbie Williams turns up. Because sometimes I get up there and he doesn't, and I have to do it myself. Robbie Williams is sort of the cloak of invincibility that I put on, and sometimes he doesn't turn up and I have to do it myself, and it's terrifying.'

He played a show in Switzerland last year where he waited for Robbie Williams to join him, and he just didn't. Rob couldn't find him anywhere. 'I'm, like, it's so *lonely* out here – how does Robbie Williams do this?' For seven songs, he did his best to make it through on his own. And then, at last, Robbie Williams joined him. 'And I thought, "Thank God he's here,"' he says. 'That might sound incredibly schizophrenic to you, and I suppose it is, but that's the way it goes.' He says that it also happened on the Knebworth night that was broadcast live on TV. 'I think there's a point in the Knebworth footage, about six songs in, where I actually say "I'm back!"' Goodness knows what people imagined he was talking about, but it was about this: 'Me noticing the moment when the gods of entertainment take over.'

It reminds him of a story about Dean Martin that his dad tells. The full version was told by Orson Welles, about the time in 1969 when Welles was preparing to appear on *The Dean Martin Show*. Before they went onstage,

Dean Martin offered him a drink, like the one already in Martin's hand. Welles demurred, said he was fine. His host was shocked.

'You mean you're gonna go out there *alone?*' Dean Martin exclaimed.

There's a logic to that, or at least a lack of logic which still kind of makes sense, which Rob understands.

'So,' he reasons, 'Robbie Williams is my whisky.'

* * *

Ayda phones from Los Angeles.

'Listen,' says Rob, 'can I call you back later, because I'm backstage and I'm doing worrying?'

But first he speaks to Teddy and Charlie.

'Ted, I'm going to do some singing tonight to a lot of people – is there anything I should sing?'

She tells him, of course, to sing 'Let It Go'.

And then she offers some further advice – not such bad advice, either.

'Don't sing it messy,' she instructs.

'Okay,' he replies. 'I'll try.'

* * *

A little while before Rob is due to go on, a cryptic teaser trailer for his new album is broadcast in an ad break during this evening's *X Factor*.

An old friend from Stoke called David Parry emails him: 'Just seen your advert on *X Factor* – what's that all about?'

'It's about a hundred and fifty grand,' he emails back.

He relays this conversation to the dressing room, and it reminds his father of what Don McLean is supposed to have said when he was asked what 'American Pie' means.

'It means,' McLean is said to have responded, 'I only have to work when I want to.'

Rob laughs. 'I'll have to lodge that one,' he says.

And he will.

* * *

Rob is told that the Liverpool manager Jürgen Klopp is in the backstage hospitality area. It's fair to say that if there were any one of a hundred famous musicians or actors that he was told were nearby right now, he would be sculpting his excuses and working out his rationale to explain why there was no way he wanted to speak to anyone just before a show like this. Someone he admires from the world of football, that's different. If everything in the world of entertainment represents pressure, football represents some kind of relief. So he leaves the dressing room compound to find Klopp and say hello.

'It's an incredible pleasure to meet you, and congratulations on everything that's happening at Liverpool ...' he tells Klopp. Soon he is explaining to Klopp that he has Mané and Coutinho in his Dream Team, the online fantasy football competition that takes up untold hours of his life in the winter months.

The Liverpool manager immediately engages with this conversation, as though he both understands its importance and would like to offer some input.

'You don't buy Lallana?' Klopp asks, incredulous.

Klopp's seat for the concert is on one of the balconies directly facing the band, and Rob will say afterwards that periodically during the show he will catch the sight of Klopp's teeth, lit up by the light from the stage, gleaming.

* * *

Some more thoughts about performing: the challenges it brings him, and how he overcomes them, or at least finds a way round them.

'I've always got stage fright,' he says. 'There's always a level of fright. If I can just make it manageable rather than overwhelming then I've won. The energy that I've used to be a showman, is: "Fuck, this is the biggest bluff ever, people are going to find out in the next three seconds ..." And that's how I live the whole show going forward: "They're going to find out! They're going to find out! Move! Keep moving! Do some stuff! Do some stuff!" I've never been that confident with my singing voice, so around that

I've built this persona of: "Watch me do this, and don't listen to me! Don't listen to this, watch me do … *this*!" And it's worked for me. It's worked. That out of necessity, I've had to entertain them, because I don't think people would come just to listen to me sing.

'What I do is an act, and it's a bluff, and it's a character, and that act and that bluff and that character only works in cooperation with the audience. I come out at the beginning of the show and I act like an emperor and I pretend that everybody is very lucky to see me. And people in the audience act accordingly and they go, yes, we're very lucky to see you, and I go, yes, thank you for playing your part. Now if the audience went "what a wanker" then I'm fucked. There is no show. So the audience brilliantly participates in the entertainment of the evening. I'm not really that brave, I'm not really that confident and I'm not really that arrogant. I'm going to play this character, and they've got to play along.

'The comedian Steven Wright says, "You know that feeling when you're on a chair and you're wobbling and it's just about to go and you can't do anything about it? That's how I feel all the time." That's how I feel all the time onstage. But I can now channel that. It used to be out of control and very fucking scary, because there's a lot of people staring at me. Now I can channel that and make it work for me.'

* * *

Some months ago, one of the fans on Rob's website forum, Upfront, suggested to him that he should bring back the tiger underwear he wore in the 'Rock DJ' video. He thought it was a good idea – 'I thank my fans,' he says, 'for reminding me I should wear my iconic underpants so I feel iconic' – so he commissioned several new pairs to be made. He started to wear them whenever he performed, initially 'to be ironic and funny to myself to go to work', and I think it's in that spirit he's wearing them tonight, though he'll soon start wearing them as his regular default underwear. Exactly what this says about all kinds of things, including the complicated and shifting lines between the pop star Robbie Williams and the man called Rob whose body he shares, is difficult to say.

Tonight, given that he hasn't performed in public like this for some time, he doesn't take long to get into it. Not only does Robbie Williams turn up from the start, but he performs like he's trying to make up for lost time. 'Rock DJ' is tonight's second song, and he decides to share the news that he's wearing what he wore in the video by unzipping the trousers of his white butterfly-covered suit to unleash the tiger beneath. This is the image, and the moment, which will dominate the next day's press coverage.

What no one seems to notice – or maybe he manages to pass it off as more deliberate showmanship – is that his zip gets stuck and he nearly can't get his trousers back up again.

* * *

The next morning, Rob seems energised by the reaction. 'It's all really positive,' he says. 'Couldn't have gone better. They all love the gig. Nobody noticed that I got Botox and fillers. *The Guardian* gave it four out of five. Which is six out of five for me …' A pause. 'I didn't read it, obviously.' He means by this that he'll have Googled it, read the headline and star-rating, and tried his best not to read any more.

'I don't think there was anything,' Michael reassures him.

'You don't know what I'm sensitive about,' Rob counters. 'I'd find *something.*'

Here's a couple of possible candidates from the mostly upbeat *Guardian* review, titled *A Perfect Meeting of Ego, Self-Deprecation and Hits*: 'Sensational' is referred to weirdly, whatever its merits or otherwise, as 'a generic rocker', and 'Rock DJ' is described as 'his worst song' and 'still thumpingly lumpen'. But I think he'd actually quite like the bit that goes: 'There really is nobody else, in pop music anyway, who combines monumental hamminess and bone-deep vulnerability quite so effectively'.

* * *

2007–2009

In March 2008, I email Rob to say that I'm in Los Angeles, and suggest meeting up on the following Friday afternoon.

This is the full text of his reply:

Any time ... I'm free all Friday and the following days ... weeks ... years.

* * *

This is how he likes to explain it:

'In 2006 I retired, but I didn't tell anybody, and I didn't work for three years, and I sat on a sofa, ate potato chips and chocolate, got fat, grew a beard, looked like a serial killer. I ate Kettle Chips, the big bags, and I would have Krispy Kreme Fridays, I just got fatter and fatter, my beard got bigger and bigger. I saw that Paul McCartney, when he left The Beatles, grew a beard, and it looked really cool, so I grew one, but I just looked like a serial killer.'

Right at the beginning, when the weight first began to pile on, he didn't even pay attention. One day he put on a pair of his tracksuit bottoms, but they didn't slip on as they should have. He was annoyed that someone had tied the waist cord much tighter than he liked to wear them, and he obviously knew who the culprit was. 'I'm like, "Babe, the next time you wear my tracksuit pants, do me a favour and don't tie them so tight." Ayda's like "... OK." It wasn't until a few months later that I realised that she hadn't been wearing them at all ...'

He doesn't know exactly how large he became at his heaviest. 'Must be two-thirty, two-forty pounds,' he says. 'It was my retirement phase, and I had my retirement party. And there was a lot of cake at that retirement party.' Eventually he found a way of dispensing with the annoyance of close-fitting clothes almost entirely. On holiday in Morocco, he bought these cashmere kaftans: 'I thought, "Wicked, Obi-Wan Kenobi, great, I'm going to get loads."'

And now, day after day, that's what he wore.

* * *

How deliberately was putting on the weight and growing the beard a way to de-'pop star' yourself? To make yourself unfit for duty?

'Well, I was eating what Ayda was eating, but her metabolism works a lot quicker than mine. So I got fat and she stayed like that. Quite often it happens in relationships where you don't have to go out hunting and gathering, so you take off the brakes. I remember at one point watching a TV show about the fattest man in the world, in South America, and there were graphs and pictures of how much chocolate he was eating, and I was, "Well, I'm not as bad as that so I'm all right." But we were going for it, the food.'

I remember seeing you then and you seemed very relaxed in yourself. You seemed quite joyous about the new you.

'Probably, because there was no work on the horizon. I hadn't got to go and do the thing that was making me ill. And I'd made a really good friend.'

And went camping in the garden?

'Yeah, there was a summer of camping in the garden.'

Why?

'We'd done glamping, and we went out to the desert, Joshua Tree, in an RV and I'd taken a chef with me – we were underneath the stars and felt as though we were on a different planet, being out there. Then we went to another place that was just near here, and it was a campsite but the people that ran it weren't very nice. They were very authoritarian, and it got my back up. We were just trying to chill out. After that, we went to an RV park in Malibu but it was grubby and the service was terrible. So after those, I still wanted to camp but I didn't want to be part of any of that. So we pitched a tent in the back garden.'

Would you be going in the house all day?

'We'd go in to pee and get drinks, but then we'd come out. I got a literal picket fence around my tent, then got an AC unit in, and got a proper bed, and basically we were just living outside. And we would spend all night sat on chairs staring at the stars. And one tent became two tents became five tents. Friends would stay over in the tents, and there'd be security in one tent.'

Why couldn't security stay in the house?

'Because we were outside, and we were scared.'

* * *

In these months that slipped into years, he rarely left the property, but one day he went in the car with a friend who'd come up for dinner to drop him back at his hotel in Hollywood. That was when Rob, looking as unlike the Robbie Williams that people knew as he ever had in his life, ran into some old friends. And though he was very pleased to see them, it would have been difficult to think of two people who would have offered a starker contrast to the man he currently was: Ant and Dec.

'They happened to be walking into the hotel, so I got out and went and had a drink with them,' he remembers. 'I'd got my Obi-Wan Kenobi on. They thought I'd gone fucking mental. They're brilliant, but they're the most normal blokes in the world. And then their crazy pop star friend turns up with forty-five extra pounds and a big beard and a kaftan – somebody from Newcastle's not going to have that, really, are they? I think they definitely thought I'd gone mad. And I probably had at the time.'

* * *

At one point during his retirement years, a story even went round that he was dead.

'Yeah, I did hear that,' he says. 'I just hadn't been out for three weeks. People thought I was dead – I was just eating doughnuts.'

* * *

September 2016

He flies to Germany in a private jet to talk about himself. There'll be a few of these trips over the next few weeks. Sometimes he only asks where he's going when he's already on the plane.

* * *

Many of these interviews follow a similar path. Generally – and as often as not it's the first or second question – he has to explain the album title *The Heavy Entertainment Show*. His usual answer involves his grandmother's house:

'The sofa at my nan's in Newfield Street, Stoke-on-Trent, terraced house with a toilet outside. I was taken care of a lot by my grandmother, and she loved me – you know, she loved me without a pointing finger. She just loved me totally. And there I would be eating carbohydrate after carbohydrate – crisps on buttered bread with a cup of tea and lots of sugar, and chocolates, and love, and the TV, and the gods on it. When I was a child there was three TV channels, which meant that the whole of Britain was having shared experiences on mass levels, and the TV screen in the corner of the room, the people on it were gods, and they made me happy. And they were aspirational. I wanted to be like them. I wanted to be in the TV screen and walk amongst the gods that reside there. But I didn't know how I was going to do it. It seemed that from where I was sitting to where they were was like me stretching an elastic band from Stoke-on-Trent to Venus, and I didn't know how I was going to get there, I just knew that I wanted to. I'm nostalgic for that, because of the naivety. Showbiz is really like the Wizard of Oz: you open the curtain, there's a little person with a speaker going like this. But before that, there really was a wizard and he really was a god, and I'm nostalgic for that time. And these people, on a Saturday and Friday night in England, what they were doing was called light entertainment. But the power of the light entertainment was so big that to me it was incredibly heavy entertainment. So much so that it spurred me on having a career trying to emulate who they were. Hence *The Heavy Entertainment Show*.'

That's the standard version but sometimes he may diverge, say something like: 'The Heavy Entertainment Show is the world that we're living in, from the worldwide crisis over everything right now, down to going for a coffee, and sitting outside the coffee shop and watching people go by. People-watching is heavy entertainment. Getting up and changing the nappy from Charlie when he's filled it full of shit is heavy entertainment. Getting onstage and trying to be the conduit of tens of thousands of people having a good time is heavy entertainment. You're entertaining people whether they like you or hate you. You're entertaining their hatred. And if they like you, you're entertaining their love.'

And then, just occasionally, you'll get this:

'I've elaborated on the title just for the fact that people ask about it in interviews, I've made up a lie. So I won't do that with you. I feel as though we're being frank and honest. It was just something that I thought: "Oh, yeah, that's an interesting, snappy title."'

In their own way, each of these answers is perfectly true. (His reminiscence of time spent at his grandmother's, for instance, is a heartfelt one that is important to him.) They're each also a spirited attempt to entertain and satisfy whoever is sitting in front of him – that third answer just as much as the first and second. One fantasy underlying the whole interview process is that people decide upon a reason for doing something and then do it. Life's rarely like that, for Rob or anyone else. Often we do things, and only later, if we have the time, and a reason to do so, do we try to work out why.

* * *

Rob and his entourage drive in silence. Maybe his brain is unwinding from talking too much about himself all day, as required – processing what he did say and what he didn't, what he should've said and what he shouldn't. Still, I wonder what winding path and sparking synapses lead Rob to finally say this:

'You know how the Queen doesn't comment on anything? I wonder how many times in her life she's really fucking wanted to.'

* * *

They keep coming, he keeps talking. Here, today, are some of the other questions he is asked, and the answers he offers.

Is the money a motivation?

'It never was. It was just something that came with. I just wanted to be liked, more than anything. I just wanted people to like me. But I wanted millions of those people to like me.'

Could you use your entertainment skills when you were young?

'I did some acting in local plays and stuff, but you couldn't really use your entertaining skills where I come from, because you'd get beat up. If you did anything that was considered big-headed, you were definitely going to get a kicking. So I tried to blend in as well as possible. But I'm a bit too eccentric to blend in. I did a good job – I didn't get my head kicked in too many times. But did I use my entertaining skills when I was a kid? Not really, I just tried to stay out of the way. I wanted to be an entertainer, but that kind of stuff didn't really happen for people from where I'm from. You would learn a trade with your hands and you'd do that. So I kind of had to keep it quiet and keep it to myself – what I thought I was going to do, and what I thought I was going to be.'

Are you the happiest you've ever been?

'I'm definitely, *definitely* not the most miserable that I've ever been.'

What is the secret behind your and Ayda's relationship?

'Chemistry, personality, trust, and laughter. We have all of those things, and it's a miracle, because I didn't think it could happen to me or for me. That I would be responsible enough or able to be in any kind of relationship. Because I just thought I was going to fuck it up – because that was my history, and I have addictions that are very animalistic, and I want to act out on them an awful lot. And I also wanted to be in this relationship, so the paradox of the two things is: wanting to be in love and to give myself to this person, but also knowing that I'm an animal that wants to sleep with everything. You know, it's heartbreaking. But here I am, and here we are ten years later, more in love than I was in the beginning. She's my best friend. We're ten years down the line and I love her, and like her, more than I ever have. And we have a lot of fun. Yeah, we have a lot of fun.'

Would you agree that nothing tastes as good as slim feels?

'No. No. It kind of did for three or four days. There was a period where I lost weight very quickly and I got into those clothes in the wardrobe that I hadn't worn for a long time. You know, *those* clothes. There was one night where Ayda was in bed and I went into the wardrobe and I got changed about fifty times, going, "Look! Look!" She's like, "That's good, babe, I'm pleased for you." So there was a moment. But it becomes one less thing to worry about, and then it comes back and it slaps you in your face and you have to go again. You just have to keep getting on the bike. You just have to keep getting up and going for it the best way that you can. Because naturally my workings and my addiction and the way I am doesn't want me to be thin. It wants me to indulge. So I'm working against Fat Robbie – I'm working against my nature. It's tough.'

Are you still smoking pot?

'No, I'm not – and I haven't for a while. I've stopped smoking weed and I'm not planning on starting again, which for me is interesting – that's something that's changed. As fun as that stuff is, it does fuck my mind. I see my life as a kind of bottle with silt at the bottom, and up here is clear, and then there's the silt in the bottom that's always there and is not going to leave. And if I take anything that's mood-altering or mood-enhancing, the bottle goes ...' – he makes a noise to represent the bottle being shaken up – '... and the mud rises, and it becomes instantly murky.'

* * *

The next morning, he is interviewed by a German media personality called Barbara Schöneberger who has her own magazine, named *Barbara*, on which she appears on the cover. That a slightly different power dynamic is assumed here than has been the case for this trip so far is signalled by the fact that she keeps Rob waiting for over half an hour past the scheduled start time before she is ready to begin the interview.

They've met before, and she's kind of flirty from the outset – though not in a 'I fancy you' kind of way, more 'as I am at work, I will now adopt my professional flirty personality'.

She puts down her recording device on the coffee table next to them. 'It's very small but it works,' she says, then adds, 'Have you heard that sentence before?'

'Listen,' says Rob, 'it fills a pram. It definitely fills a pram. It fills two prams.'

She explains that the topic of this particular issue, on whose cover she will appear with Rob, is 'luxury'. Rob immediately looks concerned, thinking that this isn't his kind of subject – as well as he lives, he's not that interested in too many of the traditional trappings and conventional consumption habits of the wealthy. But it turns out that, for this very reason, he soon finds himself with quite a lot that's worth saying.

'I live an abnormal life to the life that I was raised in,' he tells her. 'Things shift with success, money, but my sensibilities are ...' He trails off, but he means that some things stay the same. To explain, he offers an example: 'I'm constantly turning the lights off after Ayda. Still. We have this thirty-two-thousand-square-foot house in Beverly Hills, it's incredible, and I sometimes often feel like it's my rich uncle who's letting me live there. At night, Ayda, she puts the sleep mask on, I then get out of bed and turn all of the lights off. Ayda buys these candles and they're quite big candles and they have three wicks in them and she'll just light them and then we'll watch the TV, and I'm sort of watching the television and looking at the candles ... and I'm watching the television and I'm looking at the candles ... and I look over to see Ayda, and if she falls asleep, I blow the candles out.' This is far from the first time I have heard him mention these candles, and how freaked out he was when he discovered that each of them cost $250 (even though they are gigantic, and presumably are supposed to last months if not years). 'Listen,' he continues to Barbara, 'the house smells fantastic. But when I smell how fantastic the house smells, it feels like we're burning money! It's like, "Yes, it smells great, but it smells of lost money!"'

It's obvious he's torn between thinking this is silly of himself, and thinking that it is eminently sensible. 'I am still trying to enjoy the lifestyle and be the sort of person that we can economically afford to be … but I find it difficult, moving in a different economical circle,' he says. He explains how he's resistant to the constant pressure to buy more clothes. 'I've bought some clothes – I don't need to buy any more, ever,' he says. 'I've *got* clothes.'

This leads Barbara to ask about their washing machine. 'I know where it *is*,' he says. 'I've seen a stairway that leads to it. And I know there is one, because things keep turning up clean. But still, I swear that I need very little, and I would learn to be able to use it if it all went away.'

She asks about the first expensive luxury he bought. He has a story about that. 'When I was a kid and I was in Take That, I really wanted a pair of Versace jeans. It was 1990, and they meant the world to me,' he says. 'I was on £150 a week at the start of Take That, and there were heavily discounted Versace jeans in Stoke-on-Trent where I'm from, one pair that fitted me, and I bought them. And I felt really fancy.' Three years later, he saw Gianni Versace and Elton John at Versace's villa in Lake Como in Italy, and he realised he had the chance to explain to the person who had designed them just what one particular creation of his had meant to an excited teenager. 'I thought that it was very important that I told Gianni Versace, "Your jeans were very aspirational to me – I really wanted a pair of your jeans, and I managed to get a pair of your jeans, and it was fantastic."' Whatever the reaction Rob hoped for, he didn't get it. 'He wasn't bothered. He didn't care. He was, like, "okay … would you like grapes?" or whatever. He was a lovely man and I had a lovely evening, I just couldn't quite impress upon him how important his jeans were to me.'

After the interview, they go into an empty ballroom where a backdrop has been set up for photos. Rob poses, with Barbara draped over him.

'Make me look like Gigi Hadid's dad,' he instructs the photographer.

Barbara adjusts her pose so that the jewellery on her arm shows itself well as it dangles with her arm over his shoulder.

'It's all about the jewels, the accessories,' she explains.

'We're all accessories,' Rob points out.

* * *

Sometimes he flies, sometimes they fly to him. One day in London, he sits in a hotel room, meets people from around the world, answers whatever he's asked.

Sweden: *When I was told I was going here, I read a lot of interviews with you, and the impression was that big hits aren't as important today as it was before?*

'It depends which interviews you've seen and which lies I was telling in those interviews. Yeah, it's really important. I don't want to be a has-been. That moniker is something that my ego couldn't deal with. I want hits. I want to be in stadiums. I want to make news. I want to be entertaining … My ambition doesn't feel forty-two. My ambition is still young, and is still greedy, and still *needs*.'

Spain: *Would you say you're a more mature person? Do you miss a kind of irreverence?*

'Irreverence? There's plenty of irreverence. Yes, I am more mature, but we're working from a very, very small percentage of maturity. I was an infant until I was at least thirty-seven, so maybe I've just got out of nappies. Maybe I've just stopped shitting myself.'

Ireland: *Are you immune to critics?*

'No, I'm not immune to critics. Words hurt. I'm incredibly sensitive, and I wish they wouldn't, but they do. And also I'm not the most diplomatic when it comes to not hurting people's feelings, so if you dish it out you've got to expect some of it to come back. People are people, humans are humans, and we can't be kind all of the time. I try my best, but quite often I'm found lacking for who I'd like to be as a person. So no, I'm not immune. I wish I was – it'd make life a lot easier. But then if I was immune maybe I wouldn't be bothered and I wouldn't be putting out an album.'

* * *

The first stranger Rob has seemed excited to meet since he left Los Angeles was Jürgen Klopp. The second is even less likely.

He is at the French radio station NRJ where he has just been live on air. Afterwards, he is standing in the corridor when he catches a glimpse of someone passing him. Someone he recognises. At first he thinks it's someone from the boyband Worlds Apart. Then he gets it.

'It was, wasn't it?' he says to Michael, who also recognises him. They give chase, pull him back, and ask him.

'Are you Gioboy?' Rob says.

Gioboy is a young, good-looking French model.

'You're on Ayda's Instagram,' says Rob, and demands that they do a photo together. 'Ayda will love this!' he declares, accurately, though there is something fairly surreal about Rob asking someone else for a photo. They pose together. 'Nice to meet you,' says Rob, and once Gioboy has gone, he explains. 'Me and Ayda had a look to see who was following her, and there's a few really good-looking boys like that, and he's definitely someone me and Ayda have gone: "This guy!"'

By morning, Gioboy has quite naturally tweeted about this encounter:

Cant believe @robbiewilliams recognized me! He said Gioboy something ... Damn, yes that's me!

'The joy I got when I received that photo ...' Ayda tells Rob over Skype.

'We got so excited,' Rob tells her. 'We chased him down a corridor.'

They do acknowledge that there is a shameful and embarrassing aspect to this whole situation – 'We recognise Instagram followers!' she says – but it's a shame and embarrassment that, for now, they seem delighted to embrace.

* * *

One afternoon in Paris, Rob does a series of one-on-one interviews with French interviewers. The French music journalist tends to be a very particular breed – typically male, and older, and rather intense, with the kind of demeanour that suggests they'd been hoping that this was the day they'd manage to unlock a knotty philosophical problem that had been distracting them for some time, but are resigned to the fact that they won't get too much help from this pop star who seems to have off-message thoughts entirely of his own. 'In my head,' says Rob after, 'I'm going: "I'm supposed to intellectualise everything and I don't know how."'

Nonetheless, to some of their shorter questions, he gives replies:

Tell me the truth: your real dream is to be crooner?

'I want to be a crooner, I want to be a rapper, I want to be a rock'n'roll star, I want to be a skateboarder, I want to be a basketball player, I wanted to be a race car driver, I want to be a golfer, I want to be good at FIFA, I want to not eat carbohydrates – all of those things. I don't have one dream to be a crooner. I want to be *everything.* I'm finding it impossible but I'm giving it a good go.'

[forcefully] *Not more a crooner … ?*

'I want to be a rapper more than I want to be a crooner. I'm closer to being a crooner than I am to being a rapper.'

Is it a new fight with each album released?

'Yeah – it is a fight with every album that's released. You're at the mercy of the world and social media. It can be a very traumatic experience with your thing that you've carefully nurtured and loved and hoped that the world likes it, and then you get battered and rained on and kicked and punched, psychically. It can be a really traumatic experience. So you've got to be ready for the fight. Especially when you're the kind of artist that I am which is an entertainer and a celebrity. So it can be incredibly scary to go out there and put yourself out there. Because we live in a world where sensationalism rules. And it's not like sensationalist *nice* stories, it's sensationalist bad stories – that's what sells. They need you to fuck up, they need you to carry on fucking up, and if you're not, they're going to write that you're fucking up. So it's scary.'

What is your main worry?

'I suppose my main worry is that it'll all be taken away from me, and I won't have any options, and I'll have to go back to Stoke-on-Trent and live there. I love Stoke-on-Trent, but I kind of live in the promised land – it's a mythical place that I live in, and I enjoy it here. There's a lyric from a song by a band called James and it says *if I hadn't seen such riches I could live with being poor.*' He laughs, maybe picking up a sense of earnest disapproval from his interviewer. 'You asked the question, and I gave an honest answer.'

My last question: do you like promoting music or is it boring for you?

'I like being a pop star – it's fun. I got on a plane this morning, it was my plane. Nobody else was on it, other than my friends. Then I landed and then they did make-up on me and did my hair and put me in some nice clothes, and my job is being a pop star. I'm incredibly lucky. I'm tired today, but I've got this butterfly jacket on and you've come to ask what I think about shit. Cool! I could be in Stoke-on-Trent, selling drugs.'

How have you changed since you were sixteen?

'For a short answer, I'm older, fatter, more comfortable in myself, still oversensitive, still insecure, still have inferiority complexes, I am kind, funny, generous. Also, I bought a ticket to the dream, and the dream came true.'

How long have you been depressed?

'Er … how long have you got?'

* * *

As we land back at Luton from one more promotional trip, Michael goes through the latest presales statistics for the album.

'You've got wind,' he tells Rob. Meaning that everything is lined up, and everything is heading in the right direction.

Rob nods.

'I'm Robbie Williams,' he says, 'and I've got wind.'

* * *

He's done dozens of interviews, and there's plenty more to come. Meanwhile he goes back on Upfront, the membership section of his website, to see what his fans want to know today.

Rob, where do you get your drive from?

He knows the answer to this one:

'Shame and fear of failure x.'

* * *

In March 2008, the secretly retired pop star and recluse called Robbie Williams briefly broke his undeclared media blackout by appearing in the unlikeliest of places: an interview on a local radio station, Gemini FM, based in Exeter. He did so because the show was co-hosted by the singer Joss Stone, who he knew. They chatted freely, and among the many other things that he told her, he made a somewhat fanciful declaration: 'I'm stopping being a pop star, I'm going to be a fulltime ufologist'.

After that, it was open season. Endless articles, as often as not with some kind of headline like *I'm Loving Aliens Instead*, followed, suggesting that he had finally lost his mind. Mostly, he found it funny. 'I kind of liked the mischief of playing up with the fact that people might think I've gone mad,' he says, 'and so I did.' But there was also a certain amount of humbug in the way people reacted, because it wasn't as though Rob had ever hidden his interest in such things. The 2006 Close Encounters tour that had just burned him out and sent him spinning into seclusion had taken its name from Steven Spielberg's movie about alien visitations, and its elaborate stage set was designed to convey the sense that a traditionally shaped UFO might have landed at the one end of a stadium. And it went back much further than that. If his interest in this stuff made him a nutter, it was a kind of nutter he had always been, and the evidence had been staring everyone right in the face.

'I believed that stuff when I wrote "Angels",' he points out. 'That's why I wrote "Angels". "Angels" isn't *about* anybody, it's about the thoughts that loved ones that have passed on come back and take care of you.'

* * *

To find where his interest in such matters started, you need to go back much further.

'I think when I grew up I just took for granted that there was this other world where ghosts and UFOs and legends and myths are not actually myths, they're real,' he says. 'My nan used to have tons and tons of UFO books that I would read. My dad's mum. And a Ouija board and all of that kind of stuff. I was intrigued from day one, really. And my mum reads Tarot cards – she would have people round and read their palms. And there was always a bookshelf full of folklores and myths and fairies just outside her room. The world's mysteries, elves, demons and witchcraft – some frightening books on the shelf for a nine-year-old to open up and have a look at and become aware of and not know that it might not exist.' He'd look at the books, but he wouldn't really discuss any of this with his mother. It entranced him, but it unnerved him, too. 'I just lived in fear of all of this stuff,' he says. 'Maybe that's why I want to investigate UFOs and ghosts and everything. So I can work out why I get scared at night.'

His particular curiosity about the possibility of extraterrestrial life was also spurred by the stories he saw on TV and in films. 'I think that there's lots of contributing factors, like when I first watched *The Hitchhiker's Guide to the Galaxy*, the TV series, and that spaceship came over to blow up the planet. I think that kind of blew my mind as a ten-year-old. It opened up a whole range of possibilities. And I remember one of the Empire's spaceships was a mile and a half long. I thought that was incredible.'

* * *

'When I was ten years old,' he says, 'I was outside Port Vale's football ground, and I was on a BMX. And I had this overwhelming thought and feeling, to the very core of my being, that none of this was real. It fucking terrified me. I headed home as fast as I could. And I don't think I could articulate it because I was so young, so I didn't say anything.'

There are other more specific experiences that he has had, experiences which he doesn't take as definitive proof of anything except that he has known things to happen that he cannot explain. But these are the stories that Rob tends to tell when anyone interested, whether in an interview or in civilian life, asks him. Often he just gives a brief and perfunctory summary of what happened, but in 2008 he was spending time on the conspiracy-theory forum AboveTopSecret.com, and he was also in touch with one of the site's administrators, and he wrote an account to the administrator in an email which he later allowed them to post. Here, he is clearly trying to give as much descriptive detail as possible, both to contribute to the overall debate and to solicit theories, explanations or parallel stories from others about any of what he experienced. It is clearly written less to entertain or impress than in the spirit of a shared quest for knowledge. (If it helps to further judge the tone with which this narrative was offered, it is in an email that concludes, very unconspiratorially, 'I'm off to watch *Iron Man* …')

This is what he wrote:

I was facing Sunset Strip lying on a sun lounger about 11:30 at night in the yard of a hotel I was staying at. The yard area was about 50ft square (maybe less) and at the end of it are palm trees and bushes, which obscures people's view from the other side in (and ours out). I was with a friend who was lying next to me on another sun lounger and we were both staring upwards. From what I remember, an object flew over us at about 200 to 300ft high … it may have been higher, I don't know.

It was definitely black with yellow stripes underneath. Now, I'm not sure if it was square or triangle, but I do remember that it made absolutely no noise whatsoever. My friend and I both saw it. I don't know why, but I had a hunch it was one of ours.

In addition to this sighting, there was another very strange occurrence I witnessed one Friday night about 5 months ago. My friends and I were playing a song called 'Arizona' (about ufos) that we had written. It was dusk and, suddenly, a big ball of light appeared over the San Fernando valley. We were standing on my balcony at the time. When the song finished it disappeared … when we played it again it came back on … once again, when the song finished it disappeared … this happened 4 times.

During this back and forth with the ball of light, an electrical storm came in and the balcony on which we were standing was hit by the lightning. One of my friends said he saw it (the ball of light) fly straight up and out of sight. I can't vouch for this cause I didn't see it with my own eyes, but he was sure that's what he saw happen … we came in off the balcony after the lightning had just missed us and were stood back in my studio, when, out of nowhere (and everybody that was there saw this), a black strip of light a few inches thick came in through the studio door and stretched about 20 feet or so (the length of the studio) and went out through the opposing studio window.

Then 4 white large (spotlight) lights appeared in the clouds … 2 in front of the house and 2 a few miles behind it … Though the shape and look of the light did resemble Hollywood search lights, but the patterns they were making and the distance they were traveling was amazing. This happened for an hour and half from about 10 o'clock at night onwards and then again after 2 o'clock for half an hour … everything shuts down in L.A. at 2am, so I don't know if it would be legal for a club to put spotlights on at that time in the morning … maybe you could find out?

The hotel in question was the Beverly Hills Hotel; the song was being recorded in the large upstairs bedroom in his Los Angeles house, the far end of which was, for many years, his recording studio; the friends and collaborators in the studio at the time included Danny Spencer and Kelvin Andrews, the brothers from Stoke with whom he wrote much of *Rudebox* and *Reality Killed The Video Star*, who would both later separately post to corroborate Rob's account of what they all saw that night.

* * *

Back on his 2003 tour, I'd given Rob a book, both to stave off the boredom he was feeling from being penned in his hotel room for week after week, and because I figured it was the rare kind of book that he would find riveting. The book was Jon Ronson's *Them: Adventures with Extremists*. Two years later, he called Jon Ronson from the set of the 'Advertising Space' video in Blackpool and asked whether Ronson could arrange for the two of them to stay overnight in a haunted house. That never happened, but they stayed in touch and in February 2008 Rob suggested that the two of them attend a UFO conference in Laughlin, Nevada. They flew from Los Angeles on a private jet, attended lectures and presentations, spoke with people including a mother who believed that her son is a serial alien abductee and a scientist who claimed to have removed alien implants made of an unknown metal from people. The trip became a Radio 4 documentary, *Robbie Williams and Jon Ronson Journey to the Other Side.*

Rob was doing this for fun, and to explore something that interested him now that he had enough free time to dig deeper into it, but, behind that playful statement that he was giving up pop music to be a ufologist, there was a slightly more serious thought in his mind. If he really didn't want to be a pop star – and he was still telling himself that this was how things were going to be – then he was beginning to realise that he would probably need to find something else to do. At first, he just waited for it to turn up. 'I was hoping,' he says, 'that by wandering from my bedroom to the kitchen something would present itself.' When that method didn't bear fruit, he began to consider what else in the world aside from music he really cared about. 'They say that if you have a passion and you follow your passion, you don't have to work, because you're doing your passion,' he says. 'And I thought, well, what was my passion? And at that particular time it was UFOs. I thought if I followed the line of something that I was interested in, maybe I could go to work and it not hurt me.'

The half-formed notion that was taking shape in his head was partly based upon his memories of the beguiling TV documentaries he saw as a kid that the science fiction novelist Arthur C. Clarke would front. Clarke made three similar series, *Arthur C. Clarke's Mysterious World, Arthur C. Clarke's World of Strange Powers* and *Arthur C. Clarke's Mysterious Universe,* all of which followed the same format: 'I think he sat on a patio in Sri Lanka introducing the show, then the show happens, then he talks about the show at the end on that patio in Sri Lanka, and that's the show.' Rob imagined doing something along the same lines, a show investigating the world of UFOs and the paranormal in which he played the Arthur C. Clarke role. 'I thought that it would be something that would entertain a restless mind.'

The Jon Ronson programme was a way to dip his toes in the water, and maybe also to see whether he and Ronson might collaborate further.

'I thought that he'd be kind of a perfect foil for the TV show. Him more sceptical than I. I thought maybe it'd be a dry run for something later on down the line.' Rob also held out hope that maybe, once his interest in such things was more widely known, perhaps people who had information that wasn't public might approach him, and some secrets might be unveiled. 'I wanted to go, "I'll put this out into the universe and see what it attracts,"' he says. 'See who would contact me.'

In both respects, he would be disappointed. 'It attracted very little, really. Nobody sought me out – nobody with any information that I don't know.'

* * *

Around this time, Rob began posting on the AboveTopSecret forum under the name 'Chrisonabike'. Not long after he first posted, he came clean about who he really was. Though plenty of people on the site were supportive, over the period when he was an actively posting member he would also face all kinds of criticisms and prejudices. He was even attacked for his decision *not* to remain anonymous, as if motivated by vanity not transparency:

Coline: *Why did you decide to post under chrisonabike and then to say whom you are? You think that the fact of being famous makes you more credible … it annoyed you to be an unknown person among the unknown persons…*

Chrisonabike: *Would it not be better to remain anonymous on the board instead of allowing the whole world to see who you are? Yes and no. Yes, because I'm sure this will damage my very fragile credibility. And no because I find this all very fascinating. And maybe it will open a door that wasn't there before. Plus, I'm not planning on putting an album out for a very long time and I'm a bit bored. Anyways, I haven't got this far by not looking stupid to begin with …*

Mostly, when he did offer answers to things people said, these tended to be pretty honest, straightforward and self-reflexive, the voice of someone really trying to join in with a group of peers. Whatever sense of safety he felt here, alongside a desire to genuinely communicate with people he clearly hoped were both open-minded and like-minded souls, allowed him to be honest in a kind of way he would rarely otherwise be. In another post, he explained what he was getting from all this:

I think everybody wants to feel some sense of community … I guess I view this as an experiment … thinks to self … let's see what happens if I do this? But I do get a real kick out of all of this. I find all aspects of this interesting. ATS is an amazing site full of amazing info, brilliant minds and scholarly research on a subject that's very often dismissed as hogwash for mentalists. I am that mentalist and I love it!

Then there's the way that people interact with each other here. It's fascinating. All sorts of human life getting together and thrashing out the truth. You have the combatives, the submissives, the apologists, the mother/father earth types, the loving, the hateful, the unwell (and I am not above your suspicions in this category – but then again neither is anybody else here).

Maybe I am here for egocentric reasons and I have to take a look at that as well … So thank you all for every post – the good the bad the indifferent. If you stop questioning your own motives, you don't have a very firm base to go from, and you're helping me to question myself. Sure, some people's opinions do stick in my craw. But you have to review them so you can review yourself … I think that is the point of a debate right? It's reality TV for a subject I have great affection for. Even if a thread falls on its face here, you always go away with either … info you didn't have or entertainment from a bitchy fight that descends into chaos. Both are enlightening, both very entertaining.

To be honest I quite enjoy the odd bit of negativity. It's fun dissecting it and trying to understand where people are coming from. Here's the deal: I think my AIM is true, just like most people here but I am open to offers that it might not be. Because … I've been wrong before…

One ongoing debate was about whether the attention generated when a celebrity was known to be interested in such things was positive or negative for ufology, and also whether it was positive or negative for the celebrity. Not surprisingly, both aspects were things he too had been thinking about.

Do I think celebrity attention helps/hinders … ? Who knows in the long run? Maybe if a few more came forward, then yes, it would add some credibility to the subject. But I think it depends on the celeb. And the media's agenda towards that celeb. I'm not sure how much stick Dan Aykroyd gets but as a talking head for ufology I'm sure he has more credibility than myself. I'm much younger, less articulate and have had all my dirty laundry washed in public. Therefore it is easier to get their claws into me, so they do. The press didn't take it seriously before I turned up and I'm sure they're not going to on my behalf. It is not my goal to become a talking head for this subject. I'm rubbish at retaining information and relaying it in an understandable manner anyways (but maybe that will change). I'm an 8-year-old at heart and something magic's happening. I want people to at least have a look and make an informed opinion. Doesn't everybody on this site wish the same thing?

Will I make it look stupid? I hope not. Will I help? Hope so. Help/hindrance I think will be a 50/50 thing …

On: if I think it will damage my career? Well if people stop buying my albums because I saw something strange … that's fine by me. And there's nothing I can do about it. It genuinely doesn't worry me … I think I said it before but no I'm not worried about my career. I've had my time in the sun (no pun) time and time again. My career shouldn't really have happened. I've done the biggest stadiums in the world and sold more records than I could have ever imagined. If it ends tomorrow I've had beyond what we would call 'A good run'. I'd rather not have a career than have to mind my Ps and Qs (metaphorically speaking) for the rest of my life … None of the 'he's a nutter' thing has disturbed my emotions in any way. They might have a point. I might be stark raving mad. But it feels good … know what I mean?

And when other posters trotted out the 'all publicity is good publicity' trope, suggesting that anything that helped him get into the newspapers was de facto good for him, he was very unlikely to say silent:

Everybody thinks that everything is a publicity stunt. I've been to rehab twice. That was for publicity too, apparently. Why would I go away for 6 weeks for publicity? I'm lazy. If I was that way inclined I'd have thought up something less time consuming. The 'just for publicity thing' … I don't have to do or say anything. I'm in them all the time, without any input from me.

* * *

In an interview that Jon Ronson gave some years later, on a web TV station called London Real, when he was asked about his experiences in the world of Robbie Williams he offered a very succinct and perceptive summary of this whole period.

'I think,' Jon Ronson suggested, 'he saw me and the whole UFO thing as like a holiday from his real life. Some people said that it was a sign that he was going crazy, but actually I always thought it was the opposite: I thought the stadium tour was the thing that had turned him crazy, and all of this was the thing that was making him better again.'

* * *

September 2016

There's a comedian called Nick Helm who has had a BBC Three TV show called *Nick Helm's Heavy Entertainment*. Rob didn't take the phrase from him, but Rob is aware of Helm's show, or at least its title, because when Rob first thought of the phrase he Googled it to see if anyone else had ever previously flipped 'light entertainment' in the same way.

In advance of Rob's album release, Helm has been tweeting his annoyance in correspondence with a few sympathetic, outraged fans:

Yeah. Fuck off Robbie.

Robbie fucking Williams.

(I think 'Robbie fucking Williams' is supposed to be rude. I'm not sure he realises it's one of Rob's live show catchphrases.)

Rob has just read that Helm's next DVD is called *Nick Helm Is Fucking Amazing*.

'I feel like direct-messaging him,' Rob tells me, 'saying "I'm just about to embark on my world tour, the 'Robbie Williams Is Fucking Amazing' tour."'

* * *

More interviews, this time at Magic Radio. The first one is down the line to a man called Mike in Manchester. They talk about Rob's kids for a while, and Mike asks whether this is his greatest achievement.

'Apart from the seventeen Brits,' Rob replies. 'Kaboom!'

He's asked about money, and he recasts the answer he gave in Germany.

'Well, it's never really been about it – it's always been about the ego. I mean that in the nicest way about myself: *Oh I don't feel good enough, I don't feel worthy*, and the job was always about trying to fill those holes and trying to be welcomed and taken into people's hearts, and maybe that would fill this gap that's there, whatever it is. And the money just alongside it. And I love that too. But the biggest thing for me has always been about: "Like me! Like me!" And that's a sad realisation, but it's the truth.'

The interviewer tells Rob that if he had 90 million in the bank, he'd be laid back too.

'It's more than that,' Rob replies.

* * *

The second Magic interview is down the line to someone called Arlene in Scotland. This one begins on diets.

'Alls it takes is not eating anything you like ever, and even less of the stuff that you don't like, and just being confused and depressed – that's the truth about diets. I've been thin, I've experienced that – I'm just going to work on my personality now and eat what the hell I want.'

A few minutes later, she asks him: 'Are you partial to a few vodkas then?'

'Well, I would be if I wasn't sober for the last sixteen years ... only been to rehab seven times, Arlene.'

He talks over her apologies with some amused advice.

'When in hole,' he suggests, 'stop digging.'

* * *

At some point in most of today's interviews, the DJ will say something like 'good luck with the new album *Heavy Entertainment Show*'. Each time, Rob seems to flinch. I think when this has been happening in press interviews, or with foreign interviewers, he's accepted it as a kind of sloppy shorthand, or a second-language issue, but hearing the title of his album being broadcast over the air like this is troubling him. Between two interviews he says to Michael, 'I think everybody's got it written down as *Heavy Entertainment Show* – it's not, it's *The Heavy Entertainment Show* …' Michael doesn't say anything – now's not the time – but I'm pretty sure I know what he's thinking. All of the pre-publicity does say *Heavy Entertainment Show*. So does the heavy block-lettered artwork on the CD sleeve, showing two sweaty Robbies facing off in a boxing ring (because, as he will explain many dozens of times, the last great battle is with himself). The same artwork that Rob has, of course, seen and approved.

When he gets into the car after leaving Magic, Rob picks up the *Daily Mail* lying on the seat. The front-page headline has got his attention.

4 OUT OF 5 HAVE A HEART THAT IS OLDER THAN THEY ARE.

He scans the story for a moment, then discards it.

'I thought "that's me",' he explains. But then he realised it was just a scare story about the nation's physical health.

It's then that Michael broaches the subject:

'Rob, the cover artwork currently says *Heavy Entertainment Show*.'

'Oh really?'

'Does it need to have a "*The* …" in front of it?'

'Can it?'

'So everything should be "*The* … ?" including the song?'

'Yeah. Yeah. It should be *The Heavy Entertainment Show*.'

* * *

We're stuck in traffic, so he passes time by answering questions from fans on his computer.

Will any of your new songs possibly be labelled a bit edgy?

'I suppose a few will. But it doesn't take much to be edgy these days.'

* * *

143

A couple of hours later, Michael, who has been making calls, picks up the earlier conversation.

'We do have a problem with the deluxe version,' says Michael. 'In that it's printed.' He points out that the deluxe version is limited to 300,000 copies globally, and that the standard 11-track version, which can be changed, will sell many more than that. Does Rob definitely want the change to be made?

'Every time they said *Heavy Entertainment Show* I was in my mind going "it's *The* ..."' says Rob. 'I'd like "*The*" on. It's only going to annoy me. And I'm aware that I've looked at the album but I didn't think that there was a "*The*" missing. Might as well get it right. Spent so much time trying to get this album right. Right for me, in my head.'

So it's agreed that the regular version, and the lyric booklet, will be changed, and will be *The Heavy Entertainment Show* for evermore. But the initial run of the deluxe version – collector's items! – will be *Heavy Entertainment Show*.

After the album's release, this is sometimes noticed, both by fans and journalists, and the general assumption seems to be that this is a deliberate way of differentiating between the two editions. I actually don't think it crosses anyone's mind that it might just have been a mistake.

* * *

He's taking sleeping pills. Ambien.

Earlier in the summer, the basketball player Kobe Bryant, one of the most famous sportsmen in America, published a letter he had written to his teenage self. Bryant's main message seemed to be to not just shower gifts on friends and family around him, because that would ultimately bring tears and heartache to them and to him, but to find other, more durable ways to invest in their futures and help them realise their potential.

Rob thought it might be interesting to do the same exercise, so he jots down the first two lines one night just as he is going to sleep. It doesn't go so well. When he wakes up the next day, this is *exactly* what he discovers he has written; the thoughtful and heartfelt words he has decided are worthy of wishing back in time to guide the teenager he once was:

First of all i love you and i miss you little brother
yeah you are more ethan worst betting lovetdg and etoetally miabcetl

'Yeah, I know,' he says. 'That's Ambien for you. Imagine how confused I'd be as a sixteen-year-old to receive that?'

* * *

'Bit early for all this, isn't it?' says Rob to the fans gathered outside Radio 2. It's before eight in the morning.

Upstairs he asks if there's somewhere he might be able to smoke. They think that maybe there's a balcony they can unlock.

'The last time we did that,' says the producer, 'was for Nile Rodgers and the eclipse.'

'Well,' Rob asks, 'can you do it now for Robbie Williams and a Silk Cut?'

After The Weeknd's 'Can't Feel My Face' and the *Happy Days* theme, Rob is introduced on air by Chris Evans; soon he's been coaxed into doing a Frank Spencer impression and is unloading his neuroses on morning Britain as it yawns itself awake:

'Every time I've been in the studio it's been under the heavy weight of: "You're coming back, you're doing an album, this better be a hit, you're forty-two, you're fat, your eyes are droopy, you've got a big 'eleven' above your eyes, you've got to go and sort that out, this isn't a hit, oh, you've just said the wrong word, is that chorus big enough? no, it isn't, go and write a bigger chorus, come on fatty ..." It's not just the week build-up, it's the eighteen months before that when you're in the studio every day going: "No! Don't be a has-been! Don't be a has-been!" And that's where my brain idles at. But it propels me forward. It's an uncomfortable place to be, but here I am, still doing this. Still in the pop charts, hopefully. Fingers crossed. It's been a stressful eight months, trying to not be a fat pop star.' Then he talks about the transformation that has come with having a family, how his life used to be a fruitless quest to 'fill in all the blanks that were in the soul. And that didn't make sense. I got to the top of the mountain and it was like, "Ow, I'm still in pain." Then the wife came, then the kids came ... now it all makes sense.'

In the control room, where I am standing, someone from the show mutters 'such a good interview …'

* * *

In the car on the way back to the hotel, as we edge along in the traffic, Rob spots Phil Jupitus walking down the pavement next to us.

'Always horrible about me on … *Buzzcocks*,' he says. 'Just general hatred for me. He was kind of insistent that I was completely in love with myself. And other things.'

Gary Marshall, who is driving, reminds Rob that he took his revenge a long time back.

'Oh yeah,' he remembers. 'Pissed in his coat pocket. At the BBC Centre. And I wiped my arse and stuffed the paper in his video recorder.'

Rob says this in the kind of way that suggests that he wouldn't do something like that now, but that he is still quite some way from truly regretting it.

* * *

He telephones me one Saturday night about an article that has come out in *The Guardian*. It's predominantly thoughtful and respectful, even when it's not positive, and it's knowledgeable about who he has been, but part of the following passage is playing on Rob's mind:

As a character, he was simply riveting. Williams was the ideal pop star for an age when celebrity increasingly seemed like a poisoned chalice, dramatising his ambivalence towards fame as Eminem and Kanye West later would, but in the guise of a cheeky light entertainer. He doubted his own abilities, feared live performance, hated being alone, worried about his weight, displayed a Nixonian capacity to bear a grudge, and constantly fantasised about retiring.

He's still mulling it over a few days later.

'Is my grudge-bearing any worse than anyone else's?' he asks me.

I allow that it is definitely something he sometimes does quite energetically.

He thinks about this, and wonders about the different ways he and Gary Barlow seem to deal with things. Rob comes up with a theory. 'Maybe he's a grown-up,' he suggests.

Or maybe, I counter, he just deals with it in a different and less visible way.

'I suppose I don't respond well to being alpha-maled,' Rob nods. 'To my detriment.' This reminds him of something. 'There was a time when I was a kid when someone was bullying me a little bit, from off the estate, and he was walking past my drive one day when I was with my mum, and I thought, "You can't do anything because I'm with my mum" and while my mum wasn't looking I did this ...'

Rob mimes sticking up two fingers; his brief, sweet, ill-thought moment of victory.

'And the next time I saw him he got a knife out and threatened to stab me. Held me up against a tree. A penknife, but it would have punctured.'

So what do you think is the lesson from that?

'That the lesson *wasn't* learned. There's something in me that goes, "Yeah, this might work to my detriment, but ..." I think there might be a grown-up version that is still in me.'

When does it come out?

'Just when I'm thinking that there's scores to settle, even though I'm out-psychoed or out-gunned.' But it's complicated. 'For me, I think there's genuine panto involved, and genuine hurt feeling.' He laughs. 'With real life consequences.'

Which means that one reason people often can't tell whether you're doing panto or being serious is because maybe you can't?

'Yeah. Yeah.'

He mulls this over a little more.

'There's an energy in revenge,' he adds, 'that's quite seductive.'

* * *

He's back at Magic another day, for an acoustic concert where two of his new songs, 'Love My Life' and 'Hotel Crazy', will be heard in public for the very first time. Beforehand, being interviewed, he takes another stab at explaining his success.

'I think it's because I've got massive, massive low self-esteem,' he says, 'and I think that's relatable to a lot of people. I think people on the outside can hear my inside voice and just take pity on me.'

So it's just understanding that luck has played a part?

'Yeah, and, you know, not being very smart. I don't know why I've been taken into people's hearts. I just think that I'm sort of like the idiot brother to a lot of people. The archetypal class clown. I don't know how it works, but I'm still here.'

A short while later, he plays 'Love My Life' in front of an audience, and starts to tear up.

'That was an incredibly moving moment for me,' he says – and I think this is a relatively rare moment of complete uncomplicated sincerity in public – 'and it's magical, and it's those moments that I talk about ...'

* * *

2008–2009

An exchange on an AboveTopSecret.com forum, May 2008:

Isaac Tanner Madsen: *Thanks for being willing to chat with folks on this site about your experiences. We're all definitely appreciative ... What makes a person a nutter anyhow? Unless that happens to be their last name (like my cousins, and they're as 'normal' as can be).*

Chrisonabike: *I've always been scared of normal ... Normal people dropped the bomb.*

* * *

In August 2008, Rob and Ayda visited a place called the Gilliland Ranch, a location in Trout Lake, Washington, that is reputed to be a hotspot of extraterrestrial activity. They were there with some of the AboveTopSecret administrators, and searched the night sky for anomalies, with inconclusive results. A group of his Stoke musician friends were also there, and in between times they wrote songs: one, 'Deceptacon', would appear on his next album, and another, 'Soda Pop', wouldn't surface until 2013. While at the ranch, Rob says that he ran his hand blindly along a shelf of books people had left there, picked one out, then took it to the toilet and randomly stuck a finger inside the book. When he opened it fully and looked at what was next to his finger, it was the words 'underground city of Stoke-on-Trent'.

News of this trip reignited a particularly excitable and only intermittently lucid version of the debate on AboveTopSecret about whether Rob's current pastimes would destroy his music career. For instance:

Triplesod: *Rob has done enough himself in the past to ruin his career but always come out of it pretty well. He has had drug and alcohol addictions which possibly was the catalyst to a huge ego for a period which came across as quite obnoxious … certain strange relationships etc etc … in the UK for a period, he was possibly the most famous celebrity for quite a long time and, as is their wont, the press did all they could to ruin him. If they didn't manage it then, they aren't going to manage it over this.*

Anonymous ATS: *Hi Robbie, majorly disappointed to discover you've gone completely insane! Not that the men in white coats should come just yet, but you are definitely giving 1970s Elvis a run for his money. You've always come across as very intelligent in interviews – both clever and perceptive. So how could you possibly fall in with the Ron Paul/black helicopters lot? … Is it worth sacrificing your reputation and the high esteem in which so many people hold you? Why not use your obviously bright mind to pursue virtually ANYTHING ELSE? Any shelf at Borders will do! Why not read Freud or Althusser or Foucault; Dostoyevsky or Joyce or Proust? Study molecular biology and discover new mating habits of starfish. Buy an expensive camera and take artsy black-and-white photographs of homeless people and interesting gates. Write the definitive analysis of Spaghetti Westerns in 60s Italian cinema. Travel to Japan to learn the ancient art of calligraphy. Take a carpentry class and build a grand-father clock from plywood, patent the design and sell it to Ikea. Any of these hobbies would be less crazy than what you are doing now.*

0010110011101: *He's made enough money, slept with enough women and taken enough drugs and alcohol to last a lifetime! Time for a proper hobby!*

Rawsom: *For some of us it is quite clear that Robbie Williams is just a puppet to get this message of his across … This is just a stunt to make him more popular among circles he hopes to attain attention of.*

Crakeur: *Yeah, he's conquered every market except the coveted UFO nutter demographic … this should really put him over the top with us.*

Anonymous: *Hello Robbie & Everyone, I myself believe in other beings, planets/universes/galaxies and I feel that Robbie does have a connection. However, I am very aware that Robbie has been mind controlled for a long time by other people on earth. But his controllers have underestimated just how strong his spirit is, despite the numerous times of re-programming he has been through – he is a natural fighter and has wanted to be free for a long time.*

Eventually Rob chipped in, joined this conversation:

Hey folks, just reading through the posts and wanted to comment … there's no use getting angry with the unwell … leave em to it… So I'm crazy … ok … I'm crazy … that's cool… On a side note … The men in the white coats are letting me take my scratch mittens off today … whhhhooooooaaa …

* * *

'There's always been kind of a nearly thing running alongside my career that I might be a bit mad, that there might be a bit of a bonkers-ness going on,' he says. 'It's always great to play with, if you're not bonkers at the time.'

Just occasionally, it could get a little tedious. Towards the end of his time off, after he and Ayda moved into the big house he'd bought in Wiltshire, the tabloids, projecting from their new cartoon version of who he was, imagined that he'd chosen this area because it was known for its crop circles. He hadn't – not at all. But *The Sun* was sufficiently committed to their narrative about Rob's Wiltshire life that they tried a good old-fashioned tabloid stunt. 'They sent journalists down to stand outside the house dressed as little green men,' says Rob. 'I remember being in the car and driving past these guys in alien suits ... I could see them looking sheepish and embarrassed as I gave them the stink eye.'

Rob was also aware that there was a danger here. For someone like him, there's a fun and pleasure in people believing that you might have gone crazy. But there's also a collateral risk. 'If you *are* actually bonkers when they accuse you of being bonkers, it's a bit worrying, because then the game is out of your control,' he says. 'Little did I realise that I actually was a little bit mad too, but that was separate to UFOs.' A far simpler kind of crazy that was willingly self-administered: 'I was smoking a *load* of weed.'

* * *

The threads on AboveTopSecret which Rob seemed to get the most from were the ones where he was able to join in conversations about the kind of stuff that had drawn him to the site in the first place. For instance, after posting his description of his potentially paranormal experiences, he patiently answered pretty much every subsidiary question that followed, whenever other posters asked him to clarify even the tiniest detail. On another thread, he solicited the best UFO and related YouTube videos. And his voice would pop up in other unlikely places whenever he actually had something of substance to add to the subject under discussion. On a thread someone had started entitled 'Strange scratches on my body' he contributed this:

I get them all the time ... haven't had them for a few months though ... I thought everybody got them until I brought it up with a few friends ... 'you know when you wake up with scratches in places you can't reach?' 'no' came the answer ... OH ... they're about 4 to 8 inches long and they look like they've bled a little and dried up ... they don't last long ... normally gone in a couple of days ...

But more and more often, the discussions he was pulled into involved his existence as a pop star, and – even setting aside the pure Robbie Williams fans who had begun to find him here, whose presence seemed a distraction for everyone – generally his role involved having to justify himself.

One typical thread was based on two recent press reports. The first said that Rob had had dinner in Los Angeles with a visiting Lily Allen and wants to assume a big brother role in her life, a role which will incorporate, as the headline asserts, *Lily Allen to go UFO spotting with Robbie Williams.* The second was, in its way, similar: *Robbie Williams enlists David Beckham's kids in UFO hunt.* Much of the subsequent negative commentary congregated around the way that in the photo illustrating the second story, captioned 'Robbie Williams admits he's fascinated by the thought of alien life', Rob is wearing a cap, sunglasses, and an orange scarf covering his face. The forum discussion on this crucial subject is thirty-seven pages long; eventually its subject was goaded into a lengthy response:

Hey folks, can't reply to every lie in the media here on ATS, because I think it'll descend into pop star baiting ... Anyways I love ATS and feel part of all this. So, fellow members as way of explanation ... The picture is from 2003/4, maybe before ... It was a period in my life where they (paps) were everywhere ... There were a load of them waiting for me to get off a plane, about 7/8 paps ... When a plane full of people, maybe 200 or so, are getting off behind you, it can be very scary ... Flash lights go off all over the place and you just don't know what to do ... you panic ... and try to salvage some kind of privacy to protect yourself ... in hindsight maybe a bright orange scarf doesn't help the cause. But believe me, any photo like this was thought about (by me) in a panic. I was younger then and naïve ... you can't beat them so I've stopped trying ... that pic was just a long line of failed attempts to try and make their photo worthless ... it didn't ... you try these things ... sometimes they work sometimes they make you look daft.

As for the story ... I don't have Lily Allen's phone number, I don't know her, met her just to say hello to for 5 mins last year sometime. There are no UFO parties in my back garden. The thought of it actually makes me laugh. Sure, I look up from time to time but that's about it. And as for David Beckham and his kids? Really? I've met David a few times but UFOs have never been part of any conversation.

As a rule of thumb, believe nothing you read. It's all made up. And I know you think you know, but believe me, the tabloids are just a soap. And as for making 'the movement' look silly? I promise not to wear an orange scarf again. That way it should ensure that everybody takes this subject seriously.

Anyways ... I'm here, I read, I wanna know. Just like everybody else on these boards. Good luck on the hunt, folks.

RW

He adds subsidiary posts to further clarify:

Oh, and by the way, I don't walk around trying to cover myself up if there's nobody trying to take a picture. Yes, you are right ... that would make me a C2nt.

And then:

Oh, and by the way, I wasn't suggesting that everybody takes these things seriously. But as you can read here on this thread, some do. And I know I said I wasn't going to post again, but I'm bored and I've been picking puppy poopoo up all morning. So this is a nice distraction ...

And then, having to defend his thinly disguised use of foul language:

Sorry ... I forgot it is still deemed as vulgar. It's my favourite word. And seeing as I've been called it many times, I've decided to make it my own. Takes the power out it.

After a while, perhaps inevitably, it became too much.

'A lot of people were really lovely,' he says, 'but a fucking ton of people were just incredulous and nasty about my participation on there. My fingers got burned.' And so Chrisonabike went silent. Rob continued reading regularly, but his public voice was gone.

* * *

Counterintuitively, in a way what Rob was interested in exploring in this period when he focused more of his attention on ufology and paranormal phenomena was not the possibility that these things existed. He'd grown up believing that they did, as an unexamined article of faith. While a fundamental part of him still very much *wanted* everything that he'd instinctively always believed in to exist, what he was now interested in thinking about and investigating was just as much the possibility that they *didn't*.

'I wanted to go and put myself straight on the matter,' he says. 'You know, it wasn't until this break really that I looked at stuff in earnest and would have a look at the other side of the argument too.'

And, if anything, his journeys into the world of those who believe in such things ultimately ended up leaving him somewhat less of a believer. (He has a pretty good nose for bullshit.)

But he would still *like* to believe. The world would be so much more interesting that way. His faith endures that we live somewhere stranger and more shadowy than inflexible, rational modes of thought can explain.

'I'd be sad if there wasn't anything out there that was a bit tinfoil hat and whooey and weirdy,' he says. 'That's why I put myself out there – to see if I could find some truth, either way.'

And he remains hopeful that such faith will not always go unrewarded.

'Am I eight years old?' he says. 'Of course. I think everybody loves a bit of magic, and sometimes I would hope for that magic to be real.'

* * *

Here's another way, the more pure Robbie Williams way, of saying the same thing.

'There's been other unnatural things that have happened,' he points out, and kind of giggles at the absurdity of it all. 'Me selling sixty million records is one of them. If I can do *that*,' he says, 'then the possibility of life on other planets …'

* * *

September 2016

Late one night in his Soho Hotel suite, before heading to bed after another long day sharing with the world the best and worst things he can think of about himself, Rob shows me a YouTube video he's just discovered. It's of a drone flying over Tunstall where he grew up. As it plays, he offers a running commentary of Tunstall geography, and of his past.

'And that's my house – how mad is that? Greenbank Road ... Lived there from three till sixteen ... That's where the pub used to be ... It's crazy, isn't it? ... And everywhere's had their windows done. *Everywhere* ... This is where I got bullied once. A big boy beat me up, put a stick in my mouth, and went "now you know what a fucking horse feels like" ... I was ten ... he was a psychopath ... Somebody murdered their wife here ... This house used to sell weed ... draw, you know ... resin ... This guy that used to live here pissed in a Lilt can then gave it me to drink. And I thought that Lilt tasted like that and was awful, and I only realised that Lilt didn't taste like that when I had a sip of it again, and it wasn't warm and didn't taste like piss ... Our next-door neighbour, one of them was writing songs, and I found them on YouTube and I thought "Great!", I was genuinely, "Good for him!" Then I was listening to one and it went *The pop star who lives next door/looks like he's got fat again*. I was, "Oh ... it's about me, and me getting fat ... I was going to help you out, but I don't think I will now" ... And his dad used to go Morris dancing ... Drank cider for the first time in these bushes ... Yeah, there was a halfway house for mentally ill people, and one of them killed a girl in the Methodist church that's just there ... I think the man that did murder that woman followed me around the park. And I led him all the way to the police. My inbuilt fear detector saw this guy looking and acting weird. I told the police and they said they couldn't do anything ... Actually, since everyone's had their windows done, it looks quite posh ...'

* * *

2008–2009

Just as Rob never put a limit on how long it would take him to return, or if he ever would, he says that his management never put him under any pressure. 'They left me to my own devices,' he says. 'There was no asking. They just let me be.' Later, I think he came to appreciate this as an unusual act of faith and friendship. 'Other management might have been badgering,' he reflects. 'I mean, the guy that was bringing in the most money was eating cake and hunting UFOs.'

But very slowly he realised on his own that a life of retirement was not for him.

'My brain turned to Swiss cheese,' he says. 'I found out that I need to be doing *something*, at least. A man needs a purpose and a man needs something to do. I can understand why people retire and then die. I can see how that happens. There has to be some meat and bones, otherwise you will decompose, and I was decomposing. The head turned on itself ...'

Even so, he had to edge his way towards a decision. At first, he decided that he would release some of the music he had been making, but not do any promotion at all. 'I had an album ready to go that would have petrified the record company – lots of bleeps and blobs and no choruses and strange lyrics,' he says. He thought about just putting it out on the internet. But he was persuaded by the argument that this probably wouldn't be greeted as a beguiling, fascinating move, it would probably just communicate that he wasn't really bothered. And that his audience might reciprocate by being equally unbothered. He realised that if he was going to do it at all, he should probably do it properly. 'I went, right, okay, I'll just have to wait until I can get my head around being enthusiastic and confident enough to come back ...'

* * *

As he made a few first tentative steps to shake off his hibernation, he noticed that there were some ways in which life for him was already easier than before he disappeared. Maybe he'd come to rue this change in other ways, but one kind of pressure had relented.

'When I started staying in,' he says, 'there was a part of me that was like: "Fuck these paparazzi! I'm not going out! Fuck 'em!" Because they used to wait at the top of the estate for me. There used to be ten carfuls of people that used to follow me. I was *money*. And I couldn't cope with that. It was maddening and saddening and frustrating and isolating. And I waited and waited and waited, and something happened in those three years while I was away. You know ...' – he laughs, quoting the Fun Boy Three – '... the trial separation worked. By the time I'd come out they'd gone. They'd moved on. And the intense light that had shone on me had left too.'

* * *

He had been showing Ayda pictures of Stoke on Google Earth. When he showed her Tunstall Park she told him it look 'so idyllic'. It was time to see the real thing. And so in November 2008 he took her on a trip to his past.

'A magical trip,' he says. 'We bypassed London, because there's a lot of memories and shadows there of a person that I used to be. We came to go to Stoke so I could show Ayda Stoke. And up in Stoke people were really warm and friendly. I felt like I had literally come home. People are a lot different in Stoke than people in Beverly Hills.'

Earlier that year in Los Angeles, he had experienced what he calls 'a catalogue of disasters with friendships'. Coming back to the place that formed him, at least for a little while, was the perfect antidote.

'I found myself needing to reconnect with something that was real, and something that had happened before I became famous. And I managed to do that in Stoke, and it was amazing. I went round to my mum's, I went round to my dad's, took Ayda to Port Vale, took Ayda to Tunstall Park, showed her my nan's house. We went to my nan's grave, saw my Auntie Jo's grave, went for an Italian with my dad and all his friends. It was snowing, so it was lovely. And people were wonderful with Ayda and really lovely with me, and I felt a spirit of belonging.'

One day, the two of them just turned up at the door of the house where he lived from the age of three until he was 18 or 19.

'It's an Asian family who live there now,' he says. 'They were surprised, but they were really, really lovely. They instantly wanted me to come in and have a look. So I went in and saw the box room that was my old bedroom and the living room. They've built an extension on the place and there's a balcony on the back now – it looks kind of posh.'

On the same trip, he bought the house in Wiltshire. He sent an email to let me know:

Looks like I'm going to be living in Blighty for a bit … hurrah.

* * *

In February 2009, Rob took Ayda to see Port Vale play Brentford at Brentford's home ground, Griffin Park. It was Valentine's Day, the day after his thirty-fifth birthday. Port Vale lost 2-0, and his presence didn't go unnoticed. The crowd started singing at him. They had something that they felt he needed to know.

You're not famous anymore!
You're not famous anymore!

Never mind the paradox at the heart of their chant: how the fact that they'd noticed him and cared to taunt him rather undermined their proposition. It was still an interesting indication of something.

'It made me laugh,' he says, 'and it made me go, "Wow, the general public's talking about me and that's what their perception is of me – that's strange."'

Still, he gave at least as good as he got.

'I sung back, *I'll buy you and turn you into a Tesco.* And, *I've got more fans than you, I've got more fans than you …*'

But it was certainly something to think about.

You're not famous anymore.

And of course it begged the question: was he more worried that it was true, or more worried that it wasn't?

* * *

He says that there was one specific, slightly random moment when he realised that he really did want to return. He was in a car, being driven up to London, and he was listening to the charts on the radio … and he can't even really say exactly what it was about that precise moment except that suddenly, at last, he *knew*. 'There was something about listening to the charts, and being in the car, and going to London, that in that moment made me go, "I've got to go back and do that,'" he says.

With the certainty, of course, came the fear. What if whatever it was that broke at the end of 2006 wasn't really fixed? Or – something simpler, something more fundamental – what if being a pop star is something that you can forget how to be?

'I've always been terrified throughout my career, but I've always been able to mask it. And now I didn't know how to get back on the bike, where the gears were, where the pedals were, and whether the mask had slipped. At least when I kept getting into the car, I kept doing it. The muscle was working. But now I'd taken so long out ... what if the muscle didn't work again? What if they could really see what was happening?'

4

November 2016

On a private jet returning from Germany, Rob and Guy Chambers are sitting together, talking. They have so much shared history together, but there's also a ten-year gap after they fell out where Guy has very little first-hand knowledge of what was going on in Rob's life. Sometimes this history bubbles up, as it does this evening.

Rob is explaining about the one live concert he agreed to do back in 2009, when he returned from retirement, at the Electric Proms, and how, by the time it came around, his comeback had already been derailed in his head.

'I was leaving New York after working with Take That,' he explains – this was the moment when the five of them had secretly reunited, but the world was yet to know – 'and I knew that I'd got to go and do this whole thing that was terrifying to me at the time, and overwhelming.' The terrifying, overwhelming thing he had to do was to be Robbie Williams who, after a long absence, was about promote his new album *Reality Killed The Video Star*. 'I'd had a good time with the boys, and I knew that I was safe there. And then I'd got to go and do the thing that I just wasn't prepared to do. And off I went. Then "Bodies" happened on *The X Factor* and that just made me ...'

'Yeah, I remembering watching "Bodies"...' Guy begins.

Rob interrupts. 'But I remember leaving New York and thinking, I just don't want to do this.'

He has interrupted for a very specific reason.

'Mmmm,' says Guy.

Rob looks at Guy. 'Don't say what you're about to say,' he warns, with a pleading lilt in his voice. As healthy as their relationship now seems to be, there are still many fault lines that remain, running in both directions, and one is a long history of Guy saying things that Rob finds inappropriate, and often also unsettling to his peace of mind. It's a history coupled with an equally long history of Guy not quite understanding what these things are or why they should be a problem for Rob.

This is about to be one of those moments.

'How do you know what I'm going to say?' says Guy, both puzzled and slightly indignant.

'Go on – say it!' says Rob, exasperated.

'No, I'm not going to say it,' says Guy, slightly sullenly.

'Say it!' Rob insists. 'Go on. And I'll tell you which bit.' He prompts him: 'You remember watching "Bodies" ...'

'... on *X Factor* ...' resumes Guy, tentatively.

'*And?*'

'... and ... thinking ...' – Guy sounds as though as he's checking each word, making absolutely sure it is free of offence before he allows it from his lips – '... it was weird.'

Rob exclaims, in a sad sort of triumph. '*That's* why I didn't want you to say what you were going to say!'

'No, no, your *performance*,' says Guy, thinking Rob has misunderstood.

'*Yes!*' exclaims Rob, laughing at how much worse it's getting.

'Sorry … sorry,' says Guy, who now seems both nervous at, and confused by, wherever he's wandered into. 'Why's that so bad?' he asks.

Rob sighs.

'Oh, sorry,' says Guy. I think this apology is perfectly sincere, though I suspect he probably still doesn't quite understand.

Rob explains.

'Because *then* it felt like trauma when it was picked up on as being weird,' he says, 'and then it made me stop doing the promo, which was what I was talking about before you started to have an opinion, which is why I stopped you, because I knew where you were going, and didn't want to relive the shame.'

'Oh. Yeah, sorry.'

'Does that make sense?'

'Yes.'

'Because it *still* feels shameful and hurtful.'

'Okay. I didn't …'

'That's why I wanted to cancel all the promo.'

'Ah …'

'Because I didn't feel safe.'

'Understood.'

'Yeah, I was so scared.'

'Yeah.'

'It didn't feel natural anymore. What I was doing just didn't feel second nature any more.'

'Yeah. It's quite a tough song, that, to sing, though, isn't it?'

'*Any* song would have been.'

'Oh.'

'Just the performance. I didn't know how to do it. It didn't feel right. Yeah, and unfortunately it's not like the days when the BBC taped over things and burned them and they don't exist. This will exist forever.'

'Right,' says Guy.

* * *

June–October 2009

At the beginning of recording *Reality Killed The Video Star* – still months before he has to face the public – Rob has a conversation with the producer Trevor Horn about how he likes to work.

'So what hours do you like to do?' Horn asks him.

'Friday,' he answers.

Horn laughs, but Rob is being serious.

'No,' he explains. 'Friday is when I come in.'

He elaborates that his preferred schedule is to pop in for a couple of hours to hear what has been done over the previous week, to offer his input and opinions, and to an add a vocal here and there when required, before disappearing for another seven days. 'It's always felt like a very grown-up process,' he'll tell me, 'going into these big studio rooms and having professors of pop taking care of your album – I've sort of felt a bit redundant in those places.' Later in the year Rob will frequently deliver this I-only-worked-Fridays anecdote to the press, indifferent to the impression it gives that he was some kind of bystander or passenger in the creation of his own album. Which is neither true, nor the point. The main reason Rob has never seen much need to hang around during all of the painstaking labour of finishing a record – aside from the fact that he has little patience for it – is that he considers that he has already done most of his work. And that's far truer than most people who will hear his 'Friday' quip will ever realise. For instance, while Horn's contribution to these final songs will be hugely impressive, and will elevate them in all kinds of vital ways, if anyone who'd got to know the finished version of *Reality Killed The Video Star* subsequently heard Robbie's early versions, mostly recorded in his Los Angeles bedroom, they might be surprised at exactly how much they recognised – not just the basic songs themselves but in most cases their fundamental structure and arrangements.

If one tool in the magic box of being a successful entertainer is to always be ready to take credit for what you didn't do, Rob is also a part-time master of its inverse: sidestepping the credit for what he actually did.

* * *

For the first month of recording, Rob sticks with dedication to this Friday schedule. But then he begins to drift in to where the record is being completed – Trevor Horn's Sarm West Studios complex in Notting Hill – more and more often. Not that he spends most of the time in one of the big studios upstairs where Trevor Horn is doing the pop-professoring. There's a small, windowless room downstairs, and that's where I find him in the first week of June.

Danny and Kelvin are here, too – they are hunched over a keyboard and a screen, working on their own mix of Frankie Goes To Hollywood's 'Welcome To The Pleasuredome', originally recorded by Trevor Horn in this building twenty-five years earlier, for a remix project. Rob is on his laptop.

'It's a bit like the end of term,' Rob explains. 'All the dossers here gathered in the playground. You know how school's great when you don't have to do any lessons? We're all here. We're in the common room, behaving like sixth-formers even though we're not yet.'

At this particular instant, Rob is drawing up song lists and planning his next swing album, an album that is still another four years away. Anyone who spends time in his world recognises this pattern: as the pressure builds towards the launch of one project, his attention seems to be on the next thing down the road, or even the one after that. It can be a little maddening for the people around him: just as they're doing all they can to bring current plans to fruition, his attention and enthusiasm can seem to be elsewhere.

Partly I think his impulse is a genuine one, fired by ambition and forward propulsion, but it's also undoubtedly a defence mechanism and a form of denial, a way of avoiding the pressure that comes with having to acknowledge to himself how much may hang on what is just about to happen.

He leans back. His return to the public eye is, nonetheless, clearly on his mind.

'So,' he announces, 'I'm going to re-form. Me.'

With the original line-up? I ask.

'No,' he says. 'Some of us have gone.'

Trevor Horn pops in briefly to update Rob on the real work on his album upstairs, then Rob checks his email, reads a post on AboveTopSecret about there being twenty different alien civilisations monitoring Earth, and searches on Spotify, a new discovery, for weird cover versions of his own songs. He finds a choir singing 'Angels' as a Gregorian chant. 'Imagine all those nice men singing a song out of this filthy mind,' he says.

After a long while doing all these kinds of nothing, he goes upstairs to hear what progress Trevor has made with 'Bodies', a song he has belatedly realised might make a good single.

'What a noise,' says Lol Creme, a frequent participant in Trevor Horn's musical circle, enthusiastically as the song plays. 'Great noise.'

Rob likes it, but it seems he has other things on his mind.

'Saw a picture of these pigs in the sea yesterday,' he tells Trevor. 'I want to get one. A sea pig.'

'A sea pig?' asks Trevor, his voice betraying a certain amount of surprise, but little enough that you can tell he has become used to such conversations. 'What do you want one for?'

'They're pigs that swim,' says Rob, as though this is a full and fair explanation. 'Somebody's trained them.'

Trevor points out that pigs typically can be quite fierce.

Rob nods.

'I've had one attacked me on a moped,' he says, 'when I was going through the South of France. I was so drunk. The pig chased me. Wild boars.' Rob lets this final detail hang in the air for a second, then adds, because it is that kind of day, 'Like the Duran Duran song.'

* * *

The following week, he is at the house in Wiltshire, preparing for the first photo shoot of his return to public life. He sits having his make-up done in a Winnebago parked outside the helicopter hangar that is up the drive from the main house. (To be clear, Rob has no helicopter, and has no intentions or desires in that direction; this was why the house's previous owner built this shed. In years to come, the hangar will be used for band rehearsals.)

Rob is told he needs to get dressed.

'Hold on,' he says, as though everything is suddenly happening too quickly. 'It's been three years.'

Gently getting into the right mood, he turns to his hairdresser, Oliver Woods, generally known as Ollie.

'Have I ever told you about how I don't talk about myself much?' Rob says. 'I'll tell you now.'

In the afternoon, 3D from Massive Attack, Robert Del Naja, who is friends with someone on the shoot, drops by. He and Rob haven't seen each other since 1995, and 3D says he was worried that Rob associated him with lost time.

'I've had two trips to rehab since then,' Rob says.

'We did get a bit battered …' 3D acknowledges.

They share notes about their forthcoming records. 3D mentions that Elbow's Guy Garvey is on their album.

'He's absolutely kicked me in the head fifty times, but I love them,' says Rob.

Rob asks 3D what he is calling the new album. He replies that he doesn't know yet, and returns the question.

'*Reality Killed The Video Star*,' says Rob.

'Really?' says 3D.

This title, *Reality Killed The Video Star*, comes from a sad song Rob wrote some time back, but never released, about a teenage girlfriend from Stoke who he met up with years later in Los Angeles. He's been vacillating about whether it's the right title. He thought of a few. Later tonight, Rob will open his computer and read me a list of the other contenders he considered, with varying degrees of seriousness: *Il Protagonista* (long his preference until he bowed to the consensus that it was 'too pretentious'), *The Protagonist, Let Me Underwhelm You, The Very Best Of Luke Moody, Singing And What Have You, Me Singing* ('a definite contender for a while'), *Robbie Williams and the Cock Of Justice* ('Harry Potter theme,' he helpfully explains), *Politebox, Give Him Another Chance, Look Don't Make Me Beg, Hop On, Look Just Let Go, Girlfriend In A Korma, Brunch, Captain Starlet, I Love You* ('I wouldn't be taking the piss – I'm not mostly taking the piss, and that wouldn't be taking the piss at all. "I love you" – it's a nice positive thing to say'), *The One Who Done Angels, The Demos Were Better, The End Is Nine* and *The Very Best Of Roger Whittaker.*

* * *

As his comeback nears – and I suppose this album really is a comeback, though Rob will soon learn that once you are past a certain point in a pop music career, *every* album you release for the rest of your life will be greeted as 'a comeback album' – he says to me that increasingly one of his motivations for coming back is to redress the false narratives that have blown up in his absence. Just because you withdraw from public life and withdraw your participation from being defined by the outside world, it doesn't stop that world from continuing to define you. And the world has been mischievously busy.

'There's a lot of untruths out there and it bothers me. I wish it didn't, but …' – a wry laugh – '… I am a fucking celebrity, emotionally unhinged. Everybody's "don't listen to it, don't feed into it …" I do. And it bothers me. Tremendously. When they say how badly *Rudebox* did, how badly I did, how I'm desperate to be in Take That, all of those things – it bothers me. But also, in a weird way, has given me the petrol to come back and sort it out.'

That aside, he says that he's realised that what he wants back is not the fame, but the success. In an ideal world he'd like to be less famous but more successful.

'It's success, not fame, that is quite addictive. As you know I am addicted to a lot of things. And as it happens, success is one of them.'

* * *

Later that week, back up in London at the studio, Rob has a disturbing conversation. He has become friendly with Clive Black, a former record company executive who is managing Trevor Horn. They sit down one evening in Black's office, and, as Rob sees it, Black feels the need to share some home truths. He clearly sees Rob as facing a kind of creative crisis, and uses Rod Stewart as a comparison. Rob explains what happens:

'He said, "Well, Robbie, you know why Rod Stewart stopped writing songs? Because his diary started being shit. He used to have a great diary – he used to go round shagging birds, drinking, tearing up the place, and then all of a sudden he's married, he's got kids, the diary's boring. He gets other people to write his songs. Your diary's got boring. Right?" And he went off on this whole … completely destroyed me. You know, "The trick is knowing what your audience wants …" I think he thought that I'd like to hear the truth because nobody else tells me the truth.'

After Rob leaves his office, he cries.

'I cried because I thought it was true,' he says. 'I was crushed.'

And then he thinks about it some more and decides that what Clive Black has said is really daft.

* * *

On his computer, down in the windowless room, Rob reads something on AboveTopSecret that he likes.

'There's a nice thread called "They mapped the stars and the moon … and we call them cavemen?"' he says out loud, as much to himself as anyone else.

The thread is about the prehistoric astronomy that some researchers believe they can discern in French cave paintings, but Rob's mind is already analysing and repurposing.

'Good little lyric,' he mutters to himself.

* * *

Ayda arrives at the studio, and he shares his latest idea with her.

'I think I'll get a tattoo that just says "tattoo",' he says.

She is encouraging – if only, perhaps, because she judges the danger level here to be low.

'But you should misspell it,' she suggests.

'With one "t",' he agrees. 'I'll do that.'

She nods and smiles, reasonably safe in the knowledge that this will never happen.

* * *

Trevor asks Rob upstairs to work on 'Morning Sun'. This song was originally written by his four usual Stoke collaborators, but there has been a lot of going back and forth, trying to find a lyric Rob feels comfortable with and can relate to. His first breakthrough was to realise that it could be about depression, and for a while the lyric mentioned a Mr McCarren, who was Rob's religious education teacher when he was at school.

But Rob's still not happy with it, and this week he's been working on the lyrics with, ironically, Clive Black's father, who is the legendary lyricist Don Black. (Among the many famous songs Don Black wrote the lyrics to: 'Diamonds Are Forever', 'Born Free', 'Ben'.) Now Trevor wants Rob to sing some of these latest lyrics, so he does so:

Gifts from God, that's what they are
Shine for the lost and loneliest
The one who can't get over it …

I always wanted more from life
But you didn't have the appetite.

But he still keeps changing words and lines. Something's nagging him; it still doesn't feel quite right.

The following week, he and Ayda go to the Bahamas on holiday with some friends and his father. He's on a jet ski when his friend receives a text: Michael Jackson is dead. Rob's immediate reaction – perhaps understandably, as someone who people have also recently announced as dead – was that it'll be some kind of mistake or hoax. But then they discover that it's true.

While Rob knew what Michael Jackson had done in his life had been amazing, he didn't have a particularly strong or deep connection to his music. But he realises that he strongly relates in a different way.

'It hit me about prescription medication, and where I've been. And how close I must have come to being in the same place. And that scared me. And then I started thinking about his kids, started thinking about the other Jacksons, and then just became sad for him, about where his life had taken him, what he'd done to himself, how people had allowed him to be that way. Thought about myself on tours, knowing what he's been through, knowing that he didn't really want to do them. Just a few parallels …'

After the holiday, he goes back into the studio, and when he returns to 'Morning Sun' – … *after the long and sleepless night, how many stars would you give to the moon?* – he finally begins to understand his own song.

'I just pictured him awake, not being able to sleep because of the opiates,' says Rob. 'Then I understood what the song was about.'

He and Don Black work some more to bring it into this new focus:

You always wanted more than life
But now you don't have the appetite
In a message to the troubadour
The world don't love you anymore
Tell me how do you rate the morning sun?
Stuck inside the rainbow years

And you could happen to me
Cause I've been close to where you are
I drove to places you have seen
It all seems so familiar
Like they've been sent to kill ya.

When I ask him a few weeks later what the song really now says, he first answers, simply, 'don't do drugs'. But then he elaborates, and talks about the final verse, which begins like this:

How do you rate the morning sun
It's just too heavy for me
And all I wanted was the world
If you are the starlet in the sun
Don't go wasting your time
Cause there is no finish line.

'I think the last verse,' he says, 'it's just about the bollocks of show business. About how you think it means this when you go into it, and it doesn't at all. And the further and further you go down the tracks into your career, the less it all means. Also, spending a bit of time on the planet, notching up a few years between the start of my career and now, it's kind of me looking back and going, fucking hell, where did all that time go? What happened? I still feel twenty-three. Nothing's changed. Everything's changed. It's confusing.'

So, I ask, the moral is 'don't go into show business'?

'No. And yes.'

* * *

In Barbados, there was something else that Rob saw clearly for the first time.

One evening, he was listening to his father. The way his father was speaking was the way he had spoken throughout Rob's life, but only now did it really click: what his father's words really meant, and the effect these words had had on an impressionable son. Not just the language and the way of looking at the world that they taught Rob, but a whole universe of awe and ambition and desire.

'My dad was talking about Matt Monro again,' Rob explains to me, 'and my dad would talk about all these people that he admired like they were gods – like they'd arrived on chariots from the gods. Frank Sinatra was his Jesus. Matt Monro, the same way. And what's his name from *Marathon Man*? Laurence Olivier. The way he'd talk about these people were like they were gods on earth. And in some way that went into my DNA and impressed upon me about what it meant to be those people. And it must have gone an awful long way in a very young me, into: "Oh my God, how magical to *be* those people." It must have done so much for me to want to be that. I would say it would probably be the biggest driving force of my career.'

If you took that on board at that age, what did you think that feeling would be like if you could ever manage to make that leap onto that chariot?

'Just watching *Parkinson* when you're growing up, and hanging on every word that these people said, and the free rein that these people were given to be amazing – you just wanted to be amazing like those people. You only see pictures, and movies, and interviews. Parties – you see a picture of a party that was shit, it looks amazing in a photograph.'

Which is quite a good description of a certain part of being famous.

'Yeah. It all looks amazing in a photograph.'

Rob describes exactly how his father spoke of Matt Monro as they sat there in the Bahamas: '"He'd be singing, Matt, and there'd be people *talking* … and I'd be dead frustrated with them. *Don't you know what's in front of you? Can't you see what's in front of you?*" My dad would be talking like that. And that was when it clicked. Matt Monro's amazing and he's got an amazing voice and he's sung some amazing songs, but he's just a singer, and he's from London. He's a singing guy from London. I'm a singing guy from Stoke-on-Trent. With all the real normal everyday-life stuff that goes with it. You know, Frank Sinatra did a lot of amazing things on the screen and sang a lot of songs – didn't connect with any of them myself because he scared me as a man. I connect more with Dean

Martin because I genuinely think he didn't give a fuck. And all of his songs are more about not giving a fuck. But you know, they're all just *people*. In extraordinary circumstances. But the time when my dad was growing up, it was a less cynical world.'

Do you think it was a good or a bad thing that your dad instilled that in you?

'I don't know, because I didn't live a life another way. I don't know. My life is fucking absolutely incredibly amazing … on a certain level.'

And are you thinking that if your dad had been more level-headed in his admiration, you probably wouldn't have done any of this?

'Probably not.'

That's a weird thought, isn't it?

'Yeah.'

* * *

In early September, I watch as Rob does two days of interviews to kick off the promotion of *Reality Killed The Video Star* and its first single, 'Bodies'. When it comes to talking like this, the rust loosens fairly quickly.

He tells Hong Kong, who ask about the new album: 'You know, it's just, it's normal fare for me. It's me going, "Oh, I don't like me very much." And then there's other songs going, "I love me!" Pretty standard Robbie Williams stuff …'

He tells Denmark, who ask about how he does what he does: 'Ego happens in many different ways to many different people. Mine is an act. There's always a very fragile, unconfident, fat thirteen-year-old beneath the skin … And I think that fat thirteen-year-old is in everybody.'

He tells Belgium, who ask about his recent retirement: 'I was, "I'm done with this business!" I just needed some sleep and a cuddle.'

He tells Italy, who ask whether he thinks Jesus exists: 'I really don't know. I wouldn't say no. I've got a tattoo of him on my forearm. I'm a big fan of Jesus, whether he existed or not. I'm a big fan of Superman, and he didn't exist.'

He tells Ireland, who ask about his poker-playing style: 'Robbie "all in" Williams. Does that answer your question? I never fucking win, but I am all in.'

He tells Argentina, who ask what he wishes for in order to live in a better world: 'They could invent a calorie-free doughnut. That would make the world a better place. It would for me. Calorie-free cake that *tastes* like it's full of calories. I know you probably want "an end to war", and "an end to suffering", "an end to violence", but you can keep that. Just give me cake that doesn't make you fat.'

He tells Brazil, who ask about God: 'But where I'm at with all of that stuff at the minute is: I'm an atheist until the shit hits the fan, and then I'll be on my knees quicker than anyone else.'

He tells Mexico, who ask about the disadvantages of being famous: 'They're only disadvantages if you view them as such. And I tend to view them as such.'

* * *

And then he finally has to perform.

The X Factor performance of 'Bodies' is scheduled as the first big piece of TV promotion to showcase Robbie Williams' return from the wilderness. Rob is already anxious, and he has a full wobble a few days before. 'I just crumpled,' he says. 'It just hits you like a shovel round the back of the head, and I don't know why. And your girlfriend has to spend the next twenty-four hours going "it's OK".'

At the centre of his worries is a fear that he simply won't be able to do what he used to do. He already picked up the sense that performing might not feel as instinctive as it used to when he went to make the 'Bodies' video in the Mojave desert and found himself trying to dance on the wing of an abandoned plane. He replays the dialogue in his head between himself and his limbs: 'What do you *do*? ... Point! And then do this! And do a spin ... Do a spin, that always looks good ... then put your hands on your chest ... do this ... now kneel down ... now kneel down and do this to the camera ... do this, like you've seen Jay-Z do ...'

It all felt very unnatural. 'People say it's like riding a bike,' he summarises. 'It wasn't.' He's even been coming up with odd theories about why this might be, wondering whether it's because his performances were driven by sex and, now he has a girlfriend, that need has receded. But he doesn't really believe that. 'I wish I had some kind of answer,' he says, 'just so I knew what it was.'

The night before the show, he's rattled enough that he keeps putting off visiting a friend who has suffered a recent bereavement, and in the end decides he can't face going at all. (The friend will respond with an email noting that it is quite obvious that Rob has relapsed.) But the day itself begins perfectly calmly. At the London flat where he and Ayda currently stay when he is in town, he eats some lunch – ribs from a Sainsbury's bag then some chicken breast dipped into a bowl of salad cream – while his father shows him some aerial photographs of where he grew up from a pullout in a local Stoke paper. Mid-afternoon, a van takes him to the studio in Wembley where *The X Factor* is filmed. He watches Alexandra Burke rehearse then chats with her and Dermot O'Leary. Back in the dressing room he reads one of the tabloids while singing 'Bodies' to himself – then, bizarrely, morphs it into Elton John's 'Don't Go Breaking My Heart'. He says he's feeling better and calmer. When he goes to the stage to rehearse, during the first run-through he just feels his way into the song, but by the second he has worked out what he is doing, and has some graceful moves loosely choreographed. By the third and final run-through he seems to know what his plan is. It looks good: very controlled and composed.

'It's like Pandora's box,' his father observes, watching with evident pride. 'It's all come out to play. Just like all our yesterdays.'

'I was just doing an impression of what I used to do,' Rob explains back in the dressing room. But he'll add later that inside he was still worried: 'I felt as though it had left me: the language, the binary code of projecting charisma had gone. It's Superman when he went to the diner and he'd given up superpowers to go and be in love with Lois Lane, and at the truck stop that guy punched him and he was bleeding for the first time. I'm not painting myself as Superman, but …'

Afterwards, when all the judgement is raining down upon him, people will talk as though beforehand he must have been raging around backstage like a hyperactive, pumped-up madman. That couldn't be further from the truth. Once he has rehearsed, he goes to have a chat with Simon Cowell, then sits in the dressing room and discusses future home renovations, then picks at a plate of sushi and discusses clothing options for the show. Harry Hill's *TV Burp* plays on the dressing room TV. He shaves, and nicks himself, then sits down, shirtless, and makes some phone calls, inviting people to a quiz night he's holding at the flat tomorrow evening, then sings a bit of 'Moon River', then walks around, smoking, drinking coffee, half watching *Family Fortunes*. Then he goes into the corridor and chats with some of the *X Factor* contestants, telling the young Jedward twins not to read the bad things being written about them in the newspapers. 'I believed anything they said about me,' he tells them. 'It fucked my head in.' Then the contestants start queuing for his autograph, and to have their photo taken with him. Back in the dressing room, he changes his socks. The atmosphere is calm and friendly; his mood and demeanour about as far from the one some people will come to imagine. When he's just about ready to leave for the stage, Ayda kisses him on the cheek – his make-up has to be quickly retouched – and his father says, 'Go get 'em, youth.'

Behind the *X Factor* set, just before he's about to make his entrance, the father of one of the contestants, a young Essex singer called Olly Murs, comes up to him and says to him, 'Don't forget the words!' It's just a friendly quip, but it unnerves him, and starts up a disconcerting chant in his head: *I'm gonna forget the words, I'm gonna forget the words, I'm gonna forget the words*. He stands behind a screen as he is announced, waiting, and when the song's hymnal introduction begins – the part that sounds like a Gregorian chant, but is actually just him in a recording studio making a stream of nonsense words sound like a Gregorian chant – the screen is supposed to split open to reveal him, and to open up his way to the stage. Just like it did in the rehearsal. So he waits, singing the theme tune from *Rocky* over and over in his head to give himself confidence. And waits. The dirty bass line starts up, the audience roar ... and the screen stays closed.

Eventually, Rob has to force the screen open by hand. But it breaks whatever composure he had, and throws off everything that he had worked out in his head. 'I had a whole pose planned and whatnot,' he'll explain, 'but that went out of the window.'

And now he's into the performance, the one that Guy Chambers will later call 'weird'. In a way, even if Guy would have been wise not to bring it up, that description is fairly accurate. It's not that Rob sings terribly, or as if anything else is so terrible. It is just oddly ill-judged, and inappropriate for the circumstance. Perhaps because he was rattled, and already nervous, he seems to overcompensate by making every aspect of his performance bigger: this is more the performance of someone doing a breathless celebratory encore in a stadium than of a new single in a TV studio. He actually breaks off from the lyric nine times to address the audience: 'How you doing? ... What a pleasure, what a pleasure ... Let's hear it! ... Evening! ... You look beautiful tonight! ... Yeaaaahhhh! ... Wow! ... Let's see everybody! ... It's good to be back!' And though the studio audience responds to each invocation, seemingly in tune with what he's doing, the impression watching it on TV is that something is uncomfortably askew.

In the post-song interview with Dermot O'Leary, Rob seems even more overexcited: 'Yeah, I loved it! *Loved* it! Great audience. What a fantastic audience. Thank you ... It's great! I love it! Love it! Thank you very, very much! Made up!' The gratitude seems real, but sort of super-sized, exactly the sort of manic Robbie Williams overeagerness that can polarise people. And, as is often the case when he is extremely pumped up, his facial expressions are exaggerated, and his eyes at times look as though they are popping out of his head. You can see why people will, not for the last time, imagine all kinds of nefarious reasons for this, and how they simply wouldn't be able to believe how low-key and reserved he was beforehand. And even though he's still a little frenzied after, as though he needs to do a few more songs to discharge everything that's built up inside him, he soon settles down.

'It felt really cool,' he says.

There's no sense yet of how this appearance will be received. When he gets home – after his car runs over a paparazzo leaving a studio, a whole other negative press cycle to come – he writes a blog on his website detailing the day's adventures and what felt like its triumphant climax.

… It all felt so electric … Like 3 years of anxiety leaving my body. So happy right now …

* * *

What's wrong with wild-eyed Robbie? blares the front page of the *Daily Mail* with touching concern. Nobody's theory is that, through a combination of nerves and rustiness, he might have just got it a bit wrong, like a plane coming in too fast that misses the runway. It's either that he has been wheeled out onstage in an unfit state by conniving puppeteers, or that he has clearly relapsed on drugs, or both. (The second possibility is fresh in people's minds; his latest interview made the front page of *The Sun* earlier that week – *ROBBIE: I WAS 24HRS FROM DEATH ON DRUGS*.)

Never mind that the performance really wasn't all that different from hundreds he has been praised for in the past. In the days that follow, the papers simply keep reprinting the same photo – eyes wide if not wild – and the same insinuations.

As though repetition can make anything true – and, these days, usually does.

* * *

Rob didn't watch the performance back then, and he hasn't watched it to this day. But he can remember it. 'There was an outpouring of love,' he says, 'and then I just … didn't think I was enough. So I tried to go too big.'

It took him a short while to realise how people were talking about it. He instinctively expects people, especially in Britain, to be disparaging about what he does, but suddenly they were all saying the same thing. 'Every single one of them started with "after the disastrous performance on *The X*

179

Factor …" And I was, "Wow, I didn't even know that it was bad." It kind of caught up a head of steam, overshadowed everything.'

All the reasons he had stayed away so long came rushing back.

'I thought I was crazy,' he says. 'I'd just been on the television and embarrassed myself in front of the world, it seemed, and my worst fears were true: I'd forgotten how to do it. Which instantly made me want to back away from doing any of the promo that was coming up. You know, my worst fears had come true. Here I was back in the place of work where I'd got so ill last time, but now not only that, I'm back, I'm still ill and the mask that I use is broken. That coupled with the fact that I wasn't a hundred per cent confident about coming back and placing myself in the lion's mouth. And whatever that entails. The brittle ego that I have, or the huge sensitivity to any sort of criticism or hatred – my self-loathing's enough without anybody else joining in.'

He called a meeting with his management and told them that he wanted to cancel everything.

'It wasn't even to do with *The X Factor*,' he says. 'I just felt so overwhelmed with everything and so sort of powerless and energy-less and scared. It all kind of felt a bit futile.'

* * *

He relented, of course.

'There was still some part of me,' he says, 'that didn't want to fuck it up completely for myself.'

So he went ahead, and he did what needed to be done, though when he looks back now it's with the sense that he never really gave *Reality Killed The Video Star* the chance it deserved. 'I didn't want to communicate that I wasn't bothered,' he reflects, 'so I turned up and did some half-arsed stuff and communicated that anyway. I regret that.' Partly, he says, his mind was elsewhere: 'I wanted to be in Take That. Or at least I didn't want to be Robbie Williams.' And partly, after such an intense self-imposed exile, he had underestimated how long it would take to relearn to be himself.

'I didn't know how to do it,' he says. 'Getting back onstage, it just felt weird and clumpy, and I didn't know what I was doing. It took me years, especially onstage, to adjust back, and feel my hands with … "oh yeah, I do this, and then I start to walk …" I got back on the bike, and the bike felt a bit wobbly. It took me a long time to make the bike function again.'

What happened then, he carries with him as a warning for the future: he now knows that if he embraces his hermit tendencies for too long, there'll be this price to pay.

'I think I've been terrified of stopping ever since.'

* * *

July 2011

An extract from a question and answer session on the Robbie Williams website:

I have an important question for you! I really admire you when you're onstage! You seem not to be worried about anything. I am singer (in my town) and I love performing but I've got stagefright before an exhibition … and when I look at you, you're exactly as I'd like to be. Tell me your secret. What can I do to be more relaxed and confident?

With love, Annalisa.

THIS IS A TOUGH ONE …

AND IT'S ONE THAT YOU HAVE TO HAVE CONSTANT VIGILANCE WITH …

YOU CAN LOSE ALL THE TIME IN WORLD WORRYING ABOUT THIS SHIT …

I LOST 20 YEARS … DON'T DO THE SAME … YOU DON'T HAVE TO.

'MY VOICE IS NOT GOOD ENOUGH' 'I DON'T KNOW WHAT TO SAY' 'I DON'T KNOW HOW TO BEHAVE' … 'I'M NOT GOOD ENOUGH, I'M NOT GOOD ENOUGH, I'M NOT GOOD ENOUGH' 'I'M FAT' 'I'M UGLY' 'I'M STUPID'

I'VE BEEN THERE TOO MANY TIMES.

REVEAL

WHATEVER YOU THINK YOU ARE ... THAT IS WHAT YOU'LL BE ...

YOU HAVE TO CENTRE YOURSELF DAYS, WEEKS, MONTHS BEFORE THE PERFORMANCE ...

INNATELY IT IS IN ALL OF US TO CLIMB EVEREST ... TO STEP FOOT ON THE MOON ...

TO MOVE 80 THOUSAND PEOPLE WITH ONE WORD ...

TO DO WHATEVER THE FUCK WE WANT ...

IT'S NOT FOR THE SPECIAL FEW THAT HAVE BEEN TOUCHED BY THE MAGIC UNICORN ... IT'S IN ALL OF US ...

IF I HAD FOLLOWED THE RULES AND LISTENED TO 'PEOPLE' I WOULDN'T HAVE GOTTEN ANYWHERE ...

I'M FROM STOKE-ON-TRENT. I HAVE NO QUALIFICATIONS, I DIDN'T COME FROM MONEY. I DIDN'T GO TO STAGE SCHOOL, I DIDN'T HAVE ANY TRAINING TO BE A SINGER.

I REALLY DIDN'T HAVE ANY SPECIAL TALENTS ... I DIDN'T EXCEL IN ANYTHING ...

BUT I, LIKE EVERYBODY READING THIS, HAVE 'THE LIGHT'

ONLY YOU CAN PLUG INTO YOUR OWN ...

'YOU' HAVE TO FIND IT ... I CAN'T FIND IT FOR YOU ... NEITHER CAN YOUR FAMILY

OR YOUR AUDIENCE ... LIKE I SAY 'YOU' HAVE TO FIND IT. BE OPEN TO THE POSSIBILITY THAT IT'S THERE ...

FEELINGS SLIP AND SLIDE. WHAT YOU'VE EATEN THAT DAY AND HOW MUCH SLEEP YOU'VE HAD WILL HAVE AN EFFECT ...

BUT KNOW THIS ... AND REALLY DO KNOW THIS ...

YOU ARE AN IMMOVABLE FORCE WITH MAGIC AT YOUR FINGERTIPS ...

IT'S NOW YOUR CHOICE HOW YOU USE THAT MAGIC ...

IF YOU'RE READING THIS AND THINKING: BUT IT'S ONLY ME AND I'M NOT BIG ENOUGH OR GOOD ENOUGH TO ACHIEVE ...

THEN THAT'S EXACTLY WHAT YOU'LL GET ...

LIVE IN THE LIGHT OR LIVE IN THE DARK ...

YOU CHOOSE ...

* * *

July–September 2012

He has an album on the way, and a baby.

The album has had a complicated genesis. Originally, it was to have been centred around songs written with Gary Barlow. Even that idea sprung from an earlier one – in 2010, before the five-piece Take That reunion was even announced, Rob had a half-formed plan that Take That's *Progress* might be followed by a Robbie Williams and Gary Barlow project which would involve them also playing concerts together; songs were already being earmarked for that. (One day back then he even told me he'd had an idea to call their joint album *Cain and Abel* 'because Gaz said that in his book: "maybe me and Rob are the Cain and Abel of Take That"', though soon after he withdrew the idea: 'I read the story about Cain and Abel and I was like, "No way!" Who would be who? I'm not being Abel!')

That joint Rob-and-Gary project evolved into a new Robbie Williams album. 'Gaz came over and stayed at my house,' says Rob, 'and his mum came over, and we played, and got to be fourteen. And thrashed out a load of songs together and enjoyed each other's company. We just spent all day laughing about what we can and cannot say, and shit ideas, and good ideas, and shit ideas that might be good but aren't, and then we crossed them off the list and then started again on something else. Spent all day giggling and trying to come up with a song that might resonate with a lot of people.'

This album, a modern middle-of-the-road pop record, was actually recorded. But then Rob's plans were derailed by a chance meeting that his brother-in-law, Dylan Trussell, had. Dylan and his friend Dave Dinetz are filmmakers, but at the time they also had a scabrous rap group called The Connects. Rob, who often already liked what The Connects did, suddenly noticed that their music had become, as he puts it, 'forty per cent better'. They explained that they were working with these young Australians, Tim Metcalfe and Flynn Francis, who they'd met in a Los Angeles bar. Rob suggested he'd like to meet them, and they came up to the house.

'All of a sudden I've got these guys in the studio and we're vibing and we're buzzing and we're writing song after song,' says Rob. 'I think we wrote fourteen songs in ten days. That's only happened on the first album, *Life Thru A Lens*, with Guy – that took ten days to write the whole album.' Rob felt re-inspired in a different way. 'They breathed youth into the situation, and naivety, and hope, and talent. And they have got pop running through their fingers.' The Gary album was set aside. 'We made a great record together but it sounded like older guys. I just think I was aware of the impending process of my age, just getting older as a pop star, and worried about it, and I wanted it to be totally right. Tim and Flynn were young and vibrant. And I just thought, hang on a minute, perhaps I'm missing a trick.'

Some of the cancelled album's songs would later be used in Gary Barlow's solo career. One, 'Wedding Bells', would reappear on *Swings Both Ways*. But Rob did carry forward two of the songs for his new album: a powerful ballad, 'Different', and an out-and-out pop song called 'Candy'.

* * *

The baby's genesis had been, in the obvious ways, simpler. But it had taken some time for Rob to feel he might be ready to take this step.

'I was steadfast with my "no kids" rule,' he says. 'I'd concretely decided that I wasn't going to have any children, and I thought that was a sane thing to think: "Look how unable I am to cope with the world." I thought it would be insane to add a child to that mix, because I know how important it is to give them love and support, and I couldn't do that for myself. So I thought I was making a sane choice by not. But it was something that Ayda wanted, and I love her. And so it was a problem. For us both.' Eventually, he agreed, and was happy to. But as the birth approaches he says he's still apprehensive. 'There's been ups and downs in my mind: 'Oh shit ... oh shit ... oh what the fuck is this?' Lingering doubts about fatherhood, and what it meant. I'm just scared.'

* * *

'Hello, lovely,' says Rob, 'how are you?'

Rob is in his home studio in Los Angeles. On the wall behind him is an artwork by David Shrigley with the words IT IS MY DUTY TO REPRESENT THE WORLD AS I SEE IT. The man on the phone, who has just come offstage in Germany, is Elton John. Rob has been trying to get in touch with him because he has something to ask, but first they chat. I can only hear Rob's side of the conversation.

'A hundred and fifty-three gigs this year? ... Jeez ... How long did you do tonight? Three hours? ... Fucking hell ... Congratulations, number one album this week ... Fucking amazing ... Oh, by the way, I didn't tell you at the Queen's thing, I bet they got lost, but we sent you some pyjamas at Christmas ... Did you get them? ... Oh, that was probably us!'

Then he gets to the matter in hand.

'So I had this idea that other day ... I've got this song, it's called "Candy", and it's as much of a fucking hit that I've ever had. It's so poppy and it's so up and the chorus is big, and it's whimsical, deh deh deh deh. So I sent the song out to a few video people and they've come back with ideas that were expensive and not very interesting. And I was lying in bed with the missus the other day and we were thinking about using the budget just to rent a fucking great big boat and have a nice time! Instead! And then I was, "Well, I can't do that, because there's no ideas on a fucking boat." And then she was like, "What about the South of France?" And I was, "Ooh, South of France, Elton did a video there, 'I'm Still Standing'." Then I played "Candy" over the "I'm Still Standing" video and it fits, I think, perfectly. My idea is to remake your video.'

He clearly gets some kind of assent, and Elton also seems to pick up on Rob's conviction that he has a big hit ready to go.

'I think it is ... I think it is ... and fuck do I need one, and do I want one. I'm so engaged with this album, I so want it to be fucking successful. I've had my head up my arse for the last fucking eight years, it would seem. But I am back, and want it all again.'

He listens for a while.

'Ah, bless you … Oh, I'm going to have a ball … It does seem like happy-ever-after time right now, it really does. It's like: "Okay, this is who I am, this is where I am, this is what I'm doing, and I really like it. Let's go and enjoy it."' He listens some more. 'Yeah, we stop choosing things to have a problem with. And that's basically what I was doing.'

They say their goodbyes.

'God bless you, Elton, you're a lovely man … take care, darling … bye.'

Rob puts down the phone.

'Wrong number,' he says.

* * *

Rob and Elton have sometimes had a complicated relationship. They ended up having very different perspectives over what happened when Elton tried to help Rob at the beginning of his solo career when he was first facing up to his addictions, and a more recent odd moment came during the final leg of Rob's 2006 tour, when the wheels were coming off. By chance, he and Elton were staying in the same Australian hotel. It was when the four-piece Take That had just made their successful comeback. 'I'm trying to think if there was a part of me that wasn't pleased for them, and I can't recognise me having that,' says Rob. 'I was really pleased they'd had it away. The only problem that I'd got unresolved was Gary. But I was not going to bemoan Take That's success because I ultimately love them.'

Judging by the tone of the note that Elton sent to Rob's room, he clearly saw some other kind of narrative. The note said, as Rob remembers it:

Take That, number one album, number one single – funny how things work out. Elton.

But, since then, bridges have been successfully built. 'He's just the best ambassador for pop, isn't he?' says Rob today. He goes to the bathroom, and when he comes out he's singing Elton's 'Are You Ready For Love?' 'We're all dichotomies, I suppose. I don't know. He seems genuinely all heart.'

In the end it'll turn out to be too expensive, and too complicated, to remake Elton's video – and the pink-suited tomfoolery Rob films in Spitalfields instead seems to work surprisingly well – but Rob's grateful anyway.

* * *

A couple of years earlier, Rob had talked to me about him and smoking – its history, its future:

'I've been smoking since I was fifteen. The first one was with a friend, Philip Lindsay, walking from school – I think he had a B&H. And it was weird because it was like I was already a smoker and I was withdrawing and I just had to have a cigarette walking home from school. And so it started. First ones were B&H, then it was Embassy Number One, then it was Consulate and then it became Silk Cut. Now I smoke two packs a day but it can only really be deemed as one pack a day because I only smoke half a cigarette if that, each time. As you can see by the ashtray. The top bit's always the best. I've talked about stopping. I think I stopped for a week when I was about eighteen or nineteen. But then I had a drink, and drinking and smoking go together. I haven't really thought about stopping again up until last year – not this New Year gone, New Year before – and I gave up for a day, and then started again. I was depressed – really really depressed. Miserable.'

So for the foreseeable future, I asked him, you're happy to smoke?

'Yeah. But it's coming soon. The end's in sight for me and nicotine.'

That end came in March 2012, when he finally gave up what was now a three-pack-a-day habit. The simple reason was that Ayda was pregnant, he had a baby on the way, and he'd been told that he could only smoke outside. And the simple version of how he stopped is: he just did.

The longer version is that there were five weeks on patches, and there was some vaping, and he took Wellbutrin, 'and then I had about twenty-four hours where I didn't want a cigarette but I got really angry at fucking nothing'. And there was also that time when he was in Mexico and he'd forgotten his patches, and then watched the movie *Hanna*, and immediately wanted to punch its director, Joe Wright: 'I actually wanted to get on Twitter, see if I could find him, hunt him down.'

Nonetheless, when he got back from Mexico, the cravings were gone. 'And I haven't missed them since,' he says. 'I can be around people smoking.' He points out there's still 800 leftover cigarettes in his Los Angeles house, and it's not even a temptation. 'It's so weird. Because it was *me* – breathing, and cigarettes is what I did all day from when I woke up. It was what I did, it was what I was great at. And then I just wasn't bothered.'

* * *

In September, Rob does a tour of the same venues he played on his first solo tour of the UK. Their baby is due at around the same time. He will keep telling everyone that he has a special phone in his pocket, and a helicopter on standby, in case Ayda goes into labour. I see no evidence of either.

Backstage in Leeds, before the first show, he checks what people are saying about him online as he returns, and reads out an article on MSN News which says that he is no longer relevant:

But the thing with fantastic pop stars is they never quite know when enough is enough.

'The thing I'm taking out of that,' he says, 'is "fantastic pop star".'

* * *

Rob brandishes a syringe and plunges it into his leg. It's disconcerting to watch, but when you spend time around Rob you get weirdly used to it. For a while now, he has injected himself with testosterone twice a week. Last April, he was told that he had the testosterone levels of a 90-year-old man. This fixes that, and is something he credits with a huge positive change in his outlook and his energy levels.

'Life's just got better,' he says. 'I attack things with vigour ...'

Most people would leave it there. If there were also some less positive effects, they might keep these to themselves. But when you're the sharing kind, you share.

'… and I grow more hair in places you don't really need more hair. Like, I can plait my arse hair now.'

That image might be quite enough on its own, but it reminds him that he has something else to tell me.

'I had it waxed last night.'

I nod, not knowing quite where this is going.

'I filmed it.'

Backstage in this tiny and tatty Leeds dressing room, he shows me the video. In it, he is lying on the floor, face down, wearing a black t-shirt and nothing else. Gwen, his mother-in-law, is filming. Ayda and another woman are down near Rob's legs, studying the target area and discussing with great specificity how to approach the job at hand – 'the forest is going upwards,' Ayda comments at one point – and then they both apply waxing strips onto his arse. Finally they rip; Rob hollers.

'I think it's less sensitive on the cheeks itself,' he explains to me, filling in a few further details, 'but if they get to your Biffin's bridge, that's painful. They wandered down Biffin's bridge, by a corner, and …'

I believe there are almost certainly no other pop stars who will tell you this.

* * *

No helicopters, fictional or otherwise, are required. The tour finishes in Southend on 16 September. Teddy is born two days later.

'None of my fears came true,' he says. 'Something different happened that was quite incredible. Something just kicks in and you go, "I love you, I fucking love you, this is amazing." As soon as she was born, I felt genuine real … the realest of loves that you can ever feel. It was like, holy shit, I'm feeling ecstasy. I get it. And it was incredible, spiritual, cosmic, and I got to feel that way naturally in this lifetime – that was really cool.'

It's quite a change. By the time he's promoting his album, he'll be telling people: 'I've learned that maybe the fear of commitment was a bit bigger than it had to be. I've learned that maybe I don't know exactly what's good for me. I've learned that, as I always do every year, I worry about things that

I shouldn't worry about – everything's cool. I love being a dad, and I didn't know that I would. I thought it was some sort of prison sentence.'

Not that he handled every moment around the birth perfectly.

For one thing, he got a little distracted in the build-up: 'I just did the gas and air all the way through the labour. It was like when you go to the dentist and everything's nice. I must have done gas and air for a good six hours. Getting them to turn it up. And Ayda had to sort of wrestle it off me.'

And then after the birth, he had to go and do an interview with James Corden, and he felt incredibly tired so he went back to the house for a sleep. That mightn't have been so hard to understand, but when he returned to the hospital and Ayda asked where he'd been, somehow things were muddled enough in his head that he thought he'd better not say that he'd been home for a sleep.

So he told her he'd been to the gym.

* * *

He knew that Teddy was born with a bounty on her head. The first photo of her would be worth a lot of money, and people would be after it. And that made Rob think of all the years to come, all the frightening moments when the cameras and the cameramen would surround her, harass her, block her way. He'd heard a story about Shiloh, the daughter of Brad Pitt and Angelina Jolie, and how her school friends tease her for looking so miserable in photos, and how she'd retorted that of course she looks miserable, that she's really scared in those photos because there's all these big frightening grown-ups shouting her name.

So Rob's first thought was that, applying the same logic as they applied to their wedding, they should sell a baby picture. 'She might as well get her education paid for, and first car,' he reasoned. 'I think we should get something back in return, for my daughter being terrified.'

Then, he had second thoughts. She was going to get hounded anyway. And something didn't sit right with them about the idea. So he posed for a photo, shirtless, lying on his back, cradling Teddy on his chest – a tired, proud, smiling father and his daughter – and gave it away, for anyone who wanted to use it. 'Instead of having to hide her,' Rob says, 'I thought it would be best just to give it them for free – say, here it is, please leave us alone, Mommy's really tired and emotional, and Daddy's shit scared, so if you could leave us alone just to be getting on with this new experience in our lives, we'd really appreciate it.'

But we live in a world of complicated rules and codes, not all of them obvious, and not all of them obviously fair. Rob and Ayda would subsequently discover what they'd intended as some mixture of selfless sharing and generosity, and also as an act of protection, would be misconstrued as neither. They would learn that when celebrity parents fight for the privacy of their children, and for the right that their children's faces not be shown, one argument that can be used against them is any evidence that the celebrities have willingly put their children's faces in the public eye. In the months and years to come, when Rob would argue and plead with paparazzi not to take pictures of his children, sometimes they'd even come back with this argument: *But you posed for that photo.*

That's why, if you look at Ayda's Instagram feed today, you'll see many photos of Teddy and Charlie, enjoying their life, exploring, slowly growing up into the world. Some of the photos are so intimate, and the two young Williamses are pictured doing so many different kinds of things, that it could take you quite some time to realise what every single one of these photographs has in common: you never, ever see their faces.

* * *

October 2016

He is asked his earliest memory.

'I must have been about two,' he replies, 'and I remember *Happy Days* was on. And I was told I had to go to bed, and I wasn't too pleased. I can remember the credits to *Happy Days* rolling, and I remember being on Earth somewhere and I didn't know what it was. But I knew it was bedtime and I knew I didn't want to go.'

* * *

November 2012

His single 'Candy' is at number one. 'It's just like the old days,' he says. 'The credible press in England hate it, the tabloids love it, and the general public have made it number one … so it feels like 1998 again.'

He tells me that when he and Gary Barlow wrote 'Candy' – its music based, though this seems to pass most people by, around a trendy instrumental dance record by Norwegian DJ Todd Terje that Kelvin Andrews had played to Rob – Gary said to him, 'Fucking hell, you've written a happy song – that's not like you.'

You can see what Gary meant, superficially, but it's not quite that simple. And for all the success that the song is having, Rob is slightly put out that, perhaps misled by its jaunty nursery-rhyme cadence, people seem to assume that the lyrics are meaningless. Today in the car, as a dry run for a blog, he goes through the song, line by line, explaining exactly how it tells the tale of 'a girl called Candice who thinks she's the shit'. For instance:

Low self-esteem but vertigo.

'She thinks a lot of herself, but she doesn't really, because it comes from a place of insecurity.'

She thinks she's made of candy.

'You know that saying, if she was made of chocolate she'd eat herself?'

Ring a ring of roses.

'Which is the famous Black Death poem. So I'm saying, she's contagious, stay away from her.'

Whoever gets the closest.

'Whoever gets the closest to her will come away being affected by some sort of madness.'

Liberate your sons and daughters
The bush is high but in the hole there's water.

'I'm actually meaning: take time with your sons and daughters so they don't turn out like Candy. What you put in, you will get in return. It's hard work, but at the end of it you'll be rewarded. The bush is high – going through the bush with your machete. But in the hole there's water.'

And so on. His explanations only fall short with one couplet, and even that is reassuringly honest.

You can get some when they're giving
Nothing sacred but it's a living.

'That just is a few words that go into the chorus. That's nothingness, really.'

The weirdest aspect, though, about this song, which will spend four weeks at number one, is the chant that comes at the end of the song: *Do as you will shall be the whole of the law.* Because that is a quote from the notorious occultist Aleister Crowley.

Rob started reading some of Crowley's work around the time of the *Intensive Care* album, back when he was speaking with the comic book writer and magic practitioner Grant Morrison. Morrison and the artist Frank Quitely were responsible for the customised Tarot-like images and sigils on that album's sleeve, and Morrison has talked since about how he guided Rob into casting certain basic kinds of spells. Of Crowley, Rob says: 'I started reading Aleister Crowley stuff and then thought, this is too dark. Scary, dark … and I've always been scared of that sort of darkness, and I thought, well, I'll go to it and see what it is. And then I thought, even by reading this sort of stuff you're focusing an energy into it that may not be the best idea. So I stopped as soon as I started.'

By repute, the most famous Crowley authority in pop culture is the former Led Zeppelin guitarist Jimmy Page, who for many years owned Crowley's former Scottish home on Loch Ness. Rob mentions that he met Page not long ago. At first Page seemed friendly, and gave Rob a big smile.

'And I was, "Oh, I got into Aleister Crowley because of you." And he was, "I've got something to do."' He touched Rob on the arm by way of farewell, and moved off. 'He didn't want to talk about it. I don't know. Perhaps he's just sick of discussing it or explaining it.'

* * *

As Rob disembarks from his private jet in Rotterdam, the pilot asks him whether he's performing live here, or just appearing on telly.

Rob shrugs hopelessly, as though trying to convey that the probability of him knowing the answer to this question is so infinitesimal that he can't imagine why someone would waste even one of their lifetime's breaths in asking it.

'I turn up,' he says. 'They point me in the direction, I sing at the camera, I leave ...'

* * *

The first thing he doesn't know he's doing today is to be interviewed by a room of Dutch fans while a *Take The Crown* cake sits on the table in front of him.

The final question is from a woman who explains that, 15 years ago when Rob released his first solo single, a cover of George Michael's 'Freedom', and appeared on MTV in Cologne, she asked him the question 'are you happy?' She says that he replied 'yes', but that looking back it wasn't really true so she wants to ask again.

'Finish on a high note,' mutters one of Rob's entourage at the back of the room.

'Uh, I'll see you in fifteen years,' says Rob. 'You know, if you ask me on TV when I'm twenty-two, "Are you happy?" I'm not going to go, "Well, actually, no, I'm completely addicted to cocaine, and I'm having trouble with relationships with my family and poor self-esteem ..." Of course I'm going to lie. Am I happy now? I've never been happier. Your twenties are shit anyway. I think that when you leave home you sort of get spat out and you go, "How the fuck do I deal with this shit?" And then you spend your whole twenties going "Fuck ..." And I did it in public. And then I found that in my thirties shit got a bit more relaxed. I grew into myself a bit more. And also I had a sort of washing machine of being an addict in my twenties. I'm still an addict, but I'm better with it than I was then. It was completely and utterly out of control, I was trying to medicate my own depression. Back then there was moments of happiness but they were chemically induced.'

When Rob stops talking, the host says: 'You're the most honest world star I know.'

During the next interview he doesn't know he's doing, he's asked about marriage and children.

'I love it. I'm so pleased that I did both of those things. They're both the most rewarding things I've ever done.' Pause. 'Apart from being a huge successful pop star.' He laughs. 'Sorry.'

And then he explains that the longest he's yet been away from his daughter in these first two months is for a single night, as he is doing tonight, and it isn't easy.

In the van, a few minutes later, he calls Ayda.

'Any news?' he asks. 'Has Teddy said anything yet?'

He is next pointed in the direction of a TV interviewer who requires that he set a competition question.

'Who is the tallest member of Take That?' Rob suggests, and then supplies the answer.

'It's *me*! Everybody thinks it's Howard, but he's just very *lithe*. The upper part of my body is really big, and I have a massive head, so … I am the biggest. There's two at six foot, but I'm six foot one.' Pause. 'Mark's tiny.'

Driving to the airport – we're now flying to Holland – Rob has a question for everyone in this people carrier. 'Do you have weird dreams?' he asks. He offers his latest. 'I woke up yesterday making a list of nice people. Tom Hanks was one. Jimmy Carter was one. And then I was really struggling. Jimmy Carter just seemed like a really nice guy.' He laughs. 'And then I was in between dreaming and waking up this morning, and I said to Ayda, "What have I got in common with a scarecrow?" She went, "What?" And I said, "I'm outstanding in my field."'

At the end of the day, we fly to Denmark and Rob calls Ayda again, requesting further unrealistic updates.

'How's my daughter been today? Did she vogue? Does she know what she wants to be when she grows up yet?'

* * *

What's interesting about watching Rob on trips like this is that he can spend hours just doing what he needs to do, getting through the day with jokes and pop star patter, and then without warning – as though a man who was having a nice picnic on a mountainside suddenly jumped up and launched himself off a cliff edge on a hang-glider, the ground receding far below him – he'll start talking about something serious and deep and thoughtful, often at length. This next morning he is doing a Danish interview, and is yet to even indicate that he's particularly wide awake when the interviewer asks a fairly open and general question about whether Rob ever wonders when he comes offstage why he gets the response that he gets.

'I think I spend too much time thinking about that,' he replies. 'There's that saying that when you stare into the abyss the abyss stares back at you. If you try to figure it all out, you can dismantle your own brain, go into some sort of time-warp continuum. Because I don't get it at all. I know that I must have some sort of personality that radiates something that people are attracted to. I say that objectively outside of myself. I understand that. But I understand that there's a lot of people that hate me. That really fucking hate me. That *despise* me. I make people's skin crawl. So neither is to be taken too seriously. I adore the fact that people fucking love me and they smile and I make them happy, but also there's an awful lot of people that think I'm what's wrong with music, and all that kind of stuff. So I think it's important not to take either of them seriously, because if you took the positive seriously you would be an uncontrollable narcissist, and if you took the negative seriously you would be an uncontrollable depressive. And I'm trying to walk the line between the middle of them.'

Then the interviewer asks why he does what he does.

'I just think, like, if you're a horse in a field you're going to run in that field. Because you're a horse. That's what you do. If you're a kid in a sandbox, you're gonna play with the sand. It's what you do. It's what I do. I don't know anything else. Not that I'm the same sort of artist, but would you ask Neil Young? Why does he still do it? Because it's what he does. It's what I do. I enjoy doing it. It's a hobby but I get paid for my hobby. The creativity of trying to make a great album that touches people is a wonderful task and a poisoned chalice – perfect for me. I've got a private plane, when I get on it they bring me sushi and a coffee, and then I get off and I get tarmac access and I go to a TV show and show off for three and a half minutes on the TV, then everybody claps, and then I leave, and I get back on the private plane, and I get picked up and I get taken to my house, and then I watch the football. There's so many different reasons why I enjoy doing what I do – an awful lot of them are shallow, an awful lot of them are deep, an awful lot of them are meaningful, most are meaningless. I'm a very, very lucky man from a working-class town that nobody really leaves. I didn't have any qualifications. I was bound to go into the army, to be honest with you. Or the police force. Or be a drug dealer – one of those three things. But here I am, twenty-two years later, in Denmark, talking to you. So there's many wonderful reasons why I'm doing what I do. It's a wonderful life. It really is.'

* * *

As she sits down, the interviewer from *Politiken* describes her newspaper as 'the Danish version of *The Guardian*'; Rob immediately retorts, 'Oh, so you'll hate me then.' She wants to have an in-depth discussion about The Perfect Pop Song. Rob offers up some possible examples – 'Yesterday', 'You And Me Song' by The Wannadies. 'There She Goes' by The La's, 'Singing In The Rain', 'Somewhere Over The Rainbow'. 'When I Fall In Love'. She asks what such a song's topic should be. 'I would guess,' he replies, 'it would probably be want, need, longing, yearning, regret, sadness, hope, melancholy … all tied up in one little message. So incredibly simple but incredibly complex. All in one song. A mixture of melancholy, hope and sadness.'

And soon he is telling her about writing 'Feel'.

'Pop loves an extreme emotion, and pop loves big bold statements. And I was certainly having extreme emotions – the day I wrote that was probably the saddest of my life. But it would be not for any other reason than chemically something was happening to me. And it just felt like a prison – a very, very uncomfortable unpleasant place. You know, I couldn't abide life. So it came from deep pain, "Feel" did. What was special, if you term it special, was that it was from a place of very raw, very honest …' He recasts his thought. 'And also it's the simplicity of the chorus. *I just want to feel real love in the home that I live in.* Everybody feels that way. I think it was the right kind of mixture between simplicity … and there's a bit of smarts in there too, but not too much that it complicates stuff. There's the saying: write about what you know. And I do write about what I know. I don't know about much, but I know about how I feel.'

Ironically, that's one of the songs he has to sing later today on the Danish *Voice*, with a female contestant called Søs. The show has edited the song down to two and a half minutes, and so she now sings the lyric *before I fall in love, I can feel myself coming*, which apart from being surreal and weird is a mash-up of lines from different verses. Fame is also a great place to get honoured and dishonoured in the same breath. On programmes like this, your songs are mincemeat, and they fit wherever and however they're told to fit.

After, Rob rubs on some hand sanitiser. He mentions that he recently read a tweet saying 'the good thing about hygiene in hospitals is that everyone walks around like they're planning a dastardly plan'.

* * *

Take The Crown goes into the album charts at number one. The Williams family listen to the chart rundown together on Radio 1.

'I had a bit of a dance with Teddy,' he says. 'She's doing proper smiles now. She did one this morning … I think she knows I'm number one.'

* * *

Rob is playing three concerts in the round at London's O2 arena. Rehearsals are in a west London studio complex. Afterwards, Rob's car takes him back down the M40 towards town.

'It's always a grim introduction to London, this,' he says. 'Coming down from the north in Take That we always used to pass these houses, and they've not got any less grim. It's a pretty full-on road to live off. All that "it's grim up north" stuff – it's not much around here, is it?'

I ask him if he remembers the first time he came to London.

'I think it was on an anti-Thatcher march. My family were staunch socialists at the time: Auntie Jo, Uncle Don, my mum, my sister, me. On their shoulders, singing, "Maggie! Out! Maggie! Out! Maggie Maggie Maggie! Out out out!" I can't remember much, I just know that it happened. And I can remember being outside the Houses of Parliament. I would have been maybe three or four. I just loved joining in.'

He pauses, then laughs.

'I think my mum always voted conservative.'

Back at the house, Rob changes Teddy while half watching *The Young Apprentice* on TV.

'Is that the best nappy change you've ever had?' he asks his daughter. 'Number one nappy change?'

* * *

The next day Rob arrives at rehearsals early, and is annoyed to find that there are people everywhere.

'I'm not supposed to be here for another thirty-five minutes,' he points out. 'I came here to get away from everything. My wife was asleep. There was some very loud gardening next door. I'd expended the walking up and down stairs thing, I'd been asleep for long enough, and I thought that this room that we're all in now would be a nice place to get some peace. So I arrived here an hour early just to internet myself and to expand my mind about alien abduction. But …' – he says this looking resentfully around at all the people who are also already here – '… I myself have been abducted by show business.'

The obvious mistake he has made is to imagine that everyone else only turns up at the place he is going to at the time he is due.

Josie – Josie Cliff, the manager who will be with him day-to-day for many years until 2014, the role Michael now has – walks in, and Rob's exasperation overflows.

'Josie! I'm not supposed to be here for half an hour, so can everybody treat me as if I'm not here.'

He lets this request hang in the air for just a moment.

'Unless I ask for things,' he clarifies.

* * *

He's found a clip of the comedian Lee Mack's stand-up where Mack is taking the piss out of him:

'I wish someone would tell Robbie Williams that *this* doesn't constitute entertainment,' Mack says, and he pretends to be Rob doing an exaggerated slow self-satisfied walk, a lopsided smirk on his face. 'Look at me: smug as fuck,' Mack says. Then he ridicules the way Rob will hold the microphone to the audience – 'come on Glastonbury, you know this one' – encouraging them to sing the songs. 'Yeah, we know it, Robbie,' Mack continues. 'It was a hundred and fifty quid to get in. Any chance you could sing it for us?'

This isn't the kind of thing that he takes as a slight. Not at all. Rob finds this hilarious, and plays it for anyone who hasn't seen it.

As for the implicit criticism, he doesn't care. He performs his songs the way he does, because that's the way he means to do it. He understands perfectly well the argument that when he turns the song over to the audience something is lost – the opportunity to hear the artist sing every word of his song – but to his mind something far greater is created. He'll often dismissively refer to this tendency, getting the crowd to sing the chorus, as laziness, but don't be fooled. There are things that Rob isn't bothered about, and there are things that he doesn't take as seriously as other people often feel he should, but how best to communicate with and entertain and move a stadium full of people … that's not one of them. This is something he feels he can do in a way that few others can do, and it matters to him greatly. Just as he's astonished when people imagine he'll know exactly what he's going to be doing on a promo trip, he's just as astonished when people imagine he doesn't think through every tiny part of what he does when he's in front of an audience.

This is how he explains it:

'When I stop singing and get everyone to do choruses, I'm inviting them, rightly or wrongly, to have it be the biggest mass-karaoke session on the planet for that moment. People allude in a negative way to me leaving out stuff and making the audience sing, but that's part of me dragging the audience to a place that I'd like to feel as someone in the audience, to being allowed to do it. Maybe I'm wrong – maybe it's just me because I'm an entertainer or I'm an extroverted introvert, but I think that's what people really want to do. It feels as though we're in communion. It's spiritual and egomaniacal at the same time – it's for them, for me, for us. All of those things all at the same time. It's everything. It's religious, where I feel humbled and very, very small, and also massive and really, really big-headed. They show me the way and I guide them too.'

* * *

Rob is backstage at the 2012 Royal Variety Performance, where later this evening he will be singing in front of the Queen for the second time this year. In the summer he opened the Jubilee Concert at Buckingham Palace that was organised by Gary Barlow.

'Did I tell you I have a hair transplant?' he asks me.

'Only four weeks before he had a fucking photo shoot,' says David Enthoven.

No, I say, he hadn't mentioned this.

'Pre-emptive,' he says. 'I didn't even need it. I just got bored one day, and I was, "I'll have a hair transplant."'

'I tell you what, it didn't half look sore,' says David.

'Oh my God, it looked terrible,' says Ayda. 'It looked so scary.'

Did someone convince you to do it, or did you go looking for it?

'Looking for it,' he says. 'And fuck me, it's a big ordeal. There's a machine and it just takes out individual ones … It looked grimness, didn't it?'

'Rob in a bed, bleeding head,' says Josie.

'A thousand puncture marks,' says Rob.

'I can't remember, bar the day of going to rehab, seeing Rob look so miserable,' says Josie.

'It looked so bad,' says Ayda. 'So bad.'

'I really didn't know,' says Rob. He laughs.

'Amazing how much you can suffer for vanity,' says David.

'He lay down on his tummy for eight hours,' says Josie.

'Showbiz,' Rob sighs.

* * *

Rob has been avoiding celebrities all day, but not this one. He agrees, with some enthusiasm, to have his picture taken with the winner of the most recent series of *Britain's Got Talent*.

'Hello, Pudsey! Hello, Pudsey!' he says, as the performing dog is brought in by his trainer.

Rob asks whether Pudsey has been on a private jet yet, and is told he has.

'Has he *changed*?' Rob asks.

Josie and Ayda together try to post the photo of Rob and Pudsey online. They give the photo the caption 'we love Pudsey', but the text keeps autocorrecting to 'we love pussy'. Ayda, thank goodness, spots it just before she presses send.

* * *

Rob sings his latest single, 'Different', and then 'Mr Bojangles'. In between there's a comedy routine with David Walliams, at the end of which he says: 'Gary Barlow … OBE. Robbie Williams …' – and he looks up towards the royal box – '… *nothing*. You organise one birthday party …'

After, he is told he has to stay here so that he can take part in the end-of-show ritual where all of the performers line up to meet the Queen. 'Fuck me, it's so boring, waiting,' he complains. 'Haven't we waited enough for this year?' Eventually, he announces that he's going to try to find One Direction. Partly because he wants to see if they've been persuaded to hang around too.

'If they're gone,' he says, 'I'm going.'

'Robbie Williams!' he announces with fake pomposity as he walks into their dressing room. 'Just checking to make sure that you're here. Because if you are here then I'm staying for the line-up, but if you're not here I'm just going to go home. I'm fucking bored.'

'We're so bored,' says Niall, nodding.

So they chat. First they talk about video games, then Rob asks them who they fancy, and then they turn the same question back on him.

'My wife,' he says. 'Yeah. It's really fucking good. Don't be scared about having babies. In fifteen years' time though, boys.'

They ask him how fatherhood is,

'Fucking brilliant,' he tells them. 'Absolutely brilliant. I was absolutely shitting myself, I thought it was one of the biggest own goals I've ever scored, and I pretty much thought that life would be over for me. But it's completely enhanced it. I love it to bits. And don't – honestly, take this with you – if you find the right girl, and she's fucking great, when you're way into your thirties, towards the end, don't be scared about having a kid. It's brilliant.' He pauses. 'That's real talk,' he commentates, as though One Direction are no longer here. 'I did some real talk with the lads.'

After that, they talk about songwriters, and golf, and Rob asks which of them are learning instruments. When the answer seems to be that they're all learning the guitar, Rob chides: 'You can't do that – you'll be the Gypsy Kings.' Then he invites them over to play football when they come to Los Angeles. He also mentions the recent tabloid kerfuffle where one of One Direction's bodyguards sold his story. They all laugh knowingly, and say the bit they minded was when the bodyguard talked about them saying that they were 'bigger than The Beatles'.

'Yeah, but he also levelled it up by going "they're only joking",' says Rob, who clearly read the story quite closely. 'He didn't leave it going, you're saying "we're bigger than The Beatles, and we mean it". When you read it, you go: "Oh, they're obviously laughing in the van at themselves." We used to do that same thing.' He means in Take That. 'Gary actually believed we were, though,' he adds.

'Tell me some gossip before I go,' he says. 'I'm really fucking bored. Have you complained about waiting too long? Have you talked about maybe letting the Queen down?'

They all say no.

'Oh,' he says, in a knowing avuncular way, as though making a mental note, 'you're not there yet.'

* * *

'Sweet boys,' he says, back in the dressing room. Eventually Rob goes off to line up onstage, ready for the curtain call, where he's to stand next to Alicia Keys. The rest of us here with him are positioned in an ill-lit backstage side area, supposedly well out of the way, and so we're somewhat surprised to suddenly see the Queen and Prince Philip a few feet away, making their way past us. Prince Philip looks at us and comments, wryly, 'You guys are always standing in the dark.'

A few minutes later, we meet back up with Rob.

'You know, completely not what I thought she'd be,' says Rob. 'I prejudged.'

'The Queen?' says Josie.

'No!' he says. '*Alicia*. She's been here all day, she's done the dress rehearsals I didn't do, she did the curtain-call rehearsal I didn't do, and took me through everything: "Now you go here, now you do that, now you do that …" Bless Alicia Keys. What a sweetheart. What a darling.'

As for the Queen …

'The Queen,' says Rob, 'didn't know who I was. She said, "Were you the man that was on the wires?"' David Walliams came down on a wire at the beginning of the show. 'I thought, "I could have gone home."'

'What did you say when she said that?' Ayda asks.

'I said, "No, Ma'am, but I have been on them."'

'Then what did she say?'

'"It's a very difficult stage, isn't it?"'

Rob sensibly assumed she wasn't referring to his late thirties in general.

'I went, "Tonight it was a wonderful stage, Ma'am." That was it.'

There's one further detail.

'I gave the Duke of Edinburgh a Masonic handshake,' he says, 'just to see what would happen.'

And?

'Nothing. He mustn't be one then.'

* * *

By the time Rob gets to the O2, the tale of this curtain call, gently improved and embellished, has become part of his show.

'She hasn't got a frigging clue who I am,' he tells the audience. 'Not a frigging clue.' He describes the first encounter at Buckingham Palace – 'I met the Queen afterwards and she thought I was a member of Madness' – before describing their more recent rendezvous:

'... and then in the line-up afterwards, no shit, she thought I was Pudsey's trainer ...'

* * *

The O2 shows go extremely well – none of the occasional frailties that plague him turn up, and performing in the round seems to suit him. He seems in full command.

After the second night, Rob sits with his father at a table in the backstage hospitality. Pete seems particularly overcome by what he has just seen, and may have relaxed into a drink or two. I think the conversation that follows is at times slightly awkward for Rob – there's a fine line between fatherly pride and almost being starstruck – but there's something very honest and moving about it, too.

'I couldn't be any prouder,' Pete says. It takes him back to his days as a comedian. 'I was just saying to Robert, when I was working I used to work for four hundred people, five hundred, whatever. I've had a thousand. And I control them when I go onstage – that's what you do when you go onstage. You go on, and you control people, and you keep a grip on them. And I'm watching my son now do that to twenty thousand, forty thousand. From the *second* he walks on. Within two seconds of being there. And I'm watching him, I know what he's doing, I'm inside of his head, but when he walks on … that's what you do. You can't teach it. You can't teach it. You can watch it, you can learn … you can't teach charisma. There won't be another one – I don't think there'll be another one after him. I think this is the end of it all. We're not going to produce anybody from *X Factor* or bloody *Britain's Got Talent* to put forty thousand, fifty thousand in a field. That's never gonna happen. No individual is going to have that charisma. Because what he's got, you can't teach. If he turns right, it's because he *should* turn right. Not left. Because there's something inside says, "I'm going to go that way now." There's a muscle that says I'm going to smile over there, or growl over there at this moment in time. Or look whatever I'm going to look. And because that's what's inside here. That's what you do when you're a pro.'

I ask Pete when he first noticed that Rob had that.

'Tonight, about half past nine,' he fires back, then gives the real answer. 'I'll tell you something – when he was the Artful Dodger in *Oliver!* and I was in the audience and I watched him … it's a great part anyway – it's a good solid part … he *got* it. He was cockney – "awl right", and all that business. And I watched him walking round the stage, and I'll tell you when I thought, "Christ…" He picked two apples up, he nicked two apples or oranges out of a bag, and he did a one-handed juggle with these things. He was still talking to Oliver, but he was juggling with these apples with one hand. While he was still talking. Talk on your left, and do a one-handed juggle on your right, and then go into the song "Consider Yourself". He was fourteen then, and he had stage presence at fourteen. I know as a father, you can think it. No, no, I'm a *pro*. I know my game. I've still got it on video and I watch it now and I show people and I say, "That's what happens when you're that age, you've got that confidence to do that." But right now, it's upset me tonight. It's upset me in a lovely way. I felt touched … it's really touched me tonight. The lad has got so much stage presence. Stage ability. As an old pro, I've just watched my son working an audience, and it's fabulous. I mean, I used to do it, and I thought I was good at it. Which I was.'

Pete has tears in his eyes. Rob, who has sat through all this without saying a word, says, 'He's the guv'nor.'

'… I was,' Pete continues. 'I mean, I could do that. I had that. If I was losing the right-hand side of the room, I'd be on top of it. I wouldn't let 'em go.'

'So relaxed, so charming – unbelievable,' says Rob.

'I can tell you this,' says Pete. 'One of the nicest quotes that was ever said to me by a person when I came offstage – a person said to me once, "you make Perry Como look like a nervous wreck".'

'He's the most relaxed man I've ever seen onstage,' says Rob.

'Perry Como to me was the epitome of cool and relaxed: "You make Perry Como look like a nervous wreck" was the *nicest* thing I'd ever had said to me. Because that's what I did – I just wandered around. But I knew what I was doing. Wandered around, knew what I was doing – and I watch my son know what he's doing. He knows what he's doing. That puts it all in a nutshell. When you get out there, you know what you're doing when you get there. And Christ almighty did you tonight, son. And with abundance.'

'Thanks,' Rob says. 'Thank you.'

I ask Rob whether he relates doing what he does the way he does it to the way he saw his father do things.

'Yeah,' he says. 'I would say that every bit of me, apart from the aggressive bit, is my dad. Because my dad doesn't do aggression.'

'No,' Pete agrees. 'No.'

'But I would say that all movements … that, what I've just done there, that's my dad,' says Rob.

'I remember you ringing me a long time ago,' says Pete, 'and saying, "I was you all night last night, couldn't stop doing it."'

'Yeah, I'm my dad an awful lot, all the time,' says Rob. 'Onstage, even more so. And it's got to be DNA, because I'm not going, "I'm going to do my dad now."'

'It's upset me tonight,' says Pete. 'It's got me tonight. How many times have I watched him? So many times, but tonight it's really … my consideration is now my son is really genuinely a superstar. That's the business. And he'll always be my son – that's forever and ever amen. But the level of working … I love Sammy, I love Frank, I love Barbra Streisand, but he's now in that league for Christ's sake. Amazing. Can't say more than that, youth.'

'Well …' says Rob. 'Whosever's praise that you search for, there's none better than your dad's.'

'Well,' says Pete. 'You've got it in buckets.'

'And I can sit back now and go "yeah I have". Instead of "no, I haven't".' Rob stands up. 'And I'm going to go and do it all again tomorrow,' he says. 'I'm going to go and grab Ayda and go back to the hotel.'

'Go and do it, youth. I love you so much.'

* * *

'Best you've ever been,' says James Corden, after the third night's performance, which has been broadcast live around the world, as Rob puts his arms around him and Harry Styles. 'Genuinely.' Rob looks at the homemade tattoo that Styles has done that he describes to Rob as 'really shit', and says, 'I'm going to do that,' before leading Styles into the corner for a private chat.

When he returns, the comedian Jack Whitehall comes over and introduces his friend, who is an actor. His friend has something to show Rob. He pulls down his pants. He has an *I Love Robbie Williams* tattoo on his right arse cheek.

'If I win the Oscar, right, because I'm an actor,' the friend says, 'you've got to get *I love Ben McGregor*.'

'I might just get it anyway,' says Rob, laughing.

By the time we're in the car, Jack Whitehall has tweeted the photo of Rob leaning down next to his friend's bare tattooed arse. Rob explains the story he's just been told to Ayda:

'They were students and they were going to commemorate being students by getting something on their arse. One got a Pac-Man. And then there was a song of mine of the radio and he said, "I love Robbie Williams – I'm going to get 'I love Robbie Williams' on my arse."'

Rob looks at the photo. 'Oh, it's a good picture,' he says. 'Except for his hairy arse.' And he explains to Ayda about McGregor's Oscar challenge.

Or, says Ayda, defusing the idea by taking it too seriously, Rob could just do it for a tweet.

'You know I'm daft enough to do that,' Rob points out.

'I know you are,' she sighs. 'And I'd have to see it every day for the rest of my life.'

Climie Fisher's 'Love Changes Everything' comes on the radio. Rob says that he remembers it from when he was a teenager.

'There's a lyric in this song,' says Rob, 'that goes: *I was only seventeen … when she stole my heart away.* I was sixteen, and I was like: "I've got another year, and then somebody will take my heart away …" Little did I …'

'Little did you know,' says Ayda.

He nods. 'That it would take almost twenty years.'

* * *

He returns to the Royal Albert Hall ten days after the Royal Variety Performance, for a much briefer visit. This time, he doesn't leave home until after 9:30 in the evening, and has only just woken from a nap a moment before. In the car across Hyde Park, he sings along to 'God Only Knows' on the radio. Gary Barlow is playing at the Royal Albert Hall tonight and, in a reverse favour after Gary appeared at one of his O2 shows, he has agreed to be a surprise guest.

When he slips in the backstage entrance, he can hear Gary singing 'Everything Changes' from the stage, and sings along under his breath. He does the same to 'The Flood'. Then he leaves the corridor and stands just out of sight behind the drum kit.

'I want to introduce onstage now,' says Gary, 'a young man … who's become one of my best friends in the last few years … and I love him from the bottom of my heart … please welcome onstage … Robbie Williams!'

They sing 'Eight Letters' and 'Candy' together, and the place goes crazy.

'Wow!' says Rob coming off. 'Wow! That was sheer awesomeness. That was sheer awesomeness.' He leaves behind a message for Gary, because they have only met tonight onstage: 'Tell him I fucking love him – that was fucking awesome.'

He's still on a high, back in the car.

'Oh my Lord,' he says, in the car. 'Yeah, that was pure brilliance. The audience were having such a good time.' He realises something: 'It's lovely to get such a reaction, because a lot of those people have still followed the narrative … I think it's one of the most successful reunions after a bad split.'

Surreally, Rob is home around 50 minutes after he left. Ayda has been upstairs the whole time. He could just as well have popped downstairs for a moment, rather than having gone out to receive a rapturous two-song ovation at the Royal Albert Hall.

* * *

May 2016

Before tonight's Eurovision viewing party, Rob and Ayda have invited over some of the neighbours in their Wiltshire village for a drink. Most of them seem to work in finance. After they leave, it's time for the show, but the TV feed keeps going down. Rob looks like he's trying not to show how frustrated he is by this. Guy goes to the piano and says he'll play something while we wait. He sets into something jaunty.

'Not that one,' says Rob.

Finally, the TV starts working, and we watch the first few Eurovision entries – disappointingly they're neither interestingly good, nor the interesting kind of car-crash awful that Eurovision is famous for. Rob's observation, which may say more about the inner workings of his mind in the months before the release of a new album than about the talents or otherwise of those on-screen is this: 'Everyone's really thin.'

In one of the limp comedy sketches between performances, someone on-screen says, 'crazy is the new black.'

'I like "crazy is the new black",' says Rob. 'Guy? Swing song?'

In the middle of the show, Justin Timberlake debuts his new single, 'Can't Stop The Feeling', co-written by famous Swedish songwriter Max Martin. 'He's not keeping my attention,' says Rob, halfway through the performance, 'for whatever reason.' When it finishes, he's a little gentler: 'I like the song, but it seems all a bit vanilla.' After that, he goes outside for a cigarette and has a conversation with Guy that perplexes him.

The competition is a bit of an anticlimax. Afterwards, Karl shows Rob a video on his phone – I can't see it, but it's obviously of Karl's son. Rob laughs. 'My granddad used to do all that,' says Rob. 'He used to get me to dance on the bed and box him.'

Then he leads Ayda upstairs.

* * *

The next morning, Rob muses over that conversation with Guy. It began when Guy said how good he thought Max Martin is. 'I said, "Well, you're a genius,"' Rob recalls. 'He said, "I'm not as good as *him*." I'm, "*What?*" He's, "Yeah … he's a different class." I'm … "Eh? Eh? Don't say *that!*"' He shakes his head. 'Don't say that! I can't be *second* … I said, do you want me to go and write an album with Max Martin?'

When he goes out for a post-breakfast cigarette in the vestibule, he's still talking about it.

'Considering I've got a group of work that I'm obsessing about, worrying about, literally to keep the ship afloat, to keep this thing going, to go over the edge and then take it all the way through the promotion, do all the talk … It's like you come into your corner after the first round and your cornerman's going …' – Rob puts on a worried voice – '… "Stay away from him … if he hits you, stay down."'

He says that this morning it seems funny, but last night it was really bothering him.

* * *

2002–2012

There's no point pretending that no scars remain, or that there are not scabs to occasionally pick. At one point during the iTunes festival performance in September 2016, Rob fills in between songs, first leading the crowd through a brief a cappella version of A-ha's 'Take On Me' then his own 'Come Undone'. The second of these draws a particularly loud and enthusiastic audience response. Rob turns to Guy. 'See?' he says. 'I told you it was a fucking hit.' A fair amount of this is pure pantomime, but not all of it.

The relationship between Rob and Guy Chambers fell apart during the recording of the fifth album they had made together, *Escapology*, in 2002. One particular focus of their disagreements back then was the song 'Come Undone', which Rob had written with other songwriters and which at the time Guy neither particularly appreciated nor could see the potential of. But really those kinds of specific arguments were proxies for the much bigger schisms that can occur when a creative collaboration fractures: usually credit, respect, money and pride are involved, and typically much more, too. When two people work together that closely, what pulls them apart can be about almost everything and it can be about almost nothing. Once it's broken, the *why* hardly matters.

* * *

Tentatively, on a personal level, Guy and Rob mended their bridges a few years later. They'd occasionally go to dinner, and Guy and his family went to stay with Rob in Los Angeles. They even, very quietly, worked together, though no one seemed to notice. In 2008 Rob's version of The Kinks' 'Lola' appeared on a Radio 1 album on which artists covered number one singles; the sleeve credit 'produced by Guy Chambers' seemed to pass everyone by. At the same time, they also recorded a cover of Rufus Wainwright's 'April Fools' and even tried to write a song together. It was based around a sample from Ennio Morricone's theme for *The Good, the Bad and the Ugly*, but Rob didn't feel too enthusiastic about it. Eventually the song would appear as 'Let's Get Ugly' on the first album by British boyband The Wanted, but nobody would know: Rob was credited as 'McStagger'. (Presumably this was the quiet reappearance of Tipsy McStagger, an alter ego borrowed from *The Simpsons* he had occasionally used before then.)

When I talked to Rob in 2009 about this attempt at writing, he was sensitive about the possibility that people would think they'd worked together because *Rudebox* hadn't done well: 'Guy happened to be in Los Angeles, we happened to be talking again and be in each other's lives, there's no reason why we shouldn't go and have a look at it. You know, there wasn't a confidence crisis in my songwriting ability because of *Rudebox*. I hadn't gone to Guy because of that. The dumb narrative that people will have. Guy just happened to be in LA at a time I was free.'

I asked him back then if he thought he and Guy would ever try again.

'Who knows what will happen?' he said. 'I think ultimately me and Guy will write an album again, but when? I don't know. And plus, it wouldn't be me to go running back to Guy because of a perceived fuck-up. I'm too stubborn for that. Right now, I wouldn't feel fulfilled by it. I think we will write an album together at some point, and I look forward to that day, but I can't see it being in the next five years.'

He also says this:

'I love Guy. I do. I find him difficult to work with.'

* * *

The following year I go to see Guy in his recording studio in London. He's agreed to be interviewed for a celebration of Rob's 20-year career. He chats amiably about the early days: their first phone conversation where Rob told him he wanted to do 'dirty pop' and Guy replying 'I can do that'. How they arranged to write for two days. How on the first day they came up with 'South Of The Border': 'He literally walked into the bedroom and started singing. There was no "I want to do this …" I think maybe we had a cup of tea afterwards but he didn't talk much.' How on the second day he came back and they wrote 'Angels'.

'He started singing, he had the melody in the verse and he had all the lyrics of the first verse, I think. Maybe even the second verse. But he didn't have the chorus. So I started playing the piano to this melody and then I took it to the chorus and had that chorus melody, and he went with that melody straightway, he didn't question it. And I think we kind of wrote the lyric together for the chorus. It took about twenty minutes. If you actually see the lyrics written down on a piece of paper, it's very simple. There's no bridge in that song – it's two verses and a chorus.'

We talk through a few later stepping stones in Rob's career, and when we come to 'Feel' Guy mentions that Tina Turner recorded a never-released version here in this studio: 'I can't wait for when EMI have the sense to release it because it shows what a classic it really is. Obviously Rob's version will always be *the* version, the most important version, but when you hear someone as amazing as Tina sing it, it makes you hear it again with new ears.'

Then we reach the split.

'The way it ended was a bit shocking, yeah,' he says. 'It was very brutal. Maybe I deserved it. Who knows?' But he bends over backwards to make clear he understands things he may have done: taking their collaboration for granted, working on other projects in way that wound Rob up, underestimating some of the songs Rob was writing with others, both in terms of their importance to Rob and their commercial potential. And he acknowledges how annoyed Rob would be when people thought that Guy did all the work. 'Not that I ever encouraged that in any interviews or in any conversations with anyone,' he says. '*Ever*. I was always, and always will be, incredibly complimentary about his writing talents.'

214

He talks about staying at the house more recently – 'that was lovely' – and their writing session. 'We wrote a song that summer that I was very excited about, but that wasn't reciprocated, that excitement ... so that definitely knocked me back quite a bit. It came against this big brick wall of him just not wanting to really do it, and not being that excited about it. I can't get past that. That's just the way it is, and that's fine. It's frustrating for me, but you can *never* make him do something that he doesn't want to do.'

Guy's friendly and frank, but he also seems a little as though he's on one hand worried that he might say something to trip things up again, and as though on the other that he's hopeful he might say something that unlocks the future, and as if he's wondering if there's any signs that might happen.

* * *

In the autumn of 2012 Rob emails Guy to ask him if he will appear as a special guest at one of the three shows at London's O2 arena he will be playing that November. Rob says that he got a reply which said 'yeah, sure', followed by another the next day worrying about the tone of this first answer: '"I might have sounded a bit too casual with the 'yeah sure' – I'd really like to do that".'

I ask Rob why he'd come to think this would be a good idea.

'Because I miss Guy. I just want to see him.'

They meet up not long after when Rob goes in to sing on the Hillsborough tribute version of 'He Ain't Heavy, He's My Brother' that Guy is producing. They next see each other at the LH2 rehearsal complex in west London where the O2 production rehearsals are taking place. They run through the three songs they'll be performing together: 'Eternity', 'Mr Bojangles' and 'She's The One'. Guy stands on the empty floor watching Rob rehearsing the rest of the set. He looks somewhere between surprised and alarmed when Rob finishes without singing their most famous song.

'What? No "Angels"?' he says.

I explain that it is in the set, during the encores, but that Rob skipped it. 'Fucking bored of it,' Guy sighs.

Back in the dressing room, Guy goes to the bathroom. When he returns, he starts saying his goodbyes, but Rob asks him to sit down.

'Doing a swing album next – do you want to do it?'

'Of course,' says Guy.

* * *

Barnaby, the videographer who is covering these rehearsals, asks Guy some questions. Guy says that the last show he played with Rob was in New Zealand a decade earlier. 'There's an element of healing going on, I guess. Because I haven't actually done a gig with him for all that time.'

Barnaby asks how it is to see Rob.

'It's great to see him happy. That's the best thing. There's been times when I've hung out with him when he's been not so happy, and he's been quite tortured. I think the time we stayed with him in LA – was that three years ago? That was a difficult time for him.'

When Barnaby next speaks with Rob, Rob refers to Guy as 'my erstwhile songwriting partner from when I was good'.

* * *

A few nights later, they perform onstage together. Rob introduces 'She's The One' as the best song the two of them ever wrote together. It's actually written by Karl Wallinger from World Party. Rob covered it after listening over and over to the album it was from, *Egyptology*, the first time he was in rehab, but over the years Karl Wallinger has been at best churlish – and sometimes incredibly rude – about Rob's version. (A version, incidentally, that will have earned Wallinger a great amount of money.) Rob's comment tonight is but the latest salvo in a long war.

Guy, who long ago used to be in World Party, will subsequently receive a call from Wallinger. Unfortunately, it turns out that Karl Wallinger's daughter, Nancy, is in the audience tonight, and she has happened to video what Rob said. Wallinger earthily expresses his fury: 'He's, "Can you tell your friend he's a cunt." "What friend's that?" "Your fucking friend Robbie

Williams. Tell him from me that he's a cunt." I'm, "Karl, I don't think that's a good idea, I don't think that'd go down well."' (Rob will later vow to introduce it on next year's tour as 'my eighth favourite song that me and Guy Chambers have written', which I don't think is quite the adjustment Karl Wallinger had in mind.)

Rob asks Guy to return and play again on the third night. Late that evening when Rob gets back home for the first time in three days – he has been staying in a hotel near the venue during the concerts – he settles on the sofa and cues up *The X Factor*.

'I think Guy's back in my life,' he says.

A couple of weeks later, Guy and Rob have a meeting with Rob's A&R man Chris Briggs at Rob's house, going through a long list of possible songs to cover for a new swing album. That's the easy bit. They also plan to meet in Los Angeles in January to write new songs for the album. It's five and a half years since their last attempt at writing songs together, and that didn't work out, but they both seem to be assuming that this time it will.

* * *

January 2013

Before Rob and Guy sit down in a room as they used to, which is when they will really discover whether they can do what they used to do, there is a welcome distraction. Guy has already been in Los Angeles for a few days, working with Rufus Wainwright, and the three of them have agreed to try to write a song together.

Even before that, there is a dinner at the Chateau Marmont for everyone to meet. This isn't the kind of thing Rob likes to do at all, so it is a measure of the respect in which he holds Rufus that he agrees. They have met briefly before – Rob says that at a party in Los Angeles in around 2000 he mumbled to Rufus that he was a big fan and would love to work with him. 'And then never followed it up,' he says, 'which is what I normally do.'

But they've never really spoken. Tonight, they sit down at one end of the table, chatting easily, and by the end of the meal between them they have come up with two possible song titles to work on tomorrow. One is 'Swings Both Ways', the other 'Cocks And Diamonds'.

In the car back up into the hills afterwards, Rob explains how the second title came about. 'Ayda called me a size queen when it comes to houses,' he says, 'so then I said, "Well, you're a diamond queen."' His comment triggered, he says, a wider discussion of what it is that women want. And then Guy proposed an answer: 'cocks and diamonds'.

Somehow, as we near the house, this leads on to a discussion of Guy's eccentricities.

'The great thing about Guy,' says Chris Briggs, 'is that he has absolutely no idea when he's been weird.'

'None whatsoever,' says Rob, laughing.

'It's quite endearing,' says Chris.

'It is,' Rob agrees. 'I hope it just now stays at endearing and doesn't piss me off.' He's silent for a moment, then he adds, 'I don't think it's gonna.'

* * *

The next day Rob goes down to a room at the Chateau Marmont, and the three of them write a song. He takes Spencer, their white goldendoodle, with him, and a photograph of the two of them, pop star and his dog, taken as they enter the hotel, will appear in the next day's *Daily Mail*. In the story he is referred to as '"Candy" hitmaker' and 'Take That star'. Could be worse, he points out. 'In *The Sun*, three weeks ago, I was referred to as "portly singer".'

This is true. It was on Christmas Eve, only a few days after *The Sun* had named him Bizarre Man Of The Year: *The portly singer was in full-on protective dad mode during a pre-Christmas stroll in LA this weekend with wife Ayda and three-month-old Teddy.* Whether or not any of this has some bearing on the crash diet he has been on for the past three weeks, he doesn't say.

'We got something,' says Rob, quietly triumphant, when he returns to the house a few hours later. The song they have written uses the first of last night's titles, 'Swings Both Ways'. He explains what happened: 'Guy played the piano, Rufus had a melody and an idea for the verse. He's very quick. I got the melody in the pre-chorus and then just a smattering of words every now and then.' Rob starts singing some of the lyrics, almost under his breath: *I'll get out of your sandbox ... you'll get covered in shit ... getting off of your see-saw ... say goodbye to your momma ... let's get high on some pop rocks ... pop rocks and coke ... I'll blow your sock off ... teach you how to laugh at Daddy's dirty joke ...*

He goes into the TV room and watches Oprah interviewing Drew Barrymore. 'I just know the me and Guy thing is going to work,' he says. He flicks over to take in a little *Honey Boo Boo*. Then *Storage Wars*. Then Howard Stern interviewing Jay-Z. 'I'm a bit bored,' he mutters.

I ask how many songs he hopes to write this week.

'Probably three definites,' he says, then recalibrates. 'At least one definite. The song today's good as well.'

But he says that he hasn't thought of any particular ideas.

'Go in cold. See what happens. That's what we always did.'

* * *

The next morning, Rob gets up for Mommy and Me class at 9:30, and after sitting on the floor in a circle and doing his best to make himself look like he's paying attention, is back just before 11:30. He reports that they were lectured on SIDS – or, as he puts it, 'a woman tells you stuff that scares you about cot death and stuff' – and about the importance of not having smoke on one's clothing.

'That's good,' he says, 'but I was raised in a pub for the first three years of my life.'

Ayda comes in. She has to go to an audition soon, to play a slut.

'Will it disturb you if I run my lines?' she asks.

'Depends how well you do it,' says Rob.

Gwen, Ayda's mother, comes in and runs her lines with her. Ayda's character is soon describing a target of her sluttiness: 'He's six-one, a hundred and seventy-five pounds and an internet entrepreneur.'

'He's six-foot-one and *how many* pounds?' interjects Rob, incredulously.

'One hundred and seventy-five pounds,' says Ayda. 'Sorry about that, babe. My character likes anorexic men.'

Soon she heads out, encouraging words from her husband – 'Hey, slag it up one time' – fresh in her ears.

Rob joins Guy in the studio, and Guy relates what Rufus said about Rob the other night at the dinner when Rob and Ayda both left the table for a moment: 'Oh, he's so fabulous – he's just like an animal.'

'He meant it in a good way,' Guy adds.

'I suppose I am,' says Rob.

And then it can be avoided no longer. The short version of what takes place next is that today Rob and Guy will successfully renew their songwriting partnership, and today will break the back of two key songs for this autumn's *Swings Both Ways* album, itself named after their collaboration with Rufus one day earlier.

That is all true, but if it suggests something smooth and linear – two men go into a room, write a song – it is also extremely misleading. The reality is very far away from that: so much messier, so much less distinct, so much more precarious and chaotic and protracted, and so much closer to never happening at all.

* * *

Here is what really happens today:

First, Guy tries out the piano in Rob's studio.

'Sounds good,' he says.

Rob picks up an acoustic guitar. Then he suggests that they first have lunch.

Over lunch they listen to the rough recording of 'Swings Both Ways' on Guy's phone. 'Rufus was really shocked,' says Guy, 'because he said no rock star in America would do a song called "Swings Both Ways". He said it just wouldn't happen.' They return to the studio where Rob discusses in great detail the property dilemmas he faces in terms of how and where he and Ayda should live. This goes on long enough that Guy turns to the engineer, Drew, who is just sitting waiting for something to happen, and says, 'Sorry about this lack of music-making.'

Then Rob gets up to go to the toilet, and as he moves across the room, out of the window he spots his neighbour from across the road.

'There's Slash,' he says to Guy.

'That's hilarious,' says Guy, craning his neck to see the former (and future) Guns N' Roses guitarist.

'Isn't it?' says Rob.

'What are the chances,' asks Chris, 'of two people from Stoke living opposite each other in Beverly Hills?' (Slash was raised in Stoke until he was five.)

'Yeah,' says Rob.

'What part of Stoke is he from?' asks Chris.

'Fenton,' says Rob, and then fills Guy in on his other notable neighbours here in Beverly Hills. There's Tom Jones ('he pops up every now and then – you'll just be in the middle of something and then Tom'll be there, such a sweet man'), there's Brian Wilson and there's Paris Hilton. Not to forget Charlie Sheen.

'He had valet parking for hookers!' Rob exclaims. 'How great is that? That's how I'd roll if I'd had a *really* fucked-up childhood. More fucked-up than mine. That's the next level.'

By the time this digression has concluded, and Rob has recorded a quick vocal for 'Swings Both Ways' and worked on its lyric a little, Ayda is back.

'Here she is,' welcomes Rob. 'Here's my slag.'

He asks how it went; she says she can't be sure.

'There are other slags in this town,' she points out.

'It's a slag heap,' Guy comments.

Rob sings a bit of Adele's James Bond theme, 'Skyfall' – Ayda was at the Golden Globes with Adele the other night when she won – and that sparks a conversation about how strong or otherwise the song is.

'I think if we get lucky we might write something better,' says Guy. 'Maybe not right now …'

'No! Let's do it right now!' says Rob. 'Come on! Let's write a better song than that then! Do it!'

'Okay,' says Guy. 'I'd better have a piss first.'

He does, and then he starts playing something on the piano. 'You feel like doing something slow like that?' Guy asks, and plays on a while. 'This is your confession-to-the-world song,' he suggests, trying to inspire some kind of connection. 'Because that song's a confession song, isn't it? Kind of saying: this is what I'm really like.'

Rob doesn't really respond.

'You in the mood to do something slow?' Guy persists.

'Well … I think we should do at *some* point,' Rob demurs, then decides that right now they should look at the list of cover songs for the swing album instead, a conversation that devolves into a further discussion of what the album should be, and about the disintegration of the music industry. This goes on and on.

Eventually they tell Drew he can go home.

'Sorry about today,' Rob tells him. 'We're just figuring out what we're doing.'

Drew leaves, and if he has any sense of Guy and Rob's history, he could be excused for thinking that their attempt to rekindle an old flame has been an abject failure.

Rob suggests to Guy that they have dinner, and do something afterwards, which sounds like another way of procrastinating indefinitely. But Guy tries to get him interested in some ideas now. He plays Rob a piano sketch from his phone.

'Sweet,' says Rob in a way that suggests it doesn't really engage him.

'Because at the moment there isn't a waltz song on the album,' Guy presses.

'I don't fancy writing that right now,' Rob clarifies.

'You fancy something … more confrontational?' Guy says, but doesn't see the response he wants. 'Not confrontational … but with more energy …'

'Yeah,' says Rob.

Guy goes to the piano and begins to play. Rob interrupts him almost immediately. 'Guy, did we have a song called "Guns, Chicks and Booze"?'

'Yeah,' says Guy. He begins to play it and Rob sings *Guns chicks and booze – here I go again! How could I refuse …* ?

'Can't believe you remember that,' says Guy. 'There was also … do you remember?' He begins playing something else and they launch into the lyric in unison: *Between you and me, I'm not much of a man.*

'It wasn't the right chorus,' says Guy. 'It's very Neil Diamond-y.'

'It's not very swing-y, is it?' Rob says.

'No, good point,' Guy concedes. He begins to play something a bit more traditional, with a walking bluesy bass line.

'Shall we eat and then do it?' Rob says.

* * *

After dinner, they come back up to the studio.

Guy sits down at the piano once more and begins playing – as he plays, he suggests that this could be a kind of José Feliciano-style thing.

'I'm not feeling that right now,' says Rob. 'It's lovely, though.'

'Something more ballsy?' Guy asks.

'Yes.'

Guy proposes something more along the line of 'Hey Big Spender', and plays some chords.

Then Guy plays a third thing, and this one he keeps playing. Rob looks at his computer and exhales. Guy still keeps playing.

'No?' Guy eventually says.

Rob doesn't even reply.

The suppressed tension is unacknowledged but obvious. Maybe this just isn't going to work.

Guy tries a fourth idea.

'I like the vibe of "Soda Pop",' Rob interrupts. He plays 'Soda Pop', the song he wrote with his friends and collaborators from Stoke on their alien-hunting trip, on his computer. 'It's the drums, isn't it? Is it jitterbug?'

'Another song that's sort of from that era?' says Guy. 'Is that what you're thinking?'

'Yeah.'

'But not the same groove,' Guy muses aloud. 'How about something … ?'

But Rob simply shuts him off mid-sentence by playing something jitterbuggy from his computer that he has just found on YouTube. 'Play along to that,' Rob requests. For a moment, Guy struggles to find the key, then joins in. 'It's quite tricky,' he says. Rob stops the track, and Guy keeps on playing, but Rob already seems to have lost interest.

'How about something like the Charleston?' Guy suggests, and hums some notes and a rhythm. He begins to work on something, but Rob interrupts again.

'Check out the brass at the beginning of this,' he says, and plays something else from YouTube.

'Great,' says Guy. 'What is that?'

'A really weird song by Sammy Davis Jr,' says Rob. The song is called 'I Am Over 25, But You Can Trust Me', and it's an obscure album track from 1972.

The song itself seems to interest Rob little, but the remarkable brass fanfare which starts it off is what he keeps going back to.

'We could write something on that, couldn't we?' says Guy, and begins playing some piano chords to fit around it.

'I've looped it before and rapped over it,' Rob points out, and plays from his computer what he did six years earlier. It's from the autobiographical rap range:

I liked Robbie circa 1993
When he was still in a boyband doing too much E
But all those birds he's with, that's just weird
He claims that he shags them, yeah, scratchy beard
We all know Jonny Wilkes is his lover
But who plays daddy and who plays poppa
Can't break America to save his life

Because the Yanks are clever, yeah that's right.

'That's great – that's really good,' says Guy, and Rob plays some more.

Oh, that's okay though, must write hit

Can I exchange one Grammy for fourteen Brits

'Angels', the best song of the last twenty-five years?

Kiss my arse, that's not art.

Another unreleased song that mashes up egotism with self-lacerating mockery. I think there's more of these hidden away on his computer than anyone knows.

'That was the week before rehab,' he says.

A year from now, in this same room, they will return to the same sample, and from it will come 'Sensational'. But right now this, like all the other ideas, comes to nothing.

* * *

Rob says he's had enough of the studio for now, and invites us out to the balcony outside his bedroom, overlooking the lights of the San Fernando valley. He wonders whether they should try to write a song about Gwen, his mother-in-law, and suggests a lyric: *She speaks many languages no one understands.*

Back in the studio, he plays a very un-swing backing track from his computer. 'Something I did years ago,' he says.

'What do you think it should be like – the song, the music?' says Guy, clearly trying to create some momentum where none exists.

At that very moment Ayda arrives back from a cardio class in the Valley.

'It was like ballet on crack,' she explains. 'Crack ballet. I was fine until the abs section.'

When she leaves, Guy starts playing something else.

'I like that,' Rob says, and sings along for a while under his breath. 'Do that again,' he says, and sings wordlessly along. It sounds like something is beginning to happen. But, almost as though he realises he has backed himself into a corner he'd prefer not to be in, Rob announces that he wants to move on. Guy presses that they should quickly record this anyway in case they want to work on it more tomorrow, put some drums with it. He plays it again to record, but Rob doesn't sing.

'That's really good,' Rob agrees, and offers a kind of apology. 'My head's not working melodically. Nothing coming out at the minute.'

* * *

Rob will later explain what he was thinking at this moment. Nothing was coming, and he was panicking. They had both been investing in this reunion, building up to today, but clearly it wasn't clicking. It was going to be so awkward.

'I really felt a lot of pressure last night before we got it right. In my head I was going, "Oh shit, he's going to be heartbroken, I'm going to be heartbroken, this isn't going to work."'

* * *

Just then, Guy offers his zillionth suggestion.

'How about a "Candyman"-type thing?' he says.

Who can take a rainbow…? sings Rob, absentmindedly.

'Like a sad version,' Guy suggests. 'A minor version.'

He plays a pulsing chord progression, and right away, the first time that he plays it, Rob sings a melody, and half-formed lyrics begin to appear: … *is it pain for me and you?…*

'This is great,' Rob says, and continues.

Don't stop and look forward … Don't stop in the ocean … I'll come round for you …

And suddenly, at around 7:25 in the evening, after an aimless, fruitless few hours, something magic is happening. Different melodies keep forming around what Guy is playing, and they sound beautiful.

… in your penthouse … you can't put me in the … you'd better just waste it … it's all been a waste, kid … a waste, kid …

Rob holds his arms outstretched as he sings a second section:

*It doesn't matter who you are … you could be something … you could be
something … you could just get there … if we just get there.*

He keeps repeating *you could be something* and *if we just get there.*

'That's really good,' says Guy.

'Something good there, isn't there?' Rob agrees. And then he sings: *We
know who you are … we're gonna be there … be there when you get there…*

That's the moment when he realises.

'It's a song for Teddy, isn't it?' he says.

* * *

'We've got that, right?' says Rob. 'That felt really special. Sweet, right? Let's
write another one. Because that's a big lyric to do.'

Then he tells Guy he wishes he'd written 'One Day Like This' by Elbow,
and begins singing it.

'We haven't got one like this,' says Guy, trying not to lose the momentum
now things seem to be working, 'like a merry-go-round thing.' He
demonstrates what he means on the piano.

'Oh, like "Bojangles"?' says Rob.

'Yeah,' says Guy. 'A descending thing.'

Rob sings a little then says he's not feeling it.

'It's going to be hard to think of something as good as that last idea,'
says Guy.

He tries something else. Rob sings along a little then stops.

'No,' says Rob. 'Too eighties jazz.'

Guy wonders if they can do something like 'If I Were A Rich Man'.

He starts playing something quite jaunty and odd.

'I like that,' says Rob, and begins singing. '*Gather round boys …*' It's a
kind of storytelling song.

'Could be about having a riot?' Guy suggests.

'Having a riot?' Rob questions.

'I see it as you dressed as a cowboy and you go into the saloon – like,
gunfight at the O.K. Corral. Where everything in the bar kicks off. It's that
kind of thing, isn't it?'

'The last big punch-up,' says Rob. They play it again and he sings *Fuzzy Wuzzy was a friend of mine.*

'There's a lot of lyrics in that song,' he says, meaning that if they were to actually write it there would need to be a lot of lyrics; this is clearly said in the voice of a man who sees this as a problem, not an opportunity. Then he adds, more brightly, that he's been wanting to do a song where you can barely hear what he's saying, and the words sound like they're saying something but they're not – maybe this can be it. He demonstrates, singing quite convincing gibberish.

'If anybody could get away with it,' says Guy, 'you could.'

* * *

They set aside this song, the saloon gunfight one, though they both like it, and listen to the previous song again on Guy's phone.

'A sending-a-child-off-into-the-world song, maybe?' says Guy.

'Mmm-hmmm,' Rob replies.

Then Guy begins something else on the piano that he'll soon describe as 'a bit "On Broadway"' and Rob starts singing to it. It gathers momentum and Rob begins singing the verse lyrics to 'Got To Get You Into My Life', in the process finding a rhythm. Something begins to take shape. They play it back on Guy's phone and Rob starts singing an 'oh-oh-*ohhhh!*' backing vocal.

'That was good, right?' he says.

'It's got that Sammy soulful thing that he did,' says Guy. 'It's got a little of that Aloe Blacc thing.'

At this, Rob starts singing 'I Need A Dollar'.

Anyway, they decide to call it a night. They've got something after all. They hug.

* * *

And then, suddenly, Rob starts singing a cappella, a tune for the last idea they were working on, and comes up with: *Why do you love me? I treat you so ugly.*

Suddenly they're back at work. Guy goes back to the piano. Rob sings.
Why do you love me? I treat you so ugly. You know I do
Why do you trust me? I know where I must be. When I'm not with you.
'It's a licence to be a cock, this song, isn't it?' he notes.
Why do you take it? Why do you care?
You're not gonna miss me. You're not going to kiss me. When I'm not there.
They stop for a second.
'It can't be that easy, can it?' says Rob.
'It *can* be,' Guy replies.
Another half-hour or so's concentrated work on the lyric follows.
'There's three,' Rob says, then corrects himself. 'Two. The cowboy one's really good, but there's too many lyrics.'
Then they go back and work some more on the first song for a while, and as a final flourish Guy comes up with the descending melody at the end of the chorus that will be one of its most distinctive features. This song will become 'Go Gentle', the album's first single. The more up-tempo one will become 'Shine My Shoes', the first track on *Swings Both Ways* and the opening song on the subsequent swing tour.
They're back.
After Guy leaves, Rob sits a few moments longer in the studio, decompressing.
'I don't think I've sat with anyone at a keyboard and done that since doing that with Guy,' he says to Chris Briggs. 'Guy's really talented, isn't he?'

* * *

The next day Guy explains he has a chest infection, and that he was struggling to keep with it all the previous evening. There is an echo here that they're both aware of.
'That's what happened when we wrote "Angels",' Rob reminds him.
'It was. I had a massive fucking sinus infection,' Guy remembers. 'I actually managed to get a doctor to come to the house.'
'He receives greatness,' Rob summarises, 'through illness.'

Later, when Rob isn't in the room, Guy fills in some more details. 'I was in a bad way. I never call doctors out. Something happened to me that day – it's very weird. Maybe I knew. Maybe my brain exploded a bit with the thought that I'd actually written a hit after thirty-two years of being on this planet.'

* * *

This afternoon, Rob has a fresh idea.

'Guy, we should write a song called "Thin". A swing song about losing weight.'

'So would it list all the things you can't have?' Guy wonders.

'Let's write about what we know,' Rob says. 'And I know about trying to be thin. And not succeeding.'

The idea of a list song leads Guy to 'My Favourite Things', and he starts playing around with that on the piano, and almost instantly finds a kind of fairground waltz.

Almost immediately, Rob starts singing:

No dinner for breakfast
Just sadness for lunch
And a glazing of self-esteem … a thimble of air … the thinnest person
ever seen.

Plenty of lyrics cascade out – *Lara Flynn Boyle, emaciated royals … Lena Zavaroni, would I win a Tony?* – that exist for half a second and then are passed over or forgotten, but as soon as Guy gets to the chorus, he sings:

No one likes a fat pop star
Especially the pop star itself
We know you know where the shops are.

And though the lyrics will be refined, on day two already there's a third song that will end up on the album, 'No One Likes A Fat Pop Star'.

A little while later, Rob comes up with the line *the saddest that I've ever been.*

'Because it is,' he says. 'When I'm the thinnest. I'm the saddest.'

He laughs.

230

'Really?' says Guy.

'Yeah. The thinnest I've ever been was round about the time we recorded *Swing When You're Winning*. And we also wrote "Feel". And that was probably one of the most depressed moments of my life.'

'And when we were recording it?' asks Guy.

'Yeah!' says Rob.

'You masked it really well,' says Guy.

'All the way through my twenties I was *incredibly* depressed. Things didn't get better until …' – he considers this, with a chuckle – '… a couple of weeks ago.'

* * *

At dinner, Rob and Ayda sit with Guy and his wife Emma, and they talk about the pros and cons of living in the country.

'We've got our own forest,' Rob says, of their place in Wiltshire.

'Guy wanted an axe,' says Emma, remembering when they also had a place out of town for a while. 'I said no.'

'No to an axe?' Rob asks.

'No, to *Guy* with an axe,' Emma clarifies.

Rob nods, and empathises. 'I'm slightly dyspraxic,' he says. 'If there's a knife, it's going in me. If there's scissors, they're cutting me. If there's a package, it's going to be ripped. And I can't gently open a door or a drawer, it's getting pulled open and off its hinges. I never go, "Oh, this is the point where you ruin stuff …"'

They discuss childrearing, and Emma says that Guy changed one nappy.

'I have to say Rob's done more than that,' says Ayda.

'I quite like doing the nappies,' Rob points out.

'He's not *bad*,' says Ayda. 'Rob's actual wrapping-of-the-nappy technique does need some refining. But he does at least attack it with vigour, which I like.'

On the way back up to the studio, Rob detours to spend a few minutes with Teddy. She's crying. First, he sings 'Dancing In The Street', then Ol'

231

Dirty Bastard's 'Baby I Got Your Money'. She remains unconsoled, so he tries a different tack.

'We're rich!' he tells her. 'It's okay! We've got nothing to worry about!'

* * *

Over the next couple of days, Rob and Guy work steadily on completing these three songs.

One afternoon, Ayda appears in the doorway.

'I want to show you what your daughter did to me,' she says, and points to the shit on her pants and the matching shit on her t-shirt. 'She exploded through her nappy, through her clothes. I've been hosed in baby shit. And here's a little bit of vomit on the back.'

'We wrote a wonderful song to Teddy,' Rob tells her.

'Is it called "My Poopy Poem"?' she asks.

This reminds Rob of something – the paparazzi photos that were taken of him at LAX airport when he arrived back in Los Angeles before Christmas, pictures that were then published in the *Daily Mail*, including a close-up of the legs of his dark grey sweatpants.

'They said,' he explains, 'I had baby sick on me.'

In fact it was even in the headline: *It's not all rock and roll: Robbie Williams touches down in LA with wife Ayda and daughter Teddy ... wearing trousers stained in baby sick.*

A touching tale of what being a parent is like: however rich and famous and I'm-in-first-class you are, there's nothing you can do to stop your baby throwing up on you.

There was just one tiny detail, Rob explains, that they had got wrong.

'It was actually just me, eating.'

* * *

Rob posts a blog on his website:

Me and Guy worked together for the first time in many years. Funnily enough we're a good team ;). What a treat. I luvs him.

Teddy got her first song, It's called 'Go Gentle'. It might be called something else by the time it comes out. I sang it to her yesterday as we walked around the estate. She was in a papoose so she was a captive audience. I think she liked it … then she threw up. Tough room!

* * *

As they work, occasionally tales bubble to the surface about the old days. All kinds of tales. Over the years, I've heard many stories told of Guy's eccentricities and worse, but now that he's actually here, the balance is somewhat redressed.

Here's one:

'Do you remember that time in Dublin when you got into my bed?' says Guy. 'Again.'

'Yes,' says Rob. 'Yeah, that *was* weird. That was like six in the morning, off my head on fucking Jack Daniels and coke.'

'I filmed it – I thought "hello this is great",' Guy tells everyone in the studio. 'He didn't even realise it was on.'

'Yeah I did!' Rob objects.

'Did you?'

'Yeah! I thought it was a good idea to tape it too.'

'It's very funny footage. Proper, proper drunk.'

And a second:

'When we wrote "Strong",' says Guy, 'he got me up at four in the morning. I was in bed with Emma and he said, "I want to write a song." "What? Now?" He was on the vin rouge. The posh hotel in Cologne. He was, "I don't care – I want to write a song." We wrote "Strong". In about an hour. I woke up the next morning and thought, "What happened? I think I wrote a song."'

And a third:

Guy is describing Rob listening to the playback of a version of 'Let Me Entertain You' when they were making the first album.

'There was a sax solo,' he says. 'And the first time he hears it, he doesn't react at all. And then at the end of the track, he comes up to me, holds me by my throat and says, "If you *ever* put a saxophone on one of my records again, I will kill you. Do you understand?" And then just walked off. Needless to say that got removed. Fucking great sax solo that was, too. But he was right, because the trumpets are more exciting.'

I ask Guy how he felt at that moment.

'Scared. Genuinely scared. Frightened. We had moments during that album where he was, shall we say, a little bit emotional.'

I ask Rob whether he remembers doing this.

'No,' he says.

But does it have the firm ring of truth?

'Yep.'

What would you have been thinking?

'I really didn't like sax at the time.'

And a fourth (and fifth):

'Do you remember the party at my flat in Archway where you threw my guitar out the window?' Guy asks.

'I didn't throw the guitar out the window,' says Rob, dismissively.

'Yes, you did.'

'Did I?'

'Yeah. My John Lennon guitar.'

'Where did it land?'

'On the street.'

'What had you done to annoy me?' Rob wonders. 'Did it break?'

'The whole guitar was fucked. What's really annoying is that I didn't pick it up and frame it – it could have been a lovely art piece. I put it in the bin.'

'Was I aiming for a hedge?'

'I think you were annoyed about something. Once you threw a lovely guitar I had in Lake Como, because you couldn't tune it.'

This one Rob remembers, and, in his own way, can justify. 'It was a twelve-string. They're difficult to tune. The head of the police walked into my room as I was just about to throw a TV into Lake Como, because he was our chaperone. And I looked at him and he went ...' Rob mimes the unexpected encouragement he was given to go ahead. 'We both watched the TV go, and then we high-fived each other.'

'What was weird about the guitar,' Guy says, 'is we were all having dinner and he left early, and then suddenly there were these searchlights around the hotel, and police boats. And there was a fireman in full fireman gear holding my guitar: "I have got this from the water!" This completely fucked guitar. And, again, I wish I'd kept it ...'

'I think I was probably trying to get a reaction,' Rob says.

'All you needed,' Guy suggests, 'was to come back to the table and say, "listen, Guy, can you help me tune the guitar"?'

'I thought the guitar would pass by the window,' Rob reasons, 'where you were sat, which it did, and I thought you'd see it and go, "Oh, he needs it tuned ..."'

* * *

Before Guy leaves Los Angeles, a fourth song is written, this one a non-swing song called 'All Climb On', and they also rewrite an old song of theirs called 'Where There's Muck There's Brass' which Rob used not to like, but now does. At the end of the trip, they listen back to everything.

When 'Go Gentle' finishes, Rob looks satisfied. 'It's such a sweet song, isn't it?' he says.

He declares that he's made a more definitive version of an old decision.

'I'm getting Robbie Williams back together,' he declares.

* * *

September–December 2016

As Rob has conversation after conversation with people about *The Heavy Entertainment Show* and his life now, one constant question is about his renewed relationship with Guy. There are some things Rob talks about where he'll head for the security or comfort of similar words each time; by the end of the year, there are big chunks of his interviews that I could more or less do for him. It's interesting, then, that almost every time he is asked about Guy he finds new words to explain their relationship, its strengths and its weaknesses, and how they fit together and how they don't. It's as though he's always finding new words because he's still trying to work it out himself.

Listen:

'I think we're both awkward people, and our awkwardness dovetails.'

'Working with Guy is great, and infuriating, and loving, and bonkers, silly, wonderful, enriching. It's all of those things.'

'Guy's always been an older semi-mentor for me. We're both in the same place – we're both dads, and we both have families, we both have egos, and our egos are both permanently bruised, and we want to heal those bruised egos by writing hits. It's the same as it ever was with me and Guy – we're opposing personalities that seem to mesh well.'

'We have chemistry, and that chemistry I only have with Guy Chambers. He's incredibly talented, and he's incredibly silly, and when we get together we write incredibly silly, pompous, hopefully important-to-many-people songs. What me and Guy do together, I don't do that with anybody else.'

'Musically, this album is a richer tapestry because of Guy Chambers' eccentricities and musical gifts. It's just a bit more complex, because Guy's back on board and he's fucking mad and he knows all the chords.'

'Then we fell out. Which is also a pattern which happens in my life. I fall out with people, and then I bear grudges, and it all becomes part of the panto of my life. But I always knew that I would be returning to write with Guy. That relationship waited in the wings while the panto of my life played itself out. I daresay that that relationship will now last until we cease to exist.'

* * *

February 2013

Rob is in Guy's London studio. He has a song he wants to write, a song he intends to release for free on the internet as soon as they have finished it. He has something he wants to say, something that can't wait.

He holds the microphone, and begins to talk-rap over the plangent backing track, a track Guy has probably written in the hope that it would inspire something tender and epic. Another day, perhaps. Right now, Rob has other things on his mind.

He begins.

Well, that Brits night was so fucking boring …

* * *

Two days earlier, Rob is at the Brits. In the empty O2 arena, he chats with One Direction before watching them rehearse in an enjoyable ramshackle way. Someone describes them as 'like a herd of cats', and Rob nods. 'There's no sort of Gary Barlow telling them off – no Gary Barlow, no Jason Orange to pull everyone in line. It would seem that it's a band of Robbies and Marks.'

Back in his dressing room, he explains that he wants to do a joke from the stage where he offers to fight Liam Payne for charity for £100,000, in a tribute to his Brit Awards offer to do the same with Liam Gallagher. But as he discusses it, he realises with disappointment that it probably won't make as much sense or have the impact he'd want it to. It's frustrating.

'Everyone's too well behaved these days, aren't they? I wonder if it's got anything to do with the desperation.'

'I think we need a bit of … *attitude*, basically,' sympathises David Enthoven.

'Yeah, just a touch,' says Rob.

'We need something,' David adds. 'We need some angry young … I mean, if I was young, I'd be fucking angry.'

'Yeah, normally that's what happens – there's a youth movement, is there?' Rob considers. 'But I just think maybe there's just apathy and fucking chavs.'

'Since the internet's taken off, we haven't had any ...' begins David.

'Well,' Rob chips in, 'dumbing down's worked, and everybody thinks they can be a celebrity. Whereas before, you know, it was just people with Home Counties accents that were on the TV – there was nobody they could have a look at and go "that's who I want to be". Now there's the false hope, through *The X Factor* and reality TV shows, anybody can be famous. And the truth is: anyone can. There's loads of fucking reasons why there hasn't been an angry movement – apathy's one, and I think dumbing down's worked.'

A few minutes later he is chatting with Jonny Wilkes about the list of foods that he's been told he can't eat after a food-type blood test two weeks ago: ham, pork, barracuda, chestnuts, vanilla, coconut, oranges, tangerines, wheat, couscous and vinegar.

'You can't have balsamic vinegar?' Jonny exclaims.

'No,' he says, 'and that's all I am. I'm half man, half balsamic.'

He reads out some of what he can have: chicken, lamb, turkey, venison, buffalo, halibut, pineapple, plum, pomegranate, banana.

Still, some good news.

'I can drink whisky, plum wine and sake. Which is *great*,' he says sarcastically.

Jonny studies Rob's list in more detail. 'Orange roughy – what's that?' he says.

'It's a fish,' says Rob. 'Have you not learned *anything* since leaving Stoke?

* * *

Someone walks in and compliments Ollie on Rob's hair.

'I'm the one who grew it!' Rob complains, mock offended.

'You look about ten years younger,' Gina tells him.

'Yeah,' he says, 'but I did look sixty.'

Rob says that the melatonin is working for him, which triggers a discussion about whether melatonin gives people nightmares. Rob says that, for him, that's just business as usual. 'I have nightmares every night anyway. I'm either killing someone or somebody kills me. It's cracking.'

Back out in the arena, he watches Muse rehearse the opening song then James Corden runs through his show introduction. There's a lot of hanging around, and it does have the air of a rehearsal for a corporate presentation.

'It's not as magical as it used to be,' Jonny complains.

'It's because we're older and more cynical,' says Rob, 'and not as bothered.'

'Do you know what it is?' says Jonny. 'Nobody seems happy.'

'Nobody's *supposed* to look happy here,' Rob points out. 'They never were.'

'*We* used to be happy,' Jonny objects. 'We went round fighting with laser guns.'

'When we were the Harry Styleses?' Rob replies drily.

This is when the Taylor Swift security detail's over-the-top corridor-clearing etiquette starts happening. Rob is instantly annoyed and complaining to everyone. It also reminds him of when Lady Gaga's security pulled a similar stunt a few years back. He speculates what would happen if Taylor Swift and Lady Gaga, with their respective teams, were walking towards each other down a corridor. 'That's what the Hadron Collider in Switzerland is made for,' he says. 'They could have just done *that*, and seen what happened.'

Various Mumford and Sons, momentarily one of the biggest groups in the world, are mingling. Rob doesn't speak with them. Later, he'll say some respectful things about what they do and what they've achieved, but it's clear that whatever it is that he finds weird and uninspiring about the music industry right now – not so much the music itself as the whole attitude and approach – they seem to be playing their part in it: 'I can't really watch them for too long – I'm sure they're all lovely lads, but there's an over-earnestness there. It's like they've come from prospecting all day to standing onstage. And it annoys me. I think they're The Wurzels with a degree.'

* * *

Soon it is time for the show.

When you see celebrities arriving and walking along a red carpet at an event like the Brit Awards, it's usually as much a performance as what they do onstage – usually they have been in the building for hours, preparing, and then are ferried round to the red carpet entrance to 'arrive'. Rob often used to refuse to go along with this charade, but this evening he does his bit, answers the requisite sound-bite questions – 'You're nominated – how does it feel?' 'How's Teddy?' 'Are you rejoining Take That?' – then sits around in the dressing room, bored. He decides to 'go for a wander' and check out a room called, more in hope than expectation, the Star Bar. There's no one here but a few record company people, and no fun in the air whatsoever. He sits at a table, wondering what to do next.

'I'm from the nineties,' he says. 'I'm not having this.'

He steps back into the corridor, but then realises that there's nowhere he wants to go and just stands there. 'There's no buzz, no vibe, no energy.'

He sighs.

'I'm tired,' he says, 'and I haven't eaten since last year.'

He goes back into the dressing room where he can watch the live TV coverage of the show. The atmosphere looks dead. As Rob sees it, the problem is the fundamental problem with any record industry audience. 'They know the magic's not real,' he says, and then adds, 'They're the ones who killed the magic for me in the first place.'

When the time comes, he goes out and performs 'Candy', but he gets slightly unnerved because the first people he sees at a nearby table are Damon Albarn and Noel Gallagher, and all he can think about is what they're going to be thinking while he does his uber-pop hip-thrusting choreographed 'Candy' dance routine. After, he goes back to do his James Corden interview and insults Taylor Swift, then presents an award to One Direction who he refers to onstage as 'my five little brothers, show business brothers'.

Whether or not he succeeded in adding anything valuable, nobody else seems to do anything but go through the corporate, promotional motions. It's a sad state of affairs when *The Sun*'s pop columnist, in these days Gordon Smart, tweets immediately that 'rock'n'roll is dead'.

'He's right,' says Rob.

* * *

That's what has driven Rob to write the song that will become 'The Brits 2013'. Maybe it doesn't *need* saying, but he needs to say it. He starts writing it the following day, and wants to record it immediately, but first he has to film an appearance on *Ant & Dec's Saturday Takeaway*.

But before that, when David comes to pick him up at home, first he needs to share last night's dream. Maybe it's the melatonin. Maybe it's the after-effects of the Brits. Maybe it's just the wild night-time firings of the synapses inside his head ... but, even by his standards, this is a strange one.

'I had a really weird sleep,' he says. 'I wanked George Michael off. There was no cock. He had a vagina. Me, Jonny and Ayda were in a sort of quarry that wasn't a quarry, and we had a little skiff but that sank, and it was fifteen foot down and Ayda was like, "You could get that." And I was, "I can't." Then there was a houseboat, and me and Jonny got on it, on the roof and all of a sudden we heard, "It'll only take us an hour to get back," and it shot off. And it was: "Oh fuck, now we've got to tell them we're on it." So we did, and they stopped, and let us off. And then I ended up at George Michael's house. And I don't know why I started wanking him off. I remember in my head thinking, "This is my first male sexual encounter – he's never going to have that. I'm not even going to tell him." But he was like a girl, and the clothes were still on – a chiffon something. We talked afterwards and he was upset with me. He was very sensitive. Because of something I'd said previously, before the wanking. And then Andrew Ridgeley was there. Then I went downstairs, and it happened to be my birthday, and Ayda had found out where I was, and she's come and put balloons up and everything. In George Michael's house. And she's, "Boozy!" And I'm, like, "Oh my God, I've just wanked George Michael off – how bad do I feel? And now you've done this for my birthday?" And I was thinking: should I tell her? It wasn't like a proper cheat. I didn't *enjoy* it.'

'Are you taking melatonin?' David checks.

'Yeah.'

'They do work,' says David, 'but the mind does drift off into strange places.'

'Oh,' Rob adds, by way of agreement, 'yeah, and the pre-dream before wanking George Michael off was a zombie apocalypse. Frank Ocean was in that.'

He heads to the TV studios. In the dressing room, having his make-up done, he brings everyone up to date:

'Guess who I wanked off in my dream last night? George Michael. And he had a vagina.'

A while later, David Walliams, who is acting as the show's announcer, comes in.

'Shall I tell you who I wanked off … ?' Rob begins, and re-shares his dream.

'Well, if he doesn't have a penis,' David adjudicates, as though he is prepared to assume some authority, 'it doesn't count.'

Later Rob meets Louis Walsh, who is also on tonight's show. He doesn't tell Louis, but Louis compliments him on how he looks. Afterwards, Rob replays his words:

'You look great! You look great! Jesus! I mean, when you were at *X Factor* last year you were fat!"

* * *

The next day, in the studio, Guy listens to the lyric for 'The Brits 2013'.

It's like VD clinic, only pricks are in it
So fucking dull and professional and timid
To be frank, sir
I prefer this showbiz chancer.

'It's good,' he says. 'As rants go, it's good. I can see why you want to get it out now.'

'I can't wait three years,' Rob says. 'I mean, it's not going on the swing album,' he says.

'Somebody needs to say this,' says Guy. 'No one else is going to.'

And on Rob continues:

Now I know I got fat, but make no mistake
Every million that I make they bake me a cake.

* * *

In the afternoon, they take a break and go back to Guy's house for a while. Rob reminisces how he used to come over to where Guy used to live to see his first daughter just after she was born, and how he'd lie there on the couch with a hangover.

'You were on the sofa for a long time,' says Guy. 'You demanded sausages.'

'I didn't *demand* anything,' Rob protests.

'I think you said one word,' Guy clarifies. '"Sausages".'

When Guy's son Marley, who is ten, comes back from paintballing, Guy encourages him to show off his drum skills in front of Rob. He doesn't want to. Rob sympathises.

'People used to do that to me when I was little,' he says, 'and it was horrible. "Do Tommy Cooper! Do this! Do that! Do that!" And I didn't want to do it.'

But then Rob encourages Marley to have a go anyway, Guy goes to the piano, and father and son play 'Come Together'. 'Well played, Marley,' says Rob. Then he takes a look at Marley's maths homework. It's to do with averages. Rob shakes his head. 'Not a scooby doo,' he says. 'You won't need any of this, you know. Yeah, you won't. But good luck with that – don't let that put you off. I can't add or subtract. I really genuinely can't.'

This may not be the speech that Guy or Emma would like their children to hear, but it's the one they're getting today.

'I was let down by the schooling system,' he says. 'But they didn't have "dyslexia" then, they just had "thick".'

One more question for Marley. 'What are you going to do? Do you know?'

'No,' says Marley.

Rob nods. 'I don't know. I'm nearly forty, I still don't know.'

* * *

Back at the studio to finish off the song, Rob picks up one of Guy's guitars and strums some chords.

'"How Peculiar" was written on that,' Guy says.

Rob remembers that day.

'It was great,' he says. 'We wrote "How Peculiar", went back to my house, two strippers knocked on the door and slept with me. And I played that song in the background while they shagged me.' He half smiles, half sighs. 'Good days, good days.'

And then he gets back to complaining in song – complaining, and offering himself as the solution:

If they can't be bothered then I promise you this
If they won't entertain you then I'll do my fucking best.

* * *

July 2011

Post on Robbie Williams' blog, in which he is answering questions and responding to requests that have been sent in by his fans:

I BELIEVE THERE WAS A LADY THAT WAS LOOKING FOR INTELLECT AND NOT FLUFF ...

I AM MADE OF FLUFF.

MAY I SUGGEST ANOTHER POPSTAR FOR YOU. I THINK YOU MAY FIND WHAT YOU'RE AFTER HERE.

He embeds a link to http://leonardcohen.com/community.html, a Leonard Cohen discussion group.

HAPPY HUNTING ...

* * *

February 2013

For Rob's thirty-ninth birthday, Guy sent him a book, John Niven's *Kill Your Friends*, a tale of horror and homicide set in the 1990s British music industry and packed with gleeful and sordid insider knowledge. Rob read the first 50 or 60 pages, but he was struggling with the narrator.

'I was finding it difficult because there's absolutely nothing to like about him. And then there were coke moments that took me back exactly to the nineties where I was, "God, that feels bad." Then there was a bit about me. He wasn't even that rude. But he obviously saw me at the Brits doing … obviously what he saw me doing. Which was being sober. And I was "ohhh…" because he was spot on.'

This is what he'd read:

As we drink and gossip and bitch I look over at the recently clean and sober Robbie Williams, who is sitting at a table a few feet away. He's fiddling with the label on a bottle of mineral water, smoking two-handed, and nodding while some guy I don't know – some manager, some lawyer – explains something to him. Williams periodically turns away to stare hard – a hard stare I know well – at the glittering rump of some boiler standing near him. Poor bastard, I guess that's all he's got now, isn't it? The pumping. Can you imagine it? You're not even thirty and you can't do anything any more. No nose-up, no pills, no frosty beers, no warming shots of Jack or Remy. You're just sitting there, completely sober, in your fuck-off mansion, dressed head to foot in all the finery you spent the morning trawling New Bond Street with some stylist for, you've just given up trying to read some book for the umpteenth time, because it's too hard, you're turning on Sky Sports again, or forcing some underling to drink fruit juice and play cards with you, and you're thinking – another forty years of this? You're just some stage kid, some poor song-and-dance spastic with a cheeky grin who fate threw a whole bunch of sevens. And now you're staring down the wrong end of four decades with just your own thoughts for company when you don't really have two fucking thoughts to rub together. Nasty.

Rob decided he didn't want to read any further.

'Cheers, Guy,' he laughs.

It's actually a fairly savage portrait of who that Robbie Williams might have been, but even if some of Niven's guesses and suppositions are close to the bone, the real Robbie Williams has worked hard to transcend the bleak version of his future Niven saw. But there was a different part of what Niven had written which resonated the deepest, and stuck with Rob. The bit about him just being some kid who fate threw a whole bunch of sevens.

'And it really struck a chord with me,' he says. 'Yeah, this could have fucking happened to anybody, and it happened to me. I'm a lucky son of a bitch. And so is absolutely everybody else in the recording industry apart from Prince. And a couple more that can't come to mind. Apart from Prince, everybody is a lucky fucker. I just look at the Brit Awards and the people on there, including myself – we're all so very very lucky. I'm a lucky son of a bitch. There seems to be no rhyme or reason why one thing and not the other permeates whatever touches the soul of the nation. You know, how many fucking "me's" are there? George Michael's fucking lucky to be where he is, too. Madonna, lucky as fuck. Me, lucky as fuck. It's only Prince who deserves to be where he is.'

* * *

March–May 2013

In the middle of March, Rob and Guy meet up in Los Angeles. The plan is to record most of this new swing album at the legendary Capitol Studios, where they recorded *Swing When You're Winning*, with the same legendary engineer, Al Schmitt. First, they need to do a couple of days' preparation up at Rob's home studio, listening through songs and making final choices. They're discussing arrangements and checking keys when they are interrupted by a distraction Rob spots approaching through the window that faces onto the street of his gated estate.

'There's Lord Thomas,' Rob says. 'He's coming up the hill. To say hello.'

'Is that Robbie Williams over there?' booms the voice at the bottom of the stairs, and seconds later Tom Jones appears. They compare their jet lags. 'I thought I'd be all right today,' says Rob, 'but right now I feel like a bag of spanners.' Rob explains about the swing album, and Tom Jones talks about the late career success he's having making the kind of rootsier records that he'd felt he wasn't able to make earlier in his career because, he says, 'It's Not Unusual' had set him on a different, poppier track. Once you do one thing, people expect you to carry on doing it.

'Yeah,' Rob sympathises. 'You've got to hit it right down the middle every time. That's what I tried to do with this last album, the swing album is this, and then I want to go and do something mental for the album after that. But people don't want that.'

'All right, lads,' Tom Jones eventually says, taking his leave. 'Get on with it, have a good time.'

A while later, taking Teddy for a walk in her pram in the estate, Rob says, 'Wasn't it great, seeing Tom? It's great, my life, living on Stella Street.'

As though the world is determined to illustrate this point as memorably as possible, as we pass one of the houses just down the street, a car pulls up, the driver gets out and Brian Wilson walks into his house.

* * *

Rob recently saw the movie *The Perks of Being a Wallflower*. It made him think two things. The first is that, although he liked the movie, he resents the lies that certain kinds of movies sell to you, and the way those affect your life.

'It's one of those coming-of-age films,' he says, 'that once you've come of age, you go, "Fuck, the last time I watched a coming-of-age film I was coming of age ... bastards!' It's like a *Sixteen Candles* – it touches all of those buttons, and you go, "I'm nearly forty! Fuck! Film, you *lied* to me, you bastards! Life isn't like that! No one's going to just start singing!"' He has made a resolution. 'I'm not going to watch another coming-of-age movie. They fucking lie, those films. No one's ever that interesting.'

The second thought he had was that the film's star, Emma Watson, would be someone good to duet with on the swing album, so he made contact.

'She came up to the studio,' he says. 'Her boyfriend was outside in a yellow Mustang. She's like the prettiest thing ever – prettier actually than in film. If she didn't exist there'd be a conspiracy theory about her existing.'

Watson said that she wanted to get a singing coach, and felt that she'd need to prove to Rob that she'd be good enough. Rob told her not to worry. But he was impressed by her general poise when it came to her life, and to dealing with fame. 'I got the vibe that she was compos mentis and handling it better than I did.'

He laughs.

'Which isn't very difficult.'

* * *

Rob seems to be in the mood for some consternation, and an article he has just read in *The Sun* ably supplies it. The article begins:

SUEDE frontman Brett Anderson says 'cr*p' acts like Justin Bieber and One Direction are nothing new.

Then it quotes Anderson as saying:

'*There has always been cr*p pop music. I remember when we had all the crap boybands in the 90s – stuff like that has always been around. The lack of money in the music industry created a crisis. Record companies don't have the resources to take a gamble, these pop stars are created by committee.*'

'I fucking hate everybody that's having a go at One Direction,' Rob says. From the blog he has written in response, it's clearly got under his skin:

I THINK NOT ...

ANY QUARTER-DECENT 3 CHORD KNOBHEADS COULD AND DID GET A DEAL IN THE 90'S ...

I WON'T NAME NAMES COS IT WOULD BE UNFAIR ON ECHOBELLY, SHED 7, SYMPOSIUM, MENSWEAR, SLEEPER, HURRICANE NUMBER 1, RIDE, THE BLUETONES (APART FROM THAT ONE SONG), OCEAN COLOUR SCENE (APART FROM THAT ONE SONG ... HANG ON NAH NOT EVEN THAT SONG), NORTHERN UPROAR, CHAPTERHOUSE, CURVE, SALAD, ADORABLE, CUD, SPACEHOG, KULA SHAKER, THE AUDIENCE, POWDER, KINGMAKER, GENEVA (SUB-SUEDE – CAN YOU IMAGINE?).

SHOULD I GO ON? COS I CAN AND THEY SURE FUCKING DID.

THERE WERE A FEW SPECIAL INDIE BANDS THEN JUST AS THERE ARE IN EVERY GENERATION ...

AND JUST AS SOME POP BANDS ARE USELESS, SOME ARE MAGNIFICENT IN EVERY GENERATION.

I FEEL SORRY FOR THE PEOPLE WHO ARE TOO BIGOTED TO APPRECIATE THE LATTER.

THE WORLD'S A LOT MORE EXCITING WITH A ONE DIRECTION IN IT AND MORE HEARTS WILL GENUINELY RACE AT A NEW I D ALBUM THAN THEY EVER HAVE OR WILL AT ANY SUEDE ALBUM IN ANY TIME PERIOD.

SORRY ABOUT THE TRUTH.

PLEASE SAY HELLO TO YOUR DRUMMER.

HE WAS CONSISTENTLY LOVELY WITH ME.

YOURS IN POP,

ROBBIE WILLIAMS

When Rob tells Guy about this blog, and mentions that he hasn't posted it yet, Guy tells him that he shouldn't. That he doesn't need the negative energy. Though Guy does also remind Rob about the time that he, Guy, phoned up Sonya from Echobelly, asking her to sing on Rob's first album. How she laughed and put the phone down on him.

* * *

We pull up at the car park barrier for Capitol Records' legendary studios.

Here is a fair snapshot of Rob's superstar status, or otherwise, in America.

'We're in studio A – Robbie Williams,' Rob says to the man in the booth.

The man peers at him doubtfully. 'That's *your* name?'

'Yes,' says Rob.

The man checks paperwork for a few moments, then agrees that it's okay for us to enter. Some version of the same routine will be repeated day after day after day.

Inside, Rob greets Al Schmitt, who is 82 and who first worked here in 1972. History is everywhere here. (In old ways and new – the wifi password is *Sinatra1*.) Rob is told about the microphone they have set up for him today.

'It's the same mic as Nat King Cole used,' says Guy.

'The actual one?' says Rob.

'Sinatra,' nods Schmitt. 'Nat King Cole. Dean Martin.'

Michael Bublé, who Rob is to duet with today on 'Soda Pop', arrives.

'I'm so fucking excited and honoured and giddy,' Rob tells him, and they talk about the song.

'I don't know what it means, to be honest with you …' Bublé says.

'I don't either,' says Rob. 'I don't know what any of them mean.' Then he explains that it has a new middle section that was written last night.

'I'm Ron Burgundy, man,' says Bublé. 'You write it, I'll say it. "Go fuck yourself, San Diego!"' And he asks whether he can mess with the harmonies.

'As much as you like,' says Rob, then adds, 'by the way, harmonies and me is like Russian roulette – some days they're there, and then some days they're really fucking not, and it's embarrassing.'

They go into the main room and Rob greets the musicians – many of them some of the most famous session musicians in the world: 'Can I just say hello? I'm Robbie – I think I've worked with a lot of you before. Lovely to work with you all again. Thank you for having me, and I appreciate everything that you're going to put into this record, so thank you very much.'

Rob and Michael Bublé run through the song and then, in a break, Bublé quite randomly starts singing the 'hi de hi de hi de ho' refrain from 'Minnie The Moocher'.

'I'm doing that,' says Rob, meaning that he's recording it for this album, and then adds, matter-of-factly, 'it's going to be fifth song in the stadiums this year.'

The fifth song in the stadiums this year. Here's one more Robbie Williams contradiction. In so many ways, he seems to barrel forward recklessly, without preparation or apparent forethought. Often he treats Tuesday as if he has no idea that it will be followed by Wednesday. So it's easy to miss the signs that, somewhere in the background, there's also a very different kind of programme running: one that's imagining and assessing possibilities and calculating and planning, a kind of shrewdly scheming entertainment mastermind. Rob is yet to even record 'Minnie The Moocher'. But in the summer he will indeed perform 'Minnie The Moocher' on his stadium tour. And it will be the fifth song.

Rob and Bublé keep singing through the song, getting more and more animated.

'I just see us now at the Royal Albert Hall,' says Michael, 'singing this tune. Speaking of that, when you did that show it looked so expensive.'

'It fucking was,' Rob says.

'I mean, it was truly amazing – it was like a Broadway musical.'

'Thank you. And it was truly, truly expensive. And we lost a lot of money on it. And then the DVD came out and all was good.'

'And how many days did you shoot?'

'One.'

'No!'

'Yeah, it was one night.'

'Come on – but did you do stuff over and over?'

'No, it was one night.'

'No!' Bublé protests. 'I'm not that talented, I'm realising. That's amazing.'

'Lucky,' says Rob, offering a different adjective to describe what he did. 'That was performing on my nerves. By the skin of my teeth, and the seat of my pants.'

In the next break, Bublé tells him that it's nice to collaborate like this: 'I'm a loner. As a singer, I'm alone up there, just like you are.'

'Yeah – it's terrifying,' says Rob. They share notes about performing, in the way that people do when they realise that they're talking to a rare conversation partner who might actually understand the experience that they're talking about. 'It's about a thousand per cent concentration and what you're doing next and how you're doing it next …' says Rob, '… and, congratulations, we make it look as though that isn't going on inside our heads.'

'Isn't it funny how that works?' says Michael.

'I know, because I watch myself back and think the voice must be that loud that it must tell on my face,' says Rob, 'and ninety-nine per cent of the time it doesn't.'

Rob then tells Michael about his TV plans. 'I fancy doing something that's funny,' he says, 'but I don't want to do a film.'

'I don't want to do anything where it's me playing me, that's for sure,' says Michael.

'I'll play me,' Rob explains, 'as long as I'm a wanker. As long as I'm an idiot.' He sings a line. 'Which isn't very difficult,' he adds.

In between all this, they keep doing takes of the song, but they usually have to be interrupted to be prevailed upon to do so. Time and its conjoined twin money are at a premium during a session like this, with a large group of professional musicians gathered to play, so the way they both seem to be embracing this as a bonding experience with a little attached singing is not usual. In the control room Al Schmitt says, as though somewhere between baffled and exasperated by the youth of today, 'Do these guys know they're here to make a record?'

* * *

When Rob gets home, he gets Ayda to read the blog, which he has now gone ahead and posted. Even though he warns her she may not like it, I think he's expecting some kind of support for sticking up for himself.

'I'm not saying nothing,' she says once she has finished reading.

'What?' he says.

'I'm not saying nothing,' she repeats.

'*What?*' he repeats more insistently.

So she says something. Specifically that she thinks Rob is making himself look bad. 'I feel like there's ways to get your point across without making yourself look bad. Like, you're not that guy. If you were that guy, then that's you. But you're throwing out a message about yourself that's not reflective or actually who you are.'

'I *am* that guy,' he argues.

'You're not!' she says.

'I am that guy that thinks that about those bands,' he says.

'Yeah, but you're not a jerk. You came off like really angry in it. You're not an angry person.'

This sits there for a second.

'I am,' he says.

'No, you're not,' she says.

'Then you don't know about me,' he says, but laughing.

'No, you're just not that guy. When I read that, that does not sound like you. That's not my boozys. So many of your blogs are funny and truthful – they dance this fine line of funny and truthful and poignant. And that to me was just angry. That's not good. You're not better than them because you just kicked the shit out of them on this blog.'

'Okay,' he says, evenly.

'It's like punching a bunny,' she continues.

'It's not,' he says. 'They were *nasty* bunnies.'

'Okay, well that bunny's old now. It's like punching a mean old bunny.'

'Yeah,' he says. 'I don't know you.'

'I don't know *you* apparently, reading that blog.'

Chris Briggs walks in.

'I'm being told off for that blog,' Rob tells him.

'Are you going to beat me up now?' Ayda asks. 'The guy that wrote that blog would beat the shit out of me!'

There's a level of humour in this whole exchange, but not, too.

'Oh boozys,' she continues. 'It was a random quote, not even really directed at you or really even related to you. You're so clever and wonderful and funny and poignant and *accurate* with what you say, and I feel like you kind of missed the mark with this one. Not that they're not dickheads and you got it wrong, but the way you presented it I feel just makes you look like an angry person, I feel like it does disservice to the point you're trying to make.'

'I don't know about that,' he says. 'I think it's a good blog. I think it says something really lovely about pop music.'

'But I just go "he's really angry",' she says.

'By the way,' he says, 'I *am* really angry about being vilified by these pretentious cunts for fucking year after year after year after year after year. And I have got a dog in that fight. They were all fucking knobheads to me.'

'There is this terrible snobbery in the UK,' Chris Briggs points out to Ayda, explaining the ways in which, whatever its faults, this blog isn't an out-of-the-blue attack but a response to a whole mindset that used to dominate one part of British cultural discourse. 'And it's kind of been relentless for years – it's so tiring and boring. And it was particularly dreadful in the late nineties, that sort of golden era of stupidity in the indie world.'

'And you're made to feel like a fucking pariah for even *existing*,' Rob echoes. 'Just because of a fucking genre of music. You're made to feel subhuman. And practically every single one of those bands, I can name you this time that they said this, this time that they did that, this time that she laughed and put the phone down.'

'That's going to be in the papers tomorrow, and they'll make you look bad,' Ayda counters. 'They always love to make you look bad and then you've just served it up on a plate for them to trash you.'

'By me speaking anytime *ever*, or appearing in the public anytime ever, it serves it up on a plate for them to do whatever they want,' he says.

But this conversation, and the fact that Ayda thinks he has made a mistake, is making Rob genuinely sad, and after a while Ayda realises he's really quite upset.

'You're the person I care most about on the planet,' he tells her, 'whose opinion I treasure dearly most on the planet. You've got a very valid point, but I also wish you'd be like, "Good for you for sticking it to them cunts that stuck it to you, babe."'

She tells him she's just trying to be honest, and that she knows she doesn't have the British context that might make this seem different.

'Can't you do what my nan would have done?' he asks. 'If I'd have murdered someone, she would have been, "Well, he must have deserved it – come in and have a bacon sandwich."'

Eventually, Ayda tries to console him.

'I liked the blog?' she says, and he sort of laughs.

'Sure?'

'It was ... the best one you've written?'

'Was it ... awesome?'

'Yeah.'

And then they debate whether they should watch *Celebrity Apprentice* or *Celebrity Wife Swap*.

* * *

Much later that night, long after I've gone to bed and fallen asleep, there's a knock on my bedroom door. It's Rob. He wants to talk a moment.

'I feel really stupid for doing that blog,' he says.

* * *

In the morning, he says he feels fine about it now. Also, he's had an email from Brett Anderson's PR people saying that Brett didn't name any names in his interview with *The Sun*, and that what he said had been twisted by them.

Rob reads me the reply he's written to the PR people:

Yes, I have re-read the article and it does seem like I've gone off at a tangent. But I do think he's a cunt so I'll stick with what I said.

I ask him, with some trepidation, whether he really said that.

'Yes.'

Really?

'Yes. I haven't sent it yet.'

I suggest that perhaps he shouldn't. A short while later, he comes to read me his revised version:

Yes, I've read the whole interview and it'd seem I've gone off on a quite unnatural tangent. It won't be the last time, and it felt good to get it off my chest, so thank him for me, cheers.

* * *

Today, to record 'Go Gentle' and 'If I Only Had A Brain', Rob wears an Illuminati jumper to the studio, a design which incorporates a triangle and an eye.

'I am a member of the Illuminati,' he announces. 'And it's a really good club to be in. I pity the fools that aren't.'

I ask him where he got the jumper from.

'Off Amazon,' he concedes. 'I put in "Illuminati shirts".'

* * *

Back home, a man knocks on the back door – he explains that he's the man who does their rats but he's here to do the spiders. Rob takes Teddy for a walk on the estate, and talks to her.

'I wuv you, sirry birry,' he tells her, and makes Donald Duck noises. 'You funny bear. I sang a song about you today. I made a promise. Yeah.'

We go and sit by the swings, and Rob fills her in on other recent developments: 'Daddy started a fight with lots of nineties pop bands. They all hate me now. Even more than they did before. Which was a *lot*.'

He watches her.

'I can't wait to see what her personality's gonna be,' he says. 'I hope she's slightly odd. I think it'd be very difficult not being. The plan is to be very supportive and to be there for her, so maybe she'll be missing that chip of deep-set insecurity.'

Then he addresses her directly: 'Yeah, you're not going to be as broken as Mummy and Daddy, I don't think. No … you're just chilling.' He carries on, more father–daughter wisdom to impart.

'You can't be too good-looking *and* be really funny and clever – they hate that,' he tells her. 'I mean, I managed half of each one of those, and they still hated it.'

* * *

The next day is spent doing more work on 'Go Gentle', and then 'Shine My Shoes'. Guy gets Rob to sing them both, over and over.

'Are we done?' Rob finally asks Guy.

Guy nods. He's always keen not to go past the point where Rob's vocals begin to deteriorate. 'I think you shouldn't sing any more,' he says.

'What, *ever*?' Rob replies. 'So you're joining in now, are you?'

* * *

The Britpop furore continues. Various nineties music figures have commented, and Rob finds that he is slightly disappointed to have upset Rick Witter from Shed Seven. 'To be honest,' Rob says, 'he was always very nice.'

There's something particularly surreal about the fact that this week Rob is making a swing album by day, and fighting nineties indie rock fires by night, but that's how it is. He occasionally makes internet radio programmes under the name Radio Rudebox, and tonight he decides, as both some kind of continuation and some kind of penance, to record a Britpop Radio Rudebox special.

It begins with him explaining that he has hastily arranged this programme 'because I think I've made a bit of a boo-boo this week with a bit of a blog that went up', and then he reads out one particular online response to what he's said, quite clearly enjoying saying the words. The general slant taken by the person who posted this comment is perhaps hinted at by the online alias he has chosen for himself, WilliamsIsACock. This is what he wrote, and what Rob reads out:

Yeah, but you insulted Northern Uproar, OCS and MANY other great bands that are worth more than you'll ever be. Prick. Williams, you're a fucking dick. Don't comment on REAL MUSICIANS until you come up with anything half decent. You talentless fucking piece of shit. Northern Uproar piss all over ANYTHING you and your songwriters have ever come up with, you utter prick. And One Direction make the world more exciting? Do me a fucking favour? They make it a better climate for knobheads like you who have no talent. Worthless puppets. Just like YOU. You are a fucking joke.

'So we'll be finding out later on,' says Rob, 'why that happened. And we'll also be finding out why my wife thinks I'm a prick.'

He explains that he's been tired and grumpy and was looking for someone to take it out on but as new memories are prompted by each Britpop song he plays, his efforts to smooth the waters are erratic. After stopping himself saying something horrible about Damon Albarn, he meanders around the rest of the band until he's commenting that Alex James hasn't been nice about him 'but he's the bass player in Blur – my nanny could do that'. Sometimes, instead of an insult, he offers a revealing personal glimpse. After playing Elastica's 'Connection', during which Ayda comes in holding a glass of wine and some dark chocolate, he says: 'Oh! By the way! Heroin! I did heroin for the first time with Elastica. For the first and last time. In King's Cross.'

'This'll be so nice to play back to our daughter when she's older,' says Ayda.

'Hey, listen, Dad's been a few places, and I will be the first to let her know about it and talk her through it. I didn't like heroin – it made me throw up.'

And then Rob and Ayda reprise for the listening audience their disagreement from the other night.

'So I wrote this blog and I attacked a few bands,' Rob begins.

'Yes.'

'I did it with noble intentions.'

'Yes.'

'And then I read you the blog.'

'Yes.'

'And you said?'

'Well, you prefaced it by saying "I don't think you'll be very happy about this" so to be fair I had that in my head,' says Ayda. 'Now I of course am not from the UK, I am from the United States of America where the land is great and the milk is sweet and the honey is gold … We don't have this big thing about pop being crap. Now I'm understanding from the discussions that we had after this, there's a big kind of muso snobbery …'

'Systematic bullying,' Rob chips in.

'… against people in pop. Which by the way I think is really lame … so I think it's really crap that people bullied you …'

'*Pop*. Bullied pop.'

'… bullied pop, sorry. But I'm going to use you as a symbol of pop.'

'Yes, please do.'

'As you make me do in our house anyway.'

'So where did I go wrong?'

'Where you went wrong is that your response, to me, seemed angry. And the truth of the matter is, you're not an angry person. You are the kindest, funniest, most big-hearted person I have ever met in my life. And you walk the line of humour and truth and honesty, and it's all very poetic and spot on and light-hearted, and you always manage to surprise me and impress me with your responses to things and your perspective on things. And in this case I feel like you let yourself down a bit. I feel like you came off angry and then you're no better than the people who were angry to you.'

'I think you're right, boo … I write in block capitals anyway.'

'Which comes off angry as it is.'

'It doesn't mean to. It's because I am dyslexic and I can read it back better … I think you're right, I did come off as a prick, a little bit. I've upset Rick Witter from Shed Seven. This guy sent a tweet saying "I've met you three times, we've had good chats – what went horribly wrong?" Thems are the words of somebody's who's hurt – I don't want to upset Rick Witter. He's a nice guy.'

'He's *my* favourite guy,' says Ayda.

'He's your favourite guy right now,' Rob points out, 'because you're hitting me with a Rick Witter twitter-style stick.'

And then Rob explains further, and much more clearly, exactly why any of this gets to him in the way that it often has.

'You know, everybody's in their own film,' he says, 'and I think that everybody sees themselves as the underdog. I come at this not from my mansion in Beverly Hills playing in front of one and a half million people this summer in stadiums all over Europe …' – he laughs at this point, as obviously he needs to – '… I'm coming from the point of view of an eight-year-old going, "Why are you picking on me, you bullies?" And there is a lot of condescension and a lot of "check that talentless fat cunt out" and "if it wasn't for Guy Chambers etc., etc, …" I am coming from a place of: hang on, I've been picked on here, and I don't like it. And I've been holding on to a gripe for a long time, and continue to hold on to a gripe. But it's a weird and wonderful world. You know, there's got to be a Kanye in the world to make things interesting, and hopefully with my insecurities and fuck-ups that I can offer every now and again, I hope people find them entertaining. Which is first and foremost what I think my job is. And then I'll have a go at trying to write something that sticks in people's hearts and will live on longer than I will.'

Throughout this radio programme, incidentally, Rob is wearing a baseball cap he was given by Dizzee Rascal. It says FUCK HUMBLE.

The songs he plays tonight, between the chat, represent, for the most part, the songs from the era he has been criticising that, for him, transcend his criticisms. His full Britpop playlist: Suede's 'Animal Nitrate', The Bluetones' 'Slight Return', Blur's 'End Of A Century', Elastica's 'Connection', Pulp's 'Something Changed', Ash's 'Girl From Mars', Cast's 'Sandstorm', the Longpigs' 'On And On' (which he says came on at the very moment he was breaking up with his girlfriend when he was 20), Radiohead's 'Fake Plastic Trees', Placebo's 'Nancy Boy', The Charlatans' 'North Country Boy', The Stone Roses' 'Love Spreads', Manic Street Preachers' 'Motorcycle Emptiness', Stephen Duffy's '17', Oasis's 'Fade Away', McAlmont & Butler's 'Yes' and Suede's brand-new 'It Starts And Ends With You'. (Nothing by Northern Uproar.)

When 'Fake Plastic Trees' starts, he says, 'This has just got its cock out and pissed on everybody, hasn't it?', then describes Radiohead's career arc in a different way from how it's usually characterised: 'They went all *Rudebox*-y but got it right …' But even here, he has some lingering personal animosity. 'I met Thom Yorke in Abbey Road,' he shares. 'It wasn't so much of a meeting, it was a walking past in the corridor. And out of nowhere he sort of did showbiz jazz hands and went "Robbie Williams!" And I wanted to twat him.'

But it's the music, and the way it makes him feel, which wins over as time passes. When The Stone Roses come on, it sends him right back.

'In my bedroom, Greenbank Road, Tunstall,' he says. 'Me giving it the big 'un. "Love Spreads" takes me back to a time when anything was possible. And, do you know what, it still is. What a beautiful world we live in.'

* * *

Late into the evening he sits outside by the pool, still thinking it all through.

'I'm trying to figure out if the buzz from the bedevilment outweighs the embarrassment of upsetting people.'

He laughs.

And?

'And it doesn't.'

I tell him I've got a feeling he'll be figuring that one out for a while.

'The rest of my life, probably. I think it's fair to say that I'm probably hated an awful lot by marginally more people than probably any musician there is in England.' Pause. 'And loved, you know.'

As he's walking up to bed at midnight, he has one final thought.

'I did feel, as I sang "Go Gentle" today, this is better than all the people I've slagged off.'

* * *

Still, not everyone Rob disparaged in his blog took it without humour. One day he gets an email from Ross Cummins, singer in Symposium.

Hi Robbie, Ross here from the band Symposium. I'm going to get all the bands to reform and we're going to do a massive tour called the Three Chord Knobheads tour. LOL.

* * *

Rob sits in the control room at Capitol Studios. 'I'm bored,' he declares. 'I've finished the internet.'

Earlier he watched Michael Bublé's new video, 'It's A Beautiful Day'. Waiting in the vocal booth, he says how assured and charismatic Bublé is in that video. 'I used to be like that,' he tells Guy. 'Till I learned the truth.'

'You can be like that again,' Guy reassures him.

'Maybe,' he says.

Ayda and Teddy turn up. Rob sings 'Soda Pop' to Teddy, and then, to general disinterest, does a series of Donald Duck noises.

'Hey!' he says. 'Hey, remember when you used to laugh at that?'

He tries again. No reaction.

'God,' he says, 'show business is so fickle.'

* * *

One evening, Guy comes up to Rob's house, and Rob explains an idea he's had about doing twin *Love* and *Hate* albums. 'So I get all the hates in my soul out,' he says, 'and then we struggle to write an album of love.'

'You think that by getting out all of the hatred it'll be like a purging?' asks Guy.

'Of sorts, yes,' says Rob. 'I don't hold much hope.'

'Well, "No Regrets", would you class that as a hate song?' Guy asks, trying to understand the concept.

'Yeah. "Karma Killer". "Into The Silence" off the last album,' Rob says, and quotes some of its savage lyrics: *When karma reaches you, I want to be there just in case it needs help … you made me be so cruel to myself.*

'Hate's kind of one of your strong areas,' says Guy.

'Yes,' says Rob. 'It's because I'm full of it.'

They talk about old songs, released and unreleased, and listen to a few, and then suddenly, almost without meaning to, they're writing a song – a song about someone who wanted to be famous, someone who is 'the last of the great bullshitters', an Oasis-y attack called 'The Wanker' that's somehow vituperative but also quite plaintive and empathic.

Your girlfriend's seen you cry at the TV

'That should be me

'That should be me'
You think you're so good
Are you really?
Are you really?

Tomorrow at Capitol Studios, hallowed home of the classy and timeless greats of song, at the end of a day working on an abortive German-language version of 'Mack The Knife', Rob will suddenly announce that he wants to record a demo of this new song. And so that's what he and Guy do. I'm not sure these walls will have heard lyrics like this before:

Do you like who you've been?
Now you know the dreamer must be stronger than the dream
Thanks but no thanks
You're still shooting blanks
And the wanker must last longer than the wank.

'I mean,' Rob laughs, after he finishes singing, 'it's angrier than I actually am.'

* * *

One afternoon, he and Ayda, property hunting, go and see a very big house. It's been carefully staged: *Casablanca* is playing silently on the TV screen and fires are burning.

Rob tells Ayda it's not an option, because it doesn't have the kind of view the current house has.

'It's a big deal, having that view up there,' he explains. 'It gives the illusion of being amongst people … from a distance.'

* * *

More daughter snubbing:

'Why don't you find Daddy funny all of a sudden?' Rob asks Teddy. 'I used to kill.'

'I totally get it,' says Ayda.

'You used to find me hilarious,' he objects. 'Remember this?' He makes Donald Duck noises in Teddy's face.

Teddy barely reacts.

'She's just staring at me with big bewildered eyes,' he says.

'I think you need to come up with new material,' Ayda advises. 'She's like the British public.'

* * *

More property hunting. This is the conversation that Rob and Ayda have on their way to look at some incredibly expensive houses – mostly, I think, just for the fun of it and to pass some time. It starts out with the premise of trying to work out where they'd be happy if they had to live somewhere with less money than they are fortunate to have, and it devolves into the two of them continually underbidding each other on the degradations that could come if the future's wheels fell off.

'What people in Los Angeles are willing to do is *carry on working*,' Rob argues, 'and I could stop at any time.'

'We're not stopping any time soon,' Ayda predicts. 'Babe, let's be honest – you are addicted to it.'

'I don't know – I'm re-evaluating that.'

'I don't think you love touring, but you kind of are addicted to being a pop star.'

'Yeah,' he concedes. 'Showbiz is fun.'

'Your mind is always going to think in terms of music and creativity,' she says. 'It's just not going to stop because you think you want to stop. It's just in you. Your brain thinks that way.'

'I think you're right. And as the record sales decrease, I'll get sadder and sadder …'

'… and sadder and sadder,' she continues.

'… and more insecure …' he says.

'… and keep plugging away,' she continues, 'like a dog with a bone.'

'… like one of those people you said you'd never be,' he says to himself.

'Like when they go two seasons too far on a TV show, and they should have stopped,' she says. 'That'll be you …'

'We'll have thought that we've stooped to the lowest of lows ...' he says, '... and then I'll find lower places to go ...'

'That's when we do our reality show,' says Ayda. 'That's when we take it away from being a scripted programme ...'

'... to actually being a reality TV show,' says Rob.

'Because scripted is actually quite highbrow ...'

'Go from scripted where we're in on it because we're actually laughing at ourselves to ...'

'... being in it and people laughing *at* us,' says Ayda. 'Not with us. Just: pay me anything to laugh at me.'

'Yeah.'

'And then,' she says, as though she has a magic telescope pointing directly at the saddest of all futures, 'we'll be endorsing some sort of flavoured meat that comes in a package. "From the guy who sung 'Angels' ..."'

* * *

There is a famous pop-psychological theory that celebrities are frozen at whatever age they were when they first became successful.

A few days later, Rob refers to this when he offers one final thought on the Brett Anderson kerfuffle.

'Another thing that blog reminded me of is how juvenile I am – and I'm nearly forty,' says Rob. 'Just in general. I was just thinking that if Brett Anderson doesn't respond, he's more grown up than me. But then I thought to myself, well, that's okay, because I stay the same age that I did when I became successful, which is sixteen or seventeen. And when that day comes for him he'll be stuck too.'

* * *

Later, when Rob looks back at this period in Los Angeles, he puts down a lot of the emotions he was feeling at the time to the appetite suppressants he was taking. 'They can make you quite angry,' he reflects, 'and it's quite easy for me to indulge in vengeful thinking.'

At the end of the year he will attend the Q Awards, and there he will bump in Brett Anderson.

'I really apologise,' Rob will tell him. 'I was having a bad week.'

* * *

Some final swing recording takes place in London. The drama of whether Emma Watson will ever commit to singing her duet goes on and on, and eventually they decide they have to give up on her. But there's no clear plan as to who might now join Rob on 'Dream A Little Dream', the song they had earmarked.

One evening a few weeks after he gets back to London, Guy runs into Lily Allen at the Groucho Club. She's quite drunk. Guy is sitting at the piano, as he sometimes is, and she says to him, 'Give it your best shot.' He realises that she thinks he is the Groucho pianist. (Weirdly, back in 1985 when it first opened, he really was. David Bowie walked in one time when he was playing a Disney medley: 'I was doing "hi ho, hi ho" or something really uncool.')

This night, Guy eventually ends up suggesting to Lily Allen that she sing 'Dream A Little Dream'. She asks him how he knew it was her favourite song. 'Even though she was pissed,' he says, 'she sang it really well.' By then, she has worked out who he is, and he asks her if she'd sing it on this album. She says yes but sensibly tells him to ask her again when she's sober.

Sober, she agrees to set a date.

* * *

First, a day is booked for Rob to sing 'Swings Both Ways' at Abbey Road with Rufus Wainwright and an 80-piece orchestra. After Teddy has her first haircut, Rob walks to the studio. He and Rufus catch up on news, and Rufus shows Rob the family ring he wears, a lion with an axe.

'Well, I was born in a pub called the Red Lion with that lion out front,' says Rob. 'And what the red lion actually signified, when people couldn't read, was an inn.' He pauses. 'I've got loads of those,' he adds. 'If at any moment you want a non-interesting fact, just ask me. I've got loads.'

They share further history. Rufus talks about the crossovers between his forebears and the world of *The Great Gatsby* (he watched the new movie version last night).

'Well, check this out,' says Rob. 'My great-great-grandma lived in Boston with my great-great-grandfather. He used to be a drinker, and a really jealous guy. She goes out singing in a club with these black guys. He comes home, finds out, and in a fit of rage and jealousy hits her over the head with an axe, splits her head right open. He thinks he's killed her, and he commits suicide by jumping into the Hudson. She's not dead, she goes on to look after my mother, with half a face.'

Rufus looks suitably baffled and horrified, and then says, 'I'm going to go and throw an apple in my mouth.'

A moment later, Rufus mentions Chrissie Hynde, and so Rob shares his best Chrissie Hynde story. 'I was twenty, and we were at a party,' he says. 'It was three in the morning, New Year's Eve, and she said, "Do you want to come back and finish this song I've been writing? With no intercourse." I said, "I'll come back, but I don't think much of the song title."'

The two of them begin going through the song, working out who will sing which lines – none of this has been prearranged, but it goes smoothly until they get caught up in a debate over which of them should sing *just follow me and this enormous clown.*

'You should,' Rob insists. 'Because you're talking to somebody really stupid.' But then he has a suggestion for an improvement. 'Or, to throw it out there, *just follow me, you enormous clown.*'

Everyone laughs; it's in the song.

Helena Bonham-Carter drops by and listens to the playback.

'I'm so proud of you both,' she says. 'That's fantastic.'

She asks who wrote it.

'We wrote it together,' says Rufus.

'Did you really?' she says, surprised. 'That's amazing. I thought it was a classic.'

Rob compares tales with Helena Bonham-Carter of places and people they've known. The kind of stories where at one point he says: 'I grabbed Bono and George Michael, made them go into that toilet, and sang them three songs a cappella, off my head, from my first album. "Sit down! … sit down! … *I hope I'm oldddd before I dieeee!*" … I don't know what they were. Scared? I was probably standing in the bath singing to them …'

A woman comes in with a young girl, maybe three; she explains to Rob that the last time she saw him, she was pregnant. 'This is the result.'

Rob bends down to greet her daughter. 'Hello, Result,' he says.

The song is finished and Rufus prepares to leave.

'Thank you, my showbiz boyfriend,' says Rob.

* * *

About ten days later, in a different London recording studio, Lily Allen arrives.

'Nice to see you sober,' says Guy. 'But it was nice to see you drunk too.'

'I've always loved the tune,' she says. 'I mean, I might not be very good at singing it.'

'Yeah, I'm sure you'll be absolutely crap and it'll sound rubbish,' Rob says.

They compare tattoos, discover they both have Keith Haring tattoos and both have their grandmother's initials behind their ears.

'Oh my God, we're so similar,' she says.

They do a take; to begin with, she knows the song much better than Rob does.

'Sorry,' she says, after correcting him.

'No, don't apologise for being right,' he says. 'Don't apologise for me being lazy.'

Only now does he mention that he actually dreamed about her last night. 'You were being really *eloquent* explaining something to somebody,' he says. 'And I was like, "Damn, that's eloquent."'

'Wow, that's totally wrong,' she says. 'I've got no …'

'… eloquency?' suggests Rob.

'All mine is gone,' she says.

'Mine has, too, with drugs,' he says. 'I didn't have a lot to start off with. There wasn't a lot in my vocab, but Jesus, loads has fucking gone. It's like Swiss cheese up there. I remember in my dream going, "That's why I'm not a judge on *X Factor*, because I can't do that."'

And then he starts to tell her about a dream he had about Syd Little.

'From Little and Large,' he clarifies.

'I don't know who either of those people are,' she says.

* * *

Rob is multitasking by quickly recording some harmonies on a new song, 'Motherfucker', one that is decidedly not for the swing album, when Olly Murs bursts in. Rob says he just needs to finish up 'Motherfucker', and as he does it Olly sings an *oooo-oooo* backing vocal.

'That's good,' says Rob. 'I'm going to put that in.'

Rob sings it; three years later Olly's part will end up on the finished record.

'I want fucking credit for that!' says Olly.

Rob asks Olly how old he is now, and Olly says he recently turned 29. 'I like being on an odd number more than on an even,' he explains.

Rob doesn't seem to find this strange in the slightest. 'That's like the pool thing to me,' he says. 'I prefer stripes to solids.'

Olly adds that he's not looking forward to 30.

'But the thing is,' Rob says, 'shit just gets better in your thirties.'

'Yeah?'

'Yeah. But you've had a great twenties anyway, haven't you?'

'I've had a good twenties – I don't think it was as good as your twenties.'

'Oh, professionally I had an absolutely epic, like something out of a film twenties,' says Rob. 'Professionally. Personally, it was fucking horrendous. I felt horrible every day all day.'

They talk about the forthcoming tour – Olly will be supporting Rob in stadiums across Europe this summer. Rob tells him he's been looking at Olly's live show on YouTube and how good it looks. 'And you do "Should

I Stay Or Should I Go", which I used to do,' says Rob. 'I had a look at me doing it on YouTube the other day and someone had just written underneath: "Go".'

Olly is here to sing 'I Wanna Be Like You' from *The Jungle Book* with Rob.

'Tell a story,' Olly says, 'my first ever audition of *X Factor* I sung this.'

Olly is like Rob in more ways that might be obvious, because he's a familiar mixture of self-deprecation and confidence. At one point, he mentions that he has an idea. 'A complete ridiculous idea, but I'm just going to say,' he says, and Rob tells him to stop apologising. His idea is to add a new part to the song over the instrumental break. They try out what he sings – *step to the left, step to the right* – which soon mutates to *swing to the left, swing to the right*. It'll be on the record.

They sing the song over and over and over.

'How's that?' Olly asks, after many takes.

'That's good,' says Guy, in an even tone that doesn't try too hard to hide the fact that he is still looking for a better one.

Rob laughs at how intimidating this is.

'No,' he explains to Olly, 'that's his face *all* the time. I've had a decade and a half of that face looking at me, even when I've got it spot on. Don't worry. He doesn't know that that's what his face looks like on the outside. On the inside, he's really soft and loving.'

* * *

The swing album is nearly finished. After a final vocal session, Rob and Guy listen back to 'No One Likes A Fat Pop Star'.

'It's a bit Noel, isn't it?' says Guy.

'Edmonds?' asks Rob.

'Coward,' Guy replies, patiently.

5

September 2016

'I think,' Rob begins, 'Gandhi said ...'

One highlight of sitting in as Rob gives interviews over the autumn and winter of 2016 is seeing how different interviewers react when he invokes Gandhi. Some merely look puzzled. Some confused. Some maybe even slightly horrified or soiled. One Australian woman makes it so clear that she thinks he has gone wildly off track that he has to suspend what he is explaining for a moment to reassure her: 'Don't worry, don't worry, it'll soon come back to pubes and crabs.'

When Rob talks about Gandhi, he is explaining why he rebels against giving boring, safe interviews.

'I think Gandhi said, "Be the change you want to see in the world." And I really don't watch chat shows anymore, because the interviews are so boring, the people are vanilla, people stay on script and they don't give much of themselves. I'm bored with seeing people do Hollywood-style interviews, where everything is glossy, everybody staying on message, everybody being safe. With most people you could write the question, ask it and answer it yourself with exactly what they're going to answer. Sometimes you see people interviewed and you're like, "Ah, fucking tell the truth!" Or "be interesting!" Or "be entertaining!" And maybe they're smart, they're not opening themselves up so much to the public. But I suppose my childlike reaction to that is to want to mess it up a little bit. Welcome to the heavy entertainment show. If you want to have a vanilla interview, you want to watch a vanilla interview, you have plenty of places to go. I'm just trying my best not to be vanilla. The change that I would like to see is somebody talking about their neuroses, or being controversial, because I think the marketplace is bereft of that. It's much more interesting to be a little bit broken and talk about your vulnerabilities. And I don't have a choice either way, because I'm sort of built for oversharing. My filter is broken. For good or for bad, I will answer a question to my own detriment a lot of the time.'

Of course he absolutely knows the ways in which this is absurd – quoting Gandhi to justify why he will, to use some real examples, 'talk about cocks and wanking off and Botox'. But at the same time, however ignoble his cause, his logic stands up. And no matter if Gandhi did not actually speak the famous words attributed to him, because what he did say – 'If we could change ourselves, the tendencies in the world would also change' – is exactly aligned with what Rob is saying. There are tendencies in his world he would wish to be different, and he is doing his bit.

'Nobody seems to be dangerous,' he expands, 'and everyone seems to be politicking and sticking to scripts. I like my singers lonely and weird, and we seem to be getting Olympians. Olympic pop stars. And they're great, too, and they're a sight to behold, but I like my pop with dysfunction.

And everybody is dysfunctional, but a lot of people seem to be hiding their dysfunction and funnelling it into corporate behaviour.'

He knows, of course, how easily this can all blow up in his face. That's why most entertainers choose a different path.

'Do I feel as though I can say anything?' he says. 'No. But I have, and I do, and I will.'

Here's one more way he has of describing what he does and why he does it.

'I just think to myself that I want to go out and be entertaining,' he says. 'And I have meagre talents and I don't have a high intellect, so in a bar fight you grab whatever tool you can to defend yourself. And when I go on TV I feel as though it's like wrestling or a bar fight – I grab the nearest tool, defend myself ...'

And his nearest tool, his preferred weapon, is to be entertaining by telling stories, revealing truths, divulging the kind of thoughts and acts that others might recoil from sharing.

'I enjoy those moments of going too far,' he says. 'And some would think that it would be like taking an axe to crack a nut ...'

A smile that spreads to a grin.

'... but at least people know I've got a fucking axe.'

* * *

May 2016

The TV project which brings Ant and Casper here – one that will evolve throughout the year but ultimately not come to fruition in this particular form – requires Rob and Ayda to share memorable, and often memorably embarrassing, moments from their past. It won't be too much of a struggle. First, though, they exchange some convivial chat about Donald Trump, and about the recent revelation that he would sometimes act as his own spokesman under an assumed name but then would forget to keep talking about himself in the third person. This reminds Rob of the Darren Day call, which he explains. Then Ant tells a story which mentions, in passing, Paul Gascoigne.

'I did four or five days with Gazza,' says Rob.

'In rehab?' asks Ant.

'No, no, no,' he says.

'In *pre*-hab,' corrects Ayda, who knows.

'Prehab,' Rob nods.

* * *

Ant asks Rob and Ayda whether they ever go out around here, and they tell him about their disastrous trip to a well-known local Indian restaurant, The Palm. A friend recommended it but Rob had argued against. 'I'll get hassled,' he said.

'I promise you,' their friend reassured him, 'no one will know who the fuck you are. No one will care.'

Rob said that he'd go, but bet that they would. (He was right.)

'So we get there,' says Ayda, 'and literally within eight minutes the owner of the restaurant comes up, "Nice to meet you, Robbie Williams, it's an honour to have you here, come, come, pictures …"'

Soon enough, the photos were in the local press.

The story does have a surreal coda. When the photos appeared, there was some scepticism on the Robbie Williams forum that this could really be the real Robbie Williams in this Indian restaurant. A debate ensued. Some argued that it was Rob. Others maintained that it was one of his lookalikes who lives not too far from here, a man known as 'Tony from Chippenham'. An argument only resolved when one of those involved decided to chip in.

'Tony from Chippenham jumped on the forum,' says Rob, 'and went "No! I can categorically say it was *not* me."'

A relevant side note: as part of his new hobby, Rob has been going on a metal-detecting forum to learn more and ask for advice. The pseudonym he has adopted for this: 'Tony from Chippenham'.

* * *

Just bear in mind, later, once this story has been told, that it was Ayda who prompted its telling:

'You told that one, didn't you?' says Ayda.

'Which one?' says Rob.

'The maid,' says Ayda.

He does.

'I rented a castle in the countryside to rehearse in,' he begins, 'and I'm asleep in the main room upstairs. And I wake up and I haven't opened my eyelids, but from what I understand from my senses there's somebody in the room. There's somebody inside the room tidying up. And I open my eyes, and what could only be described as a toothless hag, whose age range could be anything from thirty to sixty, with a tape cassette with headphones on, one of which is bandaged, and she's listening to a cassette. And she looks at me. And I look at her. She looks down at the floor, sees my Calvin Kleins. She goes …' – Rob mimics a thick West Country accent – '… "Calvin Kleins?" I went "… yeah?" She went, "*Pussy.*"' Rob acts out how he shrugged to respond to this comment. 'She went, "You got morning glory?" I went, "Yep, I have." She says, "I'll wank you off." I thought, "I'm a young person, I'm creative and imaginative, I can just close my eyes." So she wanks me off, right?'

'I can't believe you let her wank you off,' interjects Ayda, though of course she knew where this was going. She seems suitably appalled, but also more amused that you'd expect.

'So she wanks me off, and leaves,' Rob continues. 'I'm like, "Wow, that was a weird episode." Later that day I'm with the lady that ran the house at the time, and I said, "You know, your cleaner's …" – because she had a feather duster – "your cleaner's a bit odd." "The cleaner?" "Yeah, the lady that came into my room." She said, "We don't have cleaners on a Wednesday."'

'Oh my God,' says Casper.

'It was a *fan*!' laughs Ayda.

'It was just somebody from the village who'd wandered in with a duster, wanked me off and then left,' he says. 'Listen, if you saw her, you would judge. You would judge. And I judge myself.'

'It's got to be bad if you'd judge yourself,' says Ayda, sagely.

'So ...' – he picks up the story – '... three years later, I've got a new guitarist, who came from round there, and I'm telling him this story. And he went, "That's Maureen from the pub! She tells everybody that story, but nobody believes her!"'

'If she was sixty, she could nearly be in her nineties now, babe. Imagine if there's an old lady in the corner, ninety years ...' – Ayda's in near hysterics at this thought – '... telling a story about how she wanked you off.'

'Yeah, bless her,' says Rob.

* * *

'Oh, It's half eleven,' Rob announces.

'That's like three hours past our bedtime,' says Ayda.

'That's like three o'clock for us now,' says Rob.

But they keep talking.

'Did I tell you about our running thing that every time we turn on the TV, that Rob has slept with someone on TV?' says Ayda. 'I mean, like, *every time*. Whether it's a reality show, a comedy, a drama, a commercial for Depends ... it is someone, every time. Even *Star Trek* repeats.'

The other day they went to a Gymboree class and Rob dropped into the balls, hiding.

'I slept with that mom,' he explained to Ayda. 'And I don't remember her name.'

* * *

Rob mentions another time he was at the Chateau Marmont – it's amazing, for a place that Rob has such mixed feelings about, how many noteworthy incidents in his life have taken place there – he went to the bathroom and a guy put his foot underneath Rob's stall and started tapping.

'Which I think is hilarious,' he says.

Rob was not aware of certain sexual codes. But he knows an amusingly silly game when he sees one.

'So I start tapping. Then he comes to my door with an erect penis.'

Rob managed to deflect the man's attention by making a joke out of it.

'It's not the same anymore,' he tells Ant and Casper, 'but the top Google search for me used to be "Robbie Williams gay" – you'd put "Robbie Williams" in and it would complete "Robbie Williams gay".'

* * *

One more before lights out.

'Babe, that just reminded me,' Ayda begins. 'I have to go to bed, but the chick from the record company … the hotel.'

Again, remember, a few moments from now, that it is Ayda who has prompted the telling of this story.

'Oh,' says Rob, too tired for preamble, diving straight in, 'I'm in Los Angeles, I'm really fucking horny. The most horny and lonely that I've ever been in my fucking life. I've met a girl in San Francisco and she's a stripper, and we didn't do anything because I was being charming. We went back to the hotel, but I didn't do anything because I wanted to be a shoulder, and I was sober, and I'm, "How can I defile this person now we've talked about family?" But now it's Friday night and I'm lonely as fuck, and horny as fuck – I've never been that horny ever since. So I phone this girl and she gets on a plane from San Francisco and comes to Los Angeles. And we instantly have sex, and the moment that we have sex and it's finished, I don't want her to be there. She has a tattoo on her arm, and it's a lady in stockings with a knife behind her back, right? This lady is fucking nuts and we've got nothing to say to each other. She wakes up the next day and we have breakfast on the patio, and I'm pouring a cup of coffee and she looks over to me and she goes …' – Rob mouths *I love you* – '… so now we've got a problem.'

He explains what he did next: he went into the bedroom while she was still eating, phoned a friend at his American record company, asked them to hire a limousine and to come to the hotel, burst through the door, shout at him, tell him that he needed to be in Phoenix to do a radio show or he would lose all his radio plays in Phoenix.

'So I go back in, sit down, wait for knock on door,' he says.

The scene plays out as planned. 'And I went, "I've got to go, babe ... I've got to go and do this." And she says, "I'll come with you." I said, "No, it's very important for my image right now that I'm not attached to anybody." I put my clothes and my suitcase in the limousine, drive to the Chateau Marmont ...' – yes, once more – '... check in, and stay there.'

He says that this story also has a coda.

'She then moves to Los Angeles, eighteen months later,' he says. She starts going out with a rock star that he knows slightly, but then one night she runs into Rob and tells him a bizarre story about the rock star acting weirdly, and then one thing led to another ...

'So I slept with her again ...'

'No, you *didn't!*' screams Ayda with astonishment. She encouraged the telling of this story, but this part of the story is news to her. 'You didn't fucking sleep with her again, did you?'

'Yeah,' he says, a little sheepishly.

'If you were a girl,' says Ayda, 'I'd be like, "Girl, you have no self-respect."'

'And,' says Rob, 'I told her the story the next day of her mouthing "I love you".'

'You *told* her?' Ayda exclaims. 'You never told me that!' She's some overtired combination of amused and horrified. 'I can't *believe* that after you thought she was a psycho with the tattoo, you still slept with her again.'

Rob looks at Ayda as if to ask her how she could begin any sentence about his behaviour with the words "I can't believe ..." after everything he has said tonight.

'Babe,' he points out, 'I got wanked off by a toothless hag ...'

* * *

September 2016

When Dan Wootton, *The Sun*'s main pop writer, interviews Rob backstage at the iTunes festival, he wants to know all about Ayda's new raised profile, and the attention she's drawing from her appearances on *Loose Women*.

'And she's revealing all sorts of things,' Wootton says. 'Talk to me about this – like, did she ask your permission? Or is it, "I'm off to do this?"'

'No,' Rob explains to him, 'I'm very much encouraging. Because when we met I kind of took her hostage – I kidnapped her and took her away from her career. Needed her with me. And that was how it was going to work. For the last nine years, she's kind of been my dressing-room bitch. And now I'm her dressing-room bitch. The biggest reason I fell in love with Ayda is because of her personality, and I'm incredibly proud of her … I want her to be out there, and I want people to be experiencing what I'm experiencing, because it's unique what she's got. You know, I'm like a proud parent: go out there and shine, my love. We don't have a lot of secrets anyway. We're very much oversharers. I've always been. She is, too. And I suppose that we can try to outgun each other with the oversharing sometimes, which is quite scary. But there's nothing on there that she's said that I'm embarrassed about. I'm sure there'd be things that other people would be embarrassed about, but we're kind of … there's no secrets.'

'So my favourite …' says Wootton, 'but I need to know whether it's true or not …'

'The cucumber?' Rob asks.

'Yes!' he says.

'Yeah,' says Rob. 'It was true.'

* * *

When Ayda tells this story on *Loose Women*, she tells it like it has only just happened, but in truth Rob and Ayda have been joking about it for years. On the show, it comes up during a discussion about child stars and how early fame can hinder someone's development:

'Rob, because he became famous at fifteen …' – a slight exaggeration; at 15, Rob was still a Stoke schoolboy dreaming of a magical show-business life where everyday vegetables might become a mystery to him – '… there's a certain level of stunting that happens when you become famous at the stage where you're learning all these life skills. The other day I pulled out a cucumber from the fridge and he asked me what it was. And I told him it was a cucumber. And he said, "Oh, I didn't know because I've only ever seen them sliced" … I don't think he realises they come in a full form.'

Rob likes to tell this story, too, though there is a part that he sometimes adds and which everyone always ignores, about there being a difference between American and British cucumbers. The fact is, he's actually sort of right. The only cucumbers that one sees growing up in England are sleek and long, their sides running roughly parallel to each other along most of their length. But you frequently see other varieties in American shops, and in American fridges, ones that are more bulbous and curvy and that look more like oversized gherkins – cucumbers that don't conform to the British archetype, and which aren't necessarily so easy for British eyes to identify at first sight.

Not that it matters. In the end, which is worth more? Clawing back a little unneeded dignity that'll only get squandered some other way? Or having in your armoury a really good story about a pop star so unanchored to the realities of the world that he can't recognise a cucumber?

* * *

November 2012

Ayda walks into their rented Maida Vale home. She has just been for a meeting with *Loose Women* today, about the possibility she might appear on the show as a panellist.

'It felt so weird,' she says, 'to have a professional meeting after not leaving the house … for a while,' she says.

'Six years,' Rob points out.

'Six years,' she says.

She was in there for two hours, which she took as a good sign.

'They were, "What kind of things do you have opinions about? … What is your thought on that? … How was your childhood? … How has your childhood shaped … ?" I think they were just seeing how open I was, how I talked. They said, "We normally ask people if they'd be open, but you're clearly very open."' She laughs. 'Yeah … oversharing Ayda.'

'We both overshare,' Rob sighs.

'Yeah,' Ayda agrees. 'It's kind of what we do.'

'It's *your* chance now,' Rob says.

'Yeah,' she says, 'it's my chance to overshare and embarrass myself publicly.'

'And embarrass me,' Rob points out.

'Oh yeah!' she says, as though this genuinely hasn't struck her. 'That's right! I get to embarrass you.'

'Yeah,' he says, mock gruffly.

'I did use a thing,' she says, 'where I said it'd be great to interview you and I'd be like, yeah, "Boozy, why do you leave the toilet seat up?"'

'Mmm-hmm,' he says.

'I was talking about my hands-free pumping system that I'm quite proud of,' she adds – it is only two months since she gave birth to Teddy – '… and how my nipples now look like raspberries.'

'Yeah,' says Rob. Perhaps unwisely, he then adds: 'If raspberries were massive haemorrhoids.'

'Ewwww!' says Ayda. 'My nipples do not look like massive haemorrhoids! And you're not going near *them* anytime soon. That's disgusting. You take that back.'

'I take that back,' he says.

* * *

Ayda says that she's optimistic about how it went. 'They were kind of intimating they wanted me to do it, in the meeting,' she says. 'They were like: We just have to figure out how we want to do it. Do we want to put you on trial?'

'What does "trial" mean anyway?' Rob asks. 'You only want to do it a couple of times.' Pause. 'How many times do you want to do it?'

'I don't know,' she says. 'Depends if I like it or not.'

* * *

February–November 2016

With one thing and another, it's over three years later that Ayda makes her first appearance on *Loose Women*. On the first show, in February 2016, she is a guest, and she is introduced on-screen from the backstage couch by her husband.

'I can't wait for the world to meet my wife,' Rob says. 'I'm incredibly proud of her. She rocks, and the world needs to know.'

'You might feel differently, Robbie,' says the day's lead presenter, Ruth Langsford, 'after she spills the beans.'

His answer is realistic and prophetic.

'She will spill the beans,' he says. 'She's the bean-spiller.'

* * *

And so it begins. That first day Ayda shows footage of Rob having his back waxed while they watched *Back to the Future 2*. Two weeks later she makes her debut as one of *Loose Women* panellists, and a pattern emerges. While discussions on *Loose Women* tend to range widely across issues of the day, both important and less so, and Ayda usually has thoughtful or smart or funny contributions to make on these, and while most of what she says on the show has nothing whatsoever to do with her husband, there's also often an opportunity for some quick family bean-spilling. And it's an opportunity she tends to dutifully accept.

Here, by way of example, are some highlights:

On her first show as a panellist, she's asked whether Rob is any good at home, and while she later explains how good he is with the kids, and how he changes nappies, her initial answer begins like this: 'Are you *kidding*? If it was up to Rob, we'd be eating Nando's and salad cream for morning, noon and night. Rob is now forty-two. For the first time I took him to the supermarket. He really is like a fifteen-year-old boy. He's just frozen in Take That time. He was, "This is amazing, they've got *everything* …"' Later in the show, as the panel discuss an idea that has been proposed for couples to have an annual sex review, Ayda suggests that in their case it might be superfluous: 'First of all, Rob has had so many affairs with so many women in the nineties, if he doesn't know what he's doing by now, he shouldn't be doing it …'

In April she tells her version of how Cameron Diaz inadvertently saved their relationship – 'If she's watching, I just want to say, thank you, Cameron' – and in May she describes Rob's cucumber failings. In her next show, the panel discuss, in the wake of Johnny Depp and Amber Heard's split, whether there is a right and wrong time for two people to meet.

'Rob and I talk about this,' she says. 'I had to date all those losers beforehand – God, why couldn't I have just met him? But I think it was the way it was supposed to be. If I'd met him in his twenties, he'd have completely screwed it up. He'd have been off his face, he'd have been cheating … that's just the tip of the iceberg, I think. I just think he would have ruined it … I think we would have liked each other but I think he would have just done something really daft.'

Later that same episode, they broadcast film that the panellists have made at home the night before, critiquing their own bodies. Ayda's is apparently 15 minutes long: 'Rob lovingly refers to them as Picasso boobs since I breastfed. I think if I'd known what happens to you after you have a kid, I would have had a farewell party for my tummy.'

In the studio, one of the other hosts, Kaye Adams, asks her to elaborate: 'Picasso boobs, what's that all about?'

'Picasso tits,' Ayda clarifies. 'Do you know what it is? I think when you have kids it's like you have the same pieces to the puzzle but when you put the pieces back, the puzzle looks slightly different. It's like, there's still a sailboat but the mast is slightly tilting to the left, the bow's in the water …'

In June she explains that Rob has tasted her breast milk ('not off the teat,' she clarifies) and shows Rob's failed trying-to-break-the-internet naked photo, during which she gets into trouble for saying 'bollocks' ('sorry, I've done a bad, bad live TV thing'): 'I said, babe, you're going to look like a jerk. They're going to make fun of you for this photo. There's no way you're winning from this photo. And he's like "No, I'm in shape, I want this, it's my birthday, go on, take it ..." ... We had eighteen tries, make sure every muscle is toned ... People make fun of him all the time. They say, "Oh, Blobby Robbie," and they say horrible things, and he wanted to go, listen, I look great, I'm in shape ...'

Five days later she's back and they're discussing people's worst habits, a subject she greets like an open goal.

'Where do I begin? My gentleman friend has a lot. I don't know which ones he's going to let me say ... but I'm going to say them all. The first one he does, randomly he'll just get the urge out of nowhere to manscape. But it's never consistent. So he'll just be in the bath and see his arm or part of his chest, he'll just get that bit, or on the toilet, and I'll come in and it's just like there's been a sheep sheared or a poodle attacked in my bathroom. And there's never any warning. And men's hair's quite thick. And then he comes in like a patchwork quilt and he'll be, "How did I do?" "Well, it could be better, to be honest."'

She's not quite finished.

'There has been toenail nibbling ... I'll just kind of look over and he'll have a little bit in his mouth ... "Is that a toenail in your mouth?"'

Colleen Nolan then reveals that they have asked Rob about Ayda, and he has told them that she'll get a fake tan before going to bed, and he'll wake up covered in it. Ayda concedes that this is true. 'It does look like an orange crime scene,' she says.

Rob is there at the studio that day, backstage, and during one of the ad breaks he comes on set with Teddy to say hello.

'By the way,' he says to the studio audience, pointing at Ayda, 'chronic farter.'

'I don't think so,' Ayda retorts. 'I don't think so.'

She gets support from an unexpected source.

'Daddy's a stinker,' Teddy announces loudly, 'and he smells of poo.'

'From the mouths of babes,' says Ayda. 'From the mouth of babes ...'

*   *   *

Increasingly, when Rob does interviews he is asked about the kinds of things that Ayda says on *Loose Women*. I think they expect him to, at the very least, confess that he rues some of what she says. That's not the answer they get:

'Well, we have a unique relationship, me and Ayda. And we are both classic oversharers. And I think we enjoy the bedevilment of shocking people with our honesty. It's not cynically produced, it's just something that naturally we do. We sort of egg each other on to be more outrageous. We share the same sense of humour which is so good, because that also allows me so much room in interviews where I can say shit that other people can't say. Our humour and our language and the way that we view the world is not very conservative, and we could cause an international incident at any moment from our house. And there's an energy in maybe getting ourselves into trouble that's quite exciting. There's not been anything that I've gone "babe, you shouldn't say that". There's not much that she can say that would embarrass me, and, if there is, I would kind of enjoy that embarrassment in a perverse way. And vice versa, too. There's nothing that she's done that's embarrassed me. And there's nothing I've done that's embarrassed her.'

One interviewer presses him on this. He's asked whether he's really sure.

'Yeah,' he says. 'But we'll keep on pushing that boundary. And we'll reach it, I'm sure.'

*   *   *

In July, *Loose Women* does a Spice Girls special. Near the end, the hosts come on dressed as the Spice Girls; Ayda is Posh Spice. And the other hosts quiz Ayda:

Ayda – did Robbie know the Spice Girls?

'Yes,' she says, with a meaningful pause. 'He did.'

Did he *know* Geri?

'Yes, he did.'

Did he know … Baby?

'I'm not … yes, he did.'

Did he know Sporty … ?

'Yes, he did.'

Did you make him write down all the Spice Girls that he knew?

'There's not enough paper …'

It's good theatre, but it plays right into a story that has been going on, spreading fun and offence, for years. There is a joke that Rob has often said, usually from the stage, and it has evolved and appeared in different forms and in different circumstances, but its basic form involves saying: *I'm very fortunate to have been in Take That and four out of five of the Spice Girls.* The frisson, and why it can obviously cause umbrage, relies on the fact that to the people hearing it, the line between the joke and any underlying empirical facts is fuzzy.

Rob has often tried to backtrack away from this story in interviews, but it's hard not to make it worse. Here's a typical recent attempt:

The Spice Girl thing has haunted you …

'It's one of those things you later regret, because it has followed me. And then for mischief I sort of embellish it and play with it. But, and rightly so, boyfriends and husbands weren't happy about that, and I understand that, and I regret that. But just me trying to do … me being a frustrated comedian and wanting to make people laugh.'

Is there a little bit of truth in it? Percentage-wise?

'It's not four. Make of that what you will. But it's unfair on the girls – we're all older now, and we've all got children and the joke's not funny anymore. You're thinking: "Which ones?" I'm not telling you.'

Ayda's *Loose Women* banter inspires a new round of headlines: *Ayda Field implies Robbie Williams had sex with THREE Spice Girls*, and so on. Not long after, Rob does some interviews down the phone with Australian radio stations. Typically he likes talking to Australian radio stations because he can say provocative, funny things and they seem to share his taste and sense of humour. But they're also, consequently, one of the most reliable places for him to get himself into fresh, or reheated, trouble.

The first interview today, with Fitzy and Wippa, they ask about the Spice Girl quip, and he explains that it was a joke that went too far. 'But, you know, the line was just too good to say,' he continues, 'so I said it and I can't take it back.' Half an hour later, he is on the phone to another Australian DJ team, Kyle and Jackie O. They've seen Ayda's *Loose Women* conversation. And in Australia, they don't beat around the bush.

'She sort of insinuated,' says Jackie O, 'that Geri Halliwell wasn't the only Spice Girl that you slept with, and it was Mel C as well, and Emma?'

'I've explained this, but I'll explain it again …' he says, and he offers the full explanation. Then he says, 'That joke carried on and has followed me through my career, and now my wife has taken that joke and run with it herself …'

He could just leave it there. He really could.

But he doesn't leave it there.

'… when we all know it was five out of five and not four out of five.'

* * *

This new version of the story goes back round the world. Even if the stories allow for the possibility that he was joking (which he very obviously was), the headlines don't: *Robbie Williams Opens Up About How Many Spice Girls He Actually Slept With*; *Robbie Williams Finally Addresses His Sexual History With The Spice Girls*; *Robbie Williams Says He Bedded ALL Of The Spice Girls*. After that, Mel B goes on the same radio show in Australia, where she is working as a reality show judge, and denies that she ever slept with Rob, but the language she chooses in doing so – 'I was the one he never did' – seems to inadvertently, and most likely accidentally, incriminate the rest of her bandmates. One of the DJs, Kyle, then further fans the flame, by recounting that Rob once told him that he smuggled Geri Halliwell out of his flat in a sports bag. And on it goes.

'So of course there'll be a Mr Beckham somewhere angry with me again,' Rob sighs. 'But it was a joke. And that's what it was. If people take it seriously, then I can't help that.'

The five-of-five quip, that is. The sports bag story is true. It was when Rob lived in Notting Hill Gate and his flat was besieged by paparazzi, the time when he was so despairing about what to do about this that he called the police to ask for advice and to ask what rights he had. When a policeman came round and Rob began to explain, the policeman cut him off and said: 'Let me stop you … you see, when you *start* your career, you want your press. But when they want something from you, you don't like it, do you? You don't like it …'

So, yes, Geri was round the house, and there were paparazzi everywhere.

'And we put Geri in a holdall, and I walked out with her over my shoulder, and then put her in the back of an Aston Martin, shut the boot.'

You put her in the *boot*?

'Yeah.'

Was she okay with that?

'Well, she was only in there for fifteen minutes. She's very little.'

* * *

September 2016

Adam Horton, the researcher from *The Graham Norton Show*, is here at the Soho Hotel this afternoon to do Rob's pre-interview for the show tomorrow. Most big chat shows now follow the example of the famous American late-night shows, where someone from the show will speak with the guest beforehand, and identify possible stories they might tell on air. (That's why, when it works at its clumsiest, you'll sometimes see awkward moments where the host will suddenly say, apropos of nothing, something like, 'Didn't something funny once happen with you and a cheetah?')

Rob thanks Adam for coming over to the hotel to talk in person. 'I don't like telephones,' he explains. He asks who else will be in the show; the answer is Justin Timberlake, Anna Kendrick and Daniel Radcliffe. Rob has told me that he has been dreading going on *The Graham Norton Show* every single day since it was first out in the schedule weeks ago. In parallel with that, he has also been thinking about what he could say there. That's what he and Adam will discuss today. But first they talk a little about Rob's previous appearance, two years ago, the most celebrated part of which was this exchange:

Graham Norton: Were you actually at the 'hello Teddy' moment? Were you there for the birth?

Rob: Yes, I was.

Emma Thompson: Were you down the business end?

Rob: Uh, yeah, I was.

Emma Thompson: Well done.

Rob: It was like my favourite pub burning down.

And then, after all the did-he-really-just-say-that? laughter and some further backchat had subsided, Rob looked the camera and said, 'Sorry, Ayda – you have a beautiful foo.'

* * *

'Okay, I just want to tell you a few stories,' Rob says to Adam. First he tells two Teddy stories he's been telling everywhere – the watching Knebworth story (cake version) and the story of the time he was with Teddy in the shared private garden behind their rented Maida Vale house, when Rob had to persuade some nannies to delete the photos they'd taken of Teddy, and then, as he walked back to the house with Teddy, muttered under his breath, too quietly for the nannies to hear, 'fucking idiots'. After which Teddy turned to the nannies and, by way of friendly farewell, blared, 'Bye, fucking idiots!'

Then Rob tells a complicated story about being at a New Year's Eve party at Sharon Osbourne's (old) house, and standing in a corridor for ages waiting for his mother, staring blankly ahead until he realises that he's been staring at Chris Rock, and then carries on staring while he wonders if Chris Rock knows who he is, until Rock suddenly exclaims, with irritation, 'What, motherfucker?'

'So I was obviously not in the famous club,' says Rob.

This he twins with what happened not long after at a U2 concert. He saw Chris Rock nearby with John Cusack. Cusack seemed to be waving in his direction but, mindful of the previous Chris Rock experience, Rob thought it better to ignore this. Cusack kept waving, and started looking annoyed, but Rob felt confident all of this was for the benefit of someone behind him, so he carried on ignoring it. Eventually, he looked behind him and there was nothing but a brick wall.

'So there's a story I could tell,' he suggests, 'about not being famous in Los Angeles.'

Adam says that's good, because Anna Kendrick has a book out, of embarrassing stories from her life, including awkward encounters with other famous people. So maybe that would dovetail.

This prompts another story from Rob's locker.

'Great. Well, I've got one with Joe Pesci, too, because I used to have this place in Los Angeles – I had a house just for football, boy's own, boy done good, what does boy do with money? Boy buys place for football. It had floodlights and Astroturf and it was enclosed and it had a clubhouse and it was brilliant. Next door lived Joe Pesci. One night one of our players parked on Joe Pesci's drive, and Joe Pesci was unable to get into his house. Joe Pesci turns up while the football game was on with a golf club, and does full fucking Joe Pesci: "You motherfuckers! I'll do this ... and if you don't ..." Kicks a dog. Does full-on scary gangster. Goes. Somebody runs, moves the car very quickly. The next day I get a hastily put-together sign that says, "Do not park on drive". It was a Saturday – that Saturday evening I went to an Italian restaurant in Los Angeles. I walked through the door and this Italian guy comes up to me and he goes, "That's a good thing you did for Joey." I don't know who this guy is, but he knows that I've put a sign for Joey on his driveway. And he's obviously connected – lots of people keep coming up to him, holding his hand and kissing him on his cheeks. And I'm, "Ha, ah, yes it's a good thing, I'll make sure that it never happens again." So we have a connection and a good chat, but I'm socially really, really awkward anyway, all the time, and I got to the toilet at the end of the meal and I come out to finish the meal and I'm leaving, and I go up to this guy – and I could do this to Graham Norton – and he's stood on a step above me, and I go to do the kiss thing, but I'm so nervous and embarrassed that I just go and kiss him on his Adam's apple.' Rob does this right now to Adam, to demonstrate. 'It was the most embarrassing moment. Excuse me that I kissed you. So that could be something else that I say, for another story in Los Angeles.'

'That's really good,' says Adam.

Then Rob tells another evergreen:

'There's when I was at Bono's and I was going through my mushroom phase. And it was a very wild party, and it must have been about five o'clock and the sun was coming up, and the great and the good were there, and I was just wandering around his house, sort of staring at this painting, and it was the most beautiful I'd ever seen. Ever. And I was: of course Bono's going to have the most beautiful painting that I've ever seen. And then Bono appeared, and I was like, "Bono, this painting is the most beautiful painting I've ever seen." And he said, "Robbie, that's the window." That's a Bono story.'

'That's good,' says Adam.

* * *

And then he unleashes the Maureen story.

'I've got this one that's a bit contentious,' Rob begins, 'and I'll get in trouble for saying it, but it might be good.'

And he tells it. When he gets to '… and she went, "I'll wank you off",' Adam goes 'Jesus!'

Rob finishes the main part of the story.

'Jesus,' repeats Adam. 'And how long ago was that?'

'A while ago. A long time ago. But for the purpose of this story it can be just before Ayda.'

'Just before Ayda …' He nods. 'Yeah. Okay – that's a good one.'

* * *

Rob checks his mental checklist to see if there's anything else. 'Bono … Teddy … Chris Rock … John Cusack … Joe Pesci…' he goes. And then he tells Adam about night-eating.

'So I was going to ask you the weirdest thing a fan has ever sent you,' says Adam. 'But I feel like maybe the maid story…'

'Well, my stock saying is, "weirdest thing a fan has ever given you?" I always say "herpes",' says Rob. 'That always gets a titter.'

Adam gets out a photo he has brought with him: it is of Rob and Tupac. 'I just wanted to ask you about this – I came across this picture, it's you and Tupac hanging, and I just wondered what the story was behind that picture.'

'Well, I'll tell *you*,' Rob says. 'I'm at Gianni Versace's place. Either Milan or Rome. And I'm with Tupac. There's not much of a story that I can say on TV, but we shared a lot of cocaine together and we had a very, very good time. And it was so surprising that his security guys were actually policemen, but they're working for him while they're not working at the police. I'm doing a shitload of drugs in front of the police, which was weird. But I tried my best not to be gushing fanboy about being with *the* Tupac, but I was, and there's the evidence. And he was incredibly charming. Beautiful man. Wanted to talk with me, wanted to hang out with me. He didn't know who I was – he was just being a nice person. Maybe I can say that on TV – we did a shitload of cocaine? I don't know.'

Adam prepares to leave.

'Yeah,' Adam says. 'That'll probably do it, I reckon.'

Once he has gone, Rob wonders whether he's given them anything they can use. 'I don't feel very story-y today,' he says, ludicrously. Though a while later he adds, 'Yeah, he'll definitely be going away knowing that Robbie Williams kissed his Adam's apple.'

* * *

Adam also told Rob that they'd want to talk about one of his new songs, 'Motherfucker', the song that Rob has been explaining to everyone was written for Charlie. Adam asks Rob how old Charlie will have to be before he is allowed to hear it.

'Well, we're sweary Marys in our house anyway,' Rob answers. 'We've got potty mouths. I'm guessing our household is probably going to be a bit like the Osbournes'. So I think we'll be a bit liberal where swearing is concerned. You're right, I haven't thought about it. But I wouldn't want him repeating it before his thirteenth birthday. When he's a teenager he can sing it with glee, because that's what I wrote it in mind with – for me as a teenager and how much I loved swearing in records and how rude it was, and how grown-up it was. And I used to listen to them in my bedroom and then repeat them underneath my breath so my mother couldn't hear.'

Adam says he thinks they'll be allowed to use one or two 'motherfuckers' on the show. He explains that there is a precedent. 'When we have Samuel L. Jackson on, it's obviously a thing that we always want him to say, and he's allowed one, I think.'

* * *

May 2013

Rob is staying in Wiltshire where the early music rehearsals for the Take The Crown tour have been taking place, but today he must go to Londonderry. He has recorded a single, 'Goin' Crazy', with Dizzee Rascal, which he has agreed to perform at a Radio 1 event in Northern Ireland; there's a car to Bristol airport, a private jet to Derry, then back the same day.

In the car he starts playing an instrumental piece of music on his laptop, one with a hypnotic repeated guitar motif. I've heard it before, last July, when one of the Australians, Tim Metcalfe, was in Rob's Los Angeles studio playing him a dozen or so new instrumental tracks. He'd sung a few words over this one – *oh, satellite* – but he didn't give any sign that he particularly liked it or was particularly interested in it. But this morning, he plays it over and over again as we drive west down countryside back roads.

After about eight minutes, Rob suddenly starts singing, for the first time: *I'm a bad motherfucker, bad motherfucker.*

He smiles. 'There's something in that,' he says. For the rest of way, past Bath and through the Bristol suburbs, the lyric is worked on. He only breaks twice, once to call Ayda ('I need to do a bit of romance – phone her up to see how her day's gone,' he says beforehand, mostly to himself) and once to recite the lyrics of Pulp's 'Mis-Shapes'.

On the plane, he tells David Enthoven that Teddy crawled to him for the first time this morning. At the concert venue, he goes to visit Dizzee Rascal, and when they greet there's a confusing collision of fist bumps and handshakes. Talking about this later, Rob is a mixture of slightly embarrassed and amused. 'I do fist bumps because I'm germophobic,' he points out, 'not because I'm urban.'

During the performance, Rob goes into the pit below the stage early on, to mingle with the crowd, and then, surprisingly, he just stays down there. Eventually Dizzee Rascal goes down there too to join him, so that they can at least sing some of the song together. After, Rob will explain that there was a very specific reason for this eccentric piece of stagecraft:

'I got down there, and realised that I was too old to get back up. That's the first time that's happened. I realised I'd have to do that stomach-first sort of beached-whale getting-back-on thing, so I thought, "I'll just stay down here – Dizzee can patrol the top and I just won't look too fat down here."'

No great harm done. Just before Rob leaves, he does a radio interview with Dizzee, who offers his approval: 'It's rock'n'roll, innit? It's Robbie Williams, innit? How much people never seen that in person anyway?'

As soon as Rob is back in the car at Bristol, he returns to the new song. Aside from pausing to comment on the unusual sight of two men playing trumpets under a suburban underpass, that's all that happens all the way home. By the time we're passing the last evening hedgerows before his village, the song has a verse and a chorus. The rest will be written the next day, and then he will sing it to Teddy in the kitchen as she dances inside one of those circular plastic walkers.

You uncle sells drugs
Your cousin is a cutter
Your grandma is a fluffer
Your grandad's in the gutter
Your mother is a nutter
Your mother is nutter
… one common thing you get from me and your mother
is that we're mad motherfuckers
we are mad motherfuckers, yeah!

Ayda, hearing this for the first time, looks a little puzzled.

'I'm a battle rapper!' Rob tells Ayda, with mock bravado. 'That's who you married.'

* * *

Rob will start singing 'Motherfucker' – a song that, beneath its foul-mouthed exuberance, is ultimately about how one generation's flaws can beget the next generation's strengths – live on tour in 2015, long before its final version is recorded for *The Heavy Entertainment Show*. By then, he'll be a father of two, and he'll have a spiel worked out that he'll repeat countless times – how he wrote a song of protection for Teddy to warn away suitors, 'Go Gentle', and how this, 'Motherfucker', was his song for Charlie. And this is certainly what it becomes – especially after, much later, he adds a middle eight that makes this explicit:

We all believe you're gonna break the chain
We all believe that you're the one
We all believe that the angels are watching over you, my son.

And if the truth is that the rest of it was written before Charlie was even conceived, maybe in a way that's even better. It was sitting there, waiting for him – a ready-made invitation, instigation and inspiration. He just had to come along and claim it.

* * *

September 2016

Arriving at the London TV studio where *The Graham Norton Show* is filmed, he talks with the Sony promotions man, also called Rob, whose wife gave birth to his second child the previous day.

'So you know the routine?' says Rob.

'You're blindly optimistic the first time, aren't you?' says Sony Rob.

'No!' Rob replies. 'I wasn't. No. When the second one popped out, I was, "I am now ready for my first child."'

* * *

Adam comes to the dressing room to run Rob through the expected arc of the show: talk about the album, talk about potentially tying Elvis Presley for the most number-one albums by a male solo artist, talk about 'Motherfucker', tell the Teddy-and-the-nannies story, tell the Joe Pesci story ('And are you going to do the thing where you kiss Graham on the … ?' Adam checks, and Rob confirms), give the herpes answer to 'what's the wildest thing a fan has ever given you?', and then tell the Maureen story.

'And that's kind of our closer for the show,' says Adam. 'We like to go home hard. So to speak.'

Rob nods in agreement. When Adam has gone, he watches Manchester United play the Ukrainian team Zorya Luhansk. He's clearly nervous. He raps to himself some of Biggie Smalls' 'Gimme The Loot' – *Motherfucking right/my pocket's looking kind of tight/and I'm stressed/yo Biggie let me get the vest* – then walks around the room. 'I don't think the Joe Pesci story is that good,' he says, to no one in particular. He wanders into the corridor and knocks on Daniel Radcliffe's door.

'Hi, guys, Robbie Williams,' he says.

'Dan,' says Daniel Radcliffe, 'lovely to meet you.'

They chat for a while, then Rob goes for a smoke. 'He's more nervous than me,' Rob says, though I doubt this is true. (He's an actor.) Back in the dressing room, Rob paces around, exhales, clearly anxious in a way that can't really be reached, because whatever anyone might say right now it won't alter or even touch upon the fact that he is the only one who is going to have to deal with what he is about to deal with. Then he goes to the toilet again.

'I hate this bit,' says Gina.

When Rob comes out, he tells the Maureen story to Ollie – both, I think, to sort of rehearse it, and to bolster his confidence that it's a good story. Then he goes for another smoke, and briefs Michael on what they're scheduled to talk about on the show. 'Teddy with the fucking idiots. Joe Pesci.' Michael passes on an encouraging pre-show message from America:

'Ayda just said you can talk about her vagina if you want, and you're the funniest fucker she knows, and she hearts you.'

* * *

The wait seems to go on forever – Rob's call time is moved backwards several times – until eventually he is called down to the studio floor where the other three guests have already been on the sofa for a good while. He stands in the wings, further delayed, while a lot of on-camera tomfoolery takes place with the dummy referred to as 'Dead Daniel', who was used as Daniel Radcliffe's corpse in his new movie, *Swiss Army Man*. Finally, Rob is introduced.

'Let's see what trouble I can get in tonight,' he says, as he sits down.

Introductions are made.

'Dead Daniel looks like me pre-rehab,' he says.

'This new album …' Graham Norton begins. 'I'm on-message. I'm on message. The new album …'

'I'm well and truly off-message,' says Rob.

It begins roughly as scheduled: talking about 'Motherfucker', telling the 'fucking idiots' story. Then Norton feeds him the 'what's the maddest thing a fan has ever given you?' question, he says 'herpes', and Justin Timberlake, who is sitting next to him, stands up, pretending as though he needs to walk out and not be next to Rob any longer.

Rob shakes his head, and says, as though to acknowledge Justin is just play-acting, 'Justin knows you can't get it twice.'

That works.

And then Norton steers him straight towards the finale – no Joe Pesci or Adam's apple kissing tonight – and you can kind of see Rob gathering himself.

'I might get in a lot of trouble telling this story,' says Rob.

'Not too late to back out,' quips Daniel Radcliffe.

'It *is*!' Graham Norton scolds Radcliffe. 'Shut up!'

'I'm in, I'm in,' Rob reassures him. 'Oh my God, I can't believe I'm telling this, but I will.' He begins. 'Back in the day, I was renting a castle …'

'Of course you were,' Graham Norton interjects.

And he tells it.

Aside from the story itself, part of the television spectacle that unfolds is watching the reactions of the other guests, which begin as the professional showbizzy chat-show-sofa expressions of shock and outrage that you're obliged to deliver when one of your peers is telling a risqué story and then, as the story progresses, evolve into what appear to be genuine looks of amazement and horror that someone is really telling this story in public.

Once Rob has finished, Daniel Radcliffe says, 'We can all go home now,' and Justin Timberlake says something to acknowledge that the basketball-at-the-White-House-with-President-Obama anecdote he told earlier has just been eclipsed.

'What a lovely, *lovely* story …' Graham Norton deadpans, and the show finishes.

Off-camera, Rob talks to Anna Kendrick, whose traumatised reaction will become a meme of its own. His words land somewhere between apology and simple statement of fact.

'You can't un-hear that story,' he says, 'can you?'

* * *

Rob goes out into the back car park for a smoke, where he runs into Daniel Radcliffe again. Radcliffe mentions that when he was on holiday in Greece recently, the only cassette the driver had was *Live At Knebworth*.

'Oh, I'm sorry,' says Rob.

In the car back to the hotel, Rob is somewhere between relieved and ebullient.

'It felt so good. And I felt in command. I could find the words in my head. I didn't feel confused. I didn't feel terrified. Every joke, every funny thing, was landing. Felt so good. Liberating. To go on one of these shows and just not to corpse inside. Finding confidence, false or real.'

* * *

The show is to be broadcast the following evening. At around five o'clock that afternoon, Rob calls me, troubled. The *Mirror* have written a story saying that he was slurring and made funny faces on Graham Norton. 'I was, "Ow,"' he says. He's partly calling me to ask whether that was true.

Perhaps the *Mirror* have already got a little nervous or unsure about what they have written, because by the time I look online a few minutes later, just after Rob hangs up, the slurring part has gone. But he wasn't imagining it: I can still find an archived internet trace of the headline before it was updated: *Robbie Williams shocks fans with 'slurred words' and lewd tales.*

And even what remains is not good.

The new headline is this:

Robbie Williams shocks fans by telling lewd tales in very bizarre appearance on the Graham Norton show.

The article which follows includes these details:

Robbie Williams shocked fans as he told crude sexual tales in a bizarre appearance on the Graham Norton Show. The Let Me Entertain You star – who had a well-documented battle with substance abuse and depression in his 30s – teased the presenter: 'Let's see what trouble I can get you into this time.' One audience member told the Mirror Online the Rock DJ superstar made 'odd facial expressions' before launching into a story about being given a sexual favour by a stranger. 'The story was gross,' the guest said. 'I don't think anyone could believe it.'

Rob is understandably upset, and worried.

* * *

Rob calls again around 11, just after *The Graham Norton Show*'s broadcast has finished.

'I didn't see it,' he says.

I'd watched it, anxiously, to see whether what I felt I'd seen yesterday wasn't somehow what happened, and to make sure that his interview hadn't been edited in any way that felt unfair, but neither was the case. I tell him it was good.

'Oh good,' he says, 'because I just looked at the top of Twitter, on "Robbie Williams" and it was savage.'

I had just been doing exactly the same thing when he called, and I read him some random tweets, positive and negative, from the feed in front of me.

That's a story one should not be sharing in public.

Robbie Williams' story has got to be right up there with the best ever.

Robbie Williams is a living legend – what a fucking man.

He calls again about an hour later. 'I've got an email saying "comedy genius", "funniest story ever",' he says, and I read to him a new tweet that I'd just found:

Wow. Robbie Williams' story on Graham Norton effectively renders all future chat show interviews obsolete. Will never be topped.

'Really? Okay, cool. I'm just not going to go on it for a bit.'

He tells me a couple of days later, though, that he did look, and that the reaction wasn't that bad at all. That just shows how inured he is to the kinds of things people say, the kinds of things that someone like him has to read every time they brave an unfiltered public forum. Because alongside a genuine wave of positivity, here is a random sample of actual comments:

Robbie Williams looks weird. He still looks like a twat though.

Robbie Williams is just the embarrassing sibling you like to hide away.

Imagine being Robbie Williams and having to spend every minute of every day with Robbie Williams. It's no wonder he's a cunt.

I would rather live alone in Russia, poor, naked and in constant fear of a bear bullying me than listen to Robbie Williams' new song.

Robbie Williams is a fucking dick.

Robbie Williams. Utter Cunt

Robbie Williams just needs to stop now. It's embarrassing.

In our modern world, that's the kind of routine savagery that is unleashed every single time someone like Rob needlessly provokes people by daring to appear on TV.

* * *

'Everything that you're scared of,' he says, 'and that you fear about yourself, there's somebody who will hold a mirror up to you and go: "You know that thing you hate about yourself? Here it is. It's true. It's in black and white." And it can become who you are as person, and you can carry it around with you on your day-to-day: I'm a horrendous person that can't sing, can't dance. Can't perform, I'm fat, my tattoos are shit …' Anything at all that you're "that's what I feared is the truth" and there it is. It can be debilitating.'

Of course he knows he shouldn't read any of it. It would be a kind of craziness to do so, once you have an idea of what is likely to be there.

'I read everything,' he says. 'And it's dangerous. And it crushes the soul. But I'm addicted to it. If there's ten good comments and one shit one, I concentrate on the shit one. I'm addicted to stuff that makes me *feel*, full stop.'

* * *

Though he has said that he won't, he wakes up at two in the morning and watches the show, though he turns it off before the Maureen story. He's worrying about it, scared that he made a terrible mistake by thinking he could say something like this on television. 'There is something potent and powerful about international shame, real or imagined. Terrifying.'

The Graham Norton Show post a video of just the Maureen story on YouTube, and over the next few days Rob regularly checks and reports on how many views it has. Soon it soars through a million. And the YouTube comments are almost universally positive. 'I've never had such good reviews,' he says. 'Even people in America are going: "I don't know who this guy is but I love him."' It turns out that the general feedback, from people he meets and people writing about it, is nearly all upbeat, and his fear that he has done something awful that he can't take back recedes. 'The story will have made people laugh that were going to laugh,' he says, 'and will have horrified people it would need to horrify, so … box is ticked.'

There are two reviews he doesn't go looking for, because, as he explains to Guy a few days later, he assumes that they will be negative. He mentions to Guy that he hasn't heard from his mother since.

'Did that go over a line, do you think?' asks Guy.

'Oh yeah,' he says. 'And my dad.'

'Really?' says Guy, surprised.

'Yeah. My dad'll just think, "Would Matt Monro tell that story? – no, he wouldn't." My dad wouldn't have found it funny at all,' says Rob, and imagines his response: '"He's let himself down there."'

A few days after that, though, he mentions that now he has had an email from his mother which says 'I did manage to see you on *Graham Norton* which was excellent – it was very funny' before moving on to other news.

In the weeks to come, he follows the rising view-count on YouTube with some satisfaction. But then the BBC remove the clip. They have had complaints that the story is inappropriate and should not have been broadcast. Rob says something about having been told questions have been asked in parliament. An official adjudication will have to be made as to whether Robbie Williams' story about being wanked off is, or is not, acceptable.

* * *

September 2016

The first single off *The Heavy Entertainment Show* is a song called 'Party Like A Russian'. Long before its release, Rob tries to work out how he can explain what it is about. To sidestep the issue, Ayda suggests to him that he says it's the story of a dream he had, but I point out to him that if he makes something up like this, he'll most likely say in the fourth or fifth interview he does: 'Well, there's a story I've made up about why …' What he settles on saying, which is some of the truth, is that it is a song about partying and hedonism – and that because no one parties like Russians party, that is why the song is 'Party Like A Russian'.

'When Russians party,' he'll explain, 'it's bigger and badder and bolder and harder than anywhere else in the world … They don't give a fuck. And that's the spirit of hedonism, and that's the spirit of partying … and I tip my hat to them. Vodka, booze, girls, boys, fashion …' Usually he also manages to slip in his S Club 7 homage: 'Ain't no party like a Russian party.'

But the first time he is asked about the song is by *The Sun*'s Dan Wootton, backstage at the iTunes festival, and the way Wootton brings up the subject is by congratulating Rob for how spectacularly un-PC the song is. This immediately throws Rob off his prepared narrative.

'Yeah,' he says, 'and I had to chisel and whittle at the lyrics, too. There's a lot of lyrics I took out.'

'Really?' prompts Wootton.

'Yeah, because there's a hundred and forty-seven million people in Russia and I don't want to upset them in any way. And I don't know what kind of sense of humour they've got. And I'm not making fun of anybody. But I kind of had to take a few things out just to make it more PC. This is the PC version.'

'Do you think you might be on Putin's hit list once he hears it?' Wootton inquires. This is precisely the road that Rob didn't want to go down.

'I doubt that very much,' he says. 'I hope not. I think the spirit of the record is saying "party like a Russian".' And then, at last, he gets on-message, but after Wootton leaves the dressing room Rob begins to worry a little – he says that when Wootton mentioned Putin's hit list, all he was thinking inside was how much he didn't want to be on it.

Wootton's take on this part of their conversation appears a few days later:

Rob's Putin the boot in
SONG MOCKS RUSSIAN CHIEF

Robbie Williams was never going to make a comeback without causing some trouble. And he might want to avoid a trip to Eastern Europe after the release of new single Party Like A Russian today. The track is an audacious, tongue-in-cheek take-down of Russian president Vladimir Putin and his chums …

* * *

When this story appears, Rob tweets a response: *I love you Dan but this song is definitely not about Mr Putin x*

But the storyline is set. Soon *The Guardian* are reporting:

It was not the war in Syria or the investigation into the downing of Malaysia Airlines flight MH17 that outraged Russians at the weekend, but a new music video by Robbie Williams … the video outraged viewers for its crude stereotyping of Russian culture, with some tabloids suggesting the singer would never be able to perform in Russia again …

And similar articles like this are everywhere. It's hard, after a story like this has faded and proper perspective has re-established itself, to convey exactly how unnerving it can be to be in the middle of a media storm. One morning he says to me, quite seriously, 'I couldn't sleep and I decided the Russians were going to kill me. And that I'm going to die alone and lonely.' He's actually started looking behind the curtains before he goes to bed. He knows it's also funny – another morning he tells me he's just spent the night 'neurotically worried about a ground-to-air missile launched by the Russians, worried about the chart position' – but it's also genuinely bothering him. If he has alienated a large group of people he had no intention of alienating, that is bad enough. And if, just by chance, the state apparatus of Russia, with all its well-practised ways of disseminating opinions and influence, focused its disapproval on him, that would be quite unnerving. One day he calls Guy, who knows at least one political journalist on a national newspaper, and Guy tells him that there's a sense that the Russian government are behind the backlash, which only feeds into his paranoia. And the rest of the conversation doesn't help much.

'That's doesn't make me feel safe,' he tells Guy.

'Nah,' replies Guy, dismissively, 'I think we're all right.'

'*You're* fine!' Rob exclaims.

One day, as he stands smoking on a TV station balcony, he turns to me and says, wanting to make something absolutely crystal clear: 'Yeah, I don't want to be the international symbol of freedom of speech when I'm killed.'

He's both joking and not joking. In a similar spirit, I promise to let everyone know.

'Okay. Make *sure* they know. "He didn't want to be that."' He sighs. 'Yeah, he died doing what he loved best. Living.'

* * *

January 2014

At the moment of their creation, songs have no idea of the weight that may one day be placed upon them. In the second week of January, Guy Chambers flies over for two weeks' songwriting at Rob's home studio in Los Angeles – the first songwriting sessions specifically for Rob's next pop album. On the first day, before Rob even arrives at the studio, Guy runs through some song title ideas that he has had. He mentions five. The first four are 'Nowhere To Land', 'Pockets' ('as in going through someone's pockets to see what they've been doing – about jealousy'), 'Electric Sundown' ('Gwyneth Paltrow, when they put Apple and Moses to bed, says "we make sure we have an electric sundown"') and 'The Golden Age'. None of these will be worked on.

'Oh, and the other idea as well,' he says, 'is "Party Like A Russian". The idea is "we party like a Russian". Just a party song. Like a new "Rock DJ".' It should be, Guy suggests, a song that will describe how Russians are, 'but also saying, there's something great about the fact they know how to have a good time'. He mentions that it was inspired by the last time they visited Moscow when he heard some hip hop music in Red Square;

he's already worked up a sample from Prokofiev's *Romeo and Juliet* as a possible backing track.

Rob arrives about an hour and a half later. He's been to the doctor's.

'Yo!' he says. 'I've had my sperm frozen, and they've found some swimmers.'

'"Swimmers,"' says Guy. 'That's a good title.'

Rob asks what Guy has, and Guy says that he has a song he thinks could be 'the new "Lazy Days"'. (That song, 'To The End', will get written a few days later; nothing will happen with it.) 'We've also got this Russian thing,' Guy says.

Still, Rob gives no indication that he has any interest in hearing anything quite yet. Instead he talks about a dinner he had the other night – it expanded out of a Mommy and Me meeting, but ended up including Mel B and her husband, and one of Linkin Park, and he says that by the end of the night his eczema was blaring. But eventually Guy plays the spare track based around the *Romeo and Juliet* sample.

'That's good, isn't it?' Guy says.

Rob eats his breakfast, says nothing yet, so Guy works with Richard Flack, reordering the sample, making a simpler structure.

'It's instantly Russian, isn't it?' says Guy. 'Snow. Men that march with their legs all the way up.'

Rob keeps eating.

Guy sings rhythmic nonsense words over what Richard is looping: *party like a Russian, get a gun, go shoot shoot your cousin ... percussion ... party like a Russian.* Then he plays some piano over the loop. 'Not many words rhyme with Russian,' he mutters.

'Hold on,' says Rob, and asks for the music to stop.

Then he phones downstairs to the kitchen for a shake.

Finally, Rob acknowledges what's going on around him, and begins to join in. The very first things out his mouth – *a certain kind of man who's got a certain duh duh duh* – already have the melody, the rhythm, and some of the words that will end up as the first line of the finished song.

And then the real work begins. Songs at this point simultaneously go down a rabbit hole and emerge. Some moments, such as a chorus line *party like a Russian/Elton John on percussion*, or a notion to rhyme *communism* with *jism*, or the couplet *we're the Russian boys and we don't care, make sure you've got clean underwear* surface only fleetingly, and then disappear over the event horizon into the black hole where failed lyrics go to die. But quite quickly, there's a complete song.

'That's great,' says Rob after about two hours.

'Russian pop,' says Guy. 'No one's done this.'

'Yeah,' says Rob. 'There might be a reason for that.'

As we listen back to it, Rob mentions that he has an idea for the album title.

'*The Heavy Entertainment Show*,' he says. 'And,' he adds, 'it sets up the tour.'

He laughs.

'Shame we can't put them out for another two years,' he says.

It's been a good day's work.

Before he leaves, Guy has one final thought.

'Hey,' he suggests, 'there could be loads of different ones! Do a whole series: "Party like a Dutchman!" "Party like a Frenchman" ...'

'Right,' says Rob. 'Go home.'

* * *

Afterwards, especially given the fuss that the song will trigger, people will wonder what precisely was intended when a song like this was being written? Was it intended to be satirical and, if so, in what way? Was it supposed to be pro-Russian? Anti-Russian? Who exactly is the oligarch character in the song – a real oligarch or Rob taking on the aspirations and excesses of an oligarch? What is the song's attitude to the current Russian political establishment? What exactly is the relationship supposed to be between the Robbie Williams who is singing the song and the Robbie Williams who exists in real life? And Rob, inevitably, will have to come up with answers, after the event, to some of these questions, because many of these are the kinds of questions to which, as the singer of the song, you're not allowed to have no answers.

But this is the truth: in the two days over which this song was being written, not a single one of the issues above was discussed. Often enough, that's just not what happens. There's some people in a room writing a song, and there's a kind of excitement when an idea appears that seems to work – in this case, in terms of the lyrics, an idea that everyone seemed to broadly understand without ever discussing it. It's a pop song about *Russian stuff*, and putting it together was making everyone laugh and making them feel fulfilled because they're creating something unusual and catchy that didn't exist a few hours before, however good or otherwise it would ultimately turn out to be. Nobody's thinking about what will happen when it's out in the world, or if one day it becomes a single, or it were to become the subject of multiple *Guardian* think pieces.

This is the truth, and I think it happens this way far more often than people realise: 'Party Like A Russian' was just *written* – in a fever of fun, silliness and excitement. Working out what it might mean, that came later.

* * *

That's not to say that in the months that followed there wasn't some pause for thought. That there wasn't some concern and discussion about whether the words might rile anyone in a way that would be disruptive to its healthy existence as a pop song. This is the kind of thing Rob was alluding to when he talked to Dan Wootton about how he 'had to take a few things out to make it more PC'.

There was a couplet in the first verse, for instance, that went:
Like a modern Rasputin
He goes shooting with Putin.
This wasn't some incendiary piece of political commentary. I think it just seemed funny, the convenience and crassness of the *Rasputin/Putin* rhyme, and the pop-ness and rhythm created by the internal rhyme of

shooting with *Putin*. And though it wasn't openly discussed in the studio, I'm absolutely sure that the image conjured up by *shooting with Putin* wasn't of assassinations or murder, it was more of a kind of weekend grouse shoot on a country estate; the international pastimes of the wealthy and privileged. And none of this made the song in any way *about* Putin. He had just been given a walk-on part because it made sense that he might turn up in some fictional oligarchical world, and because his name fit.

But Rob ultimately felt that even mentioning Putin's name might be distracting; given the reaction to the song even without it, an instinct that was doubtless correct. So he changed that couplet, and it became:

Ain't no refutin' or disputin'
I'm a modern Rasputin.

To be clear, even in this, it wasn't as though the song was being somehow consciously depoliticised or neutered, because it was never intended to be something that it now was not. What happened is more like this: it's as though a song that had been created in the consequence-free floating space of creativity was being pulled down to earth, checked for obvious faults and made ready for public consumption.

* * *

October 2016

More unsettling news comes with the *NME*'s review of 'Party Like A Russian'. They refer to it as 'the best thing he's done in years':

It's like something from a past era and a pop song from another dimension all at the same time, and crucially, it's interesting – and that's something we haven't been able to say about Robbie Williams for a long time.

Each of us has our own personal signs of the apocalypse.

'I genuinely thought, "Oh shit!"' says Rob. 'Whenever they give me a good review, something bad happens. Genuinely – I'm not making it up for drama or something – I was "oh *no* …"'

* * *

'There was a hatchet piece in the *Daily Mail* this morning,' says Rob when I walk into his hotel room one day. 'A proper hatchet job.'

To really understand what has happened today, you need to know a little of what has been happening recently in the music business, and to understand the evolving ways that the charts have been changing, and continue to change, in the wake of shifting patterns of music consumption. A few years back, when the singles chart was principally a measure of physical CD single sales, it was easy for any artist with a sizeable fan base, as Rob has, to achieve a fairly high chart position, even with a single that didn't connect with the wider public, because enough fans could be relied upon to buy the CD single, with its exclusive extra songs, to ensure that. That system, which suited established artists, has been eroded in two steps. First, the chart became dominated by the sales of digital downloads rather than physical sales – that change already worked to the disadvantage of artists with older audiences like Rob's who are typically slower to adopt new technologies and new ways of consuming music. But there has been a far bigger and more disadvantageous further change since Rob last released a single. With the recent surge in streaming, the way the singles charts are compiled was changed to include, and often be dominated by, streaming data. Fans like Rob's fans, proportionally speaking, hardly stream at all.

So everyone involved with Rob's new campaign was well aware that it was improbable that 'Party Like A Russian' would reach a high chart position. (In the week of its release, there was only one artist over 40 years old in the top 40, and that was the curiously ageless – and, in recent times, faceless – Sia.) What everyone was perhaps less prepared for was how easily this could be turned into a cheap story, and could be used as stick to beat him with.

It's hard to judge whether the *Daily Mail* simply don't understand these recent changes in the chart or fully appreciate their implications (to be honest, many people don't, even people around the edges of the music industry), or whether they know full well and are just cynically exploiting their readers' ignorance.

Either way, this is what they wrote:

**Let Me Disappoint You! Disaster for Robbie Williams
as new single Party Like A Russian limps into
the midweek chart at number 53**

*Robbie Williams' latest release looks set to be his biggest flop ever …
his latest chart entry will be a huge disappointment to the star and
a reflection of the fickle nature of fame … Party Like A Russian has
already caused confusion amongst his fans as the track samples Sergei
Prokofiev's Dance of the Knights, which is more commonly known as
the theme tune to The Apprentice. The outlandish and rude lyrics have
also been a turn off for many of his followers.*

* * *

Things like this are annoying, but over time, once any sense of panic that
'Party Like A Russian' has genuinely stirred up an international incident
has receded, Rob settles on a way of presenting all of this. First, that as he
knew he was unlikely to have a big hit, he chose a single that would generate
attention and court controversy. Second, that the stories people had written
– that the Russian authorities were furious, that he was banned from
Russia – were fiction, and that it had actually been welcomed and the song
looked like becoming his most successful single in Russia. Third, because
he knew he was unlikely to have a big hit, he was deeply appreciative of
all of the articles about the controversy because they were highly effective
in disseminating the message that he had a new album coming out: 'I'm
very, very grateful for the amount of press coverage that it's had, I'm really
grateful for the column inches …'

He also hits upon a slightly more focused explanation of what the song
is – and if it, too, was never discussed nearly three years earlier when the
song was written, no matter. 'I'm in character and it's a fantasy and it's a
theatrical piece where the guy that's in character wants to be like a mythical
oligarch. It's a musical piece, just like *Oliver Twist* or *The King and I* or
Guys and Dolls. It's kind of Lionel Bart-esque … it's Robert Williams of
Burslem, Stoke-on-Trent, deciding to be Russian for the evening at a party.

No satirical or political dimension, just a camp, funny song in character. You know, I'm not actually a burning effigy of everything I used to be, and you're not my rock of empathy. If we have to go back and look over lyrics and have them represent my true intent and who I am as a person, I'd be fucked. It's basically jolly silliness. International bants.'

When he's out of the country, he also adds a nice spin on not taking the hysterical British media furore about the song too seriously. This is what he tells a press conference in Paris: 'Anything that goes through the filter of the British media first comes out in the worst possible light. The British media could take a little bunny, a little orphan rabbit bunny, and then they'd be, "What we want to do is fucking make that bunny a refugee that's going to steal our healthcare and sleep with our women." That's the kind of filter that everything goes through. And so it is with everything: sensationalism, clickbait, "it's outrageous". The truth about my record is, it's just me playing dress-up. It's me in character, the musical *Robbie Williams*, and in this particular song I want to be like an oligarch. I don't mean to offend anybody in any way at all, and it's stupid and whimsical and silly, and it should be treated as such – it shouldn't be treated as anything political. It's just silly stupid pop music – here today, gone tomorrow.'

* * *

Throughout this process, Rob keenly monitors the statistics on the 'Party Like A Russian' YouTube video. One day he mentions that it's now up to 2.83 million hits. 'There's six thousand dislikes,' he points out.

'That may be normal,' says Michael.

This declaration hangs in the air between us, as though everyone is smelling it, trying to work out if it might be supportive but vacuous bullshit. Michael breaks the silence first.

'If it's not,' he adds, 'I'll find a stat that makes it look good.'

'Yeah, do that,' Rob agrees, enthusiastically. 'Yeah. Pad it.'

To emphasise what he means by this request, Rob then tells a story from his distant past: 'I had a girlfriend once, and I was trying to make her tell me who she'd slept with. And she wouldn't for ages. But I made her. *Insisted.* And then she told me, and I was fucking gutted, because I knew them. That's probably like my career and you, Michael. No matter how much I want to know, pad it with success.'

'"Candy" has got twelve thousand dislikes,' says Michael, trying to do just that, his point being that it's normal for a song to have this many.

'Yeah,' Rob quickly retorts, 'but there's fifty-six million hits.'

'I knew you'd say something like that,' says Michael, wisely retreating for now.

* * *

In the early days of the song's release, when it's still somewhat unclear whether or not 'Party Like A Russian' really has brought a nation's disapproval down on Rob's shoulders, there is an ongoing discussion about whether it might help if Rob was to give a carefully chosen interview to be broadcast in Russia. Feelers are put out, and eventually it's arranged that the host of one of Russia's biggest shows, *Pust Govoryat* (meaning 'Let Them Talk'), will fly over to speak with Rob. Michael is told that when it is broadcast, 18 per cent of the Russian population will be watching.

Rob agrees to attend band rehearsal that day, principally so that he can be filmed by the Russians. When the host, Andrey Malakhov, arrives, he gives Rob a very odd Russian clown jumper, which Rob announces he's going to put on right now. 'But not in front of the camera,' he explains, 'because of my man boobs.' The host explains that when he came through the airport and explained what he was here to do, the passport official referred to Rob as 'Sir Robbie Williams'.

'Is that what he said?' says Rob. 'It's only a matter of time. What can I say?'

After Rob rehearses a few of his new songs like 'Mixed Signals' for the very first time, and runs through 'Party Like A Russian' twice for the Russian film crew, all in the clown jumper, they adjourn to a small upstairs room for the first part of the interview. Rob's asked about the Russian iconography included in the video, and about other omissions. He says that he didn't know bears were a symbol of Russia and explains that vodka wasn't a realistic option: 'Unfortunately I'm terrible at drinking. And vodka was my great joy – I had a vodka passion, but unfortunately that passion got away with me. And I haven't had a drink for seventeen years, and the last drink that I had was a vodka.' He also says that he didn't really know what an oligarch was until he looked the word up in the dictionary after the single came out: 'I just thought "oligarch" meant somebody that had done really well. Genuinely.' The interviewer looks amused. 'I just thought it was a good thing,' Rob continues.

They do the second half of the interview in a private garden in the middle of a residential square in central London. Rob tries to get across the message he wants to communicate – 'It's very important for me that Russia knows that there is genuine love for me to write "Party Like A Russian"' – but most of the questions are about very different matters. The host asks several questions about British etiquette trends – what kind of thank-you notes people write, whether it is now normal with British friends to divide up a restaurant bill between them – and he also wants to know about porridge.

'Do you eat porridge?' he asks. 'Because we think all British eat porridge.'

'Yes, I did eat porridge every day,' Rob obliges, 'because I thought: those are my carbohydrates, and the rest of the day I won't. But as you get older and the body slows down, the porridge had to go.'

Finally Rob finds a Russian cultural theme he is knowledgeable about – Russia's over-the-top entry in this year's Eurovision Song Contest. Rob explains with great passion how annoying it is when you have people round to watch Eurovision and not everyone concentrates for the whole three hours. 'It's just a spectacle,' he says. 'The glamour and the silliness, that's what I love it for. Do Russian people love it for the same reason?'

'Russian people,' says the host, 'think it's Olympic games of music.'

This is when a mad notion comes into Rob's head. And, as with many mad notions that come into Rob's head, the mad notion immediately shoots right out of his mouth.

'Wow. Do you know what?' he says. 'I'd like to represent Russia at the Eurovision.'

Michael's expression, standing off camera, is a complex combination of amused and horrified, with maybe also a certain amount of you-put-out-one-fire-and-two-more-start.

'I'm saying it now, my management have just gone like that,' Rob continues, clutching a hand to his forehead to represent Michael's pain, 'but I'd like to represent Russia at Eurovision.'

'The biggest news,' says the host.

* * *

And that's not even nearly the strangest moment today. That comes in a quiet moment off camera when Andrey Malakhov explains that he wrote a bestseller ten years ago called *Moya Vtoraya Polovinka*, which means *My Second Half*. It's a book about how he secretly has an alter ego, a twin who nobody knows. 'He's fun, he's more open, he's more free, he's more cool, he's more famous ... everything is *more* inside of this person,' Malakhov says. 'It's a voice which I hear.'

And now the really strange bit. In the book, the alter ego goes by the name of Robbie. And, Malakhov explains to Rob, this is not some chance coincidence. 'The voice's name is Robbie, based on Robbie Williams, because I always associated myself with Robbie Williams,' he says.

'Wow,' says Rob, not quite knowing what to say. 'This is incredible. I don't understand it fully, but I don't suppose that I'm supposed to.'

'No, honestly I was crazy about you,' Malakhov explains. 'During the Christmas I was listening to your duet with Nicole Kidman for like twenty-four hours, one after one. Giving me, I don't know, memories for like you've been saying, about the childhood, about the happiness, about the Christmas tree. The book is about me and the Robbie which lives inside of me.'

* * *

In the car back to the hotel, Rob laughs about his blurted Eurovision proposal.

'It would probably be one of the weirdest things ever if I actually did that,' he says. 'More than a lot of me really wants to do it.'

When he gets back to the hotel and talks to Ayda on Skype she tells him in no uncertain terms that this is a terrible idea. He tries to convince her – I think more because he wants the fun of the idea to continue for a little longer than because he thinks that if only he can persuade her it will probably happen – but she's having none of it.

* * *

The final, even odder coda to Rob's Russian media campaign is that even though his forthcoming appearance on the show *Pust Govoryat* was announced in the Russia press, the interview didn't air as scheduled.

Not a word of it, until the following March when in Malakhov's studio he has Russia's real new Eurovision representative (who will later be blacklisted for having performed in occupied Crimea) and Malakhov plays her just the short clip of Rob declaring his Eurovision ambitions. Predictably, Rob is subsequently denounced for his presumption: a Russian politician and singer Iosif Kobzon will declare 'we have no need of British defenders of our culture'. He'll also characterise Rob's proposal as 'idiotic'.

6

November 2012

Given that Rob rarely reads books, and can do an entertaining routine about what an unengaged and unsuccessful student he was at school, it's sometimes surprising to discover just how much of the world he has taken in. Not the esoteric stuff so much – he spends enough time burrowing around odd corners of the internet that it's no surprise that he knows quite a lot of arcane weirdness. And while his memory can be selective (frequently less good, for instance, when it comes to categories like: *Lyrics of hit songs by singer Williams, Robbie*), once he finds something that interests him, his detailed recall can be impressive. But I wouldn't, for instance, necessarily have expected that he would have been familiar with the 10,000 hour theory popularised by the writer Malcolm Gladwell in his book *Outliers*, the notion being that all kinds of different people of exceptional achievement – The Beatles and Bill Gates are two of Gladwell's examples – started truly manifesting their special talent only after around 10,000 hours of practising the underlying skills that they needed to master.

But this evening, as Rob sits on the sofa at home watching Norwich play Man United, I will discover that he is. Today he was at the Royal Albert Hall, rehearsing for the Royal Variety Performance.

'You know when you have pretensions to be a footballer?' he begins. 'I had a moment like that in rehearsals today.' He explains that he suddenly remembered how as a kid he would imagine one day being somewhere like this – onstage at the Royal Albert Hall! – and how inside his young head he would run through the whole scenario: what he would do, how he would do it. And now, this afternoon, as he rehearsed his songs, Rob felt the peculiar sensation that he was both of these people – Robbie Williams now, but also at the same time the boy who was imagining what he would do at a moment like this. It was a strange feeling. 'I was, "This is what I'd do if I did that,"' he says, 'even though I *was* doing it. If I was this person this is how I'd do it … but I *am* this person. It felt like that.'

And you'd think that when you were a kid?

'All the time. You know that thing about the ten thousand hours? Well, I probably put in ten thousand hours showing off. Whether I was on my own or with people.'

What would you do when you were on your own?

'I don't know. I guess I was trying to be *magnetic*. Or charismatic. You know, walk around in a film.'

Why do you think you wanted that?

'I think there's quite a few reasons or whys. My dad's really charismatic and alluring. And you got to "be somebody". I don't know what that meant – I don't even know if I said those words.'

And did it feel like you were practising for something that would happen?

'Yes. It felt like practising for something that would happen.'

Not 'I've got a crazy dream'?

'No! Nope. A hundred per cent something's going to happen. Marie Cartlidge bet me what was in my pockets, or what was in her pockets – I think it amassed to £1.27 or something – that she'd be famous before me. I got annoyed that she even thought that she *could* be. I thought, "Oh, that's easy money."'

Have you ever collected?

'No. But she can send it to me by post. We'll call it £1.20.'

How old were you?

'Fifteen. Fourteen, maybe.'

If you were that convinced in your head that that was what would happen, how difficult do you think it would have been for you if it hadn't?

He thinks a moment. 'I'd have found some line of work to make it happen. In my own head, I suppose. I don't know what I saw as successful, really. I thought the twins on *Coronation Street* were very successful. I remember also there was a guy at school, I think his name was Martin Sims, and I don't know how it came up but he said, "I'm a better singer than you." I was like, "No you're fucking not." I actually thought he was delusional. If I'd have known the word "delusional" at the time. He said, "I am." And I just went straight out with some sort of Stevie Wonder kind of trill, and then went, "Go on…" And he went, "No."'

* * *

Let's just backtrack, and take a moment to consider what Rob is actually saying here.

The skill that The Beatles, according to Malcolm Gladwell's theory, amassed by playing for 10,000 hours in Hamburg and elsewhere was of playing and performing songs – and they subsequently became some of the most famous, successful and innovative musicians of all time. The skill that Bill Gates amassed by working for 10,000 hours at a high school computer in Seattle was of computer programming – he subsequently became one of the most famous, successful and innovative computer geniuses of all time.

And the equivalent skill that Rob has identified – and that, unnaturally precocious, and dedicated to the mastery of his craft, he also put in 10,000 hours' practice doing in his youth, in a way that few other people ever have – is for *showing off.*

* * *

This thought is still in his mind the following week when he holds a press conference to announce next year's stadium tour. Afterwards, he does some one-on-one interviews, and in one of these he is asked what he is best at.

'I'm quite good at everything – I'm not brilliant at anything,' he explains. 'I'm an all-right singer. I'm an all-right dancer. I play pool quite well. I play football quite well. I do everything quite well, apart from academic stuff. I can't add or subtract, I can't spell, I'm very dyslexic. But anything that involves showing off … showing off, I'm one of the best in the world.'

* * *

October 2016

Of all the shynesses and insecurities that plague him, a fear of being naked is not one of them. In private, at home, Rob often walks around in a state of almost complete undress. I don't think this is a matter of vanity, more some combination of comfort and laziness. Just as, if not prodded to do otherwise, he would quite happily wear the same grey sweatpants and t-shirt or sweatshirt for day after day after day, when it's warm enough that even fewer layers are required, he's perfectly content to wander from room to room in the emperor's new sweatpants.

Appearing naked in public is, of course, a rather different matter – here, other impulses come to the fore. On one side of the scales are his instincts for devil-may-care exhibitionism (as he'll say this month at a French press conference: 'I love to get naked – if I had a slightly bigger penis I'd be naked now') and for not being boring. (Most things are more interesting naked.) Pulling against that is his tendency to judge himself harshly, and a predisposition for feeling shame, all of this accentuated by the way he has enthusiastically embraced the diagnosis a therapist once gave him that he was body dysmorphic, where in the eye of the beholder everything in the mirror appears to be more flawed than it really is.

But every now and then, when he feels he's looking good, the balance decisively tips in the first direction.

* * *

You might think, after the shame and regret that followed his failing-to-break-the-internet nude photo a couple of years back, he might have let that kind of thing be. But this July he and Ayda post a short Instagram film. In it, he is naked, apart from a small cake that he is holding with two hands in front of his genitals – the conceit being that in the previous video they'd posted, Rob has had to choose between two superpowers, eating cake and invisibility, and so he now thinks he is invisible and the cake is floating in mid-air.

This time, people seem to find it funny, and the comments are kinder.

'That was kind of a proud moment,' he says. 'Rapid weight loss, cake covering the cock. Not my *proudest*, but it was a fun morning.'

Now *Attitude*, the British gay lifestyle magazine, have asked whether he would pose naked for the cover of their magazine, and he has said yes.

* * *

The shoot is in a studio in the East End of London. When Rob arrives, he sits in the make-up chair and eats some curry while his hair is cut. For the first shots, he poses bare-chested wearing a baggy coat held open. He looks at the shots on the monitor. 'You'll touch the hair and the zits up?' he checks.

Then he gets naked, posing with his genitals covered by his hand. When people see these photos, there's a fair chance they'll imagine that he's not really completely naked – that there's some modesty-preserving device being concealed. Or, if not, then that he is just momentarily naked for a few seconds while the shutter clicks. Neither is true. He's naked for nearly half an hour – posing for the shots, but also walking around in breaks, looking at the photographs on a monitor. And while he always keeps a cupped hand vaguely in place, I've a feeling that this is far more out of politeness for all the people present than for his own benefit. He seems completely unbothered.

That's not to say that he likes, or has any expectation of liking, the results.

He looks at the shot on the screen, and there's a chorus of other people gathered round saying how good the shots look.

'Do you like?' the Dutch photographer, Stephanie Pistel, asks him.

'I don't like me,' he points out.

They discuss a new pose, sitting down, and whether he needs to wear pants to preserve his modesty. He has a different suggestion: 'I could cover it with my little toe?'

Eventually, he puts on some clothes and goes for a cigarette in the yard outside the back entrance.

'It's kind of liberating,' he says, 'but hideously shameful at the same time. Body consciousness, and how fat I feel all the time. I have a filter in my head where it's way worse than it actually is. Even when it's bad.'

* * *

'Did I ever tell you that story,' he asks one day, 'about Nigel Martin-Smith saying that a gay magazine wanted me to do a naked photo shoot? And they were going to pay me fifteen grand. It was before Take That were famous. I was seventeen. And I really liked the Vitara jeeps and they were like twelve grand – I hadn't taken into account the tax. But I was, "Oh, I could get a Vitara jeep."'

Nigel Martin-Smith, of course, was Take That's manager in their boyband days, the man who put the band together, and the man who Rob associates with some of his worst teenage torment.

'It was full nude,' Rob continues. 'And I said, "I'll do it." This went on for a couple of weeks. I felt uncomfortable, but I was, "Oh, it's just a cock, isn't it? I'll get a *jeep*! …" Then we did a gig, I think it was in Scarborough, and went back to the hotel and it was, "Yeah, you've got to do the photo shoot after the gig." And it was to be in Nigel's room.'

Rob got to Nigel's room at the appointed time, and all the rest of the band were there, and everyone went "Arghhhh!", laughing.

'And it was a joke,' he says. 'That's weird, isn't it? That's weird, right?'

I ask him whether he has ever talked to the other four about it.

'No,' he says.

Sometimes when he tells Take That stories, it can sound like a one-way street in which the youngest and least conformist – Robbie – was constantly being put down and put in his place, certainly in the early days. But it clearly wasn't *all* like that, because the fake-nude-photo-shoot story stirs another memory.

'We used to break into each other's rooms, and wipe our arse on toilet paper and put it underneath the pillow,' he says. 'When I say "we" … me and Howard. And then we'd go and put cellophane on Gary Barlow's toilet. I can remember all four of us being in Gary's room. And then it'd happen to mine.'

But he doesn't think that compares.

'Naked for a gay magazine's another level, isn't it?'

* * *

A few days later he is on a private-jet flight to France that he is disappointed to learn will only take 45 minutes because he needs to catch up on his sleep.

'Can you ask them to go round a bit?' he suggests.

Instead, he studies some proofs from the *Attitude* shoot.

'I only like it when they don't look like me at all,' he says.

A few minutes later, he adds a further thought.

'One of my tits,' he points out to Michael, 'is droopy in one of those pictures.'

'We'll even it out,' Michael promises.

'Make them both droopy?' Rob wonders.

* * *

March 2013

'This is just a song I like,' Rob says to Guy one day in the studio, and plays him 'GMF' by John Grant, mouthing along to the lyrics.

But I am the greatest motherfucker
That you're ever gonna meet
From the top of my head
Down to the tips of the toes on my feet.

Rob discovered John Grant when he came across a clip of him performing his song 'Sigourney Weaver' backstage at Glastonbury in 2011. 'There are not many moments in pop culture where you're really taken aback – you can name them maybe on that many fingers throughout your life,' he says. 'And that was a moment for me. I was sort of overwhelmed with: "That's it, that's what I want to do, that's what I want to be like, I wish that I could articulate these things in songs the way he does it." He's another person that exists in the ethereal place where Rufus Wainwright exists – their talent, the way they see the world, and the way they channel that and put it into songs, is extra-special and different, and wonky, and dysfunctional. It's like dysfunctional mega-talent. And I'm sort of drawn to that more than mainstream-ness.'

Watching more clips of Grant on YouTube, Rob realised that in some of them his keyboard player was Paul Beard, Beardie, who was currently Rob's musical director, so Rob asked for John Grant's email address. 'I get the chance when I'm reading a book and I'm really enjoying it to reach out to that person and tell them,' he says. 'I got to reach out to John Grant and tell him how much he meant to me.'

They started corresponding and discovered a connection. 'We have very similar neuroses about stuff,' says Rob, 'so there was a nice back and forth: *Yeah, I'm fucked, you're fucked, this is how fucked I am, yeah, but I can top that, I'm this fucked.*'

* * *

'GMF' is from John Grant's most recent album, *Pale Green Ghosts*. Last week Rob was listening to another of the album's songs, 'It Doesn't Matter To Him'. A song of heartbreak, it begins with these lines:

If I think about it, I am successful, as it were
I get to sing for lovely people all over this lovely world
And I am nowhere near as awkward as I was when I was younger
I guess I'm one of those guys who gets better looking as they age.

A lot of things were going on that week. Rob had also been reading on an internet forum about artists' dream setlists so he started to put one together of his own songs, thinking he would blog it on his website. But he came up with a list of just 12 songs, only eight of which he'd written. 'And two I'd put on out of pity for myself,' he says. 'It made me sad'. Rob was also angry about a rude email that someone close to him had sent to Josie. And he had stopped taking appetite suppressants for a while after getting grumpy with Ayda and swearing in a fairly extreme way at a woman who kicked sand on Poupette and Walle, their Maltipoo and Havanese, when they were walking the dogs on the beach. And then he had started taking the pills again.

All of these things, and the John Grant song, swirled in the cauldron of his head, and he wrote a poem. I think it was written less out of any clear ambition to add to the literary canon, and much more out of an attempt to put down accurately in words a snapshot of how he was feeling at that moment. It would be a horrible mistake to take these words as some kind of definitive statement of what he really feels – what he really feels is much more like the aggregate of all the wildly different things expressed across the whole of this book, along with a lot more calmer, quieter, sweeter, and just occasionally duller stuff that tends to get crowded off the edges of pages like these by more dramatic and extreme moments.

But for anyone who imagines when Rob recurrently refers to self-doubt and self-loathing that it's just another kind of pantomime, here's an unvarnished look at the contours of some of those thoughts in the raw.

The poem is titled HAVE I TOLD YOU I HATE EVERYTHING THAT I'VE DONE and its first half goes like this:

REVEAL

WELL I GUESS I'M NOT GOING TO BE ONE OF THOSE GUYS

WHO GET BETTER LOOKING WITH AGE

I MUST HAVE OVERCOOKED THE DRUGS SOMEWHAT

I EVEN GAVE UP SMOKING

PRIMARILY TO FIX WHAT'S HAPPENED TO MY SKIN

IT HASN'T WORKED

ALL THAT HAPPENED WAS I PUT ON WEIGHT

AND I FELT AN INCREDIBLE SHAMELIKE DAGGER

BETWIX MY ABDOMEN AND MY BRAIN

TELLING ME TO NEVER GO OUT

NEVER GO OUT

AND I LISTENED

HAVE I EVER TOLD YOU

THAT I HATE EVERYTHING I'VE EVER DONE

I MADE A LIST OF MY FAVOURITE ME

IT WAS PITIFUL AND FULL OF COVER VERSIONS

I HAD SUCH LOFTY AMBITION FOR MY NEWFOUND

ARTY/ARCH FAN CLUB THAT I KEEP IN MY MIND

THEY ARE LEFT UNFULFILLED STILL ...

I CANNOT BLAME THEM FOR GIVING UP

AND SHE LOVES ME

AND I GET IT

BUT FUCK ME

WHAT A WASTE

I AM UP THERE PEDDLING THE BEST OF ME

AND IT FEELS LIKE SHLOCK ...

THIS IS NOT A MIDLIFE CRISIS

UNLESS I WAS MIDDLE AGED AT 16

NOTHING'S CHANGED

I BLUFF MY WAY UP YOUR NOSE

ON PURPOSE BECAUSE

IF I CAN'T MAKE YOU LOVE ME

THEN I'M GONNA MAKE YOU HATE ME

MORE THAN ANYONE YOU'VE HATED BEFORE

SOMEHOW THIS FEELS LIKE WINNING …

HAVE I EVER TOLD YOU I HATE EVERYTHING I'VE DONE

THIS IS WHY I LOVE DRUGS

THIS IS WHY I SEEK OBLIVION

THIS IS WHY I'M RESTLESS

IT'S BECAUSE I HATE EVERYTHING I'VE EVER DONE

After that, it just gets darker. And darker.

* * *

'I think it's more to do with what I felt like on speed than what I actually feel like all the time,' he says. 'I think these appetite suppressants can make you quite angry, and it's quite easy for me to indulge in vengeful thinking. And it was true.'

He sent the poem to John Grant, suggesting that they write a song together using its title, and maybe including some of the poem's lines in its lyrics. But he didn't get a reply, and that became one more thing to make him feel more like the way he was already feeling.

* * *

A few days later, he finally hears back. John Grant hasn't been using that email address. Everything's good.

'He liked my poem,' he says. 'And he wants to write. I love John Grant.'

* * *

October 2016

Tonight, Rob is to attend the Attitude Awards, where he will accept their Icon award. But first, he has an interview for the story that will accompany his naked *Attitude* cover. The interviewer, who has flown in from Iceland yesterday, is to be John Grant. Last year they finally wrote together, the two of them and Guy, when John visited him at home in Los Angeles – their song, 'I Don't Want To Hurt You', appears on the deluxe version of Rob's new album.

You get an immediate insight into their rapport when John Grant walks into the living room of Rob's suite at the Soho Hotel. This is exactly what happens:

'Hi, luv,' says Rob.

They hug.

'You look well,' says Rob.

'Thank you,' says John. 'I still prefer to complain though.'

'I'd still rather you know that I haven't had enough sleep,' cuts in Rob, 'feel inadequate ...'

'Oh my God,' echoes John, 'I was just telling everybody in the elevator that I was up all fucking night, because I just got back from the States, up all night thinking "you will surely die alone in one of these horrible hotels" ...'

'Yeah yeah yeah,' says Rob. 'So I do that as a way of saying: don't expect too much from me. I can't be brilliant right now because I haven't had adequate sleep.'

'Well, you're brilliant at your worst, so don't worry about it at all actually,' says John.

'Thank you,' says Rob.

'You look well as well,' John continues.

'Do I?' says Rob, sounding doubtful.

'Hot,' says John. 'Smoking.'

'Oh really?'

'Duh!'

'Well, thank you. Have you been ... ?'

'I'm not eating sugar ...' John says.

'Okay,' Rob interjects. 'How long for?'

'... but last night,' John continues, 'during my existential terror, there was a package of caramel and peanut butter popcorn staring at me from this luxury hotel, and I pounced on it like a puma and ... here I am. I don't know how I made it here.'

Rob says nothing, just walks away, through the door into the darkness of his bedroom. He returns a few seconds later with two scrumpled Dairy Milk wrappers.

'Does this make you feel any better?' he asks.

'Yes,' John says, with feeling.

'That happened last night,' Rob explains. 'Yeah. I had a Tuesday sugarfest – I allow myself one sort of meal of complete hedonism when it comes to chocolate. But Tuesday was in the middle of last night. So how are you finding not eating sugar?'

'Well, it's my favourite thing in the world,' John replies. 'Butterscotch pie, for God's sakes, my grandmother's recipe. How am I going to live without it? But I am living without it.'

'Also,' says Rob, 'the road narrowing, you're not allowed to do drugs, you're not allowed to drink, and you're not allowed to have sugar ...'

'I just think of it as: we were always lied to,' says John. 'That song I have, "You And Him", that's about the sugar industry.'

'So you put one fire out and one fire comes up – what's the fire that comes up?' Rob asks.

'Well, it's always sex,' John answers. 'Staying true to my partner. Because I want to fuck everything else that's walking around all the time.'

'Yeah, of course,' says Rob. 'So do I. But that's something you're not doing too – that's part of the road narrowing.'

'Yeah. But I find that to be ...' John pauses, and digresses. 'Coffee, that needs to go too. I think the caffeine's giving me a heart condition.'

'Me too ...' says Rob.

There has been no discussion between them about what this *Attitude* interview will be about, and there never will be. They sit down during this initial discussion and nothing that is ever demarcated as being the interview, as such, ever truly starts – it is just this conversation as it continues and continues, getting deeper and weirder and more honest and more heartfelt. Matthew Todd from *Attitude* is also here, and later on he will occasionally steer them towards some subjects that he'd like them to discuss, but for quite a while he barely interjects at all. It would probably seem a little rude, and anyway it is entirely unnecessary – it's hard to imagine how one would nudge them towards having a more frank conversation than the one that they both seem to effortlessly and instinctively gravitate towards.

* * *

To begin with, they mostly talk about addiction and desire and their partners, sharing notes on the hurdles they have found, and their struggles to straddle them. Eventually the conversation turns to what Rob is doing right now. He explains how releasing an album 'can be an international shamefest – and I'm too sensitive for that'.

'Has it ever *been* for you?' says John, surprised.

'What – an international shamefest?' says Rob, laughing, and explains about 'Rudebox'. '*Yeah*. I released a song in 2006 that was me rapping and there was this sort of vitriolic hatred for me, because it was my time to get a good kicking and I'd given them the opportunity to do so. It became a laughing stock, and I became a laughing stock, and it damaged me. Yeah, it did. But any given moment, putting out an album can be an international shamefest. And I'm not prepared emotionally for the job that I do: being so public and being so big. I don't have the ability to protect myself from the words and the shame. It hurts.'

'I think that's good,' counters John. Meaning not the shame, but the awareness of it. 'Don't you think a lot of people get into a crazy labyrinth of not even being able to admit to themselves that things like this hurt them? Because people say: "Oh what the fuck does *he* care, he's got millions? He can't *possibly* be affected." People don't take it seriously. Don't you believe that? People are like …' – he puts on a sarcastic voice – '… "Oh, you poor thing – this got to you, this hurt you." People don't realise you don't stop being a flesh-and-blood human. Just because of these other things.'

Rob nods, and says that he knows, because before he was famous he was the same. He has realised that somewhere inside him he has the same cruel and careless instincts he now abhors, because when he was young he did to others as is now done to him.

'When I was a kid,' he explains, 'I used to go and watch the local football team. And the abuse that I, and we, as a crowd used to give our own players, and their players ...' He shakes his head. 'It was *dog's* abuse. It was horrendous. It was the worst thing that you could shout at any given opportunity. Because those players only exist on that football field. They only exist there. It's like at school if you ever saw your headmaster cutting the garden or something, there's like a glitch in the matrix where you can't get your head round it: why is your headmaster cutting his garden? That doesn't make any *sense*. And the thing with the football players – you don't think those people go home ...'

John nods.

'They're just hung up in a closet and you take the batteries out, and then put them back in.'

* * *

Towards the end, Matthew Todd from *Attitude* says to Rob, 'So I was going to ask you some gay stuff.'

'Okay,' he replies.

'There have been a couple of controversial moments ...' Matthew begins. The first example he brings up is 'when you sued a paper when a guy said you had sex with him, which some people got a bit pissed off about'.

On the last Sunday of August 2004, the headline on the front of *The People* newspaper was ROBBIE'S SECRET GAY LOVER. The accompanying story claimed to detail gay trysts of Rob's in Manchester, talked of how experienced he clearly was at such things and spoke authoritatively about who he really was: 'Robbie is gay and those close to him know it but he is being suppressed and not allowed to come out. It's very sad and the pressure is beginning to show. His drink and drugs problems are telling signs that he is so unhappy that he can't be himself. I feel very sorry for him.' The article was published just before *Feel*, the book that in some ways is a predecessor to this one, came out – a book in which he had gone out of his way to discuss perceptions of his sexuality, and explain the truth, which involved detailing a few amusingly complicated situations but a grand total of zero gay trysts. Rob sued, successfully, but in victory he was widely criticised, the common implication being that there was something fundamentally homophobic about suing someone for saying that you're gay, because by doing so you're suggesting that you think being gay is a shameful way to be.

It infuriates Rob, of course, that anyone could think that of him. He describes how things were for him in 2004:

'That media spotlight was shining on me and there was sensationalism and untruths, and I felt really frustrated. So I concentrated on this book where I was one hundred per cent honest — hopefully, more than a lot of people in my line of work would have been at the time. And it was really important to me at the time to be a hundred per cent honest – that it was out there. Incredibly important for me to get the truth out there.'

Then these stories appeared.

'Now, the problem that I had with that at the time was that it was untrue — and I've written this book where the truth is. And it hurt me and upset me. And if there was a way to sue anybody in the press at the time for absolutely anything, I would have and I did. Whether that was about being accused of being gay or being accused of sleeping with somebody that I didn't sleep with at a certain time. It was not about the whole gay thing. There was an industry whose focus point is to hurt me, ridicule me, lie about me, and my focus was pointing a finger back at the time. Standing up to power, I thought. To point the finger back at power and say "that's not right..." And I'm sad that people – and people will because they are people – would perceive that me suing the papers that week was anything other than to do with the fact that I could sue them. Nothing to do with the gay stuff, but just they were *lying*. At the time it was really important that my truth was out there. And here was an article saying that I'm living a lie, that my life is a lie. Cause I haven't divulged that secret to the public. And I felt hurt and betrayed. But I did with all the articles that were out. It was weekly. Daily.'

He talks some more about the changing ways he has been perceived – he mentions again how he felt when the Google autocomplete of his name stopped being 'Robbie Williams gay': 'I was like, what's happened? Have I got a double chin?' – and he talks about that liberation and welcome he found in gay clubs in the early Take That days, and how it did make him, momentarily, ask himself the question. 'Being exposed to this world that I loved being a part of – I took my first ecstasy at a gay club, had the most incredible time. I was like, "Why have I lived like *that* when I could live like *this* for ever?" And I tried doing that, which led me to AA. But also because of the hatred, the homophobia that there is out there, I was sort of left as a twenty-one-year-old going, "Actually, I don't hate the gays … so does that mean that I'm gay?" And the truth is with me and gay …' – and here comes the quote, the sound bite that travels outwards from this article – '… is that I can't get round the cock thing. You know, I have crushes. Big male crushes. A lot. I crush a lot. But I just can't do the cock. I don't enjoy looking at mine that much. So I can't get round that bit.'

* * *

Rob actually wrote a blog at the time, in the wake of his libel victory, in which he spelled out his various thoughts on the subject with heartfelt clarity:

I don't think that anyone from any Gay rights group genuinely feels that my case against the Sunday People had anything to do with me being homophobic. I believe I'm being used as a tool for publicity, which is a shame … However, needless to say my actions have been brought into question. So I hope this will answer some of the queries …

A. I have never said or thought that it is shameful to be gay

B. The bloke was an absolute 'minger' – take a look at him. You'd sue.

C. Replace the bloke in the story for a woman – if it was untrue and I had grounds to sue then I would of course sue. What would that make me if I only sued when a story was of a heterosexual nature? The inference being that I didn't want to affect my 'gay fan base'?

D. For the record I have never personally profited from any libel case. I wouldn't touch their money. It'll go to Give It Sum, a charity that in the past has helped to finance a gay help line.

E. As far as I'm concerned this whole case has nothing to do with homosexuality, I'm just trying to make a stand against a media with too much power and no responsibility. I know it will have as much effect as throwing toothpicks at King Kong but they're my toothpicks and I'll throw them when I can.

F. Anyway the most offensive bit (in which if you didn't read it was a truly evil article) was the suggestion that my whole life is a lie and that I have been dishonest and insincere whenever I've talked in public about my personal life.

It has been said that the Sunday People case was about me proving that I'm straight – to be honest that's the last thing I wanted. I love the fact that there's a question mark hanging over my sexual preference. It's done no harm to Mick Jagger/David Bowie ...

* * *

There's one other story that Matthew asks him to discuss: 'You also got some online flack for saying a few years back in an interview that you were forty-nine per cent gay.'

In a November 2013 interview with the *Daily Star*, where Rob was talking about how he was interested in writing a musical including old and new songs, he was quoted as saying: 'I would really like to have a crack at it. I love musical theatre and a lot of the other things that are often associated with gays. I am 49% homosexual and sometimes as far as 50%. However, that would imply that I enjoy having a particular sort of fun which I don't.' After this was published, a *Guardian* columnist, Patrick Strudwick, piled in pretty hard with a column headlined *No, Robbie Williams, you're not 49% gay. But you are 100% stupid*, followed by the subhead: *A gay person would know how maddening all your 'affectionate' stereotyping is – we've had to listen to it all our lives.*

His column continued, in part:

Of all the statements about homosexuality, this is packed so deep with stupidity, I'm like a heterosexual at a car boot sale, dizzily unsure where to begin. (We can all cheapen others in the stereotype bonanza.) ... Robbie, gay people are only 'associated' with musical theatre by the sort of people who associate black people with 'being good at sport and music' ... Let me offer Robbie Williams some guidance: you are nearly half gay if about half the people you desire sexually have the same set of genitals as you and if you spend nearly half your life overwhelmed with love for someone with the same chromosomal wiring. That's it. Gay men may all like cock, but only a fraction like Cabaret ...

There is further cause for my venom. (Such sharp tongues, you know.) In 2005, Williams sued a newspaper and two magazines for daring to suggest he was gay. Yet here we are, eight years later, and he is releasing an album entitled Swings Both Ways, *with predictable allusions to bisexuality, thus ensuring both man and music swing in unison, hitting banality at one end and genre genocide at the other.*

On which bum note leads us to marketing. Not for nothing did our crooner add his sigh-inducing caveat about not actually enjoying 'a particular sort of fun': like a zillion other mainstream pop acts, he acknowledges and teases gay audiences, appropriates just enough gay culture to edgy-up his image and tap into a key demographic, but, at any opportunity will spell out exactly how heterosexual he really is, just in case someone at the record company gets a sweat on.

Sitting with John Grant and Matthew Todd (who is honest enough to point out that *Attitude*'s regular 'How Gay Are You?' interview quiz can trade in some of these same stereotypes) Rob says, 'the "49%" thing – I didn't sit the night before in my room going, "What can I tell them tomorrow?" It was just something that trips off the tongue. What does that mean? It's whimsy and theatre and ridiculous. But then can be isolated and sensationalised for the click or the morning commute. You know. That made me sad too. I phoned up the journalist ...' – the *Guardian* columnist – '... and he was, "well, maybe you should be more careful about what you say in interviews" ... I can't be held responsible for other people's lack of humour, and I can't be held responsible for the way that something is perceived.'

Rob told me more about this call – in which, incidentally, he also pointed out that for what it's worth he actually doesn't really like musical theatre – back then, a few weeks after it happened. While I don't think the journalist's cynicism about Rob's motives was justified – it's difficult to look at Rob's career and see much evidence of him being that controlled and calculating – there are certainly reasonable arguments to be made about how Rob's free and sometimes reckless appropriation of almost anything in service of entertainment and self-expression can also be seen as disrespectful and insensitive. But from the conversation Rob had with him, it seemed as though the writer also believed that, beneath all of this, Rob was guilty of a much more fundamental kind of self-delusion and hypocrisy. Because Rob says that during the call the journalist told him that he had it on very good authority that Rob had had a relationship with a specific well-known man.

At the very least, Rob may have got through to him on this particular subject:

'So then I went, look, the most precious thing I've just put to sleep upstairs, my daughter. Theodora Rose, I've just put her to bed, she's the most precious thing in my life. I swear on her life – I don't know how other I can say that, it just didn't happen.'

* * *

Rob has been thinking for several days about what he should say in his Attitude Awards acceptance speech. 'I wonder if I should mention about the gay clubs when I was in Take That,' he says one day on the plane, and reflects on the pervasive casual homophobia that you grew up with in 1980s England. 'I was born and raised in a society where gay was the thing you levelled against somebody on the playground when you wanted to hurt them the most,' he says. And though he thinks he was already open and ready to shake off these prejudices, when he started going to gay clubs it was easy. 'I felt instantly at home, I felt safe. Which is not something that you feel in Stoke-on-Trent when you go out.'

Michael suggests to Rob that he could mention that his first magazine cover after leaving Take That was *Attitude*. This isn't strictly true – he was on the cover of *The Face* before that, but he was on the cover of *Attitude* in August 1996. Those were the days when a journalist would describe an encounter with him like this: *We have now spent seven hours together. We have drunk ourselves into a state of glazed immobility and beyond into frenzied animation.* And when Rob, deep into separating himself and settling scores, real and imagined, would describe his former bandmates as 'selfish, stupid and greedy … I never fucking liked them'.

What Rob remembers is the cover photo.

'Yeah,' he says Rob. 'They managed to make my bloated cheeks look manageable.'

On the day of the awards, he seems to have decided that, just this once, he could step up to a podium and just say 'thank you'. But then, maybe half an hour before he leaves his room, he grins. He's decided on something else.

* * *

When he arrives, Rob goes out onto the fire escape to smoke, and runs into a gaggle of celebrities including Myleene Klass, Louie Spence and Emma Bunton. He chats with Emma Bunton about sleep-eating; she sympathises and tells him she does it all the time.

Back inside, he waits in the wings, where he chats with Alan Cummings, who tells him about the tour he's on: two hours of songs and stories. 'I want to do that,' Rob tells him. Graham Norton comes by, having just been onstage. 'You caused a sensation!' he tells Rob as he passes. 'My Twitter feed went …' and he makes a wooshing sound. 'I can't imagine what yours did.'

John Grant introduces him, and hands him the award. This is Rob's speech:

'I'd like to thank *Attitude* magazine for their constant support over the years. And, er, bit nervous, because I think this an opportunity, a perfect setting, to answer the big question about me …'

He milks the pause.

'... yep, I've had some fillers and I've had some Botox. And I've had something done to my chin that makes my double chin not so apparent. Can't even move my fucking forehead. Ladies and gentlemen, thank you very much.'

* * *

The first time Rob mentioned Botox in public was a few days ago at a press conference in Paris when he was asked if he could share his secrets for being in such good shape at 42, and he answered, 'Yeah – Botox fillers, and no potatoes. Good luck.' But no one seemed to pick up on it there, and, even now, it takes some time. The next day he is puzzled that it hasn't been mentioned. I ask him if he wants it to be.

'Only because I don't want to have to then justify or talk about it,' he says. 'If I can say it, have it be a joke, people find it funny, and then not have to go into detail about it, I would like that to happen.'

He must know it won't be like that.

It takes about six days for the story to break. The version he enjoys the most is the one in the *Daily Mail*, which has 'before' and 'after' photos. 'The difference in Robbie's appearance,' they say, 'is clear to see'. The 'before' photo is an unflattering shot from the Take The Crown tour in 2013. The 'after' photo – captioned 'earlier this month' – is a picture of him in a blue suit and matching blue shirt from an Australian promo day in October 2015. Nearly a year before his first Botox injection.

From then on, of course, he's asked about it over and over. 'I've got money, and I'm vain, and I'd like to look young, and so shall it be ...' he'll say, and repeat how inevitable it is when you live where he has been living. 'If you live in Los Angeles long enough you're definitely going to have something altered on your person. Because it's just all around you. Next-door neighbour. Over the road. You could throw a brick and hit somebody that's had something done.'

He considers this for a moment.

'That's probably why they had it done,' he says.

* * *

As Rob leaves the stage at the Attitude Awards, one of the audience jumps onto the stage and chases him backstage. He has something very, very important to say to Rob, something he seems absolutely convinced that Rob would want to know.

'Robbie, I just wanted to come up to …' he says, breathlessly, '… to tell you, you're the first man I ever masturbated about.'

Rob gives him a quick hug, before starting to move away.

'God bless you, mate,' Rob says. 'Carry on wanking.'

* * *

After Rob gets back to the hotel, he finds a nice email from John Grant saying that however anxious he feels at moments like that – just before going onstage Rob had told him 'the nerves just make me want to go to bed' – it doesn't translate to how he appears onstage. John says that he was amazed by the transformation.

'Yeah, I know, it's weird, isn't it?' Rob replies. 'I seem to have a way of turning trauma into something that looks showbizzy.'

And after Rob had typed this – *turning trauma into something that looks showbizzy* – he thought about it for ages.

* * *

The next morning, he has an interview with Alexis Petridis from *The Guardian*.

'I've just woke up and my brain's not working,' Rob apologises, words that are almost becoming his new *good morning*. 'Let's just have the espresso first.'

For a while they share stories about smoking, and about addiction. Talking about when how 'one fire goes out and another fire pops up', Rob mentions that the first time he gave up smoking 'that fire then became Minstrels'.

'What, the sweets?' asks Alexis, just clarifying in the manner of a professional journalist making absolutely sure of what is being said.

'No, *actually* …' says Rob.

As though he might have developed an unrestrained penchant for medieval musicians.

* * *

Towards the very end of the interview, Rob gives his confidence-and-bravery speech. And then out comes tumbling a fuller version of what he wrote to John Grant last night:

'I have a way of making trauma look confident, and that's my talent. That is my main talent. My main talent is turning trauma into something that looks showbizzy. I think that's my one talent that I have.'

That, quite understandably, will become the article's headline: *Robbie Williams: 'My main talent is turning trauma into something showbizzy'*. It's a thought he will sometimes return to in the weeks to come, and expand upon. 'These are all big moments of trauma, the traumatic experience that actually is what I do onstage, where I turn my neuroses and my lack of self-worth into something bigger than me, and I use that as a force to project this man that's incredibly confident. And it's not true. So I turn my trauma into something that looks like giant showbiz.'

* * *

Later, Rob opens a new email from John Grant.

'Oh,' he says. 'That's great.'

It's just a picture – a photo of a t-shirt.

Across the front of the t-shirt are these words:

I'M SORRY FOR WHAT I SAID WHEN I WAS HUNGRY.

* * *

May 2013

At breakfast in Wiltshire, during tour rehearsals for the Take The Crown tour, Rob says that in last night's dream he worked in a restaurant. There weren't enough grapes. Two boxes were available but they cost £1,700 and he didn't have any money. Then he was in a wheelchair he didn't need, out of control going down a hill.

He eats breakfast and watches a Washington Press Club investigation into UFOs on his computer. He sits with Teddy. 'Remember me, from being your dad?' he asks. There's a teapot on the table that plays 'Rule, Britannia'. He turns on the TV. 'Are you going to be raised by the TV like me?' he asks Teddy. 'Hey! I turned out all right. At least I'll be watching it with you.' This next part is in the tone of a parent who really needs to make something clear. 'As long as it's Sky Sports,' he says. On Sky Sports a Premier League literacy programme is being explained, in which kids will be encouraged to read by learning about football players' favourite books.

'I had the reading age of fourteen when I was eleven,' he says, 'and *I* didn't need Theo Walcott to help me.'

This is the first time I have ever heard Rob say anything that suggests receiving any positive academic feedback in his youth.

More quietly, he then adds: 'I dread to think what my arithmetic age was.'

I mention that there's an article in *The Sun* today that says he's a narcissist.

'Can I have a look?' he says.

* * *

At the Grosvenor House hotel in London to perform at the Sony Radio Awards, Rob sits in a hotel room upstairs, waiting. He mentions that every now and again the darts player Phil Taylor sends him ideas for lyrics. 'One of them,' he says, 'was: *they put my picture on the poster, and still they come.*'

Then he chats with David Enthoven.

'I'm in love with my daughter, Dave,' says Rob.

'I think she's in love with you,' David points out.

'Yeah, she is,' says Rob. 'This morning's news. Basically what's happened is: baby gets born, you go "woah!" and then you're on euphoria, and you're, like, Mummy takes care of baby, and you're just gliding along. Then you go to work and you come back from work and baby doesn't really *do* much. Then at seven months they know who they are and they know who you are and they start interacting with you. And now I'm a fully-fledged dad and totally fucking get it. I love it to fucking bits.'

The next day he tells Beardie how great Teddy is, now she knows who he is.

'I'm keeping her now,' he declares. 'For the first few months, I wasn't sure. I mean, everybody knows we've had her, but everyone knows tabloids lie.'

* * *

In the living room in Wiltshire, we watch a new David Bowie documentary, *Five Years*. On-screen, David Bowie is talking about 'Ashes To Ashes', explaining how he wanted to take Major Tom from 'Space Oddity' and put him in a Victorian nursery rhyme atmosphere, and refers to 'that queasiness of some of those "ring a ring of roses", "this is about the plague and we're all going to drop down dead"' kind of things.

Which makes Rob laugh, having just been at number one for four weeks with 'Candy', a song that directly quotes 'ring a ring of roses'.

'Jacknife …' – Jacknife Lee, the producer – '… wanted to take "ring a ring of roses" out,' he says. 'I don't think he could get his head around it being that inane.'

Rob laughs.

'And I could.'

Later in the documentary, the critic Nelson George says, about David Bowie's *Let's Dance* album, 'He made a record that was in many senses an experimental record that actually worked on a pop level, and that happens a lot for people. Every artist, their core group resents the fact that these outsiders are in on our secret, but that's the danger of making a good record: you never know who's going to listen to it.'

'That's really fucking great,' says Rob.

A while later, Rob declares, 'I'm going to be avant-garde next.'

I raise my eyebrows somewhat sceptically.

'I don't mean on my next record,' Rob clarifies. 'I mean when I go into the next room'.

* * *

Rob is at Wembley Stadium to play the Capital Radio Summertime Ball. He does an interview backstage in which he is asked what playing at Wembley is like. He patiently explains that, apart from that benefit show, Net Aid, many years ago, the stadium has been being rebuilt for most of his career, and so tonight will be his first time performing here.

Off camera, Josie is gesturing. Clearly there is a problem with what he is saying. It takes him some time to realise.

'Take That!' he suddenly exclaims, getting it. 'I played here with Take That! Just the eight times! That slipped my mind. Wow! How much is a pint of milk? Five hundred pounds!'

* * *

Rob is often weighing the pros and cons of whether he could permanently settle back in England. This week he realises one more con. He's working out in the gym of the Maida Vale house, and is thinking about Noel Gallagher because he'd just bumped into Gallagher's wife – they live only a few houses down, and she kindly sent flowers when they moved in.

The TV was on in the background, some quiz show. And suddenly a question on the TV cut through:

Which member of Take That did Noel Gallagher call a 'fat dancer'?

It wasn't just the question that he minded. That wasn't the worst bit.

'Everybody,' he says, 'knew the answer.'

* * *

October 2016

Last night Rob dreamed that he was with Paul McCartney. McCartney was showing him a gigantic art piece that someone had built in honour of The Beatles. It was a sculpture of a massive ear.

'I was, "I get it … it's about music."' Rob remembers.

The giant ear had these stairs that swept up into it, and it was *huge* – about half the size of Centre Point, the rectangular tower in the middle of London that dominates the view from Rob's hotel living room.

'It was gorgeous,' says Rob. 'It was beautiful. There was a tear in my eye because it was that beautiful.'

And then, in the dream, McCartney sort of winked at Rob.

'Yeah, it's beautiful,' he said, 'but we make money from it, too.'

'You make money from it?' said dream Rob.

'Yeah, different revenues,' said McCartney. 'We make a lot of money from it.'

Rob also says that McCartney seemed happy that Rob knew his last album.

'And I remember thinking,' says Rob, '"Oh, we're not talking about me …"'

He shrugs. 'It was just a dream that happened. It's quite something, dreaming of a massive ear.'

* * *

Today, he is filming a video for 'Love My Life' on the Isle of Sheppey, on the north Kent coast. In the car, he reads UFO websites then watches footage of a supposed UFO over a block of flats in Russia. It doesn't look like much.

In the Winnebago on a lawn overlooking the sea, he has his make-up done, drops hummus on his trousers and makes up a song about it:

I've got hummus on my trousers again!
Fuck you, hummus!
For being so white and spreadable!

It doesn't sound like a hit, but it may be the kind of a giddy nonsensical humour required to get through these long tired days. Vaughan Arnell, who has made many of Rob's most famous and iconic videos, comes in to greet him. There is a way that video directors used to be in the medium's heyday: kind of brash and irreverent and gruff, as if a party or a fight might be just around the next corner and either might be no bad thing. Though he's obviously also both sweet and smart, Vaughan seems to have kept some of that kind of aura about him.

'Graham Norton,' he says to Rob. 'Oh my God – that was *amazing*!'

'Yeah,' says Rob.

'Carole, she fucking choked on her wine and spat it out. And that American bird, her face.'

Rob goes out to film along the raised strip that protects the isle from the sea. Someone who has spotted Rob drives along the track that runs parallel to the inland side of the strip. Videoing Rob as they drive, they crash into a road sign and are stuck there. Rob goes down to film their efforts to get free.

'I was too busy looking at you,' the driver says, in way that sounds less like an apology and more the first half of a sentence that she would like to finish by saying *so it wasn't my fault*.

Once they've gone, we drive further up that track past a sign advising us that we're heading into 'remote areas'.

'Remote Areas sounds like an eighties band,' he says, and sits in the car while a button on his coat is fixed.

He's filmed singing the song over and over, the song playing at high speed, sounding like some kind of weird melodic jungle track, so that Rob's movements will look kind of hesitant and dreamy. At the end of the day, he goes to have his photo taken with some locals who are waiting outside the Winnebago.

'You're a lot taller than I thought you were,' one woman says to him.

'Yes,' he says, making friendly conversation. 'I'm very tall.'

'You're not *very* tall,' she snaps back.

* * *

The same day that begins with a Beatles dream ends with Rob answering a fan question on his website forum:

Who is your favourite Beatle?

'John x'

* * *

May 2013

He's angry again.

In bed, late one night, Rob reads a comment on his fan website from someone who says that she used to be a fan – who, as you'll see, evidently lives in Tiverton, Devon. She tells Rob that he's past it, that his career is over, that she doesn't know why he's bothering to go on tour, and she insults Ayda in passing. 'She made me feel bad,' he'll explain.

He's incensed enough that he immediately writes a blog. He sends what he has written to Josie to be posted – BLOG THIS, I'D LIKE IT TO BE UP WHEN I WAKE UP THANK YOU X – and also sends a copy to me. When you feel under fire and you feel under siege, you want to fight back. But when you feel under fire and you feel under siege, it is also easy to lose a sense of proportion and a sense of perspective. He reaches for other weapons later, but he begins with sarcasm – sarcasm and Google:

WHEN I SAW YOUR PHOTO, I TOTALLY WANTED TO LEAVE MY WIFE IMMEDIATELY AND START A NEW MORE IMMENSE LIFE IN TIVERTON WITH YOU AND YOUR AMAZING FRIENDS.

I GOOGLED TIVERTON STRAIGHT AWAY JUST TO FIND OUT WHAT MY NEW LIFE MIGHT LOOK LIKE (A BOY CAN DREAM!).

TO MY SURPRISE THERE WEREN'T ANY INTERESTING FACTS

BUT HERE'S A PICTURE OF THE NEW TIVERTON LIBRARY AND COUNCIL OFFICES

I DONT KNOW ABOUT YOU BUT I JUST MARVEL AT HOW IT'S BEEN PUT TOGETHER ... NOW THAT IS ARCHITECTURE

IF I'M NOT MISTAKEN THERE ARE THREE LEVELS ... MAKES THE MIND BOGGLE: WHAT ARE THEY DOING ON THAT TOP FLOOR?

AFTER WE'VE BEEN TO THE LIBRARY AND OFFICES PLS PLS PLS PLS SAY WE CAN DO THIS?

[Rob has then included the TripAdvisor link to one particular subset of 'Tiverton, Devon attractions', the Devon badger watch.]

IT'S BEEN A LONG HARD SLOG TRYING TO FIND YOU

WHAT WITH THE OTHER 38,330 INHABITANTS OF YOUR FAIR CITY

AND THE GULF THAT IS OUR LIVES ... AT TIMES IT'S SEEMED A TOTALLY IMPOSSIBLE TASK

IF I'D HAVE ONLY KNOWN ABOUT THE A361 EARLIER I MIGHT NOT HAVE HAD TO MARRY THIS AMERICAN IN THE FIRST PLACE ...

SHRUGS SHOULDERS THEN THINKS HOW I'M GONNA BREAK THE NEWS

IT'S A MASSIVE RELIEF IN ONE WAY

A TEAR IS RUNNING DOWN MY FACE AS I TYPE THIS BLOG

JUST THINKING BACK TO THE TIME ... ALONE IN A FIELD WITH PALMS TO THE SKY WHEN I SHOUTED ...

GOD!!!!! SEND ME A WOMAN THAT LOOKS LIKE ...

If, so far, the blog has just about managed to keep on the side of unlikely and funny rather than derogatory and cruel, it now launches itself full tilt in an uglier direction. The extended metaphors and comparisons he uses to describe the appearance of the person he is addressing are ingenious, memorable and comically inventive but the cumulative effect is wrongheaded and horrible.

That attack goes on for a while. Then towards the blog's very end, it calms down a little, or at least wears its withering sarcasm with a little more grace:

I FEEL I'VE ALREADY SAID TOO MUCH ...

I SHALL MEET YOU HERE

[He pastes in a picture of Tiverton high street.]

I'LL BE WEARING A TAKE THAT T-SHIRT AND KISS MAKE-UP SO YOU KNOW IT'S ME ...

UNTIL THEN

IN YOUR DREAMS SWEETHEART

X

* * *

It's with some trepidation that I turn up at the Maida Vale house the following lunchtime. Some of the words in this blog, particularly those I haven't reprinted here, shouldn't be read by anyone. It feels like this may have been a mistake he will rue.

When I arrive, Rob is downstairs, playing with Teddy.

'Did you get my email?' he asks.

I nod.

'It wasn't put up,' he says.

He explains more of what happened.

'It was a full moon,' he says. 'And I couldn't sleep. I was up till six. I'd run out of things to do on the internet, and I'd been watching battle raps.' Sometimes you know something is irresponsible, and that becomes the very reason to do it. 'I have to be politically correct a majority of the time, and not fuck up the brand or the person or the image, don't offend this person, don't offend that person,' he says, '… and sometimes that's exactly what you want to fucking do.'

But the moment he woke up again later this morning, he had only one thought in his head: 'Fuck, don't send that!' He emailed Josie, who replied that she'd already thought that she should maybe sit on it.

Later, at a meeting about his tour, he reads the blog out to everyone there.

'What did she actually say?' someone asks, wondering what foul provocation could have inspired such a reaction.

'She didn't like *Take The Crown*, basically,' he says.

* * *

In the end, it turns out that his impulses, however unwise, weren't so unfairly directed after all. After the same comment that inspired Rob's blog has drawn lots of objections and negative responses from Rob's fans, the woman who wrote it decides to post again, doubling-down on her attack. It's unpleasant stuff. She calls Rob 'a closet gay boy', and slurs Ayda as mentally ill, a gold digger and someone who 'must have a strap-on'.

After that appears, Rob tries to argue that he should publish his original blog after all. Everyone around him bombards him with all the arguments against doing so. He obviously knows that they make sense, but the one thing no one can deprive him of is the fun of complaining about it.

'Sometimes,' he says, 'you lot are so boring.'

* * *

October 2016

Rob has some New Zealand interviews to do over the phone. He knows it will come up, and it does.

'Yeah,' he laughs. 'Nobody's been that horrible in a long time. Nobody's been that horrible in a *long*, long time.'

In October 2015, Rob played at the Wellington Basin Reserve, and a local columnist called Simon Sweetman reviewed the show. His review was basically just a collection of insults from someone apparently appalled by Rob's continued – and, to him, baffling – prominence:

The whole chav-made-good, I'm-grinning-so-I-must-be-winning shtick is tiresome … can barely aim anywhere near a high note, let alone hit one … something called Me & My Monkey deserves a prize for The Worst Song in The World … showed just how far you can take karaoke if you've got the cheekbones … this hamfisted hack … his thin sketch of a voice … no nuance … as bad as being caught with the least flattering photos of yourself … Next time they might even invite a real musician now the circus has, fingers crossed, left town.

Rob has been mauled much more elegantly and expertly than this, but for some reason this really got to him. 'It was the end of the tour and I was really tired and quite emotional. So it made me angry.'

And so he responded. At his next concert, in Auckland, Rob dedicated his poem 'Hello Sir' to Sweetman, and changed its final line to *Simon Sweetman, kiss my fucking arse.* He also tweeted a picture of Sweetman that he found on the writer's social media – a photo of the writer, a fairly large man, holding his son, to which Rob had appended the caption: *Simon Sweatman: Baby eater.*

As Rob explains in these latest New Zealand interviews: 'I've given everything that I've got, and I take the responsibility of entertaining people very seriously, and I suppose that when you're tired and you're missing your family and somebody's mean about you, you're, like, "Owww …" I'm incredibly oversensitive. I have no thick skin. No thick skin has developed. I remain thin-skinned and incredibly oversensitive.'

But Rob also makes clear that there are no residual bad feelings on his part.

'God, not at all,' he says. 'I had a wonderful couple of evenings onstage down in New Zealand, amazing audiences, can't wait to come down and entertain them again – I'll be back. Listen, you know, it's all panto, and it's all part of the Heavy Entertainment Show. Be it good or be it bad. I sort of weave it all in. I was onstage in front of the people that were loving it, so it's all good, and God bless Simon Sweetman. God bless him too ...'

* * *

And so it might have remained. When one of these interviews is published in New Zealand, including some of these comments, the writer noted that 'Sweetman has declined to comment'.

But not, it turns out, for too long. Later that week, Sweetman posts an essay about the events of the previous year on the parenting section of a website called The Spinoff, an essay titled 'About that time Robbie Williams tweeted a photo of my son'.

He begins by talking about the concert itself again, and in describing that, he is every bit as arrogantly, self-assuredly dismissive of Rob as he was the year before – *Robbie struggled through his gig ... As did I* – and of the audience, too: *They were there with cloth for ears or cotton wool blocking them up.* All of that might well have enraged Rob all over again.

But Sweetman's only getting started. He describes what Rob tweeted – though, amusingly, he clearly seems sceptical that Rob is likely to have gone looking for photos on Sweetman's website himself. (I love the implied alternative: that Rob has a support team who handle all his unwise, impulsive social media responses on his behalf.) Sweetman explains that the photo Rob had used, of him and his son Oscar, was taken on Record Store Day when Oscar was five months old, and then talks through the media storm that followed, and his wife's reaction. And he explains how difficult it was – even as he acknowledges that he made the image public in the first place – to have had a photo of his son reprinted over and over in this context.

How could I respond? If I said it was funny or silly or weird and that Robbie should grow up I'd look like a twit. If I sincerely expressed my disappointment at the image of my son being shared it would be shared, and Photoshopped. And I'd be next week's meme too … I changed the picture on my website, updating it to one of Oscar and I in a similar pose. Surrounded, again, by music. He was now four years old. Can't have eaten him after all – that was my (silent) response.

And then Sweetman moves on to the heart of what he has to say:

There's one thing that I always held onto from that night. It's something I thought about mentioning at the time and which I couldn't believe others had not mentioned at all: Robbie Williams' impassioned speech, mid-concert, in which he talked about how he nearly stole the camera off someone who wanted to photograph his children. He was going to break the camera. Because, right, nothing meant more to Robbie Williams than his own kids. Not all the drugs and mansions and easily-pleased audiences, no way. It was the kids that mattered. They mattered most to Robbie. And he'd be fucking damned if anyone was gonna circulate an image of his flesh and his blood. And just then the lump in his throat grew as an indication that this banter was designed to move people. His audience gushed. They sighed. That Robbie Williams. Nice guy, bit of a lad, possibly a lout, but oh aye, he does love his kids. He knows right from wrong.

* * *

Of course Rob sees what Sweetman has written. And of course, irrespective of whether Rob's initial anger was justified, and irrespective of whatever new digs Sweetman has taken, Rob recognises the sense at its centre.

'I sent him an email,' Rob says, 'from a dad to a dad. I said, "When I read 'The day that Robbie Williams put a picture of my son' … my heart sank… Much like my choices when I order from Amazon on Ambien aren't the best, neither are my choices when I act in rage, and for that I apologise to you, your wife, and Oscar."'

Did he reply?

'Yeah. He just said, "thanks for this".'

* * *

351

June 2013

On the plane to Dublin, he's feeling good.

'It's never been like this,' he says. He means: just before the first date of a long tour. 'It's never ever been "let's do it!" It's always been …' He mimes a face of abject open-mouthed panic, anguish and desperation.

That's not to say he isn't still always searching for things to distract him. In his Dublin hotel room he finds on YouTube a TV show called *The Adventure Game*, presented by Moira Stuart; a capsule from childhood. 'It used to be my favourite programme when I was nine or ten,' he says. 'I remember Mum went to hospital to have an operation on her bunions, and she called on the telephone, and I said to her, "Any chance I can go? My favourite TV show's on." I got the biggest bollocking ever.' He watches some more. 'This was the best thing ever in my life at this point for some reason – this was it.'

* * *

He has been dipping his toes back in the water – the occasional small show, then the Take That tour, then the three O2 concerts last November – but this is it: these Take The Crown shows are the first time since the 2006 meltdown that he will appear all night on his own, onstage in a stadium, and then do it again and again, week after week. From this first show, he establishes a routine. He likes to get to the stadium early: relax, walk around, eat, have a massage, chat, spend time with Ayda and Teddy, stretch, talk to the band, play FIFA, rest. A safe bubble of repetition as he gathers himself for what he needs to do.

Today, in catering, Rob sings Neneh Cherry's 'Buffalo Stance' to Teddy, and chats to Beardie about forthcoming fatherhood. This leads to a chat round the table about choosing baby names, and how they often change at the last minute.

'I was going to be Dominic,' Rob points out. 'Dominic! I'm not sure what happened. I think my dad swayed it.'

Sarah Jane, one of the singers in the band, asks whether he and Ayda had a boy's name picked out.

'I think it was Sonny,' he says.

As it happens, Ayda's cousin, Charlie, is here today. 'Charlie's proper name is Charlton,' says Rob. He doesn't mention the name's presumed inspiration – Ayda's family were very close to Charlton Heston – but he does say 'that's a good solid name for a lad'.

Back in his dressing room Rob finds a message from Robbie Keane saying 'all the best', and also a basket of six bottles of Guinness and two of champagne (to make black velvet) accompanied by a note offering U2's best wishes.

'They always do,' he says, in a way that is appreciative, not dismissive. (If it was from a less thoughtful source, Rob would probably also offer a despairing aside at this point about having been sent alcohol, but I think he assumes that both he and they know that it is the symbolism here that is the gift.)

'Do you know who Bono is, Teddy?' Ayda asks.

'He kissed you,' Rob tells Teddy. 'GQ Awards,' he adds, as though Teddy was just waiting for more information before confirming the memory.

'I don't know who was the lucky one,' says Ayda.

'I do,' says Rob.

* * *

Dublin goes well. Next, a run of dates in Manchester.

Backstage on the first night, Rob puts on a kind of gel face mask that makes him look like someone from a horror movie – 'I started using it on the Take That tour,' he explains – and heads off down the backstage corridors to look for Olly Murs. They'll find each other most afternoons or nights, at some point, and have these chats. A lot of the time it's just like two pop music buddies talking, but there's also sometimes a sense of the disciple and the elder, the disciple eager to hear stories but also always looking for useful clues.

'I love the lyrics to "Rock DJ",' says Olly. 'When you actually listen to the lyrics, they're so rude. Fucking erotic.'

'Yeah,' says Rob.

'When someone did "Rock DJ" on *The X Factor,*' Olly remembers, 'it was "you can't do that lyric … you can't do that one because it's an innuendo …" Everything was: you can't do that.'

'Yeah, my whole career's based on innuendos,' Rob says. 'On things you're not supposed to say.'

Back in his dressing room, he announces, 'You know what it's time for! It's time for testosterone.'

'What days do you do it?' Gina asks.

'Normally I do it Tuesday and Fridays. Or Tuesdays and Saturdays.'

Then he gets the daily briefing he has during the early part of the tour where he's talked through what he might do better, and where he might go, at various moments in the set. As he listens, he changes Teddy's nappy.

* * *

'Question, right,' says Olly Murs. 'Do you think if I met you twenty years ago, fifteen years ago, we'd actually be mates still now?'

It's the afternoon of the second Manchester show. This conversation is taking place in Rob's dressing room. Rob is naked, face down on a massage table, being massaged. Olly and Jonny Wilkes are sitting next to him on the dressing-room sofas.

'You'd probably be one of those friends that I'd have to let go of when I got to rehab,' Rob answers. 'Because you'd only know me from drinking and drugs.'

'You wouldn't have liked that Rob twenty years ago,' Jonny points out.

'Oh, I don't know!' Rob objects.

'You were fun,' Jonny considers, 'but not when you're pissed. You'd have gone, "Come here with me!", and then took him on a bender, and then he would have looked at you for the rest of his life, scared to death. Terrified of you.'

'Yeah, I was terrifying,' Rob agrees.

'When he started to drink, first two or three drinks ...' says Jonny.

'That hour, that golden hour,' says Rob.

'... he was brilliant. And then all of a sudden he went, "I am now going mental." And that was it. The stuff he ended up in.'

'So basically,' says Olly, 'the answer is no.'

'You'd have probably gone,' says Rob, '"He's all right, but ... fucking hell ..."'

A while later, Olly returns. Rob is now dressed. Ayda and Teddy have just arrived.

Rob introduces Ayda to one of Olly's band.

'My current wife,' he says.

'My first husband,' says Ayda.

Rob spends some time with Teddy.

'You're just the smiliest child,' he tells his daughter. 'Like I was, until it all went pear-shaped.'

* * *

Most days there is a meet'n'greet, where Rob is obliged to go to a room and make polite upbeat conversation for a few minutes with whoever is gathered there. Most often they're either people who work for the tour's sponsors, Samsung, or people who have won competitions. It's something that he's learned to do quite graciously, and most people seem pleased with the experience he provides, but you never quite know what might be coming. Today a woman tells him that when she was 13 and he was in Take That she wrote him a long letter from Qatar. She still seems slightly disappointed, as though she hasn't completely given up all hopes of a reply.

Rob explains that the letter would never have reached him. I think few people realise the intensity and the insanity of what it is like at its peak when you're a teen star.

'One Valentine's Day,' he tells her, 'I got seventy-four thousand Valentine's Day cards.'

* * *

While Rob's in Manchester, an old slumbering rivalry reawakens. Liam Gallagher's current group, Beady Eye, are just about to release their second album, and they're in town at the same time as Rob. Not only are they only playing the 1,500-capacity Ritz in their hometown at the same time as Rob is playing a stadium here, but this venue, the Etihad Stadium, is home to Gallagher's beloved Manchester City.

Any doubt as to whether this turn of events might be even the slightest bit annoying for Gallagher is dispelled by a radio interview Liam gives, complaining that 'the bullshit is winning', and adding, in his trademark style: 'We should be playing the Etihad three nights, not some fucking fat fucking idiot. It could be any fucking clown. I think it's a shame that he's doing three nights and a band like us are doing one night in the Ritz. Poor, mate. It's not about him, it's people in general. But it's about fucking him, just in case you think I'm scared or something.'

It's the kind of provocation that's tailor-made to put a spring in Rob's step.

First there's a blog:

IN AN OTHERWISE PERFECT APPRAISAL OF ME AND MY CAREER, IT'S ACTUALLY 4 NOT 3 NIGHTS AT THE ETIHAD, LIAM ...
AND THEN JUST THE 4 AT WEMBLEY. OH, AND THE TWO HAMPDENS.
IN OTHER NEWS, HERE ARE YOUR NEW MANAGERS, POUPETTE AND WALLE.
YOURS BIGGER THAN AN OASIS REUNION, MAKING HISTORY WEEKLY
FATTY THE IDIOT X

The accompanying photo shows Poupette and Walle side by side on two of the fancy manager's ceremonial chairs, the Manchester City emblem above them.

He's not done. Onstage, the following night, Rob is talking to the crowd after the end of 'Feel', and he spots someone holding up a sign that says LIAM IS A KNOB. Rob reads it out, and then says:

'Just, Liam, know this – that when Oasis does get back together again, you'll never be bigger than I am. And when you're looking out in wonder when Oasis does get back together again and you're giving it the "look at what we've created", just remember that fatty here did four nights in your fucking backyard … Apart from that, all the best with your album and good luck with the future.'

The opening chords of 'She's The One' start up.

'Robbie Williams,' he adds, 'bigger than an Oasis reunion.'

* * *

'That was so fucking funny,' says Ayda afterwards. 'You hadn't planned to do that?'

'Yeah, I had,' he concedes. 'I thought if there was a moment for it, I would.'

Later, having an after-show massage, he says, 'I got the weight of the Liam thing right? It wasn't too heavy? Because I'm not angry, you know what I mean.'

Not, he means, like he used to be.

'You know I used to go and try and find him? I used to get in the car and go up Primrose Hill and Haverstock Hill and go in the places where I know he goes and try and find him. I wanted to fight him.'

How many times?

'Twice.'

Were they in response to specific things?

'No, I was just angry in general.'

After the brief friendship he shared with Oasis, there were many years of sustained, condescending abuse from the Gallagher brothers, and, even more so back then, he liked to give as good as he got.

Olly comes into the dressing room.

'Your fucking speech at the end was banging,' he says, and tells Rob he's been watching the footage of him on the Brits, talking about Liam, challenging him to a fight.

'Did you ever see me in the Tigger outfit outside his house?' Rob asks. 'I had this Tigger outfit and I was like seven foot in it, and I used to wear it to go out. I used to go down Camden Market in it. So I went to Primrose

Hill, and I'm lying on Primrose Hill and I took the head off and I'm having a cigarette and I look over and there's the paparazzi and I'm, "Ah, this is fucked now, because they're going to know it's me inside this." So I cunted the paparazzi off, and then I was, "Oh, do you know where Liam lives?" And he was like "Yeah." And I was, "Take us there." So there's me outside Liam's house in a Tigger outfit going like that ...' And he mimes raising his fists.

* * *

October 2016

In the car, driving to rehearsals in south London, Rob is listening to his friend Paddy McGuinness on talkSPORT, promoting his show *Stars in Their Cars*.

'Patsy Kensit, one of her cars was a Bristol ...' McGuinness is saying, 'and she was married to Liam Gallagher at the time, and that was their first ...' He explains how the celebrity doesn't know which of their old cars have been tracked down. 'And when we unveiled it, she just burst into tears. It took her right back to that time. In a nice way. It does do that – it really gets the emotions going.'

'I remember when they bought that,' Rob murmurs. And this, as happens fairly often, uncorks the part of his brain holding tales of Robbie Williams and Oasis. Today's comes from the fairly brief honeymoon period where he was an errant boyband member whose friendship seemed welcome. To a certain degree, anyway.

'Did I ever tell you,' he asks, 'the story about Liam Gallagher qualifying why he allowed himself to hang out with me? It went on for a bit.' Rob does a Liam voice: 'People ask me, you know, "why are you hanging out with him?" Something they don't know about you, is he goes longer and harder ...' He returns to his own voice. 'It wasn't those words but it was just basically: he hangs out with me because I stay up the latest. And he was sort of letting me know that he probably shouldn't be hanging out with me. But also letting me know why he's okayed it with himself.'

What did you think when he said that?

'It was twelve o'clock the next day, so I wasn't in the best shape to take on board any information at the time, I don't think, about anything. But I probably thought, "Ouch ... I know what you're saying."'

So you went straight to taking it as a slightly buried insult?

'Well, it wasn't a slightly buried insult. It was a slightly buried compliment in the form of an insult. I think it was that moment that I thought, "I'm completely not welcome in here so I'm not going to bother."'

What had you been doing all night?

'The obvious. And listening to Beatles' records. Jibber-jabbering. Trying to cajole the feral rock star. Cocaine neurosis.'

* * *

'Did I ever tell you about the time that I booked into a hotel as Liam Gallagher? I was up all night in Manchester and then got on the train the next day with all the journalists that were still awake, and pulled a journalist. I think it was *Later ... with Jools Holland* that he was supposed to be coming down for, and I knew that Liam wasn't coming, and I knew that he had a hotel room free and I knew his pseudonym – Billy Shears. So I checked in as Billy Shears and slept with this journalist.'

Did you ever tell him?

'I think he found out. I think somebody told him. "Cheeky cunt ..." I don't know if it was "cheeky cunt" good or "cheeky cunt" bad – I'm guessing bad. But, you know, I'd been up for more than twenty-four hours in the fumes of rock'n'roll. In the dying embers of the night. What seems a good idea off your rocker is not the best idea sober.'

* * *

One day we're discussing 'Cheese And Onions', the parodic masterpiece by The Rutles. This opens that same door.

'You know, I used to listen to it with Liam in Patsy's kitchen,' Rob remembers. 'But it wasn't a joke to him. I don't think he knew it was joke. He played me "Cheese And Onions" and all that, and there was no recognition he was getting it on a level of it was a joke. He just thought it was other brilliant Beatles songs. Just more Beatles songs.'

* * *

An interviewer shows Rob a series of pictures from throughout his career, and asks him to comment.

'This one's me and Liam at Glastonbury. What a wonderful twenty-four hours that was, to be with a rock'n'roll band that were at the top of their game. Very exciting, incredibly exciting. It has its own energy altogether. And I was sort of breaking out of the safety and restrictions of a lily-white boy and going, "No, I do this – deal with it." So it was very, very liberating. And I was a huge fan of Liam and Noel and the band as a whole, so to be in and around them at that time was extremely exciting.'

He picks up the same thread in another interview.

'Liam was the voice of our generation and those songs were the soundtrack to our lives. And there was a golden moment of eighteen months when it was pure high-octane anything goes and anything will go, and it was incredibly exciting. You know: *where were you when we were getting high?* Well, I was *there*.'

And then he offers the other side of that experience.

'Along with it being high-octane stuff, it was a very sad time, because you're pushing the boundaries of what actually your body and mine can do, and I pushed it way too far. And, you know, watching that film where everybody's at a party and they're having an ace time and everybody's doing drugs, and if they don't show you the next day when everybody's waking up with a hangover and feeling terrible, you can leave with that feeling of "I want to be part of that". Then you see the hangover the next day and you're: "Oh yeah, I'm glad I'm not part of that."'

* * *

'I had really weird anxiety once,' he tells me, 'watching *Mickey Mouse Clubhouse* on the telly. I imagined that I'd got stuck in Mickey Mouse's clubhouse and those were the only people I knew and they talked like that. It actually gave me a panic attack. And then every time *Mickey Mouse Clubhouse* comes on, I go back to that panic attack where I worry about living with him in a 3D world. I know that's really odd.'

He pauses.

'And that's what hanging out with Liam Gallagher's like.'

* * *

June–August 2013

The Take The Crown tour continues. 'It's going well,' says Rob. 'And I've vanquished the demons of 2006. That's serious – there's been a lot going on in my head since 2006 about this whole thing, and it's just evaporating.'

It is also ten years this summer since his triumph at Knebworth.

'When you consider the age from ten to twenty, how big that is,' he says, 'I think you spend your second twenty working the first twenty out.'

* * *

In Scotland. Rob orders a fried Mars Bar on room service, which is brought to his room under a silver dome.

'We're the first ones apparently to have ever ordered one in this hotel,' says Ayda. 'It looked like a fried shit.'

'It was good,' says Rob. 'Nine out of ten. I couldn't understand how the batter and the sweetness were going to melt together, but they do marry each other very, very well. I mean, I'll never have another one.' Then he looks to his daughter. 'Actually, never say never again, because I might have to have one with you, Teddy Bear, when you're older.'

* * *

The next morning, everyone is woken by a fire alarm. The whole hotel has to be evacuated, though Rob, once he has established that there is no fire, refuses to leave his room and goes back to bed. But all of the rest of the band and the touring party – some of them quite bleary and irascible, because for them anytime in the morning is too early to get up after an enthusiastic night off – have to gather on the grass and gravel outside for 15 or so minutes. Apparently someone's overflowing bath has triggered the fire alarm.

Well, to be more precise, it's my bath. I make my apologies quietly where they most need to be made, but it's really not the thing you would wish to have happen. When you're on a tour like this, the less your own needs or actions require anyone else's attention, the better you fit in. Not least, it provides the set-up for a joke whose punchline can be stretched out almost indefinitely. Most days, for weeks to come, I will open my hotel room to find a plastic duck, or some other kind of children's bath toy, or on one occasion a printout of the lyrics to 'Yellow Submarine', sitting on the carpet outside, a thoughtful gift and reminder from Rob's security team.

* * *

Maybe it's some kind of avoidance mechanism, given what he has to do later in the evening, but the back-and-forth dressing-room chitchat often ends up in some extraordinary places. Today, a conversation between Rob and Jonny about what the world's worst superpower would be (being able, they conclude, to tell that you're in a disabled parking bay with your eyes closed) somehow leads Rob to suddenly remember how, when he was 14, he and his friends were taken hostage by some bullies who made them pretend to be furniture. Who made them bridge their bodies so that their backs became a chair to sit on, and then sat on them for several hours.

'It was these people that were out burgling,' he says. 'We were camping, a few of us – Lee, Lino, Emo, Speakers – and we'd bought booze, very cheap lager. We were camping a mile away from the house at the back on some houses on Parkway. They were rough boys from the council estate. Chell. We were there at four o'clock in the morning and they just happened upon us. And they drank all our booze and they threatened us with knives and I was made to be a chair and they then sat on us for a few hours.'

Normal robbers, I suggest, don't go for the surreality of saying: these people would make excellent furniture.

'How do you know?' he challenges. 'They had nowhere to sit.'

Were you scared?

'Yeah. They were guys. With knives. It was horrible.'

How long did someone sit on you for?

'A couple of hours. They got off, had a pee, came back.' He seems bemused, and almost annoyed, that I find this odd.

'It just does what it says on the tin,' he exclaims. 'Some big boys made me be a chair!'

So what happened at the end?

'They just got up and left. By that time, it was light, they'd drunk our booze.'

And you just went home?

'Yeah.'

And did you tell anyone?

'No, I don't think we did. I don't think we mentioned it to each other.'

* * *

Teddy is backstage during the shows, wearing ear protectors. At the end, Rob runs offstage while the band is still playing the outro to 'Angels' so that his van can leave the venue before being blocked by the departing crowd. And so usually he bundles himself, just seconds from full-on stadium-entertaining mode, into a silent van where Teddy is sleeping; pumped with all that adrenalin, but having to whisper about whatever is percolating in his head.

'That was so much fun,' he whispers tonight.

Some nights those around him can tell that he's having a difficult time – usually the sign is that he's pushing too hard, trying to do too much, to be more manic, more demonstrative, more communicative, in order to overcompensate for whatever shortfall he is feeling inside. But everyone around him has learned that on all the other nights they just don't know. He will seem in perfect command, and joyously in tune with the audience and with what he is doing. And then, when he comes off, he will either confirm that this has been the case, or tell a story so bafflingly different that it's hard to believe – except that, as you look at him and the remembered fear or anxiety in his eyes, you couldn't for a second doubt it. It's something he himself acknowledges. 'Even to the trained eye – my management, my wife, my friends – they can never tell when I'm stuck right in the middle of abject terror in front of tens of thousands of people,' he says, adding wryly, 'It's a gift, I suppose.'

It can certainly be confusing. Tonight in Scotland, he seems to have been majestic, and he has nothing negative to say about the experience afterwards. But Josie will explain later that when he came into the quick-change tent for the second time in the middle of the set – at the point where he seemed consumed by the show and in total command and in the moment – what he actually said to her was this:

'Josie, do I really need to do passport pictures tomorrow?'

Likewise, a few days later in London, another triumphant show, and I don't imagine there could have been a person in the stadium who could have been able to tell that during 'Angels' one of the thoughts going through its singer's head was that there was a live eviction on *Big Brother* later that night.

* * *

In the car on the way to Wembley Stadium – twenty years ago to the day, someone has told him, since Take That's first number one single, 'Pray', was released – Rob reads out an email from a friend's mother, saying that she has some friends at the show tonight, and it's their anniversary, and could Rob wish them a happy anniversary from the stage. This won't be happening.

'It's not panto, love,' says Jonny. '"We'll all end up in panto" – who said that again?'

'Jason Donovan,' says Rob. A few nights ago Rob chatted with Jason Donovan in the bar of the hotel in Scotland. Donovan was performing in

Glasgow in the musical version of *Priscilla, Queen of the Desert*. As drily fatalistic as Jason Donovan's words were intended to be, it was also clear that he still saw himself safely on one side of the line that divides real performing from panto. But of course Rob doesn't see it that way.

'We will all end up in panto,' he says. 'I'm *in* panto. This *is* panto.'

'It's a big one, though,' says Jonny.

'It's big panto, but it's still fucking panto. So is everybody else at Glastonbury this weekend – that's panto, too. It's all panto. I think maybe Jason saw panto as a diss, but I don't.'

The conversation moves on to discussing a legendary soul singer they saw on TV who has had, they agree, 'a lot of work done'.

'He's gone from having a kind face,' says Rob, 'to having kind of a face.' He smiles. 'That's what I'll look like in twenty years' time.' Pause. 'Ten years.' Pause, and a sigh. 'Five years ...'

* * *

Rob walks round the grounds of the country hotel, the Schloss Lerbach near Cologne, with some of the band. There's a general conversation about how nice it is here.

'Drugs would make it better,' Rob says, wistfully.

'You could say that about anything,' one of the band counters.

'Yeah,' Rob says, and thinks this through to its logical conclusion. 'Drugs,' he decides, 'would make *drugs* better.'

That night a woman will be spotted trying to climb a ladder into Rob's room. Unsuccessfully. He sleeps through the commotion.

* * *

The long-distance verbal fisticuffs with Liam Gallagher continue. Rob has been quoted in *The Sun* making some disparaging comments about Liam's songwriting, going through various Beady Eye songs, saying what he likes about them, but then concluding, 'When you listen to them you think, "Please put a chorus in – it will be brilliant." They are not going to have a character brave enough to tell Liam that.' The conversation quoted here is one that Rob had considered private but, no matter, he did say these words, and it is what he thinks. And, inevitably, it gets right up Liam Gallagher's nose.

'Robbie Williams said the record's good but the songs have no chorus,' Liam retorts. 'I'd rather shoot myself in the balls than follow his advice.'

A couple of days later, Rob does a phone interview with a Croatian journalist, and inevitably they ask about this ongoing Liam Gallagher tabloid kerfuffle. Sometimes Rob just can't be bothered to not say what he thinks.

'I just think he's limited as a human,' Rob says. 'You know, our paths have crossed a few times, especially when we were younger, and Oasis have always in general, even though they wouldn't know that that's what they're doing, have kind of always been bullying. They have a lot of opinions about a lot of artists, and some of those artists can't stick up for themselves. And I decided that I would stick up for me, and I would stick up for other people that they've bullied. So I've got under his skin, God bless him. It's very, very childish, but I very, very, very much am a child still. And I get off on that kind of energy.'

He lets this hang there for a second, as though he might have finished. He hasn't.

'So,' Rob concludes, 'he's a limited remedial moron.'

* * *

On a long bus journey in Germany, Rob and Ayda have the following conversation. It's very difficult to adequately describe the mood when they talk like this. The hurt and annoyance expressed, and the jockeying over what is and isn't acceptable to say, is absolutely real, and though it's not a dialogue that many couples could have, there's also a lot of laughter on both sides as it happens, even if it's sometimes exasperated laughter, and there's a blanket of lovingness and unity that sits over the whole conversation in a way which may be hard to detect from the words alone.

It begins with Ayda saying to Teddy – who is currently nine months old and so is blissfully oblivious to this and everything that will follow – that she is going to tell her all of the bad things about Daddy, and Rob deciding, perhaps unwisely, to prompt Ayda by bringing up the circumstances of their last break-up before they finally got together for good.

'Remember when we got in the car and you got the news that you'd been fired from that job … ?' Rob says, with a kind of reckless glee that might not be quite appropriate.

'And you were *so* supportive,' says Ayda.

'I thought, imagine her shock when she finds out only I'm going back to my house …' says Rob.

'I don't think that's a joke you want to make,' Ayda suggests, 'because that's a very sore subject right there.'

'Oh, boozy …' says Rob.

'No,' says Ayda, 'there are some jokes you can't make, because you were such an arsehole. You fucked with me so bad. There are certain jokes you can't make, and that's one of them. Let's see, let's go reverse. I got fired from my show and you responded in kind by dumping me. Winning move. Winning fucking move.'

'Yeah, "This one's broken …"' teases Rob.

'You shouldn't be proud of your behaviour,' chides Ayda.

'Yeah,' says Rob, in a way that sounds dismissive.

'Babe, you've crossed the line with that joke,' she says. 'I'm not laughing at it.'

'Oh, no!' he says, with fake distress.

'Yeah, you hurt my feelings. Because you were so mean. You broke my spirit.'

'But,' Rob argues, as though this is really going to help his case, 'I was already going to end our relationship before that news came …'

'Wow,' says Ayda.

'It's not my fault that that news came!' Rob objects.

'You were the most insensitive asshole ever,' says Ayda, pushing Rob's leg off her. 'Get your fucking foot away from my body!'

'No! No! Boo!'

'No. It's *mean*. I can't laugh at it, because you actually put me on meds. You actually broke my heart. You can't laugh at your behaviour. I'd like you to feel the pain for a second ... and then me laugh at it, and see how you feel about it.'

'Ah, *no* ...'

'No, you can't make that joke. The fact that you then took me on that trip and were going to dump me anyway is even worse!'

'No,' he argues, again seeming to imagine that this will help, 'I only made my mind up on the trip!'

'Get your fucking foot away, please. Honestly. I can't. It's not funny. Like, I want it to be funny – I truly want it to be funny, for the sake of dark comedy, but actually it's so painful, because what you did was so painful that I actually can't even go there in jest. I'd love to. I'd love to take a trip to funny.'

'I'm so sorry,' he says, for the first time actually sounding contrite.

'But actually you were so cruel in your behaviour, and it was such a horrible time.'

'It's a bumpy road to love!' he says. (A little too breezily, perhaps.)

'Not for you, it wasn't,' she says.

'Yeah, it was,' he replies.

'It was like the whim of a dictator,' she says. 'It was like Nero and his fucking fiddle! It was not a bumpy road for you. Get your foot away from mine.'

'You can't help who you do or do not fall in love with.'

'Get. Your foot. Away. From mine.'

'Ah, Mummy, don't punish me.'

'I truly think you should take your foot away,' she says.

'You can't make me feel bad!' pleads Rob in a baby voice. 'That's what I do to you.'

'Do you know that your daddy's not a very nice person?' Ayda tells Teddy. 'It's okay, Ted, I'm not even sure he's really your dad.'

'Mummy, I'm so sorry that I caused you all that pain,' says Rob.

'No, you're not,' says Ayda. 'You were so awful to me. That first year and a half, my God. Daddy almost broke Mummy completely.'

'And now, for the rest of our lives, Mummy's going to break Daddy,' says Rob.

'Yeah, that's right,' says Ayda. 'No, Teddy, I just punish Daddy periodically.'

'She doesn't even do that, Ted,' Rob confides to his daughter.

'No, I don't,' Ayda concedes. 'I take the unfortunate moral high road.'

Rob looks at me. I have been sitting next to them throughout this conversation, as has Gwen.

'This has all got to go in,' Rob tells me.

I suggest that might not be wise.

'Why can't this go in?' he says.

I say that Ayda would need to want it to go in.

'This is *funny*,' Rob argues.

'You can put it in,' says Ayda. 'As long as you promise to reveal that Rob's a complete asshole.' She laughs. 'That's my only condition, is that the moral of this little paragraph is that Rob's a complete asshole.' She turns to Rob. 'The readers will obviously already have understood that you're a complete asshole, but in case, for whatever reason, they've only suddenly picked up on the notion, the message can be here in bold writing.'

* * *

Another show, backstage beforehand, Rob and Olly talk about the odd things that people say when approaching someone they recognise in public.

'This geezer,' says Olly, 'was, "Can I have a picture? I'm a bit of a Metallica fucking Led Zeppelin kind of guy." I'm, "Well, why are you getting a picture then?" "Just for the fucking crack."'

'It's just so weird when they come over and go, "You're a bit of cunt, but I want something from you." Then don't! Just don't! If I'm a bit of cunt, you stay over there, leave me alone. I won't bother you.'

'Exactly,' says Olly. 'Or what's the one they do? "I don't really know who you are, but can I have picture?"'

'I came out of a bar in Ibiza,' says Rob, 'and there was twenty-five guys, singing:

We hate Take That, and we hate Take That
We hate Take That, and we hate Take That
We hate Take That, and we hate Take That
We are the Take That – haters!

'So I went and I stood in the middle of them, and I went

I hate Take That, and I hate Take That
I hate Take That, and I hate Take That ...'

* * *

The first European show of 2013 that Rob cries at is in Vienna. It's just from the atmosphere and the way that the audience respond.

'It was ridiculous,' he says in the van immediately afterwards. 'It was like 2001 ... it was too much to comprehend. Mind-bending. It was really fucking special. I kept thinking, "For me? For *me*?" Seriously mind-bending. I had proper tears at the end. It's overwhelming and confusing and everything, because you think: I'm just fannying about.'

'But you felt the love?' Ayda checks.

'Yeah, I did,' he says. Then, fake cocky, he adds, 'Yeah. You know who you're going out with now.'

'Yeah,' Ayda says, taking her cue, 'I'm going out with Robbie fucking Williams.'

And then they say 'I love you' to each other.

We drive on in the dark, until Rob breaks the silence.

'I wonder what the tax situation in Austria is,' he says.

* * *

This morning Rob reads a horrible article in the *Daily Mail*, headlined: *Want to be as big as Elvis, Robbie? Bloated pop star bears resemblance to King in later years as he takes the stage.*

'That's not nice ...' he says. 'It's really cruel. And, you know, even suffering with incredibly poor judgement of how I do or don't look at any given time, I know that I'm not Elvis' weight before he died. I know I'm not even anywhere near that … Good job I'm in a good mood. I don't want to have my picture taken or go out or be seen out a lot of the time because of things like that. That just kind of cements that … Makes me want to smoke.'

On some level, he can joke about it. This afternoon there's a game of football on the training pitch out the back of the stadium, Rob's team versus Olly's, and his first words when he comes off are 'Elvis wouldn't have scored that last goal'. But a while later he sends me an email that he wants to send to the *Daily Mail* writer. It is a picture of Liam Neeson's face from the revenge drama *Taken*, over which are imposed the words: I WILL FIND YOU AND I WILL KILL YOU.

There's a tricky undercurrent here. Rob does look nothing at all like Elvis in his final years, and the article uses preposterously unflattering photos that are a completely unfair representation of what his audiences are seeing at every show. But he'll also look back on this tour as one where his preparation went badly askew. Earlier in the year, he was taking human growth hormone and doing unrealistically strenuous workouts for three hours a day, and then he would load up on chocolate. 'I looked,' he would later say, 'like a doorman.' Then he discovered that the workouts were unsustainable, so he cut back on them, but the chocolate-eating continued, and he knows he's not at the weight he'd like to be on a tour like this. Later, after the tour's long over, he'll talk about how the narrative in his head onstage would sometimes become 'sorry, everybody, as I'm pointing at you suggestively, and pretending that I think I'm sexy …'

So the *Daily Mail* have hit him in a sensitive spot. But that's a far cry from saying that they're right, and Ayda points out how supportive all of the comments underneath the article are.

'I wanted to give up the tour,' he says in a sulky voice.

'No, boozys. This is just one nasty person writing one nasty article,' says Ayda. 'It doesn't mean it's true. They've got a job at the *Daily Mail*, and the reason they had a job at the *Daily Mail* is because they're nasty … You're not some Las Vegas fried-banana-sandwich act.'

'I scored a cracking goal today,' he says.

'Yeah, they don't know about your prowess on FIFA,' consoles Ayda, misunderstanding.

'No, no, in real life,' he says.

'In real life?' she says. 'There is no such thing as real life outside of FIFA, babe. Now you're talking crazy talk.' Then she points out that there were 'like, a thousand people' waiting outside the hotel earlier.

'Shouting "Fattie! Fattie!"' Rob says.

His friend Jamo, who has come in to say hello, joins in the conversation.

'The good thing is, they're comparing you to Elvis, mate,' he says.

'I know,' says Rob. 'I thought that, too.'

Jamo asks Rob about his necklace: 'I love that – what is it?'

'It says CUNT,' Rob explains. 'It was a present off my wife.'

'What's the subtext?' Jamo asks.

'I don't think there's a subtext,' says Rob. 'It's literally all text.'

* * *

In Hanover, Rob does an interview with a man who reminds him that Mick Jagger, who turned 70 the previous day, once said he would never perform again after the age of 45.

'I've seen that interview,' says Rob. 'I can understand his mindset back then, but I think we're both full of shit, to be honest with you. I retired in 2006. Whatever plans that I think I may have are irrelevant, because probably something else is going to happen. I'm most definitely in show business for life. I'm a lifer. I'm just guessing ahead because the next step is for me to retire again, at some point in the next few years ... but I'm guessing a few steps ahead of myself; this is a lifetime game I'm sure. And it's just starting to be fun. In the last three years, show business is really good fun. It's stupid and it's shallow and ridiculous, and for all of those reasons it's amazing. It's better than a proper job.'

And he counsels the interviewer to expect Rob to continue to do that job much as he has so far.

'I'm ad-libbing,' he says. 'I'm the chief writer for the Robbie Williams story, and I'm not that smart. I do things to fill in spaces, and the things I sometimes do to fill in the space embarrass me. Not only onstage but in social situations. Where there's nothing to say, I fill that space with idiocy.'

*　*　*

Not tonight. Just before 'Angels' he spots someone holding up a German flag and reads out what it says on it: *Can you sing 'Angels' for my mum who passed away in 2013, and for my dad who passed away in 2011?*

'This is for you, this is for your mum and dad, this is "Angels". God bless you, God bless your mum and dad …'

And his voice begins to break. As he describes it later: 'I was thinking about her family, I was thinking about my kid, and the audience had such approval for me, and I sat on the stage and started to cry. And then it was like: oh no, this is one of those huge humungous "you look like a mental person" crying. I just started to absolutely weep.'

He is still in tears as he gets into the van.

'I saw you weeping,' says Ayda. 'It was amazing. It was so good, babe.'

'There was this woman with a flag,' he says. 'I don't know why that just set off something in me …' He starts crying some more.

'That's so special,' says Ayda.

'There was something about how hot it was, and how much love there was, and my bad back, and just what a nice time we're having, and that flag …' he says. 'I was overwhelmed. Literally.'

These are the thoughts with which he leaves the Hanover stadium and heads towards the airport. Well, these thoughts and one other. He turns to Ayda in the dark.

'I've thought of a good name for a dog,' he says. 'Showbiz.'

*　*　*

For the second half of the tour, he is staying in a house high in the hills above Nice, in the South of France, commuting from here to the rest of the concerts. It's a long, windy journey down from the house to the airport, and as we make our way today he shares what's on his mind.

'Barry Gibb,' he begins, 'was saying that they weren't allowed to get big-headed because everybody told them how shit they were all the time.' Pause. 'I think that's worked for me.'

I point out that the set of his current show – never mind his latest album cover – is literally made up from lots of big Robbie Williams heads. But he's not deflected. 'All joking aside,' he says, 'I wonder if I'd be so humble.'

No one in the car chips in to endorse this point of view, a silence that becomes very apparent.

'I am fucking humble!' he says, almost annoyed.

Important to resolve this issue, I suggest, before we get to his private jet.

'Anyway, that's my story and I'm sticking to it,' he says, dismissively, adding, 'I've got loads.'

Then he turns to Ayda. 'I am humble,' he says to her. 'Tell him.'

'He is humble,' Ayda tells me, obediently passing the message on.

On the plane, Rob fills Josie in on this conversation, and my insufficient response. 'I said, perhaps if it was different for me I wouldn't be humble. To which Chris almost had a turned-up smile.'

As he's talking he accidentally dips his salmon sashimi in some Coca-Cola.

'For a man in my position,' he pronounces – and from now on you'll need to unpick the multiple levels of irony at your own leisure and jeopardy – 'who's so fucking ace in almost every way, I'm really fucking humble about it. I mean, I'm a great singer-songwriter, I'm probably the world's best entertainer, a really good friend, great lover – used to be – and despite from all that, I'm still really humble. Listen, I'm not a million miles away from being the most humble man you've ever met.'

We listen. He figures we must be wondering how he manages to perform in these stadiums the way that he does, given the hurdle presented by his great humility. So he offers us the gift of his answer.

'I have to *pretend*,' he explains, 'to be un-humble.'

It's just his life and how he lives it.

'If I didn't have to be the world's greatest entertainer,' he explains, 'I would probably be the world's most humble man. But I have to be the world's greatest entertainer. It's my lot. *You* don't choose *it*."

The world's most humble man says this, incidentally, with soy sauce on his upper lip.

'Once you're in, you're in,' he says. 'You have to do this for the people.' A short pause. 'Mainly of Europe,' he concedes.

He seems satisfied now with the agreement that he has decided we have all come to.

'I understand me a lot better now,' he says, 'now I've had this chat.'

* * *

Sitting in an airport lounge, his private jet awaiting.

'It's good fun, isn't it?' he says to me.

What? Life?

'Yeah.'

He lets this hang for a moment.

'I'm so pleased I stayed,' he says.

* * *

November 2016

One subject that any celebrity gets asked about, routinely, is their regrets. I don't think that Rob's reply is the one that most people expect.

'You know, people often say, as the answer to "Do you have any regrets?", "No, because it's made me the person I am today." And I always think that they don't know what the fuck they're talking about. I've many regrets, from the light regrets – social behaviour where I've behaved in a certain way and said something that's embarrassing or cringe-worthy that I wish I hadn't said – to actually how I've treated people. Or been allowed to be treated. Big regrets. I'm not a sociopath, so when I've said anything that's hurt somebody, I feel really bad about it. And although there's an energy that's addictive when you are saying something that is funny, the energy of regretting what I've said is worse than the energy of me saying something funny.'

* * *

A new day, a new dream. Even in his dreams, it seems, there's a widespread potential for humiliation, and also the ever-present danger that he might take something, or everything, just a little bit too far:

'I was sort of levitating, and there was a guy that was an Inca or something – he had the look of somebody from Peru. Do you ever levitate in your dreams? I always levitate. And I think I was kind of boasting about "look what I can do!" And he quickly grew these little wings and did the most intricate flying, sort of like a tiny dragon. Blew me out the water. And before this happened, I can remember I was levitating in front of a crowd of people, and I skidded into view, and I went "*Smokin ... !*" And I thought, "Oh, *no*! I've just fucking *ruined* that! I've ruined my big moment! I didn't have to say 'Smokin!', a Jim Carrey reference from *The Mask* ..." I didn't have to say *that*.'

* * *

And another day of interviews. As he often does, out of some combination of interest and politeness and anxiety deflection and diversionary tactic, Rob today besieges the first interviewer, Becca from MTV, with his own questions. Before she has learned anything about him, he knows that she used to be a personal shopper at Topman, and that she lives with her parents in Essex, a detail she seems to find slightly embarrassing.

'You don't have to justify it,' says Rob. 'I want our kids to live with us forever.'

Her questions are from viewers, and, after the standard ones, she moves on to what she calls 'the random round'.

'Some of these can get a bit out there,' she warns him.

'Listen,' he says, 'I'm so far out there they might just bring me back.'

She asks where he would like to go back in a time machine.

'I probably would go and sit on the grassy knoll in Dealey Plaza when Kennedy was shot, just to see what went on – see if there was one gunman or three. But apart from that I'd go and get *nutted* at a rave, a quality rave somewhere out in the countryside, in 1990. I'd love to combine the two …'

Then she asks which Mr Men character he would be, and why?

Rob is probably better on this subject than Becca anticipates. His first answer is 'probably Mr Tickle – he makes people happy and he makes people laugh'. But then he starts assessing his other options. 'Mr Greedy, Mr Bump … There's a bit of all of them inside us.' He settles on a new choice: 'Mr Topsy-Turvy! He's wicked – he lives in an upside-down house, and the house rests on the chimney, and he does things back to front and he's quite eccentric and surreal. And he's got some wicked brogues. So I think I'd be Mr Topsy-Turvy.'

Afterwards, having a cigarette break on the balcony, he explains that there's actually two reasons why he's so comfortable in Mr Men territory. One is that he's recently been reading the books to Teddy. But the second is that he used to have a vinyl LP when he was young of the Mr Men stories being read by Arthur Lowe, the actor most famous for his portrayal of Captain Mainwaring in the sitcom *Dad's Army*.

He sits in the cold November sun, looking over the London rooftops, thinking about the important stuff.

'Mr Bump!' he declares. 'He bumps into trees! And the apples fall off!'

* * *

Most of the day, whether he is in his hotel room or on his way somewhere in a car, talkSPORT is on. That's the way he likes it.

'It's my go-to comfort blanket, I suppose,' he says. 'I really really like football, and the ins and outs and the whys and the whats and the opinion and the stats – it's been a constant of mine all the way through my life. Where you would normally have Radio 1 on or Capital or something like that, and it's just music so you don't even think about it, because that's what normal radio is, I have talkSPORT on instead. Sometimes I tune in and sometimes I don't. I've noticed that a lot of the time I'm not even listening to it, it's just background noise. There's been long lengths of time where I've listened intently to it and been a participant, but I've just noticed recently that now it's just on in my daily life in the background, and I just hear words. I think there's a comfort with the white noise – it's my version of those things that you can buy from a Sharper Image where you press the button and it sounds like the sea, or wind, or whatever. My version of that is talkSPORT.'

* * *

The next morning he has an interview at Radio London. There are quite a lot of fans waiting outside. He stops to talk and sign, but they have complicated questions about ticket sales.

'Don't ask me!' Rob exclaims. 'They just point me, and I get in the car, and I turn up. I have *no* idea.'

So they turn to Craig, who is on security this week, and is standing next to Rob, and start asking him the same questions, something about presales and different website access codes.

'*He* doesn't know!' Rob interrupts. 'He just stops people from killing me.'

* * *

This afternoon there's a rainbow out of his hotel window, arching up over Centre Point. Rob stands on the balcony.

'See if you can make this disappear by looking at it. The rainbow. I can do that. Can you do that? I know you can't see what I'm seeing. I'm thinking it away … I told you I had that moment in Egypt where I thought everything away and it disappeared? The person I was there with was massaging my toe and she put her thumb in my toe at the base of the toe and her thumb started acting like a drill bit. Like, weird. Inhumanly possible. It freaked us out so we went and stood on the balcony, and it was hotel, road, river, feluccas, the boats, the lights. And then all of the sudden the boats disappeared and the lights disappeared for me, and then I could bring them in and out. And I can concentrate on that rainbow and make it disappear.'

I ask him to explain.

'For the longest time, I thought I was seeing the past. Not in this moment, but in Egypt when that happened.'

It makes him think about that time they were playing the song 'Arizona' back and they all saw a black strip come through the room. 'I think when I'm fifty I'll go and do paranormal-y stuff,' he says. Before I can even ask, he says, 'I don't know what that means. Probably make Teddy come with me: "Dad's doing his fucking weird stuff."'

Then he tweets a photo of the rainbow, in its full, beautiful, undisappeared form:

This made me really happy today x

* * *

Ayda and the kids finally arrive. The new house still isn't ready, so they have to spend the first few days at the Soho Hotel. It gives Rob one more story to tell: of Teddy running through the hotel lobby holding an umbrella between her legs, shouting loudly, 'Look everyone, I'm holding it with my vagina.'

For better or worse, this story is immediately added to the heavy entertainment show repertoire and goes into high rotation.

7

January 2014

Josie comes up to the studio, where Rob is writing with Guy, to tell him that he has been offered the Freedom of the City of Stoke-on-Trent, but that he'd need to accept it in person. This would be a part of a programme of events around Stoke, already planned, to celebrate his fortieth birthday next month. Rob reads the details she hands him – there's even a cake competition – and doesn't say anything for some time.

'There's the bit that's going "I don't want to go" and that bit is prevailing,' he says. 'And there's another bit going, "Oh that's really sweet, that's fucking great, I'm made up." But there's another bit that's going, "What does it mean anyway?" I mean, there's a plaque going up – I'm happy with that.'

The blue plaque is being put up on the gates of Tunstall Park, near his old home.

He makes a definite decision that he doesn't know what he should do.

* * *

He works on a song called 'The Cure', looking for a lyric.

'Shall we have it be about the nineties?' he wonders.

'Which part?' Guy asks.

'The part where I win,' he replies.

Guy suggests a slightly different direction for the song: 'How about your first date with Ayda?'

Rob considers this. 'Oh yeah,' he says.

'And the conversation,' says Guy. 'You know, a real conversational song. What was said.'

Rob sings: *I felt revolting ...*

'It wasn't a very positive evening, to be honest with you,' he says.

'Can you remember the conversation and how it went?' Guy asks.

'Yeah,' he says. 'It didn't start off good. I was dropping her off back at a party.'

'Just recount the story really simply,' Guy suggests. 'Shall we do that? See where it leads us.'

So Rob begins:

You turned up drunk. I was too. In a way, but not like you.

And then:

I took you back, from whence you came.

'We broke up three times,' he points out.

* * *

One piece of karma somewhat restored.

'I made up with Professor Green,' he explains. Last year he recorded a song, 'I Need Church', with Professor Green, and promised him that his planned collaboration with Dizzee Rascal wouldn't be released first. But, however much other reasons may have justified it, he ended up breaking his word. After, Professor Green sent him emails using curse words he didn't even know. But on his last trip to Britain, when Rob was on a radio station event in Manchester with Rizzle Kicks, and they mentioned how much Professor Green hates him, he decided he should get back in touch. He sent an email titled 'Amends'.

'I said, at the pearly gates, if I'm asked to feel sorry for what I did, you'd be in my top five,' Rob explains, 'I said, I've got excuses blah blah blah but the bottom line is I let you down after I made a promise, and for that I'm truly sorry.'

Rob says that Professor Green's reply was gracious. 'He said, if I'm in your top five, you haven't done much wrong.'

I ask him about the other four.

'Geri Halliwell,' he begins. He doesn't just mean the Spice Girls joke. He's made plenty of other quips over the years, usually from the stage, ones that he has often quickly regretted but which have invariably brought the house down. And he knows that they have not been appreciated.

So that's one. He's not giving the full list.

'I'm just talking celebrity ones,' he clarifies.

* * *

The young singer and songwriter Taio Cruz comes up to Rob's house for a day's writing. Cruz's world is the modern world of pop songwriting where songs are often formed from their constituent parts, from contributions from different songwriter worker-bees, and pieced together with calculated and almost mathematical precision. Cruz knows plenty of the important players who do this – his soft-voiced conversation is littered with references not just to the Dr Lukes but to many of the other collaborators on such records who Rob and Guy haven't heard of.

At one point Cruz stops and says, insistently, 'It's got to be simple.'

'That's your mantra, isn't it?' Guy observes.

'That's my mantra,' Cruz confirms. 'I always say: show me a complicated song, and I'll show you a simple one that outperformed it.'

Guy laughs. 'There's an evil logic to that.' By which I think he means: an evil logic that runs against many of my most ingrained songwriting instincts. Rob doesn't say anything, but I'm pretty sure this just isn't the way he is interested in thinking about creativity.

That's not to say Rob and Guy aren't open to some new input, or to learning about how Cruz approaches things. And when Rob and Taio sing over some tracks, at moments there seem to be flashes of magic, of exactly what you really want in a collaboration: something emerging that is different from what either person could create on their own. But there are some problems. First, these moments seem to fizzle out quite quickly, partly because Cruz's judgement as to what's worthwhile seems fairly different from Guy and Rob's. Second, Cruz seems bemused in the first place at this haphazard, unsystematic method of trying to write a song – it feels like there's a sentence going round his head the whole time that he's striving not to say out loud: *I don't know how you old guys ever did anything if you all do it like this.* That, and maybe also, with the sadness of the airline pilot talking to the steam train driver: *Don't you old guys know the world has moved on?* And third, the best progress they make is over some backing tracks Cruz produces from his computer, but it soon becomes clear that not only are these tracks not Cruz's to freely dispense in this way but that permission to use these from whoever created them may not be forthcoming. Both creatively and financially, that's not the kind of collaboration Guy and Rob had in mind.

Guy, particularly, is annoyed about this. But at the end of the day it's agreed that Cruz will be back in touch about the tracks, and send on the constituent parts for one of them, over which they've written the rudiments of quite a promising song.

'Has Taio been in touch?' Rob asks the next afternoon.

'No,' says Guy. 'I don't think he'll be in touch.'

To this day, they're still waiting.

* * *

Work has to wait today until Rob returns from the sperm bank – or, as he calls it, 'the cryo wank bank'.

'It's so degrading,' he says, explaining that he read for a little bit afterwards so he didn't seem to be out of there with inappropriate speed. He also mentions that the man who you have to hand your contribution to asks you whether you've spilled any.

In the studio, Rob and Guy talk about the new season *American Idol* premiere.

'I got so bored I turned it off,' says Rob. A while back, a fairly serious approach was made to him to be one of the judges, and he did entertain the idea, but backed off. They discuss what effect doing one of these shows can do to your career if you still have one.

'Sometimes it's good to be mysterious,' Guy suggests. 'People see too much.'

'Yeah, that's a big risk,' Rob agrees.

'Real rock stars, I think, should be untouchable,' offers Guy.

'Yeah,' Rob agrees. 'Unless you're being paid a lot of money. A *lot* of money. Then I'll be touchable.'

Tea is made, and Richard Flack, at the mixing desk, ends up with the mug that says 'Teddy's Daddy'. He asks Rob whether he should go ahead and drink from it.

'You're not going to be weirded out?' he checks.

'No,' says Rob, dismissively. A moment later, he adds, 'Unless it's the *truth* …'

* * *

Last night Rob went to a party at the actress Kristen Johnston's house where he was surprised to find himself having a cigarette.

'Ayda went straight for a cigarette because she was uncomfortable, and I just went, "Yep, I'm doing that," and I'd smoked nearly all of it, then Ayda turned round and was, "*What* are you … ?" Um, don't make a scene. It's embarrassing.'

Was that your first cigarette since stopping?

'Yeah.'

'How did it taste?' Guy asks.

'Great. I don't think I can just have one – I know that. But I was just so uncomfortable.'

* * *

Working on a song called 'Pentatonic', Rob suggests a lyric:

Oh, she hears voices, when sounds are supposed to be asleep.

'Don't you think it makes her sound a little potty?' asks Guy.

'No, it's her own voice,' Rob says, explaining that the idea is based on what often happens when he's trying, and struggling, to get to sleep. 'It's that neurotic voice, when all you can hear is Radio Rob. Or all you can hear is Radio Ayda going, "Well, you know you should have de de de, and if you don't do that then you shouldn't do this and if you didn't do that then you … then they will hate you and they probably hate you anyway … so don't do that, because you're too fat …" Those are the voices I'm on about.'

Asked, answered.

Rob and Guy then have an obtuse debate, or argument, about the varied use of the musical terms 'middle eight' and 'bridge'. Puzzlingly, these are used differently in the US and the UK. (A quick summary: in Britain the bridge comes between the verse and the chorus, but in the US this is referred to as a 'pre-chorus'. In the US the bridge is the musical variation in a song that typically comes after the second chorus; in the UK this is known as the middle eight.) Also, as Guy now points out, 'often middle eights aren't eight bars, and that confuses everyone'.

As this discussion continues, Guy extends a metaphor he is trying out to say that a bridge 'goes across the lake of joy'.

I object that you typically don't get bridges across lakes, and challenge anyone to come up with an example.

Wrong crowd.

'There was one in the place I used to have outside Stoke,' says Rob. 'There was a bridge across a lake.'

'I didn't know you had a place outside Stoke,' says Guy.

'Yeah. I bought it, and then I couldn't find it,' he says.

'You couldn't find it?' says Guy.

'No.'

'What do you mean?' says Guy. 'Didn't you have a driver? Couldn't he find it?'

'No, I went up with some mates from London, and I just couldn't find it.'

* * *

Rob has decided he's not going back to Stoke for what they are calling 'Robbie Day'. Three streets in a new housing estate will be named after his songs: Angels Ways, Candy Lane and Supreme Street. A tourist trail will lead people around 11 significant locations in his early life. There will be an exhibition, Portrait of a Potteries Pop Star, and a charity concert featuring one of his impersonators and, at the Red Lion pub, an eighties/nineties disco and a 'Robbioke'.

The official reason is that he has just found out about a surprise fortieth birthday weekend Ayda has arranged for him in Palm Springs (which is where he actually will be). Rob instead blogs a mixed-purpose greeting, thanks and apology:

So it would seem that something truly fantastic/surreal is kicking off in my home town next week … It all feels like it's happening to someone else who comes from the same place I come from, someone who's far more deserving … I wear where I'm from like a badge of honour, always have done always will do … In fact nowhere has truly felt like home since I left. I am a Stokie born and bred … I can only imagine what Grandma Bertha and Grandad Jack would think of it all. Like them I hope I make you all proud. Before I start blarting I'm off to mix with these nesh buggers here in LA. Here's to you in oatcakes and love.

Robert from Green Bank Rd, ST6 7HA.

* * *

One more day in the studio.

'You know that sound?' says Rob, and sings a weird kind of two-note rhythmic oscillation that goes *dong-a-long-a-long-a-long-a-long-a-long*. 'That's what happens inside your head when you sniff gas for the first time.'

He thinks back.

'There was something that I could only think about whilst I'd done gas, and then when the effects wore off I couldn't remember what it was.'

It was when he was a teenager, still at school. They'd go to the park.

'Where I used to do gas, and take lighter fluid,' he says, 'they're just about to put up a plaque outside it.'

* * *

October 2016

It is announced that the latest recipient of the Brits Icon Award – only the third ever, after Elton John and David Bowie – will be Robbie Williams. The award will be presented at a concert to be broadcast in primetime on ITV in November. Also included in the programme will be some segments in which Rob and others talk about him, his past and his life. The provisional idea is that Rob will be filmed as though he is interviewing himself, and that while everyone else will presumably be nice about him, as people generally are when speaking for something like this, this dialogue between the two Robbie Williamses will provide an unusually realistic counterpoint.

Today there's a meeting in Rob's room at the Soho Hotel where Vaughan Arnell, who will direct these interstitial pieces, wants to pin down what Rob might be able to say in conversation with himself. At the agreed time, Rob appears from his bedroom, still sort of staggering and rubbing his eyes, and when Vaughan starts asking him very straightforward, open-ended questions about his life, it's as though, almost because he's not quite awake, the questions drill down into some rarely disturbed part of Rob's brain; as though he's so weary that it's easiest just to lower all the barriers and allow the memories to flow out. In fact, all Vaughan really says to begin with is: 'Are there any points from your childhood that you'd like us to go near or focus on?'

To that single question, this is only part of his answer.

'Well, my dad won his round in the show called *New Faces* – my dad was a policeman, and he was seeing lots of different comedians at cabaret places, because that's what was happening in the sixties and the seventies: The Talk of the Midlands, Jollies … And I've read my dad's diaries from when he was a kid – I haven't read them in ages – but to my dad these people on the silver screen and on TV were gods, and he obviously fell in love with the mythology of what was going on down the tube, and on the cinema screen … There'd be pictures of Doris Day that he'd taken out of the newspapers, and so on and so forth, and be gushing about these people … My dad would see people onstage and think "I can do that", and then he stole a few jokes, and he went and did a talent competition at a pub in Golden Hill in Stoke, and he won. This was before I was born. And he got a booking here and there and he gave up his job to go off to be a comedian. And to have an extra five quid you would be a Scouse comedian, because Scouse comedians were the rage at the time. So my dad became a Scouse comedian. That's what happened – he was a policeman and then he became a comedian.

'My dad used to talk about Frank Sinatra like he was a saint. Dean Martin, Sammy Davis Jr. And they were gods. That mixed with the fact that my dad was doing something like the gods rubbed off on me. I don't think there was a time before me knowing or feeling like that I'm going to do that. There wasn't a day, there wasn't like a moment of clarity that you get with an alcoholic where you've gone too far. It was just my life. This was what I was going to be like – and if it wasn't being "Robbie Williams at Knebworth" it was going to be "Robert Williams at Haven Holidays". Or Ladbroke Holidays. Or Butlin's camps. It was going to "Robert Williams at Skegness" or "Robert Williams at Great Yarmouth". It was going to be either that, or this, or somewhere in between. Because that's what my dad did.

'My dad, when the cabaret rooms became defunct, there was nowhere for him to ply his trade, which is when he got offered a job working for the Ladbrokes holiday camps, and he became a compère, comedian, singer, to entertain the holidaymakers. And that was where I spent all of my holidays when I was growing up. I'd spend three weeks with my dad around entertainers that were entertaining the masses, if the masses are a caravan park full of working-class people. So I'd be around Paper Lace, The Dallas Boys, The Ivy League, a band who were called The Mad Hatters, four of them playing instruments, like The Barron Knights ...' He trails off. 'Sorry – I've just been asleep ...' he says, and then continues. 'My formative education into the entertainment world was being around these acts from the seventies and the sixties that were still trying to ply their trade, with no home to play, so it would be these holiday camps. And my dad's reverence towards Hollywood ... I'm just riffing ...'

This morning, that's how he likes to say hello.

* * *

It swiftly becomes clear that the planned structure, where Rob offers correctives to others' rosy-spectacled perception of what was happening in his life, isn't really going to work. 'The truth is,' Rob realises, 'at that point in my life it wasn't much of a contradiction. All of those start coming when I sort of get into Take That.'

But, in the meantime, the childhood story-cellar in his brain has been opened:

'Oh! I know what I *did* do! When I was three we were in Benidorm on holiday, and I went missing. And I think in the seventies it was more liberal looking after your kids: off they went, and they'd sometimes come back. I couldn't be found anywhere. And I'd entered myself into a talent competition. Which I *won*. So I won this talent competition, singing "Summer Nights" from *Grease*. Three years old. And after I'd won that, I had a hat, and I walked around the swimming pool, and put the hat in front of people, and sang, and then people would put money into my hat. And this was all without being told to do it.'

He laughs.

'I had a hatful of money. And I'd have to wait another fourteen years for that to happen again.'

He reminisces about a picture his father has that was in a Jersey newspaper of the four of them – him, his father, his mother and sister – promoting his father's comedy appearances. Roy Orbison was also playing, says Rob, and it cost 50p to get in.

'We lived in a pub when I was under three. And I know that I used to perform in front of the jukebox for the punters – to "Summer Nights", bless,' he says. 'The truth is that the discomfort only came from performing, which I found natural to do obviously since I was born, when it was regarded as being big-headed, and different, and weird. Because my peers didn't do it. "And who do you think you are … ?"'

In the next couple of weeks, Vaughan will interview Rob's mother, Jan, who corrects some details – she says it was Torremolinos, not Benidorm – but echoes most of this. Rob had run away while she was attending to her 80-year-old Aunt Bet – 'she was as slow as he was fast' – and she came downstairs as he mimed to 'Summer Nights', doing the moves he'd practised on the platform by the jukebox in their pub: 'He would dance exactly as he saw John Travolta on the telly. The staff, they used to laugh about it, because he was just so enthusiastic. But I knew then. I thought to myself: "Do you know, he's going to go in that entertainment business."'

* * *

Rob will repeat and expand on much of what he says today in a filmed interview with Vaughan, and his parents and others will also speak in some detail, but in the end only very brief clips from any of these interviews will fit into the TV show. Here are some other particulars about the early life of Robert Peter Williams that are never broadcast:

Jan: We were told we couldn't have children. Peter had no sperm count. So we'd decided that was it. So he was a bit of a miracle baby, really.

Rob: I was born on a Wednesday, and Wednesday's child is full of woe. But I was delightful.

Jan: He was born in the local hospital. Premature. About three weeks. And for six hours Peter told jokes and everybody laughed while I was in labour.

Pete: It's been wrongly reported that he was born in Burslem in a pub, which he wasn't. He's been responsible for that reporting. We didn't move into there until he was nearly two.

Jan: He was the most pleasant child. He was just a joy to have, because he was never ever miserable.

Rob: I was born into a world where my parents weren't doing very well with each other, they weren't getting along. I think there's a story about my dad going to an FA Cup final with the Liverpool players and he sort of didn't come back. Which upset my mum, as it would. My mother's of Catholic Irish descent – when my mum and dad got divorced, Grandad Farrell, my mum's father, was so embarrassed that she had to walk five paces behind him, as not to be seen by the rest of the town. How odd is that?

Pete: He used to watch people on the television and copy them. He was barely talking, he was in his romper suit and he was doing Brian Clough. I think he did Maggie Thatcher as well.

Rob: *Happy Days* with the Fonz … *Wonder Woman* – Linda Carter, she was my first crush … Frank Spencer in *Some Mothers Do 'Ave 'Em* … *Mork and Mindy* … I can't remember the first time that I went: I want to be like that. It just always seemed to be part of my make-up. I would just watch the TV and go: that's what I'm gonna do.

Pete: Bill Wayne and Tony Trafford were a big star attraction on the holiday parks and they had him onstage when he was about nine. He came off and his eyes lit up. I'm sure he thought, 'I think I like this, this'll do for me. Whatever that was, I'll want some more of that.'

Jan: He only failed one audition. Everything that he went for, he got.

Pete: When he was 11, Rob was in *Chitty Chitty Bang Bang* at the theatre – he was Jeremy, the lead juvenile. And he was very good, and then he went from that. He was the Artful Dodger when he was 14.

Jan: His main one was the Artful Dodger.

Rob: I was the fat boy – type-casting – in *The Pickwick Papers*.

Jan: Not that he was fat – they had to put a cushion up his front.

Pete: He did *Fiddler on the Roof,* quite a few productions in the theatres in Stoke-on-Trent. He had a great leaning towards acting at that time.

Rob: There was no way I was going to be a singer. I always wanted to be an actor. That was what I thought I was going to do. I didn't dare dream of being a singer, because I didn't think I had a voice to do it.

* * *

Another extraordinary tale Rob will tell during the filmed interviews is the history of his mother's great-grandmother.

He begins by addressing the camera.

'I'll ask you a question, dear viewer – have you got an axe murderer in your family? I have.'

He actually doesn't. But near enough. He tells the story he told Rufus Wainwright that time in the studio – how her husband cut her head open with an axe, then, believing he had killed her, drowned himself in the river; how she survived, but with a scar down her face – though this time he refers to her, unfortunately, but not entirely without reason, by the name of Great-Granny Halfhead.

'Well,' sighs Jan, when she sits for her interview and is asked about this, 'he's so naughty about calling her Great-Granny Halfhead. That's his statement. She wasn't Great-Granny Halfhead. She was my great-grandmother. We were from an Irish family, both sides of the family are Irish. Her father had come over from Ireland, and there was some talk about him being in the IRA – but with Irish tales you don't actually know the total truth. But I do know the truth about Great-Granny Riley. She was married at seventeen, her and her husband decided that they were going to America, try and make a life there.'

The rest of the story is much as Rob told it.

'Her father sailed out and fetched her back along with her son George and my grandmother, and brought her back to Stoke-on-Trent. I can remember her very vividly because I used to go and see her with my grandma. She lived in a little terraced house at this time in Tunstall, while across the road was the White Hart, a pub, and I used to go across there with a jug to get her some beer. She also smoked a pipe, a white pipe. And took snuff. And she had this scar all down her face.'

* * *

August 2015

Rob's father, Pete, has an unworried attitude to life that is often enviable. (This is a man who when he was much younger used to have business cards which said on them *Call anytime, except when Star Trek's on.*) But sometimes he can seem to stretch this approach to disconcerting extremes.

One afternoon, he and his son are watching football together, and a piece of information comes into his mind that he decides to share. He clearly considers it interesting enough to say out loud, though clearly not important enough to have ever mentioned before now.

'You know your granddad?' he tells Rob.

'Yeah.'

'Well, he was adopted.'

'He was *adopted*?'

'Yeah. He's not a Williams.'

'Well, if he's not a Williams,' Rob points out, 'then I'm not a Williams.'

'Oh,' says Pete. 'I don't supposed we are ... I hadn't really thought about that'.

'So my real name might not be Williams ... ?' Rob says.

This whole identity he has – never mind the name of Robbie Williams that he has made renowned and notorious around the globe – might be based on foundations that only now, quite casually, is he learning are muddier and shakier than he ever knew.

* * *

In the wake of this revelation, Rob has some proper research done. He'd like to know. It turns out that there is a far less dramatic disruption in this part of his family tree: it appears that Rob's grandfather's mother died of tuberculosis when he was six and he was subsequently brought up by a stepmother. There seems to be no evidence that anyone was adopted.

So Rob is still precisely who he thought he was. In this respect, at least. And as for 'Robbie Williams' – well, the 'Robbie' will forever be the bouncy twist on his real first name that he was ordered to adopt at the age of 16 by Take That's manager. But 'Williams', it seems, remains his own.

* * *

July 2012

Unless a memory just bubbles up, the surest way to learn something new about Rob's life story is to ask him about a song.

People get this so wrong. The popular misconception with someone like him is that his songs, particularly the ones with big tunes, are just pop words linked together to sound as though they mean something emotional and semi-coherent. Just occasionally, they are. But not often. And if you ask about a specific song – though, tellingly, when people talk to an artist like Robbie Williams, for all the questions they do ask, they tend not to ask these kinds of questions – there's usually something far deeper and far more intense, and very often something much more personal, at the song's root.

Here, as an example, Rob is talking about 'Gospel' – one of the best songs on *Take The Crown*, and also a portal into his world before he became famous.

'Very simply,' he says, 'it's about the expectation of what being a grown-up is going to be about. In my version of being a grown-up when I was thirteen, fourteen, fifteen, I wanted to be an actor, or I wanted to a pop star, and I wondered and dreamed about what it would *feel* like to be that. Or, more simply, I wondered what it felt like to pass your driving test and be able to leave the house and go somewhere by yourself. Those simple things. And then in the chorus …'

He pauses, and begins to explain the precise moment he was writing about. Exactly the kind of very specific, charged, instant lighting of the beacons that link together the days, weeks, months and years of our lives – but the kind that might have little reason to surface in any other context.

'I fingered this girl, right, when I was fourteen,' he explains. 'This was on holiday, and I only met her on her last night of the holiday. And she'd let me do this thing to her that was fucking amazing, and I thought I was in love. Anyway, she left the holiday camp, without a telephone number or as much as a goodbye, and I sat outside the caravan on the step, in deep depression and remorse that she'd gone. And that's the image that I've got in my head when I sing the chorus. It was a bittersweet moment. It's about this girl that was way out of my league but let me touch her. I'm thinking of her fondly – and sadly.'

* * *

October 2016

This bleary-eyed morning in his hotel room, encouraged by Vaughan to move on to the Take That years, Rob explains how much Nigel Martin-Smith terrified him at the first audition. But there was one key moment that supposedly got Rob the job: 'He often says that I wouldn't have got into the band if it wasn't for me walking out of the audition, turning back to him and winking at him as I left. If it wasn't for the wink, I wouldn't be there.' He quotes Nigel Martin-Smith. '"There was a cheekiness …"'

I ask him whether he remembers doing it.

'Yeah. It was something that I did because I felt uncomfortable. I don't know – it was a nervous twitch, where I was looking at him and he was looking at me as I was leaving. And out of nowhere I just decided to go …' – he winks – '… like that. And it was the wink that did it …'

Next he tells the more famous story of the second audition, the proper one, at the La Cage nightclub during the day. 'I could sort of dance a little bit like MC Hammer,' he tells Vaughan. 'I could do the running man.' And he says he now understands Gary Barlow's unease with what was being created around him. 'In retrospect I know what Gary Barlow was thinking. Gaz had been making more money than his teachers at school since he was twelve, by working the clubs. He'd got an act. He'd been a working professional for nearly ten years by the time that this audition had happened. And he didn't want to be in a band. He wanted to be Gary Barlow, singer-songwriter. And yet here he was being made to do something that I know he didn't want to do. "Why've I got to do it with these bozos?" And so it was.'

That was, he says, Nigel Martin-Smith's insight: 'He kind of knew that Gary was the singer-songwriter talent, but he needed padding. Because his stagecraft at the time wasn't on point, to put it nicely. So he needed the padding of us muppets behind him. Looking back, it wasn't Gary's fault that he was indulged. And it wasn't Gary's fault that I was, or we were, psychologically damaged. But he was sort of part of that process. He was the poster boy for Nigel Martin-Smith. There was Nigel Martin-Smith and then there was Gary and then there was the rest of us.'

Famously, the call came on the day that Rob was told he'd failed all his GCSEs apart from English (he got a D). 'Until we had our reunion,' he says, 'that was the best moment in Take That – the moment that I was told I was going to be in the band.'

Rob describes the discomfort he felt from the start. 'It was the first time, early days of the band, where I found myself in a situation where nobody liked me. I'd never experienced that before. Other than the psychos around town whose only talent was to be psychos – they didn't like me. But they didn't like anyone, or themselves. And now I was in a position where I was in a band with people who were just terrified about everything, where, apart from Mark, there was no kinship. There was no kinship, friendship, encouragement. Right from the early days there was a sense of divide and conquer, and it didn't come from us. It was uncomfortable – the constant threat of being sacked, and the bollockings that we received about anything that we could be bollocked about. It made us all fearful for our own jobs, and we'd been given a golden ticket so it was the only one out.'

Rob had a fantasy of what kind of a band he was in, but it was just that: a fantasy. 'In Take That I imagined an all-for-one-and-one-for-all thing,' he says, 'and that's just not what was happening. I thought I was in a *band*, but we weren't. There was a lead singer and we were, for all intents and purposes, backing dancers, and it was a stepping stone for someone's career, and we were viewed as such. Obviously that's going to rankle with me, because I've got ambitions and dreams of my own that were sort of being usurped.'

* * *

He has a lot of Take That stories.

'We did gay clubs for … it was probably a year. I suppose, I'm guessing that he hoped that we were a band for gay people. Reluctantly I think he gave over to the fact that we should do an under-eighteens club, and it went mental. It was in Hull. Anyway, apart from gay clubs the first club that we were booked to do was on the Isle of Wight, and it was a straight club and it was over-eighteens. We'd performed, and the place went mental, and there must have been a meet'n'greet booked into the contract, because after the show, members of the audience were allowed backstage into our dressing room. I'm barely seventeen, I might have still been sixteen, the room fills up with girls, I'm in the corner over here, and then all of a sudden this girl comes over, she backs into me, puts her arse into my cock, grabs my cock and starts wanking me off in the corner of the room. I'm … "jackpot … oh my God … this is incredible … this is everything that I thought it might be. I've found the promised land. This is why I got into the band, this is all part of it, oh my God … but if Nigel Martin-Smith sees this happening, I'm going to be sacked." She was fit. She was so fit. I couldn't believe it. And to qualify again, never happened since. I'm: "I'm going to get into so much trouble." Then Nigel's "right boys, out".

'We went on the beach and we had a few tins, and Nigel was with us so we were all chatting, and we weren't far away from the club, and the club emptied and the girls saw us on the beach and started to walk over to where we were on the beach. And Nigel's seen them and he went, "Right boys – bed!" So we went off to this B&B, the owners weren't there at the time. And this girl had got in the back and I was the first one into the corridor, and she started pulling my pants down – to repeat, never happened since! I'm, "What do I do?" So she hides outside, I go to my room, Mark Owen's there. Nigel's gone to bed, and there's a tap on the window and it's the girl. And I go to Mark, "You know, this isn't right – we're young men and we have impulses and this should be okay, to do this – I'm going to tell Nigel." So I get the courage to go and knock on his door, and I'm, "Nigel, there's a girl outside, she just wanked me off, and I want to sleep with her and I think that should be okay."

'And he used to do this thing when he'd curl his hair like this, and you'd see him thinking. And he went, "All right, then". In that moment, I'm guessing I was sacked, looking back. I went back into my room and I was, like, to Mark, "He said all right!" And Mark was, "What should I do?" I went, "Go in the cupboard." So Mark gets in the cupboard. Then there's a knock on the door, and I open it, and it's Nigel: "Look, the thing is ..." And Mark starts laughing from the cupboard. So we opened it: "Mark, you go to bed ..."

'I'm in so much trouble. I'm now without a job. I don't think he said I was sacked, but I knew I was. Mark goes to bed, and I'm in my room and I've got a t-shirt on and my underpants, and I get angry about the situation: "This isn't fucking right." So I go out, and the door locks behind me with no key in a bed and breakfast where the owners are somewhere else. And I'm just about to knock on Nigel's door and I start to get the fear, thinking, "This is not the thing you should be doing is knocking on the door and having a go at him." Can't get back into my room. Fuck. I went out of the B&B, walked round the corner, the girl yet again comes at me, taking her pants down. I'm: "You got me in so much fucking trouble! You don't understand! Fuck off!" She's bemused. I go round to my room in this courtyard, and there's a window above the window, and it's ajar. I hoist myself in, and there's half of me in the room, and half of me outside the room, and I'm stuck. I can't get into the room, and I can't wake anybody up because I'll definitely be sacked. The latch stuck into my groin, right – little did I know Howard and Jason are watching me from across the courtyard, pissing themselves laughing. I'm stuck there for about twenty-five minutes – the only way I can get in is by pulling myself into the room and ripping my groin. I then fell into the room – luckily I was young enough and lithe enough to not break anything. So I sat there, bleeding, just about to be sacked from my job. I've still got the scar on my groin.'

* * *

I do feel obliged to point out that he now has two stories that go "then she wanked me off …"

'Yeah,' he says, drily. 'That's my catchphrase.'

* * *

One more Take That story for today, before he moves on. In this one, he's not the victim. It was the early days and they were meeting up to get in the van to London for a *My Guy* shoot. Jason was late, and when he pushed back at Nigel Martin-Smith's anger about this, Nigel told him he was sacked, and they drove off to London without him.

'In silence,' says Rob.

Until, halfway there, he said the question that was most on his mind.

'Can I have his jacket?' Rob asked.

Rob is actually wearing Jason's jacket on that *My Guy* cover – Jason, who didn't remain sacked, appears on the cover coming into the image sideways on a lollipop stick.

Did you give him the jacket back?

'Yeah.'

Did he mind?

'Well … we still laugh about it now.'

'It sounds awful,' says Michael.

'It was,' says Rob. 'I've stopped telling the stories of the Take That stuff, partly because things were in a much better place with me and the boys but also because I was sort of reliving those stories where the trauma was definitely with me as I was retelling it, like it happened yesterday. But during it, it was fucking horrible.'

* * *

November 2012

Rob sits around at home, playing songs from his computer, then watches part of a documentary about the legendary American record label Sun, in which some old artists sit round in a café discussing what did and didn't happen in their careers.

Someone on the screen offers up some wisdom: 'Like I said, the music business is chicken today and feathers tomorrow.'

Soon it's time to watch *The X Factor*. Rob, Ayda and Gwen gather on the sofa but wait until 20 minutes after the broadcast has started before pressing play, so that they can fast-forward through the adverts. Gary Barlow is one of this year's judges. That's why, to illustrate the fact that his contestant Christopher Maloney will be performing in France, a photo comes up on the screen of Take That at the opening of Euro Disney in June 1993.

'Ah, there's my boozys!' Ayda exclaims.

Rob pauses the TV.

'*Why*,' he asks, in a voice that suggests he hopes it might not be too late to rethink this decision, 'am I wearing shorts?'

'How much do you remember of that trip?' Gwen asks.

'Nothing,' he says. He shakes his head. 'I look like a *tit* in those fucking shorts. I'm wearing a Planet Hollywood jacket. Stussy shirt.'

'And some sort of workout-gear shorts,' says Ayda. 'Plus it looks like you're wearing the glasses thing that holds your glasses around your neck.'

'I probably am,' he says, a touch defensively. 'What's wrong with that?'

'It just looks cheesy,' she says.

'That's early doors,' he explains. 'It's all right for you! You lived in Beverly Hills! You could afford clothes. Everything I was wearing there's a freebie.'

'The best,' says Ayda drily, 'is the Planet Hollywood jacket.'

'Freebie,' he repeats. 'We were over the *moon* with those Planet Hollywood jackets. Let me tell you. We really were, babe. We were, "Oh my God, thank you very *very* much." We were grateful and humble. We were true to our working-class roots. Yeah.'

He un-pauses the broadcast. The he pauses it again.

'Yeah, I know you've got it in your locker to be mean,' he says to Ayda. 'I remember when we first met I showed you "Do What U Like", and you went *on* and *on* …'

'I was actually more protective of you,' she points out. 'I was afraid you'd been taken advantage of as a youth.'

'Yeah, but before we got to that, there was the "oh my God!"s. I was with you for about half an hour – "I know, I know, I know" – and then after about two hours it was like, "All right, you can stop now …"'

* * *

October 2016

Isle of Sheppey, the 'Love My Life' video shoot. The beautiful but windy and desolate English seascape sends Rob back. 'If I was eighteen and we were Take That it would be like this. This could definitely be *Smash Hits* at Camber Sands – we were in shorts and t-shirts because it was the beach. But it was this weather, because it's England.'

He says it's also like when they shot the 'I Found Heaven' video on the Isle of Wight in weather like this. 'And it was supposed to be not,' he says. More memories. 'You know that's the song with me not singing a couple of notes in it? I couldn't get a couple of the ends of the lines where I'm supposed to be singing, I think it's Billy Griffin does it instead.'

For some reason, this reminds him how many dinners they were forced to have around the world with people from the local record company – 'being made to have our third meal with the South Korean record company that week, and not being able to go to bed, because you're jet-lagged' – hence his enduring aversion to such things.

In the car on the way back to London, he finds a photo on the internet from the beginning of a Take That live show.

'That was the bit where we came up through the middle of the floor and I was asleep one night. It was the first song. I'd fallen asleep standing on my feet. Because I was so fucking tired. It wasn't because of drink and drugs, just because there was no chance for any of that in the middle of that tour.'

What woke you up?

'A lot of screaming. It was instantly confusing and then I instantly realised what had happened. I'd forgotten to march off, and the boys were on the other side of the stage.'

* * *

September 1993

When Take That are about to release their second album, *Everything Changes*, I write an article about them for *The Face*. The first words Rob ever speaks to me are: 'I've been on the wagon for a month. I was getting puffy around here.' He pulls the skin away from his cheeks. 'If I had one pint, I'd have eight.'

He's 19. That first day, Take That are being photographed at Click Studios in the City of London. Before the band arrives, the studio clock is set a few minutes slow, to encourage them to stay as long as possible. Because teen groups are always in a rush. Their measurements are pinned up: according to the sheet, Rob is six-foot-two, has a 38–40-inch chest, a 34-inch inside leg, takes size 10–11 shoes, and is a 32-inch waist. The second thing he says that I write down is 'I feel like a celebrity now I've had my hair done'. When Elton John's 'Bennie And The Jets' comes on the radio, he shouts 'Tune!'

The photographer asks Rob whether he wants to tuck his shirt in.

'I've got a big bum,' he says.

'There's nothing wrong with that,' he is told.

'It's a big horrible bum,' he insists.

When he changes his clothes, he says, 'Red and green are seldom seen, except upon a fool,' then asks me, 'Is that an analogy? Is that the right word?' He really wants to know, and quite seriously asks me to explain. 'So if I said that chair is the Sugar Puffs monster circa 1972,' he checks, 'is that an analogy?'

They pose for photos. He has a bullet on a chain round his neck.

'I wish we could have done the serious ones earlier on,' he says, 'when I was depressed.'

He lights a cigarette. 'I've stopped smoking B&H, Rothmans. I just smoke Silk Cut. I'm looking to give up, but not yet. I enjoy it too much.'

* * *

A few days later, at the *Daily Star* offices, just south of the Thames, Take That answer phone calls from the newspaper's readers. Outside the building, there's at least a hundred girls. Upstairs, the five of them are offered champagne. They get on the phones, each talking to different fans, one by one. I wander round, listening in:

Rob: 'Who is it? Seedy? As in Seedy Movie? Oh! Sadie ...'

Gary: 'That's a lovely name, Tiffany ...'

Rob: 'You better get your smart knickers on to throw them at me ...'

Howard: 'Have you bought our single ... ?'

Rob: 'I looked at you in Portsmouth? Have you got blondish hair? ... Brownish-blackish? I remember! Were you with someone with blonde hair? ... That's it!'

Mark: 'Say "hello" in German ...'

Rob: 'Hold a banner up saying "I'm the one you spoke to on the phone ..."'

Jason: 'Mark's on the phone. Don't you like me? ...'

Rob: 'Hello! McDonald's! Can I take your order, please?'

Howard: 'Our album is good, but I bet you thought I'd say that ...'

Rob: 'I don't think I'll be able to make it. But just in case bring one of those double-duvet sleeping bags and I'll share it with you ... you're not having any alcohol are you? ... Just some spirits then, okay?'

Mark: 'We'll stay together as long as you want us to ...'

Rob: 'I was talking about my trouser snake ...'

Howard: 'I've just bought a Russian hat, so I'll be nice and warm.'

Rob: 'You're through to Robbie. I'm funny. What do you mean "too young"? Too young for what? ...'

Mark: 'If you make me a nice cup of tea I'll come round ...'

Rob: 'Are you an alcoholic? Come on, let's talk about it. I'll give you some counselling ...'

Gary: 'My favourite song I've written is on the new album, "Love Ain't Here Anymore" ...'

Rob: 'Where are you phoning from? Hull? Do you smell of fish?'

* * *

The next month I meet them in Maidstone, where they are appearing on the Saturday-morning TV show *What's Up Doc?*

The evening before the show, Rob meets me in the hotel bar for an interview. 'You won't get nothing out of me, pig,' he says, as he sits down. Soon he is telling me about the Take That audition, and how he was all right at singing but poor at dancing. 'I think what got me into the band was MC Hammer, God bless him, because I could do that bit of a running thing that was quite street and quite cred at the time. So thanks to MC Hammer I am now in Take That.'

He tells me about his acting ambitions. 'I'm a bit of a Bonnie Langford, aren't I?' he says, 'Without the ginger hair. I suppose. I never wanted to be a pop star, I never wanted to be a singer, I never wanted to be a dancer.' He says he dyed his hair blond and auditioned for *My Family and Other*

Animals when he was 12. 'They said I was too small, but I was probably crap. And I went around looking like a complete twat for eight months.'

Do you still hanker to be an actor?

'Yeah. A lot. Very seriously ...'

I ask if he'd leave the band to do it.

'No. Because what I'm doing is what I'm doing. I've got to do this to fulfil every schoolboys' pride ... do you know what I mean? Every ambition. And it's my ambition to achieve everything I want to achieve with the band. After the band, if there is an after the band, or during the band when we get some time off, I would love to go and do some acting. I really want to act.'

Are you good enough?

'Probably not. Probably not, but I'm Robbie from Take That. I don't mean that in a conceited way. You get presenters with big tits that are crap, but they've got big tits. Do you understand what I'm saying? I'll probably be crap but people will have me anyway, because I'm a name. Which is unfortunate. Because I've got my foot in the door ... people that will be ten times better than me will not get their foot in the door. And, who knows, I might do a very good job.'

Funny roles? Serious?

'Everything. Anything they want to give me ... who knows? Funny mainly, I suppose, then I'll move on and do a bit of Kenneth Branagh, luvvie, much ado about everything.'

Loretta, Take That's press officer, interrupts. She says Howard has gone to bed, but Gary, who I spoke with earlier, would like to come back and talk some more tonight. He joins us.

'I better not drink any more,' says Rob.

'You've got the two opposite ends of the band here, really,' says Gary.

'The bookends,' says Rob.

'You've got Robbie who really doesn't care about anything in the world, and you've got me who worries about everything,' says Gary.

Is that true?

'Yeah,' says Gary.

'Yeah,' says Rob. 'Would I lie?'

We talk about 'A Million Love Songs' and 'Could It Be Magic?' for a few minutes, Gary doing most of the speaking. Rob chips in the odd thought. 'We were famous for being famous,' he says. After a few more minutes' chat, Rob asks, about this bit of the interview, 'Chris, is it all music?'

Not all, I say.

'Because I'm just bobbins on the music side of it,' he says.

A few minutes later, Rob gets up and leaves us to it.

* * *

The next morning, when he first sees me at the TV studio, Rob puts a poster over his face. 'No comment,' he says. Then he asks, 'Was I okay last night? I don't like interviews like that, because I can't be funny.' He stands up. 'Right, I'll go and annoy somebody.'

I speak to Nigel Martin-Smith instead. This morning he has been outed by the *Daily Express*; he seems more perplexed than annoyed. He talks about the band.

'There's talent there, in various forms,' he tells me. 'Like, Gary has got the songwriting talents, they've all got really good vocals, as lead or backing, Robbie's great with this presenting thing – he's got good timing – and they look great and they've got great personalities and they work really hard.'

* * *

I also asked each of the group, separately, a series of the same questions. These were some of Rob's answers:

Did you always dream of being famous?

'Yeah. This might sound very conceited of me, but I came home – and my nan used to look after me – from school and I was about ten, and it was decisions time, which school you go into, and my nan says to me, "Are you worried about your decisions? Are you worried about what's going on?" And she's told me this – I'd forgotten – and I said, "Nan, whatever happens, by the time I'm twenty-one I'm going to be very famous and I'm going to be a millionaire.' And that does sound conceited, but that was just confidence then, I suppose. I'd never realised how it would happen or if it would happen.'

And why did you think it would be nice?

'[Slightly sarcastic.] Why would I think it would be nice to be famous and a millionaire? Because that's everybody's dream. That was my dream when I was growing up. I didn't know – I thought, that is my picture of nice. That is my picture of happiness.'

How did you think it would make you feel? Why would that make you feel good?

'Why would that make me feel good? It's a sense of achievement, and it's a sense of power, I think. Power that you always strive for. I hope people respect me.'

How smart do you think you are?

'What – intelligence-wise? Or dress sense?'

Intelligence.

'I don't think I am. I've got a bit of a complex about it. Everything I say, I think, "God, that's made me sound so ridiculously thick it's untrue." Serious, I'm not kidding you. And I really find it difficult to express what I'm thinking. I'm slightly dyslexic. It's probably me being lazy, actually, but I am slightly dyslexic, I find it difficult writing "p"s and "b"s and things like that. I find it difficult expressing what I want to say. And sometimes when that happens and I start to stutter and I can't get it across. In an interview one-on-one like this, I think "he's thinking I'm thick" and then you've got the cliché "thick pop group" and that's going around in your head. That's probably the thing that I worry about. When I see these people in bars and we're all having a chat and we're having a drink and everything and then all of sudden the conversation becomes all political, I'm like, "Can we talk about football?" I really do want to be intelligent. Can somebody help me? Seriously. Honestly.'

How good-looking do you think you are?

'There's always something wrong with my appearance, in my own mind. I never think I'm good-looking at all. And that is that. I'm not saying "look at me, I'm so down to earth and a nice lad from Stoke-on-Trent". I never do think that I'm good-looking. Serious. People find me attractive; I don't find me attractive.'

If you were gay, would you hide it from the public?

'If I was gay would I hide it from the public? If I was in Take That – yes, I would. Because that's not part of Take That, I suppose. I don't know. Let me rephrase that. [Thinks.] If I was gay … I would like to think that I wouldn't. I would like to think that I wouldn't. If I was. I don't know. That is a difficult one, actually. I don't know, to tell you the truth. I would like to think that I wouldn't.'

When did you last cry?

'I've been in rehearsals and I felt like crying there, but I actually haven't. Because I'm the one out of the band that could never get the routine. I'm very lazy. I do very little. But the trick is, doing very little very well. Hopefully.'

What do you think of the tabloid press?

'Very worrying. Very worrying. Quite stressful. But I mean it's the thrill of the chase as well. It keeps the adrenalin up there anyway …'

What's your favourite rumour you've heard about yourself?

'A few gay friends of mine – all their friends have slept with me. Yeah. They've all slept with me. [Pauses.] And I was crap. I'm not so bothered about them saying that they've slept with me, but it's the "crap" that I'm worried about.'

What would make you happier?

'Seeing my mum secure is of utmost to me. That would make me happy. And also a little bit of time off, just a little bit of a break, that would make me happy. And for people who come up to me in pubs not to want to glass me but just come up and say "how's it going, it's all right, yeah". Even though you're not into the band, if you're going to come across, don't punch me. That would make me happy.'

What's your main contribution to Take That?

'Not a lot, really. All the lads go through the ideas for the tours and everything, and I'm probably watching basketball in the other room or something. I should contribute more on the side of the artist's … what's it called? … well, the artist's vision. On that front I should contribute more, but I don't. That's because I'm lazy, again. So my part in Take That probably is – it's probably a cliché but – "he's the funny one". Do you know what I mean? And I don't try to be the funny one.'

* * *

April 2017

'Well, that end bit's not true,' Rob says. 'I tried desperately to be the funny one. It makes me sad, the bit where I say I don't want people to glass me. I didn't want people to glass me so much that I stopped going out. The lazy bit – there wasn't room for me to do what I wanted to do, so I didn't do anything. There was one time I phoned Gaz and sung him a song down the telephone and there was silence, and then, "That's all right, lad – if we were in a rock band." That was the end of that. But it's telling that I say I'd like a bit of time off. I'm saying: I need a holiday and I don't want people to beat me up. But I couldn't say what I really wanted to say.'

* * *

November 2012

The Take That years, first time around, are something that Rob often returns to, at the most random of times, as if it is something that he is still processing, still trying to work out.

This evening, in a car going home, he remembers something he used to do with Paul, his security guy back then.

'He had a fear of heights,' says Rob, 'so I would always go to the top of the hotel and stand on the edge of it. He'd be on a helicopter landing pad, holding on to the floor: "Rob! You fucker!" And the higher we'd get, the lower down he'd get. I was in the tallest hotel in Seoul, standing on the edge, having a piss over. And he was, "Rob … ! Rob … !"'

The car drives on.

'You know everything then, don't you, when you're in your late teens, early twenties? *Know everything.*'

He thinks on this some more.

'I'm not young enough to know everything anymore,' he says.

* * *

November 2016

In every interview Rob has done for the past few weeks he has been asked how he feels to be given the Brits Icon Award. He finds it a difficult question to answer. Part of the answer, a part he will talk about in private but which just seems too ungrateful and mercenary to say in public, is that his principal interest in it is how the award, and more specifically the ITV special, will promote his new album. The other part of the answer is that if he really thinks about it, he feels overawed but it also activates that part of him always ready to drown any praise in his endless inner oceans of unworthiness.

'My lack of self-worth comes shining through whenever I'm given an award,' he'll say. 'Whenever I'm given an award, I'm faced with this brick wall of: *you don't deserve this.*' The higher the mountain, the further to plummet. 'Back in the day, I remember winning three Brit awards one evening, and it may have been one of the worst nights of my life. Just because my own lack of self-worth couldn't squirrel this away. It's like being given a mirror and going, "You know how much you hate yourself? Well, triple, quadruple that, because you're getting an award." I can never make it make sense. I'm very honoured but it sort of triggers something in me that's innately me, and I'm hoping innately human on some level, that just makes me go: I don't deserve this.'

He explains this patiently, again and again, and they always listen, but I don't think many of them understand what he is saying, or really believe him.

* * *

Tonight, Rob plays at the Troxy, a small theatre in east London, a full concert with an elaborate production that is being filmed for the ITV special, and during which he will be presented with his award. At one point José Mourinho had been lined up to hand the trophy to Rob, but he has had to pull out – his first season as Manchester United's manager has not been going smoothly, and the presumption is that it wouldn't be smart optics for him to be seen gallivanting outside the world of football right now. Anyway, everyone's realised that there's a much more obvious and better idea that's been staring them in the face.

First, though, there's a press conference at the Savoy in the centre of town to announce next year's tour. Rob bounds in and greets everyone, receives silence back. About the tour, he tells the journalists: 'It's still a work in progress. Garth Brooks, he says that an audience needs seven wows for a show, so they can go back and say, "Did you see that bit? Did you see that bit?" I'm currently working on my seven wows.'

Near the end, Rob is also, as ever, asked about Take That.

'Reunion at some point?' asks Jo Whiley, today's moderator.

'Reunion at some point definitely,' he says, 'but we just couldn't get our diaries to work in the next twelve months.'

* * *

'… at some point.'

For someone who's not always the best at keeping secrets from the press, Rob did pretty well there. Considering that the next Take That reunion will be taking place in a few hours, onstage at the Troxy

Mark arrives first.

'Are you going to have any chocolate?' asks Rob when Mark walks into his cramped dressing room, as though this is a familiar partner-in-crime ritual.

'Oh yes,' Mark replies, and they both hit the Green & Black organic milk chocolate. As they snack, they catch up about their latest home renovations.

'I chose the toilet,' Rob says. 'The only thing I asked for.'

Mark says he took a similar tack. 'I didn't really get involved. They asked me questions but they don't really want answers.'

'Yeah, they didn't even ask me questions,' says Rob. 'Well, a major one – the budget.'

He quizzes Mark about the next Take That album: how many songs they wrote, how many songs they're now working on, how happy they are with it, how much they have to do. And then he quizzes him about the TV show, *Let It Shine*, a reality show to cast a boyband for the forthcoming Take That musical.

'There's a Rob impersonator,' says Mark. 'You might even know him. Unbelievable. He was brilliant. Really good. But the mad thing was, even when he wasn't singing, he was you.'

'Oh God,' says Rob, 'even I can't stand that.'

Mark asks about tonight: 'How are you feeling about it? Are you excited?'

'I'm fine.'

'It's a great thing. An amazing thing. An *amazing* thing.'

'Yeah,' Rob agrees, uncertain. 'Yeah.'

'It should be really good. "More Brits than any other artist!"' Mark laughs heartily.

'It's a TV show,' says Rob, 'and I've got an album out. And it's hopefully going to be a great bit of telly.'

'Yeah, try and enjoy it tonight,' Mark suggests.

'Yeah, but what do *you* do?' Rob retorts. 'You just deflect, deflect, deflect ...'

'I know ...'

'Yeah, *exactly*,' says Rob. 'It's impossible for that to penetrate or mean anything other than I've got a bit of work to do tonight and I'll try to enjoy myself, and if I don't that's not what I'm here for.'

'But when you look who's won it ...' Mark argues. 'When we started we were round at Elton John's and he's won it. And David Bowie. It's incredible.'

'I know,' says Rob. 'It is. But you know as much as I do that it doesn't matter – receiving that kind of praise, you just deflect like some kind of mind kung fu.'

'Yeah,' Mark concedes. 'You don't actually believe it.'

'Yeah,' says Rob, and adds, sadly, dismissively, as if he's addressing someone he barely knows: 'Good for Robbie Williams.'

The two of them go and stand in a stairway that smells of piss where smoking is allowed, and the discussion continues.

'It's amazing though,' Mark insists.

'It's great, but, you know, awards,' says Rob. 'If you turn up, you get them, if you don't, you don't.'

'No,' Mark protests, 'but I think this one's special!'

'Stop it!' Rob says. 'I'm not having it!'

* * *

Howard arrives next – he and Rob go back to the piss stairway – then Gary turns up.

'Lads, now that I've got you all here,' Rob tells them, carefully and sincerely, 'thank you very, very, very, very, very much.'

They go to rehearse. It's amazing what an instant camaraderie they have onstage – arms around each other, a bundle of revolving hugs – as they sing 'The Flood'. No one's filming this, and there's no audience; this is just them. The first half of 'Back For Good' features lots of back-and-forth horseplay between Rob and Gary about who is going to sing most of the lines. Then the music Rob's band are playing accelerates, and mutates, to the three others' evident and genuine surprise, into the punk version of the song that Rob sometimes performs.

'Fucking sacrilege, that,' says Gary once it has finished.

In the corridor, Rob apologises to Gary. 'Sorry – I didn't mean to surprise you with the end bit of "Back For Good" – I thought you'd been sent it.'

'Oh, we probably just didn't listen to it,' says Gary. 'It's absolutely fine.'

* * *

Rob's show is pretty triumphant all round, but the emotional high point comes with Take That, first their performance and then when they return to hand Rob his Icon Award. Mark does the heartfelt faux-poetic stuff – 'sometimes we walk together, and sometimes we watch from afar, but wow, what a journey it has been' – but the line that Rob mentions afterwards is when Howard says, 'Rob, whether you like it or not, you will always be a member of Take That.' It's the 'whether you like it or not' that makes Rob laugh.

'Wasn't that lovely?' his mother says afterwards. 'I couldn't believe the boys. That was so reminiscent of when he came in as a teenager and said, "I've got these brothers." He was so happy that he'd found these four brothers.'

It's a romantic version of the story, or a conveniently truncated one, but it seems to make some sense tonight.

During 'Angels', dozens of Rob's fans, in a coordinated move, all hold up pieces of paper which simply say: PROUD OF YOU. It's all the sweeter for being so low-tech and evidently sincere. In the car, going home, he tweets his reply:

To all my friendlies; from the heart … I'm proud of you too x

* * *

'You deserve a thousand Crunchies tonight,' says Ayda in the car.

'May a thousand Crunchies be your reward,' says Rob as though he were Russell Crowe in *Gladiator*.

'Yeah,' she echoes. 'I grant you unlimited chocolate tonight.'

They discuss how well the show went.

'I feel like there's nothing you can't do,' says Ayda.

This comment sits there.

'Spell,' says Rob. 'Maths.'

'Yeah,' Ayda agrees, picking up this ball. 'Identify vegetables. Cook. Clean.'

'Yeah,' says Rob. 'Get an erection.' And laughs.

'Yeah, you know when you were doing that thing where you were grinding on the pole and it looked like you were doing something sexual?' says Ayda. 'I turned to Susie and said, "That just means I'm going to pick up all the chocolate off the floor tonight."'

There are a couple more of us in this car and, understandably, given the nature of the conversation we are overhearing, Rob is suddenly concerned to make sure we know that what has been conveyed so far may have been entertaining, but it is not all factually accurate.

'Actually,' he clarifies, 'it's going to be Cadbury's Celebrations.'

* * *

March 2013

During the recording of the *Swings Both Ways* album in Los Angeles, Rob has an idea, an idea he's gleefully excited about. He has realised that both he and Gary Barlow are planning to release new solo albums towards the end of the year. He thinks they should release them on the same day, and engineer a high-profile media battle, just as 50 Cent and Kanye West did some years ago, or, more combatively, like the notorious Oasis versus Blur face-off. Rob's view is that a stunt like this would be bound to raise the sales of both records. He obviously thinks it would be fun, too.

He emails Gary, excited. Gary answers, much less so. Rob reads out part of his reply: 'I would do anything for that not to happen. It brings up too much of the past for me. I would love after thirteen years just for a record to have its own story.'

When Guy comes down for lunch, Rob mentions this, and Guy reminds him that it all might seem a little like when *Life Thru A Lens* and Gary Barlow's first solo album *Open Road* came out.

'His album came out way before,' Rob says. 'I went and bought it.'

But, as Guy points out, this leaves unsaid a rather relevant detail.

'Yes, but you took it back and said you wanted your money back,' Guy reminds him.

Not just took it back, mind. Told the person who served him at Our Price: 'This is crap – I want my money back.'

And while Rob wasn't the one who told the press what he'd said – he assumes that was the staff behind the counter at the record shop – once the story was out there, for years afterwards he would be quite happy to repeat it.

* * *

After lunch Rob walks into the studio, shampooing his hair. He seems to be surprised that any of us would consider this unusual.

'It's made me pleased that I'm eccentric without thinking about it,' he beams.

He carries on shampooing as they listen through three or four more songs.

'Oh bollocks,' he suddenly says. 'I don't want to upset Gaz.'

Rob goes outside to piss, and when he returns he says that where he normally pisses, mushrooms are growing.

After that he goes back to bed.

Later he'll write again to Gary, letting it go graciously.

I hear you and it won't happen. I really thought it might be a laugh, but it's only a laugh if both of us think it's a laugh. Gaz, you'll be surprised how your album does. The songs are going to be quality, and you are loved. I keep my fingers crossed that we both sell really well. And that you sell two more than me. But only two, mind.

* * *

It's difficult to tell what might have happened if they'd gone ahead with the plan. There definitely wasn't a certain winner. In its first week of release, that November, *Swings Both Ways* will sell 109,000 copies. The following week, as overall sales climb towards Christmas, Gary Barlow's *Since I Saw You Last* sells 116,000 copies. But it is *Swings Both Ways* that climbs back to be number one at Christmas itself. So it looks like it would have been close.

But most probably it was a situation best avoided. When a fake war echoes a real one, it's far too easy for the two to get confused.

* * *

January 2016

Rob is playing pool with Stuart Price. He fouls. 'Two shots,' he says, and while Stuart takes over at the table, Rob talks about what he and Ayda did last night.

'We started to watch *Take That: For the Record*,' he says. 'The original documentary that started the whole comeback. We were only eleven minutes in, and I'm such an angry entitled prick. But it's my chance to say what I needed to say about Nigel Martin-Smith.' Pause. 'Charismatic, though.'

Stuart laughs. 'Charisma forgives a multitude of shortcomings, doesn't it?'

'Thank God,' says Rob.

But he also says that Ayda had an interesting analysis of what she was seeing. He repeats the conversation that took place last night between the two of them:

'So the boys were a bit older than you, right?'

'Yeah'.

'There's a big difference between sixteen, and nineteen or twenty. They probably all bonded because they were of a similar age, and they probably thought you were annoying, because you were younger. And you knew that they thought you were annoying, so you were more annoying.'

'Oh. Yeah. That did happen.'

* * *

2005–2006

It's difficult to remember or imagine now just how cold the careers of the other four members of Take That became in the ten years after the group split. Gary Barlow's burned brightly for a short while, then it faded, his record company dropped him and he became a jobbing songwriter and producer with modest prospects. Mark Owen also had some solo success, but that also dwindled. Howard Donald made an album he never released then worked as a DJ. Jason Orange did some acting for a while, then stopped. So when Rob was approached to appear in a Take That documentary in 2005, at his post-Knebworth height, he couldn't help but be aware how much difference his participation would make. 'I felt as though by me taking part,' he concedes, 'I would be doing them a sort of favour.' It was not exactly a peace offering, because as the interview he gave for the documentary would demonstrate, he was only intermittently open to anything like that, but it was still a gift of sorts: an acknowledgement of what they had been through together, and of their shared history. Less nobly, it was also an opportunity for Rob to get a few things off his chest.

His principal target was Nigel Martin-Smith. 'Nigel ... I haven't got a nice word to say about him,' he'd say in the film. 'He's definitely in the top three most disturbed individuals I've ever worked with ... I only wanted him to love me. That's the really sad thing. I only wanted him to love me. And he never did.' Gary Barlow, he alternated between praising and deriding. For instance: 'Gary Barlow's a wanker! No, I'm joking ... don't put that in. No, but I sincerely mean it. He is a wanker.'

Nonetheless, the finished film, *Take That: For the Record*, was, Rob says, 'a bit of a stitch-up'. The key narrative device at its climax involved the other four waiting in a hotel, apparently on tenterhooks as to whether Rob was going to turn up to join them. The film makes it seem as though he, too, knew that this would be the scenario, and that he had made a conscious choice not to be there. The truth is that he had no idea that anything would be presented in this way. He had sat for an interview but he had never seriously entertained any thoughts of getting together with the other four for this programme; aside from anything else, he already knew that if the day could ever come where he and Gary Barlow would sit down again in a room, he certainly wouldn't want a film crew to be there.

This was compounded on-screen, after they broke the news of Rob's non-appearance on camera to the others, by what the filmmakers showed next. Rob had been asked to film messages to each of the other four, but he had been told that all of the band members were filming messages for each other. The things he said were nice – conciliatory customised apologies to Howard, Jason and Gary, and straightforward compliments for Mark – but he didn't know that what he was saying would be shown in the context of: *Here's your famous former bandmate – he's decided to stand you up, but he's got a few filmed words for you instead.* Watching the programme, which was a big ratings success and reignited Take That's popularity, Rob was upset.

'I wish I'd known that's what was happening,' he says, 'because maybe I'd have done it differently. I was sad that I wasn't there at the end. I was also sad that the lads were led to believe that I might be there at the final meeting. They really thought that I was going to come out from behind the door.'

* * *

November 2006

Rob's unresolved feelings about the Take That years had never gone that far away, but the documentary seemed to stir everything up again – particularly the part where Nigel Martin-Smith said: 'Well, what have I done? What did I do, Rob? I took you out of Stoke-on-Trent … I made him massive … and look where he is now … I gave him his career, as far as I'm concerned.'

Nigel's question – *well, what have I done?* – was one that, now it had been asked so nakedly, Rob felt compelled to answer. Away promoting his new album *Intensive Care* in Mexico, Rob sat down and wrote his old manager a very long letter. 'It was just an outpouring,' he says, 'and I cried all the way through writing it, and there's spelling mistakes and paragraphs didn't make sense – I couldn't even fix it. I just sent it.'

I'm just writing as the memories come back, so please bear with me. Most of the stuff you did has been blocked out. But for the purpose of this email and your fascinating question – what did I do? – I shall endeavour to explore the darkest recess of my brain. Let's see what's in Pandora's Box.

Pandora's box turned out to be pretty full: out poured bitter, angry, sad memory after bitter, angry, sad memory, but also a chain of very specific, detailed and carefully described incidents with explanations of how each of these had made him feel. Sometimes you write something knowing full well that there's little chance what you're saying will really get through to the person it's addressed to in the way that you need it to – because if words like this could get through now, most probably much of what you're describing would never have happened in the first place. But sometimes, even so, every word still needs to be said.

Once he'd got it all out, Rob emailed the letter to Nigel Martin-Smith. He received no reply.

But he also sent the letter to his four former bandmates. What he would hear back in time, directly and indirectly, would be the most important thing of all. Because he'd been alone with his memories and his truth of what had taken place for so long, and what he most needed to be told was what he would now begin to hear:

Yes. All of that happened.

* * *

In the preceding years, Rob had somewhat rebuilt his friendship with Mark, who had been his closest friend in the band, but around this time he established a less likely rapport with Jason, with whom he used to have a difficult relationship. This was when the four-piece Take That were starting to plan a comeback tour. Rob and Jason started talking regularly on the phone. 'It was weird,' says Rob, 'because it seemed like the only person that I could have any sort of clarity with was Jason. Because for whatever reason we needed each other right then. He was uncertain whether he was going to do the whole thing and he was asking me what I thought, and we just had the most amazing telephone conversations that would last two or three hours and I didn't want to get off the phone. And it was great to be in contact with him again and to not bear any malice – that had gone.'

Several years after this, when all five of them did finally get back together, Rob and Jason exchanged a series of emails in which they tried to recreate what they each said in these 2006 conversations. Here are some extracts:

Jason: *What say you join us on the tour? I reckon we'd stand a better chance of not looking so ridiculous with you onstage next to us. Selfish reason, I know but it might also pave the way for some reconciliation too. At the very least we'd surely have a right laugh.*

Rob: *I'm really pleased you've decided to do it, mate ... I know it's taken a lot of soul searching but you've made the right choice ... As for me I'll be honest with you, bud. At the end of the documentary when you four were walking away I was a bit gutted. I should have been there. But there's too much to say to each other and I don't think our first meeting back together should be a public one. Re: joining the band – look,* Rudebox *(my album) has just been given an almighty kicking by the press. I'm a bit bruised from it, to tell you the truth, and I want to go and make it right ... I've got a 3 year plan and it involves releasing a couple of albums by myself. I'm just not going to have the time. It does pull at my heart strings to do something with you but I've got too much to sort out.*

Jason: *I am gutted that you won't be with us but half expected you'd say no. I am surprised at your feeling 'bruised' with the criticism* Rudebox *has received. I would've thought you were long past caring about what the press and, to an extent, what the public think about your work ... With all the concert tickets and albums you've sold, and with all the awards you've won, haven't you proved yourself enough to critics and fans alike? When does it all end?*

Rob: *I feel like I'm being judged for wanting to do well. Maybe I didn't explain myself correctly ... Look, I've never received critical acclaim ... The music press and the broadsheets hate me. I stopped wanting or expecting that a long time ago, and what do awards mean at the end of the day? ... It's just that the kicking I got was mixed with a more than lukewarm response from the people that usually want to put one of my albums in their homes ... and it hurt. I care about what my fans think about my music ... Pathetic or not I want them to like it ... There is a certain intangible safety that you feel when things are going well ... Elton John just released* Peachtree Road. *It's the best album he's done in ages. It didn't perform as expected. I'm sure he's not going 'well, I wrote "Candle in the Wind" ... that'll do'. Believe me when I say at his age and with everything he's done he'll be gutted. On an intellectual level I'm aware that it's an un-winnable game but emotionally you still want to play. As for now, I'm still in the game. You asked 'when does it all end?' And my answer to you is hopefully, 'When the fat lad sings'.*

'Jay's a great soundboard,' Rob reflects, 'and he makes you look at things differently, more so than anybody that I've ever met.'

Rob didn't seriously consider rejoining the group then, but he did offer another olive branch – he agreed to film a hologram of himself that they could use on that 2006 tour, so that each night 'Could It Be Magic?' began with Robbie floating in the air above the stage. As though he was almost there.

* * *

November 2012

Tonight, Gary Barlow is being honoured with the Music Industry Trusts Award at a fancy dinner in a London hotel ballroom, an evening which ends with him performing. Rob will guest-star twice. First he goes onstage to perform 'Candy', something he and Gary have never rehearsed or performed together before tonight.

'Ladies and gentleman, this week's UK number one!' Rob shouts after the first chorus. 'Written by myself and Mr Barlow!'

Then, at the end of the night, Rob reappears with the rest of Take That to perform 'Never Forget'. After, he will relate the conversation he has with Jason, who hasn't seen any of them for a while:

'Jay was like, "Have you lot been hanging out?" and I went, "Yeah, we went on a barging holiday together in Norfolk, and then we all learned how to fly."'

In between his two songs, Rob waits behind a curtain round the back of the stage. The other four members of Take That are singing one of the biggest hits of their initial comeback, 'Shine'.

You, you're such a big star to me
You're everything I wanna be

But you're stuck in a hole and I want you to get out.
Rob sings along backstage.
Stop being so hard on yourself
It's not good for your health
I know that you can change.
'It's about me, this song,' he mentions.
He sings some more:
Don't you let your demons pull you down
'Cause you can have it all, you can have it all.
I ask whether he knew that at the time.

'I guessed,' he says. 'And then I said, "It's about me, isn't it?" "Kind of … yeah."'

* * *

2006–2008

The simple version of how the five members of Take That finally got back together, the one they usually now tell, is that they had a reunion at Rob's house in Los Angeles in the summer of 2008, in which old grievances were aired, common ground sought, and healing initiated. That did happen, but the path there was slightly more complicated.

The first time all five of them actually got together was in May 2006 at a hotel in Chelsea Harbour, a few months after the documentary aired. Take That were staying there while they played their comeback shows at Wembley Arena; Rob's London home at the time was a short walk away. He waited in the lobby for them to return from their concert that night, and they went up to a hotel room to talk. There was some laughing and shared remembering, but there was a lot that was left unsaid. As Jason would later describe it: 'There was a lot of water not under the bridge, lying stagnant.'

Rob was well aware of the hovering discomfort but one of the things that would most upset him when he read Gary Barlow's autobiography would be the account of this reunion. 'To read that our meeting had not been …' – he hesitates – '… the semi-beautiful thing that I thought it was.' In his book, Gary details two nights of conversation that were intense but often friendly, but there's a particularly uncomfortable description of a brief episode when everyone stood up at the same time, all five of them. He describes how Rob then said, 'Look, it's Take That.' But after quoting these words, Gary simply adds, making the moment seem not so much heart-warming as awkward, 'No one contradicted him.'

Anyway, his overall portrait of Rob from those encounters is not a tender one:

As I'd walked into the hotel I hadn't had time to think about how I was going to react to Rob. Time may be a great healer, but still, whenever I thought of him I thought, you absolute cunt. I've never had anyone do so much damage as you've done. No one has said or done such awful things as you have said or done to me. No one has even come close. Yet as I sat there I felt nothing. I looked at him and thought, you're just a bloke like the rest of us … With everything that Rob has – all the money, all the fame, all the trappings of success – he's not a very positive person … Being with Rob again reminded me of how I used to be: completely self-obsessed, working, working, working just to stay where you are, blind to the world.

* * *

In 2008, when Rob was living in Los Angeles and still torn between remaining a hermit or someday rejoining the world, he got a message that Take That were coming to town to record their album, *The Circus*. Did he want to meet?

'It was like a date scenario with a very pretty girl,' he remembers. 'Should I go or not? Or will I be shit? Will I be unsocial? I didn't want to present myself in a bad light, I didn't want to do anything wrong. And there's four lads here and one of them, me and him, have a big problem together. And I hadn't seen Howard and I didn't know how he was going to react to me, and Mark and me were best mates and now we don't know each other. There was all of these things. And there's four of them and one of me.'

He arranged to go down to where they were staying, at the Beverly Wilshire Hotel.

'And I nearly didn't go,' he says. 'Plus the fact that I had toothache and I'd taken a painkiller, and I'd got all my togs on to go down and this painkiller kicked in and I was, "Right, I can't go now, I'm off my fucking head."'

In the end, he turned up. And it was fine, aside from one thing. But it was a major one. 'I still couldn't look at Gary,' says Rob. 'I couldn't look at him. There's things that I had to say, things that I had to get off my chest. And I was probably embarrassed about things that I *had* said, publicly, that weren't kind. I wouldn't have known where he sat with that. But also, more importantly for me, there were things that I needed to say to him: this, this, this, this, this and this.'

But not here, not now.

The next night they came up to his house. He took them into his sunken living room, where sofas formed three sides of a square, and that is where they had the conversation.

'I said, "Lads, for anything to happen and for us to go forward, I need to get this off my chest and I need you all to hear it." I remember Gaz going …' – Rob mimes a sharp intake of breath – '… "Go on, then." It was really important that I said my side of the story, and why I said what I said, and why I did what I did, and why I've thought what I've thought, and we sat down on my sofa, and I purged myself of everything that I'd been keeping in for ten or fifteen years. That I'd kept in and needed to tell. To the boys, and especially Gaz. And I got it all out. And he had his say. And it seemed that we were both mature enough to be in the right place to hear it.'

And in that one discussion, it all melted.

'We were like, "OK, I can live with that …" "Yep, okay, I can live with that …" "I'm sorry, you're sorry – done!" And then an hour later Gary and I were rolling about laughing, in my kitchen, on the floor. Hearty big laughs. And I think a weight had been released from both of our shoulders.'

* * *

In Vaughan's interviews for the Brits Icon film, Gary, Mark and Howard discuss this night.

Mark: We got in a room, didn't we? And that was the thing. That was the hardest part, about getting us all back together in a room, I think. It always probably is. Dealing with things like this face-to-face is always the best way.

Howard: Proper deep talking it was, as well. We'd never ever spoken to each other like that, as grown men.

Gary: It was the chat we needed, wasn't it? It was the chat we hadn't ever had.

* * *

'After we had this meeting,' Rob says, 'we were best mates. I felt with Gaz like I'd never felt in Take That: I got him, he got me. It was fucking lovely. And there's all these bands that can't fucking get together again because of dumb stuff that goes on when you were a kid. And there's me from Stoke and him from Frodsham and we got to a very, very happy medium very quickly. And it was beautiful. There was a long period of really, really not liking him because of the person that I thought he was when he was younger. It all came from a place of real hurt – and then the sort of anger died down, and it became part of my schtick. It became something that I did without even thinking about it. People always go, "You should get over it, you should stop it, move on …" People don't. Normal people in everyday lives hold a gripe against somebody in the pub from twenty years ago. Just cause I'm a fucking celebrity doesn't mean I'm mature emotionally because of that fact.'

But now he'd finally found a way to release it all. 'I didn't realise how *much* of a weight was on my shoulders,' he says. 'All the things that had been left unsaid from a major part of my life. Five years, your first soiree into adulthood. The formative years, as they're called. It's fantastic not to have that.'

The next day, giddy with the experience of what had just happened, Rob went to a local tattoo parlour.

'I'd spent so long not being proud of being in Take That, I finally felt as though I could be proud of what we did, and what we achieved,' he says. 'It was a huge part of my life, and there was so much sadness but there was so much success, and I felt as though I could finally celebrate that success.'

He had the Take That logo tattooed on the outside of his right forearm.

'It's a pretty cool symbol – I like it. And it was me saying to me, and them, that the weight's gone: "Look, this is etched on me for life – and I can do that now because I'm freer." It's a demon slayed, as far as I'm concerned.'

He'd see the four of them again while they were in town, more evenings 'of laughter and bonding', and on the first of these he showed them. Over the years, Rob has described his former and future bandmates' reaction to this new tattoo in slightly different ways, all variations on a theme:

'They thought it was silly.'

'They all just went "you're mental".'

'They just looked at me like I was a dick.'

'I'm sure they thought it was a mixture of brilliant and daft. As I do, too.'

* * *

November 2012

Gary has agreed to make a special guest appearance with Rob at the O2. Today, there's rehearsals. He arrives before Rob, and sits in Rob's dressing room.

'It's got to come to an end soon, this,' he sighs. 'Can't keep chasing this forever.'

Rob comes through the door, and sees that he's already being filmed. 'Morning!' he says. 'You know how I love a fucking huge camera crew.'

'I don't go anywhere now *unless* there's a camera crew,' says Gary, drily.

'Well, it's not worth living life,' Rob agrees, deadpan, 'unless it's going to be filmed, documented and then shown on TV.'

Gary nods. 'It's a waste of effort. If you're getting up, cleaning your teeth, it should be shown … How's it going, Rob? … What's that you've brought with you on your forehead?'

Rob has a spot. More than one, actually.

'Or this on the side here,' Rob points out.

'What's *that*?' says Gary. 'A relation?'

'They're like promo pimples,' Rob explains.

Gary asks Rob about the shows, and Rob describes the challenge of performing in the round: 'Most of the gig's going to be spent wandering around trying to figure out what I'm doing with my left hand.'

'I've got a few ideas,' says Gary. 'Probably not usable.' Then he further considers the predicament of a 360-degree show. 'Yeah, your back's on display. Back's usually safe, isn't it? Now it's fifty per cent of the show, your back.'

'Yeah,' says Rob.

'You have got a *big* back,' Gary points out. 'It's a big back, isn't it? He's V-shaped, Rob. Big back. Lot of back.'

'There is a lot of back happening,' Rob concedes.

They banter some more, very obviously playing up to the fact that they're being filmed.

'Have you been true to yourself, though?' Gary asks Rob. 'That word gets used a lot, doesn't it? Being "true to yourself". What does that *mean*?'

'I don't know,' says Rob, and adds, flatly, 'I've given a hundred per cent.' He pauses. 'I haven't really. At best I've probably given ninety-five, but most of the time I'm sort cruising along on fifty-five, sixty per cent.'

'Yeah,' says Gary, 'but your fifty-five, sixty per cent is most people's hundred per cent.'

Rob laughs. 'Gary Barlow, ladies and gentlemen! Hey, I'll tell you what, you're good at this …'

'I'll tell you what, I am,' banters Gary back.

Barnaby, who is directing this documentary footage, asks which of them is the better talker.

'He is – he speaks more sense,' says Rob. 'I've no filter. I don't think about what I say. And it just comes out.'

'I've been there,' says Gary.

'Really?' says Rob. 'But only for a split second. Mine can last a career.'

As they go down to the stage, Rob turns to Gary.

'Thanks for doing this, by the way.'

* * *

2009–2010

In the summer of 2009, Gary Barlow was in Los Angeles with his wife, Dawn, and his kids, on holiday. Rob invited him round for quiz night, a semi-regular Sunday-evening gathering of friends at the Williams house. An English journalist, Alex Bilmes, who had just interviewed Rob for *GQ* magazine, was also there. Rob had told Alex in the interview that when he had finished with all his current plans, 'I want to go and play with my mates.' Meaning Take That. And he asked Alex to reaffirm to Gary that that was what he had been saying. Then, as Gary left, Rob suggested that, while he was over, they should write a song together.

'He said to Alex from *GQ*,' says Rob, '"I don't even bloody know if he'll turn up – you never know with him." And I did – I turned up.'

Officially, this would be the first song that they ever wrote together. In fact, there had been one previous attempt, around the time of the first Take That album: 'We did this song called "Our Music", a rappy song. I went up to Knutsford to his bungalow.' But that was never released, and the first time around it became very clear that Gary was to be the sole songwriter in Take That. This would be the first time that they would sit down in a room together as equals.

'I went down to Malibu where he was renting a house. And he was really lovely, really welcoming. Really sort of open arms. He had this little office where he had a little computer set up with two speakers, and he said, "I've got this idea." And he played me "Shame", the instrumental version of it, and then sang the melody over the top. And then he had to go to the loo, but he put it on repeat, and by the time he came back in I was singing a different melody. And he was like, "Oh dear ... what are you doing there?

… No, no, no, listen to this …" But very jokingly and it was very, very funny. And as it happens he was totally fucking right because there was no need to change what he'd got – the melody's fucking great. And then we both sat together as I came up with the lyric. And it was very easy, very instant. Ayda went out with Dawn while we wrote the song and by the time they'd come back we'd written it.'

Rob had a half-formed idea in his head that they would write a duet that would be an 'anything you can do, I can do better' kind of song. But almost immediately it turned into something else. 'It became the story of us,' he says. 'It was one of those songs that come every now and again that kind of make you cry as you're writing it.'

They swapped line after line, Rob going first, and told their story:

Well there's three versions of this story, mine and yours, and then the truth
Now we can put it down to circumstance, our childhood, then our youth
Out of some sentimental gain I wanted you to feel my pain, but it came
back return to sender.

'It's two people spending a lot of time together, falling out outrageously, spending a lot of time not liking each other, and then realising through the folly and the hubris of youth that maybe we'd got it wrong. Maybe there was an opening for healing. It has that lovely symmetry that the song is about healing and *is* the healing. We were so excited that day. There was just a buzz of: "Fucking hell, it's *happening!*" For the pair of us.'

A day or two later, they wrote another song, 'Heart And I', its title inspired by a song they listened to together that morning, Prefab Sprout's 'When Love Breaks Down'.

'It was instantaneous that me and him were supposed to write together,' says Rob. 'It just really fitted so well.'

* * *

With this new rapport established, soon there were discussions about whether the five of them might work together. Ironically, one main impediment for Rob was the infuriating perception in the British media that he was desperate to do so. Let's allow the ever-graceful Piers Morgan to make the argument as he did in his end-of-2008 newspaper round-up of the year's 'champs and chumps'. (You should just about be able to work out which Rob was.)

Nor is my cup of forgiveness overflowing towards Mr Robbie Williams, the man who heartlessly ditched his old Take That bandmates as he conquered the pop world (well, bits of Europe anyway) and made himself stinking rich in the process. After his last album did so badly that unsold copies were used to – genuinely – make paving slabs in China, the self-styled 'Robster' has desperately been trying to hitch a ride on the astonishing new Take That bandwagon and revive his shot career. I'd love to see Gary and the boys shove him off the back, and rub dirt in his face as he lies face-down in the rubble. They won't, of course, because they're too nice. But one can live in hope.

'I feel a bit bruised and saddened by it,' Rob would say at the time, about what people somehow seemed to believe, 'but that's what's out there. A load of bullies that in a recession want to make their pennies too.' First, it simply didn't make *sense*. 'But it's like, hang on, I've done sixty million albums, and won fourteen Brits, broken a world record for ticket sales, done three nights at Knebworth, and I'm nothing and I'm on my arse? It's just sensationalism for the sake of sensationalism. It's fucking pathetic – and horrible to be perceptionally cast aside like that.'

When you really thought about it, it came down to simple mathematics: if a relative failure like *Rudebox* sold over two million copies, a five-piece Take That album would have to sell over ten million copies to earn him the same income. And there's also geography: Rob has a healthy career in many countries where Take That are barely known. It was so insulting both to believe that he would need to do it for career or financial reasons, and to believe that he would do it because he needed to do it. Perhaps there *were* reasons that he did need to do it, but they were very, very different from the ones that were being used to taunt him. 'I need to go and hide in public,' he explained to me at the time. 'And also I just want to be part of Take That, it looks fun. I've wanted to be in a band ever since I left Take That. So I might as well rejoin Take That.'

* * *

At the end of September 2009, I get a message that Rob is in New York, where I'm living. I'd seen him a couple of weeks earlier, and he'd not even mentioned that he might be coming here. Even now when I meet him at his hotel it's almost like he doesn't want to say too much, as though it might somehow spook what has been happening. He explains that he has secretly been in the studio with Take That, and plays me a little of a song.

He'd been quietly preparing for this first meeting for a month, writing down lyric ideas on stickies: 'I knew it was a big deal and I wanted to impress. And I especially wanted to impress Gary, because he's a proper singer-songwriter and I wanted to come with a heart full of lyrics and a head full of melodies.' That first day it had just been Rob, Gary and Mark. Gary already had backing tracks. 'It was wonderful,' he says. 'I just see Gaz as a balladeer and he turned up with all of this 1980, 1981 stuff from when he loved his weird synth music.' They made a start on about seven songs, and Rob will tell me that he'd figured what his role might be. 'Take That had been writing some pretty epic pop songs that were genuinely touching the heart of the nation,' he says. 'And I saw how I could add to that. Still have it be that, but bring a slant to it that isn't there – slightly crazy, dystopian, apocalyptic. A different way than your straight-up *today will be the greatest day of our lives*. Conspiracy theories and all sorts of wacky ideas and unhinged mentalness in the lyrics that wouldn't have been there.'

One of the seven first ideas, the song he plays me, is called 'The Flood'. Rob can sometimes begin to build lyrics like a magpie's nest. Here he borrowed its first line – *standing on the edge of forever* – from the title of a 1960s *Star Trek* episode. The beginning of the second verse – *back then we were like cavemen but we mapped the moon and the stars* – came from the AboveTopSecret forum discussion he'd noticed that day at Trevor Horn's studio. But just as 'Shame' had been about him and Gary, 'The Flood' became about the five of them:

Although no one understood
We were holding back the flood,
Learning how to dance the rain.

We were holding back the flood
They said we'd never dance again.

A year later, it'll be the song with which they announce their return, and I'll listen to them explain:

'It uses moments from history and time,' Mark will summarise, 'to tell the story of the band. And the breaking down of the wall.'

'The first time around,' Rob will say, 'although it was precarious and unsafe within the band, there was still a safety in numbers against this pandemonium and hysteria that we faced everywhere we went – from our fans, to journalists, to our friends becoming used to us being famous, to our parents being used to us being famous. The only safe place really was us five together. And even that was unsafe. But the flood for me was all the outside forces trying to break the dam. And we were the dam.'

* * *

At the point when they first met up in New York, this wasn't actually a Take That reunion. They had a different idea altogether. 'We were going to reform as a band called The English,' says Rob. 'It was my idea basically to call it something else and they really loved it. The idea was that we'd all be playing instruments and be a proper band and stuff, and they liked it, because I don't think any of us really like the name Take That, and they were excited about the prospect of it being a totally new thing.'

And then Rob pulled the plug. On all of it. This was in the aftermath of the difficult time he'd had promoting *Reality Killed The Video Star*. 'I just went off the idea completely – of even being a pop star let alone being a pop star and being in Take That again.' There's some footage in the documentary *Look Back, Don't Stare* of a clearly exasperated Jason, who sounds as though he had half been expecting this kind of let-down, explaining that he has pointed out to Rob how 'your whims have a direct effect on us'. Rarely has the word 'whims' sounded so disparaging.

'I got scared,' Rob says. 'And I'd kind of let everybody down in Take That again by saying that I wasn't going to be doing what I'd said we'd be doing.'

Mark went to talk with Rob, to make the case that they should carry on. All he needed to do was to commit to enough days in the studio. Any kind of other stuff, that didn't matter. Rob finally agreed.

The English were now forgotten. They were Take That, and they were coming back.

That spring, Rob described to me his new relationships with the other four: 'Well, Jay's kind of the sage. He's kind of your Buddhist hippie that talks in Pink Floyd. Howard … he doesn't say much, Howard, but every now and again he'll get on a roll for a couple of hours, and he'll be the funniest fucker you've ever met. He still does stomach-hurting funnies. But the rest of the time he's shy – he's shy and unsure of himself. Mark thinks he's shit, and at the same you go into work with him and he comes up with these brilliant melodies and he's obviously really talented. He's also never happy with anything that he's done, and always thinks that it could be bettered. But we all think we're shit apart from Gaz, who doesn't reckon he's ace but he's quite happy in his own shoes. Gaz is so black and white: "Why would you think that?" "Gaz, I hurt when things are said …" "Who *cares*? … It makes me laugh when they say that … It makes me feel sorry for them when they say that … Why would you even take it on board?" He can swat things away. Or at least you believe he can.'

This is what Gary would say: 'We were all writing, throwing ideas in. It was the album we'd always wanted to make that we were making, and we were all excited, and proud. It was gorgeous, is what it was.'

'Making the record,' says Mark, 'we were able to talk all the time. Many afternoons we'd just sit around and talk about the old days, and piece things together.'

Or here's how Rob explained it in an email he sent to one of his bandmates while they were finishing the album:

I'm buzzing about being back. Sometimes when everybody's in the room I get that excited that I can't look at anyone. I get a bit blushy.

* * *

REVEAL

May–July 2011

In a dressing room at the Sunderland Stadium of Light, where tomorrow Take That will begin their stadium tour, already the most successful British tour of all time in terms of the number of tickets sold, Es Devlin, who is responsible for the remarkable stage set down below, shares some worries.

'We're about two weeks behind,' she explains. The giant man-robot that dominates the stage, who Take That will christen Om, arrived two months late. 'It'll be ready for the DVD,' she says, breezily.

'That's all that matters,' says the Pet Shop Boys' Chris Lowe. They're the opening act on this whole tour, and this is their dressing room.

There's a knock on the door.

'This is fun, isn't it?' says Rob. He takes a seat, and starts chatting, then looks around him, puzzled and uneasy. Something is missing.

'Did Mark Owen not follow me in?' he asks.

He has come up here with Mark, and accidentally left Mark standing in the corridor. Mark, with impossible politeness, is – it turns out when someone checks – just standing out there. He's now ushered in.

They catch up a little. Neil Tennant mentions that he's recently redecorated, and Rob says, 'I've got a wife who does that sort of stuff.' Eventually they discuss the show. Mark explains how much time they've lost this week through bad weather, and Rob talks about the stresses of the dive he does from the top of the stage structure.

'I'd find it hard climbing up there,' says Chris.

Rob looks at him as though he's crazy.

'We've got a lift,' Rob says.

'Remember when you said "nothing dangerous on this tour"?' Mark says to Rob, laughing.

He nods. 'And then I saw that …' he says. Meaning that he saw a daredevil entertainment opportunity he didn't know how to resist.

Rob then shares a weird dream about being at Neil's house, and Neil says that there's been a weird rumour going around near where he has a house in the north-east that his car had broken down and then had been seen being pushed near the local reservoir by Rob and Elton John. And there was also a rumour that Rob had been into their local butcher's in the village.

'That was in 2007,' says Rob, deadpan, getting up to leave. 'The pork tour.'

* * *

Aside from some small promotional shows, Rob hadn't been back onstage since the grim end of the Close Encounters tour in December 2006, and he hadn't given any indication that he was ready to face doing more solo shows of that kind. Yet for some reason he assumed he would be able to do these Take That shows. I can understand his theory of why the five-piece Take That part of the show might be easier – the idea that people aren't just looking at *you* all the time, and the notion, even if only metaphorical, that there might be, as he fancifully put it, 'your bit where you're just playing the tambourine'. But he would also be doing a half-hour or so of his own hits, just him on the stage. Whatever demons he associated with being on a stage alone in front of a huge crowd, why wouldn't this summon them as before? Somehow, he felt this would be different.

Perhaps the new routines he adopted helped. Every night, he would do long, structured vocal warm-ups with Gary. He'd also watch inspirational speeches on YouTube: 'locker room stuff where the coach is going like that … just using tools to give myself some confidence.'

Whatever the reason, he was right. He sent me an email after the first show:

LAST NIGHT WAS FRIGGIN AWESOME … AND I WAS SO RELAXED. LOOKS LIKE THIS MIGHT BE FUN.

After, he'd explain at more length.

'That's why being in Take That is so wonderful,' he says, 'because it's so easy. There's no pressure. There's nobody stepping on anybody's toes in the band, and you sort of shoulder the responsibility of being stared at by a lot of people, and that feels really cool. When I'm with the boys and we're onstage, you get to look at the audience and take it all in, as opposed to when I'm by myself I'm constantly thinking of what to do next, how to present myself next, what shape to pull, what face to pull etc., etc. And before you know it you've been thinking and concentrating for two hours. But with the boys you get to sit back and almost be the audience as well. You can wander about, stare at the audience, have time to yourself. The responsibility's evened out. It doesn't feel like you're giving too much of yourself. It doesn't feel like you're being drained.'

Or, putting it another way, 'It's simply a case that I've been lonely out there, doing it by myself.'

* * *

The tour wasn't completely without drama. Towards the end, in Copenhagen, Rob ate a bad hotel-restaurant lobster and was as ill as he'd ever been. One concert had to be cancelled.

There was also a small disagreement over what should happen to the large man in their midst, the £1.5-million robot called Om. Mark suggested they gave him to the city of Manchester, but Rob said that he wanted to put him in his garden in Wiltshire as 'a memento for all the time together'. The disagreement was a little awkward. At one point Mark asked Rob whether he wanted Om out of ego.

'Yeah,' Rob replied, considering the question, 'at some point I'll go: "Look at this! How amazing's that?" I can't deny that there will be some ego wrapped up in something. But that's not the main reason I want it. It'd just look great in the garden.'

And now, if you walk out the back door of Rob's Wiltshire house, past the shoes and boots and umbrellas and neglected metal-detecting equipment, and start walking uphill along the curved driveway, then on your left, halfway to the helicopter hangar, amidst the shrubs and trees, hidden from public view, crouching but still imposing, there it is: Om.

'I always say hello to it,' says Rob. 'I go and stand with it. Talk to it.'

Does it talk back?

'Not much. It's thinking. Still thinking.'

* * *

2013–2014

Jason had been privately saying for some time that he wasn't going to be part of Take That's next plans. The Music Industry Trusts Award concert for Gary, the five of them onstage at the end singing 'Never Forget', remains, for now, their final performance all together.

This only exacerbated a difficult situation for everyone after the Progress tour, in terms of communicating what Take That now was, and who was in it. Whenever anyone was interviewed, they were always asked: would Rob be involved in the next thing, or would he not? It was understood that Rob was going back to his solo career, as he had always intended to, but that most likely they would all work together in the future. Even so, each time any of them said anything at all, it seemed to create a new headline. Either Rob was back, or he was snubbing them, or they were snubbing him, round in a circle, over and over and over.

Meanwhile, in their private discussions, tentative plans would sometimes be made, usually somewhere in the mid-distance, and then would often be unmade. Everyone seemed to agree that at some point there should be some kind of tour, presumably pegged to some kind of landmark anniversary. But when, and which anniversary, kept changing.

* * *

All of this could be awkward enough; Jason's as yet unannounced departure made it harder. It came to a head in early 2014 when Rob was beginning his Swing tour. At the end of the previous year Rob, after seriously considering it, had told Gary that he couldn't be involved in Take That's next project. There were a number of reasons, one being that it didn't seem quite so enticing without all five of them.

'In March,' says Rob, 'Gaz was on *Chatty Man* with Alan Carr, and I didn't watch the interview, but the upshot of it was: he had left the door open for me still, saying "well, it's down to Rob whether he wants to". And then it was in the newspapers, and I Googled myself and in two hundred and fifty news stories was: "Robbie's been given an ultimatum". Gary said, "Well, we've got till May till we know what we're doing." So I got the hump with that, because I thought: I know where this is heading. This is heading towards: Robbie Williams spoils reunion and he's a nasty bastard again. That's how it felt, anyway. And I don't want to look like the bad guy. So I was a bit angry about that.'

That's what was in his mind when *The Sun* came to interview him in Vienna.

'I'm stressed at the start of the tour, and she's, "So where are you with the ultimatum?" And I went, "What fucking ultimatum? I told them in December I'm not doing it." I said, "It's Jason who's not doing it, not me."'

He wasn't supposed to say that. Nobody knew about Jason's departure. Rob's management quickly had to let Take That know what Rob had done. For a while, it was almost back to the bad old days.

'Gary sends an email back to Josie going, "Why does he want to do something like that? It's so destructive. Does he want the band to implode?" I woke up in Austria and I'd got an email from Howard and it was really short and it just said, "look, I know it's probably good for you, but that wasn't good for us, didn't like what you did". I thought, "What the fuck?" Then I sent an email back that was a bit terse and angry. And Gary sent an email. Then I wrote this needlessly long email, detailing other superfluous stuff: "Well, when you did this in deh deh deh … I said deh deh deh and you said deh deh and it's because of deh deh deh." I shouldn't have sent it. You'd have thought I might have learned by now. It was an emotional response. And the foundations of it weren't built on solid ground. It was just, "I don't like the fact that I've been given this ultimatum. I said that I'm not fucking doing it – just say that I'm not fucking doing it." They were, "This has to be engineered in the right way." In my head it was just: "Why don't you just say Jason's not doing it?" But to them, and quite rightly because it's them and their feelings and their career and their life, it had to be handled with kid gloves.'

More emails followed, with more recriminations and no solutions. Rob credits Gary with being the one who eventually calmed the waters, and persuaded everyone that these fractious exchanges were going nowhere and solving nothing. 'He's the bigger and better person than me,' Rob says. At one point, he adds, Gary also wrote: 'I hope this doesn't stop us speaking for years (again).'

And it hasn't. Growing up, it turns out, isn't necessarily about learning how to always get along; it's about learning what to do at those times when you don't.

* * *

Rob is not sure how or why, but at the time *The Sun* didn't announce the news about Jason that he'd blurted out. The news broke five months later when Jason issued a gracious statement thanking the band and the fans in which he stated it bluntly: 'There have been no fallings out, only a decision on my part that I no longer wish to do this.' Rob makes no secret of the fact that he would have wished Jason to feel otherwise. 'It's a shame,' he says. 'Because the magic is the magic when it's the five. And also I like his company.' But he also remains supportive and protective of whatever decision Jason chooses to make.

When the Jason news did finally become public, Nigel Martin-Smith added to his impressive track record in sensitively and accurately interpreting for the media his ex-charges' motives.

'I think that Jason's behaviour is deplorable,' he pronounced. 'This is about him wanting attention.'

Just after this interview appeared, a new tweet just happened to appear in Rob's Twitter feed:

Attention-seeking man claims man is attention-seeking.

8

October 2016

Rob has spent years trying to understand, and trying to explain, the peculiar nature and particular features of the fame he has – fame which at times he has chased with gusto, which at times has simply been bestowed upon him as he got on with other things, and which at times has pursued him relentlessly despite his best efforts to evade it. He's well aware that there are many who don't understand why he, and those like him, can't just accept what has come their way as nothing but a magnificent gift, and who think any complaints or reservations they might have are just the indulgent bleating of those too spoiled, selfish and stupid to know how lucky they are.

But the truth is that Rob knows full well how lucky he is. He doesn't need to be senselessly self-deprecating about all the talents that he does have to appreciate all the luck that was still required for those talents to find the place and the time and the opportunity where they could combine and allow him to do all he has done, and to become all he has become. There are always far more ways that a life like this might not have happened than ways that it could have. And his gratitude for the life he has, and has had, is deep and real.

That doesn't mean that there aren't aspects to it, aspects intrinsic to what fame and celebrity bring along with them in the modern era, which can't be difficult – and especially difficult for someone like him who, with whatever constitution and set of personality traits he has found himself with, happens to be particularly ill-suited to some of what comes with his marvellous life. And so it's also perfectly natural that he's always searching for new ways to explain the aspects of this that he knows people struggle to understand.

Here's an analogy he has been using recently:

'You know what showbiz is like? You know when everybody is singing "Happy Birthday" to you in a restaurant. Show business is like that uneasy feeling you get when they bring the cake out and the whole restaurant is singing "Happy Birthday" to you, and everybody's well-meaning, they mean it with love, but for that moment, you can't wait until "Happy Birthday" stops being sung. It's that *all the time*. That's how fame feels. That's how I feel like when I'm out walking anywhere in England.'

But, meanwhile, you're supposed to recognise that it's your birthday and that something great is happening?

'Yeah, but you're just like, "… Oh God, no, not this song! … Get to the end of the song … Thanks! …"'

It's your special day!

'Yeah. That's fame. It's like people are doing a really nice thing, but you want it to stop.' He laughs. 'So you can just eat the cake.'

* * *

November 2016

Rob has a connection with his closest fans, mostly conducted via the internet, that he knows some people might find odd. The way that this has functioned has evolved over the years – in the *Take The Crown* era, for instance, the main way he would communicate with people was chatting in the chat box while playing an online poker game through his website. More recently that's been replaced by the membership area of his website called Upfront. It has a forum where members ask questions of him and each other, and he tends to chime in fairly frequently on anything that interests him. There's also a chat room, and he'll turn up there, too, at random, every few days, and spend maybe half an hour exchanging thoughts.

Ayda used to find it odd. 'You share intimate details at about three in the morning!' she complained to him once. 'He'll say, "Babe, so would you be happy if I got *Acieeeddd!* tattooed on my body?" And I'm like, "Yeah ... why?" And he says, "Cool," and he starts typing! I'm like, "*Really?* You're actually typing our intimate dialogue to some fan at three in the morning?"'

But then she joined Instagram and started doing it too.

'I suppose it is weird,' Rob says. 'I'm a bit weird. But it's therapeutic being able to talk to a bunch of people about the truth. And who doesn't want to be in a room full of people that enjoy what you do, and like you? Especially where it seems there's, like, a world of hate in a similar sort of place ...' – by which he means a large part of the rest of the internet – '... that doesn't. I suppose the truth is way weirder than I'd like to be public: I'm agoraphobic, I don't go out. I have an outlet sometimes where I chat on chat rooms too, like other people do. And this one happens to be mine, about me. That's where I find myself. I like talking about my music in there. I like understanding that the way I feel about that song when I wrote it is the way that they feel about it too. It feels great. When they mention songs from my catalogue that the general public don't know about and they do, and it means the world to them, that feels brilliant. It feels better than somebody not being nice about me.'

I've spent quite a lot of time reading and observing these back-and-forths, and the general tone is perhaps more thoughtful, sensible and calmly supportive – in either direction – than you might expect, rather than overexcited and sycophantic (though of course there's some of that, too). There are very few complete loose cannons, though Rob can be surprisingly unsettled, and almost despairing, when anyone does rock the boat with provocative unpleasantness, as though they're spoiling one of the few quiet, safe places he knows.

So if it seems a little mad, a 42-year-old pop star spending time on his computer talking to his fans, understand that it also often allows an antidote to a greater madness. Here's where he can explain, to people who care to listen, the truth about whatever latest drip-drip insanity or inanity might have been reported elsewhere. You can't attack every misstatement that is made about you, or reasonably hope that they could be corrected, and some of them would seem so trivial that you would get judged all over again just for caring about them. But even if it doesn't really change anything, I think it may be useful to his own well-being to constantly be leaving a trail of truth somewhere out there; just to know that there's a few more people who know.

Most of what he says is in quick replies or quips – a few words here, a short sentence there. Just occasionally, though, he finds that there is something he needs to get off his chest. It's a complicated relationship, the one between a fan and the object of their fandom, and it is laden with unstated expectations and hopes on either side, expectations and hopes that often don't match. And occasionally, when that gap becomes too evident, and especially when he feels he is being unreasonably attacked for falling short, Rob feels the need to say something.

After he visits Italy for some promotion, one fan posts about how upset she is at the way she feels she has been treated, criticising Rob for not stopping to sign autographs, or even say hello, to her and four other fans outside a radio station. 'What have we done?' she complains, at the end of a screed of upset. 'We have shown you love.'

It hits a nerve. What he posts as a reply is as clear and as detailed an insight into one person's navigation of the convoluted contours of celebrity life, with all its layered responsibilities and misunderstandings, as you could imagine:

Speaking as a human and not as a pop star for a moment. In a world where it seems most people want a photograph or to meet me, not only 'fans', it's made me agoraphobic. I don't go out at all. I don't go to the reception or bar of any hotel. I stay in my room. When I get home, I stay in my house. This is okay, it's my life and my life is beautiful but there is a cause and effect to everything. Think about that for a second. As a human I'm agoraphobic. For real. Not a joke or an excuse. I'm also a chronic people-pleaser. If I did everything that people want/expect from me I feel exhausted. If I don't do everything people want me to do I feel guilty. So I don't go out. I think you will find that after a very long day of promo I stopped outside the hotel and signed everyone's albums. I was very happy and grateful that the songs have reached their destination. But I also have to look after my own well-being too. And I will. And I do. My job is to write the best album that I can do in hopes that it finds a place in your hearts and hopefully becomes the soundtrack to your lives. This I've spent the last 3 years trying to do. Agonizing at every turn. Hoping and praying that I'm getting it right. Then I will go on tour and give everything that I've got so we all 'hopefully' have a very special shared experience. I take being the conduit to your good time VERY seriously. Those two things are what you can expect from me. Anything else after that is on you. This is written by a man in a hotel room in Cannes looking out of a window at a beach I can't go on and a street I can't walk on. I say this not for your pity or sympathy. I share this so maybe there can be some empathy between the two of us. An understanding. I don't want to be considered rude. It hurts me. But I also can't do everything that people expect me to do. That hurts me too. 'But there were just 5 of us'. Yes, and 2 hours ago there were 30 and yesterday there were 50 and in the last 25 years there were 500 thousand. If you think by buying my album we are entering into some sort of contract, where I also have to meet you and have my picture taken outside a hotel that I've personally told no one I'm staying at, then I ask you kindly and with love to rethink your terms and conditions. I'll say it again, I'm agoraphobic and I have a fear of meeting people or being met. Go easy on me. Expect me to give everything I've got for you when I'm onstage. Expect an album written with you in mind. But please from the bottom of my heart expect me to protect my privacy and well-being too.

Hand on heart, with love.

Rob

'I decided to write that,' he reflects, 'to let everybody know: look, this is the situation with me.'

In keeping with the general tone of the forum, most of the members rally around, empathising with his viewpoint, though a few, inevitably, take it as a rebuke, one that they resent. What he didn't write, because it made no difference to the general point that he was trying to make, was just how crazy it can routinely get in situations like that, in situations where fans wait for him in public, something he never solicits or encourages. And how especially crazy it had been on that particular day – though just the special craziness he sees new examples of all the time – when he supposedly let down those five Italian fans.

'What they didn't see, as well, is that when I left the radio station that she was talking about,' he says, 'a man ran in the middle of the road through traffic with a child under his arm – literally a baby – and a camera in the other. Begging me to stop and open the door to have a picture taken.'

* * *

February 2017

One day he gives an impromptu tutorial to several dozen fans in his chat room about the banners people bring to his concerts, and how frustrating he finds it when people demand that their specific banner be acknowledged while he is trying to entertain 70,000 other people. But he does also offer some advice:

I think surreal banners would be ace ... just one that says 'my knees smell' ... something like that ... 'I LIKE car parks' ... or 'golf sale this way' ... banners that confuse me … or just one that says 'banner' … or just the price of bread in your local shop … 'I've not come very far to see you' … you know, I'll totally forget about this chat and in the summer I'll be 'what the fuck? Why are people so mental?'

* * *

November 2016

Finally, over three years after they bought it, the Williamses' new London house is ready and they have moved in. Rob does an interview with the BBC there. 'It's an old artist's house,' he explains, 'Luke Fildes used to be the guy that owned the place. I think he painted George V upstairs in the bedroom. There's plenty of space for my head and my neuroses to flutter about.' More recently, this house belonged to the film director Michael Winner. The papers are quickly full of stories that Rob has had healers in to banish old spirits, picking up on something Ayda has said on *Loose Women*.

'I think we did a bit of that,' he says. 'I wasn't aware that that happened but I was told after the event. Yeah, you never know. Every little helps.'

Not, just to be clear, with banishing the spirit of Michael Winner, as some of the papers seemed to be implying. More just to freshen the old, and to air out enough space to allow new lives in.

The grandest room in the house is the master bedroom, with its two-storey ceiling, imposing windows and staircase up to a second level behind the bed. It has its own balcony, facing towards the street, where Rob goes out in the winter air for a cigarette. On one of their first days there, he is doing this when he notices a white-haired man walking up the street carrying two white plastic bags. If the man sees Rob, he doesn't acknowledge him.

It is Rob's next-door neighbour, former Led Zeppelin guitarist Jimmy Page.

* * *

The tabloids have been enjoying the great Robbie Williams versus Jimmy Page property wars for the past couple of years. On one level, the story is a mundane one. Page has submitted objections concerning proposals to renovate Rob's house, and dealing with these has considerably delayed the renovation. The delays have been frustrating, but Rob's main attitude towards all of this has been that it's a funny tale to tell.

Unfortunately, things get a little messier this month when Rob is in Italy, appearing live on a big Italian radio show called *Deejay Chiama Italia*. Early in the interview Rob explains how they moved into this London house two weeks ago. The host says something in Italian from which two words clearly stand out – 'Jimmy Page' – and Rob laughs.

'Yeah, my next door neighbour is Jimmy Page ...'

'He doesn't want you to renovate or something?'

'Oh, he doesn't want a lot of things.'

'There is still some beef going on with Jimmy Page?'

'Not from *me*. Not from me.'

'We can tell from your facial expression that Jimmy Page is kind of like an asshole.'

Rob doesn't actually rise to the bait. He smiles slightly, but shakes his head to indicate that he won't be going there.

'No, no, no. Let me tell you. Let me tell you. Our next-door neighbour isn't happy with us trying to renovate our house, and it's caused a problem, and it will probably continue to cause a problem, but what is great about this whole thing is that it's Jimmy Page with Led Zeppelin, and it's not Jimmy the accountant from Chelsea. So at least we've got a good story.'

'What's so big about the renovation?'

'Nothing really. Genuinely. No, no, no, no. So we bought this house and it was dilapidated ... It just needed a lick of paint and new stuff to be added ... But I'm next door now, I've got a studio in my house, we could write songs together.'

At this point, the DJs play 'Party Like A Russian' for the listeners, and Rob assumes that their conversation in the studio is no longer being broadcast over the airwaves. And it isn't. But what Rob doesn't know – and what would be very unusual anywhere else in the world – is that this show

450

transmits a continuous live internet stream of whatever takes place in the studio. What Rob says next, he clearly has no idea that he is also sharing with an audience – look at how careful he has just been in what he has said so far on air. But he's less careful now, and these words will go round the world. Page, inevitably, isn't happy. Lawyers get involved.

'I was advised very strongly by my wife to swallow, apologise …' says Rob a while later. 'So I have. Considering it's not my game to be diplomatic, I have been.'

Time – and perhaps also future renovation plans – will tell whether calm now settles upon their road. The two neighbours have yet to run into each other face-to-face.

'A lot of me will be embarrassed, too,' says Rob. 'Because I'm a people-pleaser, and I've offended the great Jimmy Page. I still am like, "Oh! We've upset the next-door neighbour and he's a grown-up!" It would be nice just to have an awkward conversation – you know, conversation's awkward anyway – with the next-door neighbour as we're walking in and out of the park with the kids.'

* * *

Rob has noticed a brief interview by Liam Gallagher, the gift that keeps on giving, at the premiere of the Oasis documentary *Supersonic*, in which he derisively refers to the absence of his brother Noel: 'He's probably in his big house, eating tofu and having a face peel. That's what posh people do.'

This makes Rob laugh.

'My second meal in my big house,' Rob observes, 'was tofu and lentils. That's what actually happened in my big house.'

* * *

On the private jet to Amsterdam, Guy asks Rob how the house is.

'Oh my God,' Rob replies. 'It's fucking incredible. And doesn't look like anything I've done. I'm so glad my wife has got amazing taste. What she's done with it is magical … I had zero input. Thank God. It would look so much different if it were left to me, and it's so much better.'

He tells Guy that they also had a good family day out at the zoo, all things considered. 'Petted a pygmy hippopotamus called Nicky,' he says.

'Were you in with the public?' Guy asks.

'Yes.'

'It was okay?'

'Well, I was in disguise,' Rob says. He wore a hat and glasses.

'And it actually worked?' asks Guy.

'Kind of, kind of not,' Rob replies. 'There were moments when it nearly became me that the zoo was about.'

* * *

At the end of the week, *The Heavy Entertainment Show* will enter the British album charts at number one, his twelfth number one, behind only Elvis Presley and The Beatles. ('I feel relieved,' he says afterwards. 'I remember people saying "how are you going to celebrate?" and I thought: well, I'm just going to celebrate by being relieved.')

But first there are the reviews. Rob may have imagined that the warmth with which his return has so far been greeted, even in areas of the press that have traditionally been suspicious of or hostile towards him, might also extend to the reviews of his album. But though there will be some very good reviews, in general that expectation, it turns out, is a stretch too far. You might sensibly wonder if this means nothing more than that the reviewers just don't love *this* album, but that's not the predominant tone of their reviews. Their principal criticism seems to be that Robbie Williams has made a Robbie Williams album. And sometimes they express a kind of bemusement that anyone would think to do that in this day and age.

Typical, overall, is what Rob refers to as the 'begrudgingly good' review by Kitty Empire in *The Observer* which concludes with the sentence:

If ever something was needed to reconfirm his pop star status, here it is: you still want to biff him.

'I'm glad she used the word "biff",' he says.

* * *

Rob has been asked to duet on 'Imagine' with Chris Martin at the NRJ Awards as a tribute to the victims of the terrorist attack at the Paris venue the Bataclan. The original proposal was for them to sing 'Tears In Heaven', but Rob's not even sure about the whole concept, or whether the two of them singing 'Imagine' is a good idea. He asks Michael to contact Chris Martin's people so they can discuss it. (In the end, they'll decide to perform separately.)

Rob mentions that he just read that 'Imagine', a song that holds an enduring power over him, was recently named as the worst song ever in a Twitter poll, and says how weird that is. The other songs he noticed on the list are 'Love Shack' ('I enjoy "Love Shack"') and Nickelback's 'Rockstar'. 'I think I've got three songs on there,' he mentions. 'I didn't see. Probably "Angels".'

I call up the list – 337 songs curated from tweeted suggestions received by a 37-year-old artist from Brighton – on my phone.

'Don't read mine,' he says.

I tell him he's got a couple.

'Is "Angels" one of them?'

I concede that he's actually got more than a couple.

He laughs, and asks for the list. It's 'Angels', 'Millennium', 'Rock DJ', 'Candy', 'Freedom', 'Mack The Knife' and 'Rudebox'.

'Wow,' he says.

I don't bother to mention that he has more entries than anyone else on the whole list. The Beatles have six, and no one else is even close. It's the kind of confusing hybrid of insult and compliment that in some ways characterises his whole career.

* * *

In a break this evening, Rob checks the comments on his Instagram.

Next to one post, someone has written a one-word comment: 'Horrible'.

Their user name is spoonfulofpositivity.

Clearly not a very big spoon.

* * *

453

On the plane from Holland to Germany, he ponders something that perplexes him:

'Quite often in reviews or interviews, it's 'he can't need the money'. That's something that's said a bit. Which is a weird way of thinking. That you'd do it till you get a lump sum and then you fuck off because you couldn't possibly enjoy writing songs or the job? It's such a weird way to view it.'

* * *

This evening's show in Germany is a big TV special all about him, and it'll turn out very well, but the making of it turns into a bit of an ordeal – once the cameras are rolling, all kinds of things are sprung on Rob that hadn't been agreed to. In the post-mortem afterwards, he brings up his worst TV-show nightmare in recent history, when Take That were to perform 'The Flood' at the San Remo Music Festival in 2010:

'So Take That, we're in Monaco, we're waiting in our hotel room, and then we're told to go, and then we get in the car and we go. Because we're all good working-class lads that do that shit. And that's what we do. Nobody's a diva. Or has no concept of time. We go to San Remo – it's a weird festival, the show goes on for about ten hours and the audience is asleep – and we get out of the van, back door and straight onto the stage to do our rehearsal. And there's George Clooney's at-the-time missus, some other guy with a microphone. And he comes up and goes, over the microphone, huge orchestra, room full of TV people, "Robbie, this is not *good*, you are *late*, and you should not be late …" On the microphone so everybody can hear. Me having zero clue. Having a go at me over the microphone? You know how I am with time? I'm good with time. I pride myself … I don't even *pride* myself, it's natural, it's just what we fucking do. Because it's rude not to. I'm told to go, I go, I arrive.'

Rob was so angry that he just walked off the stage. He went upstairs and declared that he wasn't doing it. But then, because he was in a band with four other people, he relented. He took his revenge in a more obtuse, and possibly pointless, way. You can see the footage on YouTube. The opening chords of 'The Flood' boom out, Rob steps to the microphone and begins to sing. What comes out of his mouth, and the reason for it, will make sense to almost nobody, but it is what he feels he needs to do. That is why, for one night only, the song begins:

Standing on the foot of our Trevor
But our Trevor was clever
Shouting love at the world.

This evening's German show does at least give him an opportunity to recycle the Don McLean line his father told him about.

'You ask, what does "Angels" mean to me? It means I only have to work when I want to.'

* * *

However hard someone who is not famous thinks about what it would be like to be famous, I doubt that anyone who hasn't lived that life could actually think through some of the smaller, odder consequences. This, for instance, is something which Rob just happens to mention one day by chance in a German hotel when he is talking about the awkward moment when you meet a gaggle of people from the local record company or from radio stations, and they just stare at you, expecting you to lead the conversation. And then he mimes the inevitable mass shaking of hands that you do in such circumstances.

'And I've just been for a piss. I didn't wash my hands. I never do. Because I'm always going to shake somebody's hand when I leave the toilet, so I never want my hands to be wet, because that's awful when you shake somebody's hand and they're wet. So you're probably shaking a bit of my piss. "How's your day been?"'

It's also another way of describing the messed-up Moebius strip of fame: when you're famous and in public, because you're always only seconds away from having to shake someone's hands, you can't wash your hands after using the toilet because, however well you dry, your hands will inevitably still be damp for a few more seconds, and if you are famous enough then those seconds may invariably involve a handshake, and the next person that

you meet will then think that you-the-celebrity has piss on your hands …
and so the only way to avoid that is to leave the toilet without cleaning off
any actual traces of piss that might really be on your hands. He'll use hand
sanitiser when he can, but in the meantime …

Or, to put it more simply:

Fame – always creating the problem it claims to be solving.

* * *

Rob makes a trip to Australia. He feels more comfortable being Robbie
Williams in Australia than anywhere else in the world. 'They really embrace
me,' he says. 'I feel really good. I'm allowed to be a pop star there, and I
don't really have to worry about what I say. It's not used against you. It's not
taken out of context.'

Which often, of course, involves him saying or doing things that
nonetheless stir up plenty of trouble elsewhere. He already did a fair bit of
that with the evening of Australian radio interviews at the beginning of the
campaign. That's what reignited the whole Spice Girls hullabaloo, but there
was more. He prefigures the other fuss in the evening's first interview.

'I'm starting on another round of promotion,' he explains, 'and I'm
sure that I will offend a lot more people on this round of promotion. Let
me just get my apologies in before I do that. All pop stars and actors or TV
personalities, let me just apologise for everything I say about you in the next
few months. I don't mean it – I've got a sort of twat Tourette's thing that I
do. And I full-on apologise to everybody in showbiz.'

To which one of the DJs immediately responds, 'Do you want to
apologise to Kylie in Australia? You could probably do that now.'

'Do I need to apologise to Kylie?' Rob asks.

And he doesn't – not yet. But the night is young.

An hour later, he's explaining to another Australian breakfast show
about the song 'Disco Symphony', which has become a duet with Kylie
but which he hasn't yet released. The hosts, Kyle and Jackie O, have just
been reminiscing with him about the time he gave them one of his pubic

hairs to give away, and, right in the middle of this conversation about Kylie Minogue, Rob now suddenly blurts out, for no entirely obvious reason, 'Maybe you could get her to cut her pubes and then send them to me?'

'Happy to ask her!' says Kyle.

'There you go, press boys!' Rob exclaims. 'There's an article for you: Robbie wants Kylie's pubes. Sorry, Kylie. I'm starting my international tour of apologies early. Sorry, Kylie, for saying that.'

At the end of the interview, Rob hands the phone to Michael.

'Kylie's pubes will ...' he says, and needs to say no more.

A couple of days later, Michael mentions that he's had an email from Kylie's manager. 'Doesn't mention the pubes,' he reassures Rob.

'Oh good,' says Rob. 'Yeah, I just hope if she does see that, she sees it in context – them getting my pubes ...'

But as he says this, I think he's realising that it's not really a context that explains much of anything at all.

There's plenty more like this once he's arrived in Australia. He goes on a big TV show called *The Project*, and when the host, Pete Helliar, explains that Rob is his wife's 'leave pass' – the liaison she is notionally allowed to have without consequences – and one of the other panellists suggests Rob could give Helliar something to pass on, Rob grabs either side of Helliar's head with his hands and kisses him firmly on the lips, then says to the camera, 'Hi, Bridget ... I just pashed your husband.'

The next day, Rob is doing interviews on the red carpet at the Aria Awards, and he has just told someone about Ayda's post-motherhood 'Picasso tits' and is telling an interviewer called Jonathan Moran, 'I do think Australia is definitely my spiritual home – people seem to get me here.' Moran tells Rob he's just jealous about last night's TV kiss. Naturally, Rob immediately grabs either side of Moran's head ...

* * *

Back in London, Rob accompanies Ayda for a date night to see David Bowie's art collection, which is being exhibited prior to being auctioned.

They're given a personal private tour while the exhibition is closed. Almost too much attention, in fact – Rob has to shut down the whole 'David's journey began ...' contextual speech that the person escorting them wants to deliver. Rob also finds some of the art quite disturbing. 'There was a huge one,' he says, 'which was a woman being raped by two guys.' The women escorting them started to explain – 'what David thought was, this is an important piece and ...' – but Rob couldn't get past the fact that it was somebody being raped. (The picture he's referring to is war artist Peter Howson's *Croatian and Muslim*, which depicts two men raping a Muslim woman while forcing her head into a toilet, a portrait that was rejected by the Imperial War Museum, who had commissioned it, and was bought instead by Bowie.)

Still, there are some pieces Rob likes, and he wonders whether he should try to buy anything. One of the thoughts going round his head is that he knows the artworks' prices will inevitably be higher than they would have otherwise been because of their unusual provenance – the 'Bowie tax', as he calls it – and he isn't sure how he feels about that in light of that article he read that mentioned him after David Bowie's death. 'I was walking around thinking about the thing Dylan Jones had said,' he explains, 'And thinking, "Yeah, I'll just get a piece of his art, stick in my house." And then I thought: he might be thinking I'm paying the Bowie tax on it and be laughing at me.'

* * *

Today Rob's back at *The X Factor* to perform 'Love My Life'. He sits in the dressing-room trailer. 'It's a weird thing being here, you know,' he says. 'Just a discomfort I don't find anywhere else. I don't know, maybe it's because it's a judging competition show. I think the energy there is a bit weird. It's like doing a tabloid gig.'

I'm pretty sure that everyone around him is thinking of Rob's awkward *X Factor* history, but no one wants to bring it up. But then, indirectly, he does.

'Also,' he says, 'it's like I'm returning to the scene of the crime. And I felt like this before that.'

Today, it goes smoothly. He feels awkward performing on his own in a wide space, fixed to one spot, while some childlike line drawings play on the screen behind him, until at the very end drawings of two small children are framed behind him, but it's effective. As hoped and expected, this song will be the kind of success his album needs – it will be on the radio for months, and, despite all the forces against it, even make a sustained appearance in the singles chart.

His performance is pre-recorded in the afternoon, and inserted into tonight's live show, so by the time it is broadcast he is back at his new house, on the sofa with a group of people, including Ayda and his mother. When the time comes for his appearance he covers his face with his shirt, turns his head away and blocks his ears. This isn't done in a theatrical, funny way to draw attention to himself. He really doesn't want to see it. As Robbie Williams performs on the TV, Jan rubs her son's knee.

Afterwards his mother says, 'Well done – great, that was.'

'It's over,' says Ayda. 'You did it.'

'Did I?' he asks, uncertainly.

'It was great,' she says.

'Yeah,' he says, unenthusiastic, unconvinced.

'You looked amazing,' Ayda continues. 'You looked skinny. You didn't look like you were on drugs. You looked handsome. The screens were good.'

At this very moment, a mouse scuttles across the room, pauses in front of the TV, then runs off.

* * *

At 7:25 the next morning, Rob arrives at the breakfast table, sits Teddy down for breakfast, cues up his *X Factor* performance on the computer in front of her so that she can see what Daddy got up to yesterday, and then lets himself out through the doors that open from the living room into the garden, so that he can smoke, and so that he can avoid watching himself.

I go out with him to chat and keep him company. It's cold.

'Not necessarily really up right now,' he mutters.

It takes time to get used to a new house, and there are details that he is yet to master. When he tries to reopen the door to let us back inside, he realises that we are locked out. We have to tap on the window for some time before someone hears, and lets us back in.

* * *

One day when Ayda is busy she sends Rob on his own to check out a school for Teddy. He finds this a disorienting experience.

'I so felt out of my depth, because I'm so uneducated, and it really wasn't my thing, school, and I'm at these incredible schools, they're just so much different than what I grew up with in the seventies in Stoke. The headmistress took me around, and it was such a mix of social awkwardness – being at this school, these intellects, teachers, and me having 1970s Tunstall, leaving school without any qualifications. And she was talking and I was just sort of doing my best to look as though I was concentrating and nodding, and there was turmoil in my head. I'm desperately trying to not look mental, to look as though I'm listening and taking in information, because it's really important because it's my children. And the headmistress stops speaking and asks me, "Have you got any questions for us?"'

Rob knows he needs to have one. The voice inside his head starts hectoring: 'Come up with a question! Come on! It's so important that you come up with a question, because they're interviewing you too!' But he just can't think of anything that sounds right, and so his mind somehow defaults to his own schooldays, and to something that might have made much more sense in the Stoke of his childhood than to a fancy private London school in late 2016.

'Do the school,' he finally asks, 'fight other schools?'

(For the record, he was told no. No, they don't.)

* * *

There are no photos of Robbie Williams on show in this house, or any of his houses. No gold discs. No awards in cabinets or on mantelpieces. Just because the career has paid for the house, no reason that the house should be a shrine to the career.

There is actually one of his 18 Brit Awards within these walls, the most recent, the Brit Icon Award. Ayda has that in her dressing room, having forbidden him to do with it what he has done with all of the others: give it away. Most of them have just been gifts – to his parents, for instance. Phil Taylor, the world champion darts player from Stoke, has one. Rob can't even remember who has all of the rest. For a while he had the idea that he would swap them with other entertainers and sportsmen for awards that he could never himself receive, but this idea foundered, probably because other people tend to be rather more attached to their own awards than Rob is. When Wayne Rooney was injured before one World Cup, Rob sent him a note which said, 'Come on, Wazza, get better, we need you to get well', and to accompany the note – 'I was having a mad moment' – sent him a Brit Award as extra encouragement. (Rooney would respond with some signed boots that he wore in the tournament, though Rob's gift didn't inspire the trophy-winning outcome he'd hoped for.)

The reason he gives for not wanting the awards around is the same one he gives for why they make him feel uncomfortable in the first place – the same exhausting counter-logic that for years and years has fired up, then sabotaged, then reignited his career.

'It's a mirror for my neurosis and my self-worth. I don't think I deserve them, so they're monuments to my lack of self-worth.'

He has all the reminders he needs, good and bad, of who he is inside his head. He gets plenty more whenever he leaves the property and steps into the outer world. There's a limit to how much control he has over either of those, and he spends plenty of time in both of those places. But in the space in between, the house in which he lives, it's nice to imagine that there can be a calm place where other things are more important, if only for a while.

* * *

October 2016

Towards the end of their hotel room meeting, Vaughan asks Rob about one more famous moment – the time in 2002 when, just after signing what was always talked of as 'his eighty million pound' record deal with EMI, Rob appeared before the waiting photographers in a sleeveless Mötley Crüe t-shirt, raised his arms, pumped them and exclaimed, 'I'm rich! Beyond my wildest dreams!'

Rob is more than keen to explain – not because it is a proud moment, but because he'd like people to at least understand what happened that day from his perspective.

'I've just got off a plane,' he says. 'I've just been given this contract that I've signed, and it's for eighty million – as you do – and it just fractures my self-worth,' he says. (A familiar pattern, you might note: this kind of paralysis and doubt that comes at the times of greatest acclaim or reward.) 'Because how do you perform like somebody that's worth eighty million?' he continues. 'How do you do that? Why am I being bestowed this? How has this happened? It's surreal. So I'm walking into the IE offices and there's a throng of paparazzi come to see me sign this record-breaking deal. Of course I have to mask the fact that I don't feel I'm worth it. I sign it and then I'm having my picture taken and I'm saying nothing, and then they're, "Come on, Robbie, give us something, tell us something – give us a quote! Give us a quote!" In my mind, I was thinking: how surreal is this? All that's missing is the massive cardboard cheque. Is that what they want? For me to stand with a massive cardboard cheque that says *To Robbie Williams, 80 million pounds, from EMI*? So instantly I'm thinking about the lottery. And so I'm thinking, "Oh yeah, what did that lady say when she won the lottery?"'

He was thinking of the story of Viv Nicholson, who after her husband won the football pools in 1961 (a jackpot of £152,319), declared, when asked her plans, that she would 'spend spend spend!' But, regrettably, Rob misremembered the most important detail.

'I thought she said, "I'm rich beyond my wildest dreams!" I thought I was going to say something that people would get, and that they would understand that I was doing a Viv Nicholson. I thought it would be an interesting witticism where people would understand the reference immediately. So I said, "I'm rich beyond my wildest dreams!" and then it left my lips and I thought, "What was wrong with that? Why haven't they got what I was on about?" I thought I was doing the funny, aping Viv Nicholson. But of course I wasn't.'

It is something that continues to make him wince.

'I was in bed once in my apartment in Chelsea, and the windows were closed, and I woke up to the sounds of somebody cleaning the windows outside.' The window cleaners knew who lived here, but they clearly thought that no one was home.

'And they were singing the chorus to "Angels",' he remembers. 'And after they'd sung it, one of them went, "I'm rich beyond my wildest dreams!" I didn't open the curtains, I was so embarrassed.'

* * *

November 2016

At the press conference to announce next summer's tour, someone asks Rob: as an entertainer, what are your thoughts on Donald Trump's showmanship?

These days, people are often misunderstood quite deliberately. What happens here is a relatively harmless example. This is how Rob answers the question:

'I think he's got something that I can take from his performance. Like, if you say things enough, that it becomes true. And this tour is gonna be huge. My tour is gonna be yuge. And my temperament is incredible. Nobody's got an entertaining temperament like me. And my respect for women, nobody respects women more than I do. Which you shall see through my two-hour performance each evening where I'll be respecting every single lady that's there. And nobody does that like me. Nobody sings "Let Me Entertain You" like me or "Angels" like me.' He pauses. 'But he's a great showman. And he sells it really well. And like I say, if you say it, I think, twelve times, loud enough and confidently enough, it becomes the truth. So I'm the best entertainer on the planet. There's one. And I'll be doing it twelve times over the next twenty-four hours so it'll become truth.'

Quite obviously, this is – in keeping with the slightly arch spirit of the question (Trump is yet to be elected, incidentally, and at this point the indications are that he will not be) – a routine in which Rob talks about himself parodically as though he were Donald Trump. Some reports of today's press conference will accurately reflect this, but others will simply take quotes from this speech as though Rob has just said them, without mentioning the context, so that he becomes a man who might simply turn up at a press conference and say – this is a real example from the website ContactMusic – 'This tour is going to be huge, my temperament is incredible, nobody has got an entertaining temperament like me and nobody respects women more than I do.'

A lot of this kind of thing happens these days. Maybe sometimes it's out of laziness and maybe sometimes out of incompetence, but mostly it's a kind of deliberate cynicism. The process involved is a little bit different from making something up. It requires some real-world basis for the story – Rob did actually say those words when he was pretending to be Donald Trump, for instance – and then either deliberately ignoring information or context that might make the story wrong, or showing a world-class lack of curiosity about what might have actually happened or of anything that might inconveniently make the story less true. This is a fairly trivial example, but many aren't. Any story which makes a celebrity look weird, or crazy, or rude, or stupid, or out of touch, or off his or her head, or delusional, or – ideally – amusingly flawed in some combination of the above is a good story. A life lived like Rob's has reliably supplied a flow of real stories that fit this format, but however great the supply, the demand will always outstrip it. Deliberately ignoring, or deliberately failing to find, the context of something that has been said or something that has happened is a very efficient way of creating these stories.

Rob has been noticing one particular tendency. 'What's started to happen in the last five years is the removal of irony or the joke from a situation. And that's head-fucking weird. You're so terrified of doing anything or saying anything because you just know that there's going to be a choice made to remove all sense of gag or funniness about it, and just report it as being "How weird: bizarre Robbie went on a rant yesterday".'

* * *

Here is another fairly harmless example. The following story appeared in the *Daily Mirror*, describing Rob's behaviour onstage at a big German awards show.

Robbie Williams grimaces as he shoves hands down his trousers onstage at Bambi Awards 2016

Robbie Williams is a true performer and will rarely let anything get in the way of a good performance, and that's why he appeared to adjust himself onstage while performing at the Bambi Awards 2016. Belting out his new track at the event in Berlin, Heavy Entertainment Show, Robbie grimaced as he stuck his hands into his trousers mid-song, even spinning around so the audience couldn't really see. The 42-year-old continued with the song and hit those high notes after appearing to do up his zipper.

Weirdly, in this case, if they'd worked out, or had found out, what really happened at the Bambi Awards, it might have actually shown Rob in a worse light. But why bother? They have their routine crazy-reprehensible-rude pop star story already.

This is the real story. A few months earlier, the German football manager Joachim Löw had been embarrassed by TV footage during a game against Ukraine which showed him on the touchline putting his hand down both the front and back of his trousers and then smelling his fingers. As Rob performed 'The Heavy Entertainment Show' at the Bambi Awards, he spotted Löw right in front of him, and acted on instinct – his kind of instinct: 'I undid my flies, had a root around my bollocks and then had a smell of my fingers and then made a disgusted face. To ape him, you know. And of course the British press completely missed out the Joachim Löw bit and was just, "Robbie was scratching his nuts and his fingers smelt".'

That misfire was to come, but the misfire in the room was instant. The hope was that, on some level at least, Löw might be amused, but Rob immediately knew he'd been wrong about that: 'There was zero banter on his face. He got it, and was instantly not amused. *Instantly* not amused. In a split second I realised, because he's very stylish good-looking man, he's probably not great at having the piss taken out of him, and it was probably very embarrassing. So I instantly understood that it wasn't a good moment for him.'

If the press had worked that out, it would have probably been a better story for them. But it would also have involved a train of thought – *when a celebrity does something that looks weird, most probably there's a reason for it* – that is going out of fashion. And sometimes the consequences can be much worse.

* * *

December 2016–January 2017

During his New Year's Eve concert, broadcast live on BBC One on either side of midnight, the most watched music TV programme of the year, Robbie Williams shook hands with members of the audience, trying his best to fake some sincere man-of-the-people bonhomie, and then, not realising that the camera was still on him, went to the back of the stage, applied hand sanitiser and was caught making a face that showed just how much this close-up physical encounter with the general public had disgusted him, and how much he needed to cleanse away the awful contagion of the proletariat.

Wish all you want that the world think of you one way, but in the end every fraud will get caught out.

Welcome to 2017, and a brand new year, and the reality of who Robbie Williams really is.

* * *

Or, as we'll see, not. But that's pretty much what you could have believed from the firestorm of derision that rained down after Rob's New Year's Eve show. The fact that it didn't happen like that is, looking at the big picture, just one of those annoying little details. With a story that perfect – all the vanity and insincerity and remoteness and self-righteous pomposity of the worthlessly famous condensed into in one magical GIF – the truth is just a distraction, a forlorn, lone figure trying to keep its feet amidst a stampede.

Even before that, it had been a rough few days. Coming into December after nearly three months' promotion, Rob is beginning to struggle. 'I was tired and confused and disorientated and generally burnt out,' he says. 'A lot was done and lot got done and a lot got done well. But I was frazzled.'

Then, just before Christmas, Rob makes an unwise, or at least poorly timed, series of decisions. He has been extending his deadline to give up smoking again, but now he feels ready. He has a final cigarette in the private-shopping smoking area in Harrods when they take the kids to see Santa, and that is that. Meanwhile, he's been overusing his sleeping pills, taking one and a half rather than one each night, because he feels sure that a single one no longer works. So his prescription has run out early, and his doctor is demanding to see Rob in person. Rob knows how that will go: 'I knew that he was going to give me a bollocking. I was, "I'm not leaving my house to go to you just so you can give me a bollocking."' So Rob decides to just give up the pills, cold turkey, instead. 'I was just like: fuck you, check this out. I give up everything! And then no one's got nothing on me!'

From the start, it doesn't go well. I'm supposed to come round for lunch a couple of days later, but he emails me at seven o'clock that morning, saying that he's still awake from the night before. He sends a further update on Christmas Eve – 'Very messy in the head … tough detox' – and that's how Christmas continues. 'I genuinely would like a redo of Christmas,' he says after. 'I feel as though one of my Christmases was stolen.'

Another email update comes the day before the concert, this one explaining how he's had to relent and reintroduce the sleeping pills for the time being. 'Just,' he explains, 'so I feel my normal confused self tomorrow.' But he offers a disheartening overview of how he is feeling: 'Not good … Life has been futile. Badly depressed … Which got me worrying about the nye gig.'

This concert is the final part of his relentless promotion schedule, and it has been easy to allow it to become an afterthought. 'It was "oh, and we do the New Year's Eve thing",' he says. 'You get there and you're, "Actually, this is massive. This is bigger than everything else. Ooops."' He also realises that while he's spent most of the past few months in front of TV audiences where, for the most part, he could at least have a reasonable expectation that many if not most of them would be watching because they like him, this is different. He is being beamed into millions of British homes, and, given how divisive he can be, he's only too aware that plenty of those who will instinctively turn on the BBC for New Year's Eve won't necessarily be well disposed towards who they find there, however good he is.

'Psychically,' he says, 'that really affected me. It just affected my performance. I couldn't stop thinking about people that hate me. It was like: do a show in front of the biggest TV audience of the year for a music show, and do it in front of a large amount of enemies. And I was detoxing. Which doesn't help your inner emotional state. So it was a mental battle, to retain the painted face.'

From the outside, the performance that results is erratic – at times commanding and serene, and then suddenly you can see a little of the manic surface that tends to signal some kind of underlying distress. And then back to commanding, like a flickering light bulb that can't make up its mind whether it's blown or not. But for him, internally, he's having a bad time. 'It was just like, that was awful for me. Inside my head. And that's all

I took away from it. I took away from it: *that really fucking hurt*. Doing that. It felt emotionally really taxing.'

In the middle of the show, when they break for the New Year's countdown, Rob has to do an interview with the broadcast's presenter, Melvin Odoom – literally singing the final line of 'Feel' while walking out on a balcony overlooking the Thames, and then going straight into having to talk. It's not the kind of transition he finds natural – whatever false bravado he's been channelling to get through the first half of the concert has left him amped up in a way that leaves him ill-suited for conversation. It doesn't help that he called his interviewer 'Marvin'. Five times. He gets through the rest of the show, and is glad to go home.

'With Take That,' he reflects, 'we'd just see these burnt-out pop stars with confused looks on their faces. It's like, "Oh, that's me now ..."'

* * *

Just in case you think Rob might be paranoid, or perversely self-regarding and self-important, in imagining that there really are all these people at home, hating him ... well, unfortunately, these days we need no longer speculate about such things, because the worst of it is funnelled into a feed where anyone can read it. Some of the comments after *The Graham Norton Show* might have seemed bad, but at least those were from the kind of people who had sought out *The Graham Norton Show*.

But don't think for a moment, if any of what is printed below shocks you, that this is just *him*. Rob may have an unusually polarising persona, and maybe over the years all that he's done and how he's done it have seeded particularly fertile lines of attack for the mean-hearted. But for just about anybody who dares to stick their head above the parapet, some version of this exists, if you know where to look. On the surface, this is about him ... but it's really about us.

These comments are just from Twitter. (Other channels of abuse are also available.) To be clear, there are also kind and enthusiastic comments here, too, plenty of them, but the sheer volume and intensity of bile is frightening. While a lot of people attack him tonight for specific sins – for being, as they saw it, obviously coked up (though, of course, he certainly wasn't), for his appearance, for his voice, for chewing gum, for using an autocue – most of the abuse is broader and more definitive. It feels as though for the people writing many of these comments that there could have been no Robbie Williams performance, however magnificent, that could ever compensate for what they see as evident and important truths, truths that this evening they feel compelled to share.

Take a deep breath:

Robbie Williams is a fat, talentless, chav cunt. Suicide is the only entertaining thing this tone deaf twat could do!

Fuck off Robbie Williams you absolute thundercunt! #cantsing #cantdance

The best thing that could happen with the rest of 2016 is if Robbie Williams fell off that balcony

Would rather slice my tits off with a rusty penknife than usher in the first minutes of 2017 listening to Robbie Williams

If Robbie Williams was dead we wouldn't have to watch this shit

Robbie Williams really is the most insufferable cunt to ever exist

Robbie Williams has ruined the whole year

I'm hoping ISIS are locked on Robbie Williams right now, let's get 2017 off to a flying start

Robbie Williams, shit then, wank now

Saw Robbie Williams trending, so disappointed he isn't dead

Robbie Williams is a total twat. That is all

So, Robbie Williams trending in Twitter. First thought, he died, but apparently it's just his career …

Robbie Williams, the musical equivalent of thrush: just when you think you've got rid of it, it comes back more irritating than ever

Well, Robbie Williams isn't the start 2017 needs. Honestly, who booked that? It's like the terrorists have already won

Robbie Williams. Wow, what a load o shit, dad dancing, old hat money grabber. I think deep down he knows he's shit. He must do. I would!

Is Robbie Williams the wanker of 2017 already? No, he's the wanker of every year

Actually thought (hoped) Robbie Williams was dead

… I always thought Robbie Williams was a fat talentless twat. Nothing has changed my mind to the contrary

Didn't that guy used to be Robbie Williams?

Dear celeb Grim Reaper. If you saw Robbie Williams in London 2nite dad dancin', please have a think bout ya next victim

Robbie Williams has already ruined my year

Robbie Williams' performance makes sense if you imagine he thinks the crowd are dragons that'll eat him if he doesn't keep performing

The list of the top, say, million singers doesn't include Robbie Williams

Everything awful on Earth > Robbie Williams

I want to dangle Robbie Williams in a pool of acid by his feet

As much as I hate the useless cunt, I can't turn Robbie Williams off because I'm enjoying slagging him off too much

Robbie Williams is a cunt, not a talented cunt, a fucking stone in your shoe kind of cunt.

It'd be great if the first celebrity death of 2017 was Robbie Williams

Watching Robbie Williams pulling mad monkey faces on the telly, where's the 2016 apocalyptic meteor that was forecast when you need it?

I reckon Robbie Williams would actually fuck himself if he could. Bloke's so far up his own arse he wears himself as a hat!

Robbie Williams looks like an Elvis impersonator who's given up impersonating Elvis.

It's 2017 and Robbie Williams is still a cunt

I don't want to drown the good vibes of 2017 so early … but it's clear to me that one day Robbie Williams will die on the toilet

None of the fireworks hit Robbie Williams in his fat fucking head. Waste of money.

I hate Robbie Williams more than I hate almost anyone else

When I can afford my rocket to blast all of the people I hate into space, I'm strapping Robbie Williams to the fucking tip

Robbie Williams is so bad that our cat just threw up. I finally like the cat
Happy New Year to everyone. Except Robbie Williams
Fuck life off to die fuck Robbie Williams stupid cunt
Am I the only person who thinks Robbie Williams is a twat?

There's plenty more. Plenty. The next time you come across some pampered celebrity who seems a little thin-skinned about the things that are said about them, and your instinct is to think that they should just get over it, maybe also remember what the rest of us can actually be like.

* * *

And we haven't even got to the hand sanitiser part of the night yet. There seem to be two schools of thought, online anyway, about what people imagine that they have seen. Either Robbie Williams is an idiot pop star who can't bear to touch the unwashed – by far the majority view – or, to his defenders, he is a modern man and parent who has adopted a perfectly sensible and responsible attitude to hygiene. The outpouring from the multitude who take the first view is instantaneous, all separately sharing within minutes their thoughts on what they believe they have seen.

Back in we go:

I never knew Robbie Williams was a savage. The face he made when he slapped on the sanitizer was of absolute disgust

Man of the people Robbie Williams … Shaking hands & touching his fans. Then realises he hates peasants and decides to use antiseptic wash

When the BBC accidentally broadcasts Robbie Williams grimacing as he cleans his hands after touching the filthy commoners

We all saw Robbie Williams wash his hands after touching the audience. Twat

Anyone else see Robbie Williams' disgusted face after shaking hands with the crowd?

Robbie Williams liberally squirting the Carex hand sanitizer after touching the dirty oiks. Rumbled, twat

Love Robbie Williams using alcohol hand wash – thinking he was off camera – after shaking hands with the crowd

The best part about BBC's live programme was accidentally seeing Robbie Williams put on hand sanitizer with this look of disgust on his face

Robbie Williams hand sanitizing after touching mere mortals!! What a dick!!

Robbie Williams using antibac hand gel on live television after high-fiving fans has cemented my dislike for him. Horrible man

Highlight of 2017 so far: Robbie Williams using hand sanitizer after touching grubby civilians in the audience

Robbie Williams sanitizing after touching the poor

What a grade A cockhead Robbie Williams is! Scrubbing his hands with hand sanitizer onstage immediately after touching the common folk

For me, the image of 2017 will be Robbie Williams disinfecting his hands after touching the filthy public.

The saddest thing is that very few people at all, even those trying to defend or stand up for Rob, seemed to realise the truth. Though Rob is a modestly enthusiastic user of hand sanitiser as he goes about his life, this was *a bit*. A bit of entertainment. And it was a bit he had done plenty of times before: shake or palm the hands of people in the audience, and then openly and somewhat melodramatically apply hand sanitiser, and while doing so make a comic, pantomime, face-contorting expression of disgust, as though upset at having been soiled by human contact. It might not represent the highest pinnacle of comedy genius ever scaled, but it is one of many of these kinds of things that Rob does, in his mission to amuse and entertain. 'I was, now I'll go up onstage and do my hand sanitiser gag, and it'll be picked up on camera,' he says, 'and people will think it's hilarious.'

What the world thought of as his embarrassing, humiliating blunder was actually his joke.

One of the things Rob will find most offensive about all of this, when the dust has settled, is that people could imagine that he would *ever* be unaware of what he is doing onstage. He might often find being onstage nerve-wracking and exposing, but he knows that his every move is being watched (that's a big part of what is so nerve-wracking), and it's the totality of every move that he makes that will, or won't, add up to entertainment.

Perhaps some performers really *lose themselves* onstage; Rob can have transcendent moments up there but I don't think even those involve losing himself. He's too busy finding himself. He's too busy calibrating each new move, and what effect it might have. To a large degree it's that very effort that makes performing so demanding and stressful.

And so to suggest that he could make some huge facial expression *without realising that millions of people are watching?* That's almost more of an insult than the insult itself.

* * *

Nevertheless, when Rob did eventually see the footage, he could at least see how people might have been mistaken. In the way the BBC cut from camera to camera – and this was done live, so there was no intention or malice in it – you don't see any of Rob's panto movements which set up his facial expression because, while he was doing all of that, the broadcast feed at first showed his backing singers then cut to the crowd. It cuts back to Rob only at the exact moment when his face is in an exaggerated, contorted grimace and he is squeezing hand sanitiser into his hands, a moment – perhaps most important of all – when his eyes are looking down at his hands. So that, if you haven't seen him telegraph with his eyes to the audience beforehand that he's about to *do* something, you might easily interpret this as being someone caught in a private moment.

For a while, the reaction – and the public's reaction was soon picked up and amplified by the media – passed Rob by. He kept to himself, still feeling rough, and only had the most minimal idea of what people were saying. When he made an Instagram video which seemed to address the subject, in which he theatrically hand-sanitised himself after shaking hands with Gwen and wishing her Happy New Year, it was greeted as a masterful comic piece of crisis management – and, in many ways, it actually was, helping to diffuse and redirect the story – but he still had no idea what a big story there was to diffuse and redirect. The Instagram film was just a quick, light-hearted, funny response to something that at this point he'd only vaguely heard about.

But eventually he realised.

'Days later, I was, "Hang on, it was a *what*? It was a *thing*?" I didn't even realise it was a thing. And I suppose that's why I wasn't bothered. Plus, I was detoxing on so many fucking things I just didn't feel great anyway. And then I realised it's a thing. And it's made me angry that there's so many things that I do where they take the humour out of it and just display it as being wacky or weird or … it's kind of terrifying. And angry-making. It was a lot like the pregnancy videos. Yeah. It affected me.'

* * *

October 2014

Yes, and then there's the pregnancy videos. Here, in part, is how the *Daily Mail* reported events surrounding the birth of Rob and Ayda's second child, Charlie:

As Robbie Williams tweets his wife giving birth … Isn't ANYTHING private these days?

Not so long ago the very presence of a father in the delivery room was virtually unheard of … surely times haven't moved on so far that the father – even a multimillionaire pop star father – expects to be centre of attention on a global scale while his wife endures the agonies of labour?

No wonder, then, that Robbie Williams' tasteless video diary and inane Twitter commentary from his wife's bedside as she gave birth to their second child has triggered such a negative reaction.

There cannot be a woman in the world whose deepest sympathies did not go out to Mrs Williams, aka Ayda Field, as the singer filmed her during her most private moments. We even saw her in red spangly Louboutin stilettos while her legs were in stirrups. Most husbands would be happy to let their labouring partners relax in a pair of comfy old slippers and a flannel night-gown. Not so Robbie, who seemed to be telling the world that Ayda was a sex object for his delectation, even while giving birth.

Then we were forced to watch the pain of her contractions. Hard to stomach? Yes. But perhaps most bewildering was the way in which Williams turned the birth of his own baby into a series of clips – one showed the 40-year-old former Take That star doing a lengthy dance routine at his wife's bedside – in which there was, very clearly, only one star. And that certainly wasn't Ayda …

It doesn't appear to occur to Robbie that he is personally invading his wife's privacy by filming her. While no doubt at the start she's capable of giving her permission, by the end she appears helpless and drugged up.

Labour is the moment at which a woman is at the most vulnerable she will ever be. Yet instead of reassuring his wife, the former Take That singer simply tunes out her moans by turning up the volume on a succession of cheesy ballads.

At one point, Ayda throws her head back in distress, with a look that says the only show she wants her husband to put on is a disappearing act. But Robbie is too busy miming and dancing to one of his hits to notice.

Dismayed she is concentrating on her contractions rather than him, he taps her on the arm. Finding himself ignored again, he tells whoever is filming the scene to stop, before flouncing off … Never mind the little life waiting to emerge – it's clear the biggest baby in this room is Robbie himself.

It wasn't just the *Daily Mail*, either. It was everyone. The story of this stupid pop star who had subjected his wife to this weird, narcissistic harassment while she was trying to give birth, that story was everywhere. That poor woman. What must it be like to be married to that scarily, delusionally self-obsessed pop star husband?

'We were just having fun,' he says. 'Charlie was born to the sound of laughter. And the next day it was, "Outrage! Women should kill and burn Robbie Williams! How dare he? Burn him! She should leave him! He's a bastard!" I was, "What have I done?" It was meant to be a beautiful moment, it was meant to be funny. You know, my wife went into labour for a long time and we entertained ourselves by doing those clips and we had a good time doing it. It was just me and my wife having fun. I suppose I'm a frustrated comedian – I like making people laugh, and l like making myself laugh, and I love making my wife laugh and she loves making me laugh. We have a unique relationship, which is telling in the birthing videos. I can assure you she was the one saying, "You should do this! You should do this!"'

* * *

This is how Ayda explains what happened to her *Loose Women* co-panellists.

'Poor Rob,' she says, 'he took a lot of flak that he was a bad guy for doing that. It was really all my idea, so I feel bad for that. It was a very organic … we didn't set out to do any videos. It started with me putting my heels on – it was a joke that I brought heels to the labour room, and we were just laughing. It was about three in the morning, because it was about seventeen and a half hours in, so I put them in the stirrups and we took this picture and he said, "Can I tweet it?"'

That's how it started: with a picture of one upraised bedbound leg, one red Louboutin. There were a further series of tweets, and nine Instagram videos. In the one which got the most attention, Ayda has her legs splayed, and is beginning to give birth, and Rob, who is holding her left leg, is singing 'Let It Go' until she finally snaps: 'Babe! Will you stop singing *Frozen!*'

'Even that was my idea,' she points out. 'And actually I am pushing Charlie out in that actual scene, and I tell him to shut up. But it kept me distracted. We were coming up with all sorts of funny bits – I wasn't thinking about the outside world, or what was happening on the outside world, but if you know us and our sense of humour, we were just getting goofy and doing these funny things, kind of taking the mickey out of ourselves. And it got me through the labour. It was only after I gave my birth, about an hour afterwards and they were wheeling me into a private room and some lady passed by us and she went, "Oh my God, those videos are so funny." And I was, "It's been an hour, what's happened?" And the next morning a woman came in to clean the room and she was, "Oh my God, I saw you on Spanish TV this morning." And the lactation consultant came in, "Yeah, you were on *Good Morning America*." And I was, "Babe, what's happened?" And he went, "Oh…"'

* * *

Rob, also, has been asked to explain this, over and over. People genuinely still believe that he was tormenting his wife.

'I know,' he says. 'I know! Even in interviews when they bring it up, they still don't get it when I say, "Look, it was us joking. Ayda was coming up with the ideas for these things." They still don't believe me. I can see it in their eyes.' He'll now sometimes refer to anything that might turn out this way – a story that either is or has the potential to spin out of control like this – as 'one of those hospital moments'.

* * *

But there is a separate question that can be asked. Even though anyone looking at all this footage with an open mind couldn't really fail to see what was really happening, was it realistic – at this point in the twenty-first century, at this particular moment in the history of technology and celebrity and unanchored storytelling – to expect that you could make this kind of footage public, and expect any other result?

Maybe not. The truth is that 'a pop star and his wife do something quite weird and funny' – that's a small story. A pop star does something monumentally stupid, insensitive and ill-thought-out to his wife, with memorable and entertaining footage you can broadcast that you can say shows him doing it – that's a huge story. Especially when the pop star is someone like Rob who many people are only too ready to believe might have completely lost the plot. It's the kind of experience that could make you very careful. It's the kind of experience that could make you second-guess everything.

Or you could decide that you have to live your life as your life, and follow the instincts that are your own. You know: wherever it may take me.

'There'll be others,' Rob reflects. 'Basically, I'm writing and directing the script for the pop star Robbie Williams, and my taste's a bit wacky. There'll be more stuff coming from me, and there'll be more stuff coming from me and my wife, and it'll be funny and bizarre and weird. But it's exciting because me and my wife, we don't have a normal relationship, we're a unique combination, and we like to do naughty things, and we like to be cheeky and we like to provoke a reaction. And knowing that something that we find funny could go out there, and be a worldwide fail, is exciting.'

* * *

January–February 2017

In the new year, Rob lies low for a while. He carries on not smoking, and also goes vegan. Almost vegan, anyway – it's not a cast-iron moral decision, and if he fancies the occasional burger, he'll have it – but day-by-day nearly all his meals are strictly vegan. 'Just got a hunch that meat's not great for you,' he says. 'I'm kind of really into this plant-based stuff now. I'm enjoying it. There is a vanity bit too, cause hopefully I'll lose weight. But actually my body feels better without it.'

While he's resting, there's a new fuss. A story appears in the papers saying that when he sung at the Queen's Jubilee concert in 2012, he smoked weed in Buckingham Palace. Rob'll say that when he first heard, his reaction was one of fury: 'Somebody told me that I had been in the news and I went and had a look and said, excuse my language, "Okay, which cunt has told them that?"'

An hour later, he realised exactly who the loose-lipped culprit was.

Rob had recently appeared on an Italian TV show, *E poi c'è Cattlelan*, where they had asked him to play a quiz: Right or Wrong. One of the questions had been: *You threw up in Buckingham Palace?* He hadn't, so he could have just said no, but his need to entertain is too strong.

'It was a surreal and weird question,' Rob says, 'so I was trying to fill in a moment and make good TV. And grabbing anything.' What he grabbed – 'No, I smoked a spliff in Buckingham Palace' – certainly worked as short-term entertainment. It was also true. More or less, anyway. He smoked just outside the palace building itself, in the grounds, then, adequately stoned, went inside. 'It appealed to my naughty schoolboy side,' he remembers of the day. 'It was: look at me being naughty.' And while he didn't particularly mean to announce this to the world, he doesn't mind much that he did.

His wife felt otherwise.

'Ayda wasn't very happy with me. Because it's "disrespectful". She's American and they've got a different concept of royalty.'

* * *

The last big event to promote *The Heavy Entertainment Show* is an appearance at the Brit Awards, where Rob is to close the show. He has to do some interviews in advance. One is with the *NME*.

'I fucking hate the *NME*,' he reminds Michael, as Michael is just about to hand him the phone, though the sentiment sounds more like muscle memory than genuine vehemence.

Recently, Michael points out, their coverage has been perplexingly positive. 'They almost hero-worship you now,' Michael teases. 'How does that make you feel?'

'I preferred it the other way,' says Rob. 'At least I knew who they were. It's confusing.'

He gets on the phone, and their interviewer, Jordan Bassett, who seems to be becoming the *NME*'s Robbie Williams correspondent and who is provocative but clearly enthusiastic, is soon asking about *Rudebox*. (Bassett will end up trying to persuade Rob that, were it released today, the album would be acclaimed; Rob argues otherwise.) First, Rob shares a relevant family snapshot. 'Out of nowhere last night,' he says, 'before I went to bed, weirdly, just as I went to the loo before I went to sleep, I just turned to my wife and said, "I stand by *Rudebox*, you know." Out of absolute nowhere. And she was like, "Me too." And then I went to sleep.'

That leads him to reminisce about what happened next, from his view. 'Listen, inevitably in the UK if you're really successful you have a kicking at some point. And there was a chink in the armour, and it was at that point it was my time for the major kicking, and I got it ... "Well, fuck you, die, you bastard" – that's what it felt like.' He puts on a high traumatised voice on the point of breaking: 'Oh no, I was only trying to make words rhyme ...'

Rob also explains – you can tell that he knows he's speaking to someone much younger – how he comes from a different generation, a different world. 'I'm from the nineties and we were a different breed back then, effing and jeffing and cussing and dissing and needing to say things in order to be interesting. I don't think people do that now. It was de rigueur, and expected for everybody to be off their face on cocaine and drunk ... if people did that now they'd look a bit sad.' At the end of the interview, the writer will try to persuade Rob to come down to the *NME* Awards that night. (The notion that he would receive an award this year somehow evaporated.) 'God no,' Rob replies. 'My back's fucked. And I'd end up snorting cocaine and losing my wife.'

Before that, the interviewer asks Rob about his quip on *Graham Norton*, after watching Ayda give birth to Teddy, that it was like 'watching your favourite pub burn down'. Turns out, Rob's been waiting for someone to bring this up again.

'No, it's great,' he says, 'because just recently there's been an off-licence that's been opened round the back ...'

* * *

There's a pop music gossip website called Popbitch which sends out a weekly newsletter. Rob's only ever been bothered once about something they've written about him, back in the pre-rehab days, and that only bothered him because it was true. But he's a little puzzled by something they've printed this week:

Robbie Williams has been out on the town celebrating his return to Take That. Presumably he knows he has at least two tabloid hacks tailing him?

Rob has no idea what it means: no idea what kind of coded indiscretion 'out on the town' is supposed to allude to, and no idea why 'tabloid hacks' should be taking a particular interest in him right now. It seems a clear hint that someone is on the verge of revealing some kind of scurrilous behaviour. When you've been up to some kind of mischief, then at least you know what you're scared that people might find out. But when you haven't, it can make you even more fearful, and certainly more confused. He has his security checking the road outside the house to see who may be lurking, and he sends an email to me, trying to think it through.

It's made me paranoid, cos I've only been out of the house a few times in the day and they have all-ish been caught on camera ... like at the Dr's ... or on my bike ... or in the park. And they look like surveillance footage rather than actual good photos ... or maybe I'm being paranoid about that.

They're going to have long waits and nothing stories, specially now I know they may be there. Shan't/won't go out. I'm good at that ;)

The only 'out on the town' I've done is two weeks ago, and we went for a curry ... fucking GREAT curry ...

But that's all ... x

When there's something you know that you've done, you know what to protect. You know your quandary, you know your foe. But when it comes to the things you haven't done but which someone might think you have: that could be *anything*. Either you aimlessly strike out around you at an invisible adversary, or you resolve to carry on as though there's no one there. But it's hard.

* * *

Rob comes downstairs in the London house wearing a t-shirt with a picture of a UFO on it.

Teddy studies his outfit.

'Do you know what it is?' he asks her.

'An alien,' she says.

Her proud father high-fives her, genuinely delighted.

'How did you know that?' he wonders.

* * *

Over lunch, Rob and Ayda discuss a notable barbecue they attended a little while back. It was at Adele's house in Los Angeles, though Adele was stuck in the studio and didn't make it.

'I got out of the car, looking at the scene, and was, "I have to embrace this, or I'm going to run off,"' says Rob. What he saw – what made him want to run off – was that, aside from their host, Adele's partner Simon, there were precisely three other adult guests: Jay-Z, Beyoncé and Chris Martin. 'So I embraced it,' he says, 'and it became a good moment in my life.'

It was the first time he'd met Jay-Z. 'It's the president and first lady,' Rob says. 'It's on their terms, but you happily let it be on their terms. It's not like I met Jay-Z down the pub and we had a right old laugh. It's like meeting an idol of mine, and he can be whatever the fuck he wants, if he wants to be. He was very nice and he was charming.'

'I sat next to Beyoncé, as you do,' says Ayda. 'She says, "Hi, I'm Bey." We talked about the kids. She really liked Teddy. Teddy kept bringing her toys and everything, and then I was, "Hold on, it's just occurred to me, Teddy's favourite song is 'Single Ladies' and we play it all the time – I think she might recognise you."'

Over the years, there have been more than a few awkward moments in Rob and Chris Martin's relationship, but this time it went well. 'He was really lovely,' says Rob. 'But so was I. I think we might have both been doing fake humility. If Jay-Z wasn't there, I might have been a bit different. I knew that I was pissed off with him, but I couldn't remember what for. He did say, "Why has Jason left Take That?" And he was really upset about it. And Jay-Z said to me, "You're in super good shape." and I said, "Yeah, well, you know food? I don't eat that anymore. Because I got to forty, and I was fat, and the future looked bleak ..." And Chris said, "You were fat at twenty ..."' Also, when Rob was talking about some financial toing and froing, Martin quipped 'but aren't you rich beyond your wildest dreams?'

But somehow even that didn't bother him. Maybe he was just too surprised at finding himself out at a gathering like this and having a good time.

* * *

Charlie's not feeling well, so Jan accompanies him to the doctor.

'He's got exactly what you had at his age,' Jan tells Rob when they return.

'What?' he says. 'Rhythm?'

Jan explains that Rob had adenoids, and grommets in his ear, and tells a mother's story about him staying overnight in hospital: how she had to go home to check on the pub, and when she came back Rob was hanging from the bars above the bed that are supposed to be used to haul yourself up, swinging.

* * *

In the days leading up to the Brit Awards, Rob's back – which has been a problem, on and off, for years, and which has been particularly troublesome in recent weeks – gets significantly worse. After he attends the Brit Awards rehearsals, news of this leaks out, and there are stories in the press about it. Rob's annoyed. Who's told them?

'It could be anyone,' Michael points out.

Rob considers this.

'You know like in New York you're supposed to always be five foot away from a rat?' he says. 'It's the same in show business.'

* * *

In his dressing room at the Brit Awards, Ed Sheeran pays him a visit.

'I've got a really bad back,' Rob says. 'What's wrong with you?' I'm not sure whether he's heard that Sheeran is nursing an ailment, or just assumes that everyone doing what they're both doing usually has something.

'Just jet-lagged,' Ed replies, and explains his manic promo schedule, then asks Rob, 'When are we going to do this pub quiz?'

Ed's house is close to Rob's, and they have a plan, which Rob has been announcing in interviews, to have quiz nights.

'Let's do it before I go back to LA,' says Rob, and they compare new scars. Ed's is on his right cheek; Rob's on the right side of his upper lip.

(According to the papers, Ed Sheeran's was caused when Princess Beatrice pretended to knight James Blunt at a party and the sword went astray.)

'Yeah, what do you reckon?' says Ed, showing off his.

'Yours is great. Mine's a bit not great.'

'What was yours from?'

'Diving onto a bed with a Mac, and the Mac planted and my face hit the edge ...'

It happened on a short break in Abu Dhabi. Rob fills in some more details later. 'I did a Superman dive on the bed,' he explains. 'My body jumped into the computer.' There was so much mess, and so much blood, that at first he thought he had split all the way through his lip. 'It was the shock more than anything,' he says. In the end, he didn't even need stitches but, unless he takes remedial action, the scar looks to be here to stay. Ayda wants him to have work done on it.

'I want to keep it,' he says. 'I like it.'

* * *

Rob closes the Brit Awards with a medley of new songs, then returns to the stage to sing 'Feel', which is being broadcast as part of the after-show on ITV2. This last part is a bit of a shambles. First, there is a long delay. Then, when he starts singing, Rob seems to sense that he doesn't have the room's full attention now that the main part of the show is over, and he changes the words before the first chorus:

If you could all stay a bit
So I could beat the traffic
Out of the O2
That would be perfect, thank you.

But there's no discernible reaction, even to this. There's a reason why – the arena audience can't hear anything he's singing or anything the band are playing until halfway through the song, when someone flicks the correct switch back on. The sense of disorder is heightened by the fact that, in the absence of security, some of the audience have got up on the far end of the stage that extends in the audience, and have started dancing in pairs to Rob's song.

All quite odd, but the main performance goes fine. One of Rob's dancers apparently falls off the stage, but he doesn't even know about that until he reads about it in the newspapers the next day. Some people will also complain that Rob only played new songs, and they may have a point – it's a slightly strange finale for such an event to have someone play three songs off their new album – but there'd have probably been complaints, too, if he'd played a predictable selection of old songs.

The truth is that he's just glad it's over and that he got through it without calamity. He's been running on fumes for too long.

'I'm very brave,' he says, 'because I felt mental. I just needed nobody to know that I was crazy. I just need this to be a seven out of ten, and me to not look as weird as I feel in my head. Because I was Winona Ryder weird.'

* * *

Sometimes the best way of dealing with words intended to insult is to reclaim them and repurpose them. Or retweet them, as Rob did with this:

Robbie Williams looking like somebody has tried to draw Morrissey from memory.

'Made me laugh,' he says. 'It's also sort of "Ow!" But it made me laugh.'

* * *

Rob once nearly made an unlikely appearance with Morrissey. One version of the story is related in Morrissey's notoriously capricious *Autobiography*:

Robbie Williams sticks two notes in my front door. His handwriting is so bad that I can only make out one central line that shouts 'Let's do something TOGETHER'. And then another note shouts out 'I LIKE YOU!' He fragments further with scattered lyrics from You Are The Quarry, adding, 'If we sing together it would really confuse them'.

I am then invited to sing with Robbie at the upcoming Brit Awards, of which Robbie has somehow collected eighteen (it need hardly be said that my own award cabinet remains polished and empty). I politely refuse the request, but the ever diplomatic British tabloids jump in with MORRISSEY SNUBS ROBBIE. It is inconceivable to the press that a refusal could submit good terms and accord instead of sizzling spite.

Rob remembers a slightly different story. He's not sure where the initial idea came from, but he was told that Morrissey wanted to duet if Rob would agree to Morrissey's two stipulations: 'We sing one of his songs, which was great, it's a song called "I Like You". And at the end he wanted to kiss like Britney and Madonna.' Perhaps Morrissey imagined that this second request would automatically kill the idea, but of course Rob immediately agreed. 'I was bang up for that. Kissing Morrissey! That would have been great. Because he's just got, like, a fiercely brilliant face. You know, watching the idolatry that surrounds him, thousands and thousands of straight men I think would sleep with Morrissey. And I might not sleep with Morrissey but I'd have a cuddle and a kiss. It would have been amazing.'

But it was not to be.

'I think he was probably maybe a bit bluffing. Maybe. But I wasn't. I'd have wrestled him to the floor. And dominated him. I don't even know if I'd get a kick out of thinking that he tried to call my bluff. But I'm un-bluffable when it comes to stuff like that. I think it might have been something that he considered that day, then quickly rescinded. Like he does.'

All that remains, instead, is the assessment of Rob that Morrissey gave to *The Word* magazine two years before that.

'A fantastic quote about me,' says Rob, 'even though it was horrible.'

What Morrissey said was this: 'Personally I think that almost everything about Robbie Williams is fantastic … apart from the voice and the songs. He seems to have everything in place, the photos are fantastic, he's reasonably amusing, he's undeterred and he's not precious about what he does. I admire all of that.'

'Except,' Rob says, laughing, 'the voice and the songs.'

* * *

February 2017

His back is getting worse. This Saturday he's supposed to appear on the finale of *Let It Shine*, the reality show to find a boyband for the forthcoming Take That musical – he's scheduled to act as a judge, and to perform 'The Flood' with the other three current members of Take That. It's the first of these, the judging, that he's most worried about, because he thinks he won't be able to sit in a chair for an hour. And, even if he can deal with the purely physical problem, I think he's also worried that it will throw him off. If he's going to be a judge, he wants to be great at it, and to come over as having been great at it. 'I mean,' he says, remembering back to his last *Graham Norton* appearance, 'they had me as slurring when I was on good form.'

Michael starts making calls. But Rob, mindful of Take That's chequered history, is insistent that Michael makes one thing clear. 'I *cannot* let them down,' Rob emphasises. 'If I'm there in a wheelchair, I've got to do it … I will do it. You did impress on them that I'm not bailing?'

Word comes back that Peter Kay has agreed to deputise as a judge. As long as Rob can perform, it'll be fine.

* * *

Rob sits in his dressing room on the afternoon of the filming, having his make-up done. 'You know when I jot things down before I'm falling asleep to remember?' he says. He's found one, presumably from the night before, that says:

You're not the real Buzz Lightyear.

He has no conscious memory of having ever thought otherwise.

As he gets ready, he mentions how surprised he was when he looked at last weekend's episode of *Let It Shine*. 'In my mind,' he says, 'I was like, yeah, we performed like our lives depended on it, and the boys can't possibly be performing like that, like their lives depend on it. That was all we had. And then I watched a bit of the start of last week's show. And I was, "Oh, yeah, they're performing like their lives depend on it – they are doing that. They're all doing that."'

Howard, who has just become a parent again, comes into the dressing room.

They discuss nannies and sleep routines, and then talk through the performance. Rob shares his plan. 'I'll only fuck up fifteen per cent,' he says, 'if I just look at Gaz and just do what he does.'

Rob actually has to begin the song on a podium, then walk down some steps, go a short distance through the audience, up some steps and onto the main stage. He's not too bothered by the walking, or the standing, but he's worried that being grabbed at by the audience will put his back out. Security are put in place to protect him.

'The Flood' is a song Rob is really proud of – he mentions beforehand how surprised Elton John seemed when he visited Take That in the studio and realised that Rob had written all its words. And the atmosphere when the song begins today is quite remarkable – it feels more like the emotional highlight of a particularly special concert, not a song being recorded in a TV studio. At the end, the four of them get a standing ovation that just goes on, and on, and on. Eventually, when the noise has finally died down, they answer some questions from Graham Norton and Mel Giedroyc. 'It's very emotional,' says Rob. 'Seeing how much it means to everybody. It's only because I'm on telly that I'm not welling up.'

Afterwards, he says that there actually was a tear. 'I was genuinely choked, and I was genuinely overwhelmed with the love that beamed on us when we walked onstage. I got to take the stage with four showbiz brothers that I have a lot of history with – it means a great deal to us all. You could just see it in people's eyes – how much we mean to them, and how much we've meant to them. I was overwhelmed by it. It was an incredible moment. And I instantly went on a time-travelling journey in my mind. When we stepped upon the stage and the place just went mental, instantly I was transported to a yellow Salford Van Hire van with me and the boys on our way to Hull to go and perform at an under-eighteens club, way before we were famous.'

In the car, heading back into London, he's still on a high.

'It can be fun, showbiz, can't it?' he says. 'Yeah, that's the awesome bit.'

One other thing:

'The lads were having a Nando's when I left,' he says, 'and chips.'

* * *

That evening, Dylan Chambers, Guy's brother, comes over with his family, and he makes pizza and doughnuts. Rob's dietary restrictions take a one-night holiday, and everyone settles in front of the TV in anticipation of watching the *Let It Shine* finale. As we wait, Rob finds himself fielding questions about the rough early days, and tells tales of Nigel Martin-Smith, and of all the intra-band dynamics. At one point Susie Amy, another friend who is over tonight, asks Rob for a clarification: 'Would you say Nigel disliked you or Jason more?'

Rob considers this for a moment. 'Me.'

'Really?' says Susie. 'Because you were cheeky and challenging?'

'No, at the start I wasn't challenging at all, in any shape or form,' Rob replies. 'Just shit fucking scared.'

The conversation rolls on until Susie says, as though clarifying something that has already been established, 'He's very normal, Gary, isn't he?'

'I actually thought that until just recently,' Rob says. 'I've actually gone: actually you're really eccentric. He's *incredibly* eccentric. And I'm saying this from the perspective of somebody that knows that they're eccentric themselves. But it's actually shocked me that my perception of Gaz was that he's the most normal. The most reliable – he *is* the most reliable, but you just think that he's straight down the middle, but actually he's got -isms. Especially on the "Mixed Signals" video shoot, I was: I haven't noticed this before – you're completely eccentric. Which I thought was great. I can't even describe it, but it was like, oh, you're like me, you're eccentric. Maybe even *more*.'

One possible example recently came to light when Gary tweeted that he had just washed his hair for the first time in 14 years. As it happens, Rob doesn't find this so weird, partly because he believes he knows exactly where it comes from.

490

'All I can remember is back in the days in Take That, Jason in particular was like, "You know, lads, shampooing your hair's not good for your hair, and anyway your hair washes itself." That's what we all thought in Take That. And I'm lazy, so I took that as a cue to, "Yeah! I'm not gonna wash. I'm not gonna do that." So I didn't for a while. And maybe with Gaz that just stuck.'

* * *

We watch the show. At the beginning, Rob's replacement, Peter Kay, enters with 'Rudebox' playing in the background. Dressed as *The X Factor*'s enjoyably car-crash rapper contestant Honey G, Kay explains why he's here. 'I'm standing in for Robbie! He's hurt his back! And we wish him a very swift recovery!' And then a sly, deadpan dig. 'He's gonna be up singing and dancing later. He couldn't sit and judge, too much that. But he's gonna get up and sing and dance.' As he speaks, Kay's sunglass visor has letters moving across it, spelling out ROBBIE'S BACK NO GOOD.

Even though this performance of 'The Flood' is one that Rob knows he loves, when it begins he still puts his fingers in his ears and shuts his eyes. Ayda takes a photo of him like this and shows it to him after. She wants to post it on Instagram. Rob says she shouldn't, because people will think he's joking.

'And,' he adds, 'the chin's horrendous.'

* * *

The next day there's a shoot to photograph stills and a filmed advert for the Take That musical, which is called *The Band*, with the winning boyband, Five to Five, and Take That.

Rob arrives before anyone else. He's shown the sleeve to Take That's first album, *Take That And Party*, which the photographer intends to reproduce with Five to Five. Some slights never fade. Rob is on the far right of the sleeve, half cropped off the edge in the first place, and he says that whenever there was a reduced price sticker, Take That become a four-piece.

'Reduced to £8.99, there was no me.'

The photographer wants to know some background information about the original shoot.

'Did you all jump at once?' he asks.

'Yeah,' says Rob.

He's then asked if they were on a trampoline.

'No,' he says, 'on the ground. We were just on youthful exuberance.'

'How many times did you do it?' he's asked.

Rob knows the answer to that one.

'However many times the master said "Jump!"'

* * *

Rob chats with Five to Five. 'Genuinely, lads, you're the real fucking deal,' he says, encouragingly. 'We took forever to be ready to go. You guys have got something really special. Be kind to yourselves, and each other.'

Howard, Mark and Gary turn up and they do the shoot, the new boyband appearing from behind the old band, then the old handing microphones to the new, as though passing on the baton. Rob gives his a spin before passing it on.

Teddy runs around the studio, then runs into the shot, telling Rob she wants to play hide and seek. He says she'll have to wait a moment. Then she runs back in and pulls Rob's trousers down.

'Get off!' he shouts and pulls them up. So she pulls them down again.

In between shots, the four of them, Take That, mingle and chat; they seem to have that particular kind of comfort with each other that you have with people who are not necessarily your best friends, but with whom you've been through some kind of intense shared experience.

Later, back at the house, Michael asks how he's enjoyed these two days with the boys.

'Yeah, I loved it. I really loved it. Safety in numbers.'

Their path hasn't always been a smooth or easy one, and doubtless it won't always be in the future. But it's certainly a path that Rob imagines he'll continue to rejoin from time to time.

'There is an invisible cord that keeps pulling us back,' he says. 'And it's a cord that I'm quite happy that the universe tugs occasionally.'

* * *

December 2016

Upfront question, and answer:

Rob, what would you like to be your legacy? x

'I hear the word legacy and all I think is: "Who cares? I'll be dead" x'

* * *

February 2017

Rob and Ayda have a temporary falling out, a disagreement over some plans, and he goes downstairs. Tomorrow is Valentine's Day. He doesn't have a present. He needs to write a good card.

Once he catches the thread, it's easy to keep going. He knows that this is working. It's the truth, too: a catalogue of his world and of his desires, and of where Ayda stands within – above – them all. It's to her, and for her, but right now this message also talks back to its author.

'Writing it,' he says, 'I went from the fury to "Oh, God, I love this person so much …"'

I love you more than …

FIFA, football, Man Utd, Port Vale, sweet and sour chicken, rock shrimp tempura, chocolate *all, music, being right, being wrong, 1st class travel, private planes, private villas, private islands, any one else, life, MDMA, weed, alcohol, me, Mohammed Ali, Freddie Mercury, Frank Sinatra, Dean Martin, Sammy Davis Jnr, The Beatles, Morecambe and Wise, the feeling Back To The Future/ Grease/Star Wars gave me when I first watched them, UFOs, my beloved grandma * and I can't even quantify how much I loved/love her, my back when *it worked, my metabolism when it rocked, my serotonin when it was abundant, my chin when there was one, my six-pack for the 4 hours it existed, raving, early hip hop, the Exumas, Mustique, the Pyramids, truffle burgers, sleep, butter cake, red velvet cake, angels, I did yesterday … and the day before …*

So will you please be my valentine?

* * *

'The back's been horrendous for quite a while,' he says, 'but last week I couldn't sit down …'

Rob has to do a day of local radio interviews, to promote the summer concerts and the new single, 'Mixed Signals'. He's currently explaining his physical problems to Boogie and Arlene from Bauer Radio in Scotland. 'It does get to that age,' he says. 'It's weird. Just by putting a belt on and coughing, your back could go.'

'I wet myself when I do that now,' Arlene sympathises.

'Yeah,' Rob acknowledges. 'Yeah. I've got a mother-in-law that does that.' The DJs start laughing. 'And a wife that can't go on trampolines anymore.' The DJs are now laughing more or less uncontrollably. 'Yeah!' says Rob. 'She gets on *Loose Women* and talks about me! Have that! Have *that*, Ayda! Yeah! That felt good.'

* * *

Carl and Rachel from *The Big Welsh Wake-Up* want to know what tips Rob has about fatherhood, both with the birth itself and dealing with the sleepless nights to follow. He throws out some general advice – 'Good luck with that. Good luck with creating care of that human. For the rest of your life' – but stops himself from being drawn into the nitty-gritty.

'Buy a book,' he says. 'I'm a pop star.'

* * *

Between interviews, Rob shares a thought.

'Fucking chocolate makes you happy,' he says. 'It's so sad.'

* * *

494

In the next two interviews, Rob's asked whether he's worried that people will have had enough of him, and that all of this will go away. I suspect that they already have a sense from other interviews that he does worry about this stuff, and they ask because they're incredulous about it. I think he'll have to keep on explaining this for far longer than he'd have to if his fears happened to come true.

'Yeah, all the time. It's dreadful, the neuroses … it consumed my thoughts in the studio for the two years of the making of that album. "So this is the time they're just going to go no and they're going to take it all away from me and I'm gonna end up working in Carpet City in Stoke." And everybody's going to go, "Ah! You see! We were only joking!" So, yeah, is the answer. It terrifies me.'

That's what he tells listeners in Lincolnshire. He fills in a few more details for the Bauer group.

'I'm always terrified of everything going. I've always had that imposter syndrome that people talk about: "When they find out who I really am and what I'm really worth, all of this will go!" So I've always had that, and always will have that, and I'm always worried about the rug being taken from underneath me, or literally everything being taken away. And it all being a dream, and people pointing at me and laughing at me in the fifth year at school, going, "Ha! Ha! Ha! Ha! It was a dream, fatty!"'

* * *

He finishes with an interview with a Welsh newspaper.

Do the kids know what Daddy does?

'They know what I do. They don't know what it means. Teddy knows that Daddy goes and sings and that's what his job is, but she doesn't know what it means.'

And then he's asked a question he's been asked over and over, about how he'd feel if Teddy went into the entertainment business. There are two standard answers that well-known entertainers tend to give to this, either singly or in some combination – either that they would rather their kids do something else, or that they would support them in whatever they choose to do. Right after Teddy was born, Rob gave an answer which was a little like that: 'If she wants to go into the entertainment industry then I'm fine with that – it's better than a proper job, it's more fun,' he said, 'but I would hope that she would want to be a professional person, whatever that means. Maybe one day she will manage her father. I would rather her manage me than me sing with her, actually.'

That answer has evolved. The answer now goes more like this:

'I'd feel shocked if they didn't want to be in the entertainment industry. I'd be shocked if they wanted to be lawyers or doctors. I'd feel really let down. I'm the opposite of, you know, normal parents: "You want to be a *doctor*?... Don't do that! It's going to be such a hard life for you. This is fun! It's better than working. Why wouldn't you want to do *this*?"'

* * *

April 2017

Back in Los Angeles, he prepares for his Heavy Entertainment Show summer tour. Mostly, this involves endless medical consultations and treatments for his back. 'I've tried all of the above to remedy the problem,' he says, 'but unfortunately I find myself in pain.' He's determined to do the tour, whatever that requires. His creative director, Es Devlin, has been designing contingencies in which he can perform seated, and he notes that both Dave Grohl and Axl Rose have successfully toured in this way. 'Whatever I do do,' he says, 'it'll be part of the heavy entertainment show.' He's also planning to delay his flight to Europe until the last possible moment, skipping most of the rehearsals, but in truth he normally doesn't turn up often even when he's around. 'My life has been best when there's been not a lot of rehearsal,' he reflects. 'Not preparing in the way that people think I should helps give me the adrenalin to deliver my form and my brand of entertainment. And it's worked for me so far. Why mess with that formula?'

He's also been spending time in the sunshine with the kids, long days swimming at home in the pool, and he has been reading through the words that are in this book. He wonders whether people will think that it sounds like hard work to be him. 'But isn't it hard work just to be?' he says.

He has one principal thought, one main wish: 'I'd like to be more kind, less lacerating, less brutal to myself,' he says. 'If there was another book like this in ten years' time, I hope that I'll be more gentle with myself in my head. I can joke about it more now, and there's more levity, but how difficult it is for me to say nice things about myself. To myself. I just want to try to figure out how to be a bit kinder to myself.'

* * *

A few updates, loose ends. He has never been allowed his Twitter password. He has yet to go metal-detecting again. He has not been invited to play at Glastonbury. He and Guy are still waiting for those backing tracks from Taio Cruz. He's worried about what kind of story he'll need to tell the next time he goes on *The Graham Norton Show*. He didn't buy anything from the auction of David Bowie's art. One of the newest of their ten dogs, a Bernese mountain dog, is called Showbiz (or, in fact, to give him his full name, Mr Showbiz OBE). Rob plans to put out some of the unreleased songs mentioned in this book, including 'Speaking Tongues', on a new edition of his for-fans *Under The Radar* album series, and he has a new Robbie Williams album planned for the autumn of 2018. He's started eating meat and fish again, but remains on a careful pre-tour diet. He's not smoking.

One Los Angeles afternoon, sitting in the shade of the back garden, he decides to do his first ever live Instagram chat. But first Ayda starts doing one of her own, so he grabs her phone and runs away with it across the garden. 'Help me!' he shouts to Ayda's followers, 'I don't want to be in this relationship!'

Then he starts his chat. Mostly it involves just acknowledging the messages that come up on the screen, though he answers the occasional question. '*Will you get back with Take That?*' he reads out. 'Not right now, Ivan.'

Someone asks him to sing 'Love My Life' so he does, going straight into the chorus.

I love my life
I am powerful
I am beautiful …

Ayda starts laughing, and he scolds her: 'I'm doing a live gig!'

'Teddy says to stop singing,' Ayda points out.

Rob ignores this, soliciting more suggestions, doing impromptu versions of 'Me And My Monkey', 'Candy' and 'Morning Sun'.

Then he reads out a new request, feigning puzzlement: '*Sing better man.*' He requests clarification: 'Are you saying "sing 'Better Man'?" Or "sing better, man"? As a singer?'

'Telling you to sing better,' echoes Ayda, in the background.

More random requests, half-remembered lyrics: 'Putting On The Ritz', 'Tripping', 'Supreme' and 'Get A Little High'.

Perhaps understandably, as casual and haphazard as this is, it seems that not every one of the 6,000 people watching believes that this is really him. He reads out a new comment:

Robbie, my husband say you are fake.

'True,' he says. 'I am. A bit.'

But then he sings some more anyway. As if he's decided that, given how well most things seem to be working out for him these days, Robbie Williams might as well carry on pretending to be real for a while longer.